Migration and Cultural Inclusion in the European City

Also by

William J.V. Neill
URBAN PLANNING AND CULTURAL IDENTITY

RE-IMAGING THE PARIAH CITY: Urban Development in Belfast and Detroit
(*co-authored*)

William J.V. Neill and Hanns-Uve Schwedler
URBAN PLANNING AND CULTURAL INCLUSION: Lessons from Belfast and Berlin

Migration and Cultural Inclusion in the European City

Edited by

William J.V. Neill
Professor of Spatial Planning, University of Aberdeen, UK

and

Hanns-Uve Schwedler
Managing Director, European Academy of the Urban Environment, Germany

First published 2007 by
PALGRAVE MACMILLAN
Houndmills, Basingstoke, Hampshire RG21 6XS and
175 Fifth Avenue, New York, N.Y. 10010
Companies and representatives throughout the world

PALGRAVE MACMILLAN is the global academic imprint of the Palgrave
Macmillan division of St. Martin's Press, LLC and of Palgrave Macmillan Ltd.
Macmillan® is a registered trademark in the United States, United Kingdom
and other countries. Palgrave is a registered trademark in the European
Union and other countries.

ISBN-13: 978–0–230–00764–2 hardback
ISBN-10: 0–230–00764–3 hardback

This book is printed on paper suitable for recycling and made from fully
managed and sustained forest sources.

A catalogue record for this book is available from the British Library.

Library of Congress Cataloging-in-Publication Data

Migration and cultural inclusion in the European city/edited by William
   J.V. Neill, Hanns–Uve Schwedler.
     p.   cm.
   Includes bibliographical references and index.
   ISBN 0–230–00764–3 (cloth)
   1. Sociology, Urban—Europe.   2. Multiculturalism—Europe.
   3. Pluralism (Social sciences)—Europe.   4. Culture conflict—Europe.
   5. Urban policy—Europe.   6. Europe—Emigration and immigration—
   Social aspects.   I. Neill, William J.V.   II. Schwedler, Hanns-Uve.
   HT131.M54 2007
   307.76094—dc22   2006044697

10   9   8   7   6   5   4   3   2   1
16   15   14   13   12   11   10   09   08   07

Printed and bound in Great Britain by
Antony Rowe Ltd, Chippenham and Eastbourne

Contents

List of Figures		viii
List of Maps		ix
List of Tables		x
Foreword		xi
Notes on the Contributors		xiii

1 Introduction: the Challenge of the Plural City
   William J.V. Neill and Hanns-Uve Schwedler — 1

Part 1 Urban Mixing in a Changing Europe: Policy Context

2 Rethinking the Path to European Citizenship
   Elizabeth Meehan — 17

3 A Place for all our Citizens: the Council of Europe and Shared Cities
   Robin Wilson — 33

4 Setting an Agenda for Cultural Inclusion: the Work of EUROCITIES
   Heidi Jakobsen — 47

Part 2 Evolving Ideas of Citizenship: Theoretical Perspectives

5 Civic Republicanism and the Multicultural City
   Iseult Honohan — 63

6 Multiethnicity and the Negotiation of Place
   Jean Hillier — 74

7 Participatory Citizenship through Cultural Dialogue
   Brendan Murtagh, Michael Murray and Karen Keaveney — 88

Part 3 Governance and the Accommodation of Difference: City Profiles in a Cold Climate

8 The Dutch Approach to Planning for Multiculturalism post Fortuyn 103
   Hugo Priemus

9 Being and Living Together in French Cities: a Conflict-ridden Path Paved with Euphemisms 118
   Claude Jacquier

10 Berlin: Urban, Social and Ethnic Integration – an Urban Policy Challenge 136
   Ingeborg Beer, Alev Deniz and Hanns-Uve Schwedler

11 The Socially Integrative City: Results of the Interim Evaluation of a German Programme 148
   Hartmut Häussermann

12 Paradigm Shift: the Experience of Berlin's Commissioner for Integration and Migration 159
   Günter Piening and Andreas Germershausen

13 Embracing Multiculturalism: the Case of London 167
   Janice Morphet

14 Immigration to Italy: National Policies and Local Strategies in Verona and Turin 179
   Vanessa Maher

15 Fearing to Speak: Segregation and the Divided City of Belfast 191
   Peter Shirlow

16 Some Way to Go to a Shared Future: Groundwork in Belfast 206
   Mary McKee and Sylvia Gordon

17 Bosnian Nationalism and the Rebuilding of Sarajevo 218
   Sten Engelstoft, Guy Robinson and Alma Pobric

18 Cultural Divisions in a Changing Lisbon 234
   Graça Moreira

19 Beyond the Pale in Dublin: Asylum Seekers, Welfare and Citizenship 241
   Declan Redmond

Part 4   Conclusions

20 Within the City Limits: Tolerance and the Negotiation of
    Difference   257
    William J.V. Neill and Hanns-Uve Schwedler

*Appendix 1: EUROCITIES' Contribution to Good Governance Concerning
    the Integration of Immigrants and the Reception of Asylum Seekers*   268

Bibliography   274

Index   295

List of Figures

1.1	Globalization and migration: the world is becoming a smaller place – Berlin	3
1.2	Foreign population in EU member states	7
1.3	European population change 2000–2100	8
1.4	Passers-by? Place de la Bourse/Beursplein, Brussels, Spring 2006	11
7.1	Equity, diversity and interdependence: the planner as resolver	97
8.1	Street cartoons: The Hague	108
8.2	Living together in the Netherlands	114
9.1	The writing on the wall: protest on the Petit Bard estate in Montpellier, August 2004	125
9.2	The French fragmentation process 1945–1975	127
9.3	The French fragmentation process 1975–1995	127
9.4	The French fragmentation process 1995–present	128
10.1	Composition of Berlin's non-German population in 2005	138
10.2	Neighbourhood management area 'Kottbusser Tor'	143
10.3	Composition of (new) Neighbourhood Councils	145
12.1	Living together in Berlin	162
14.1	Semiotic mosaic: San Salvario	186
16.1	Tigers Bay: before Groundwork intervention	210
16.2	Tigers Bay: after Groundwork intervention	211
16.3	A 'peace wall'/interface in the project area of Short Strand, Inner East Belfast	213
18.1	Monument to the Portuguese discoveries erected in Lisbon 1960 commemorating the 500th anniversary of the death of Prince Henry the Navigator	238
20.1	Agonism in the city: public art in Berlin	262
20.2	Towards common principles?	265

List of Maps

10.1 Non-German population and urban neighbourhood
     management   140
11.1 Towns and cities participating in the programme *Soziale
     Stadt*   149
15.1 Prominent interfaces, segregation and politically motivated
     deaths in Belfast from 1969–(October) 2005   195
17.1 Important ethnic communities of former Yugoslavia   219

List of Tables

7.1	Strife in community settings	92
8.1	Population of the four major cities by ethnicity (the Netherlands)	104
8.2	Migration between Rotterdam and the region, the rest of the Netherlands and overseas, 1999–2002	105
8.3	Proportion of non-western ethnic minorities in Amsterdam, Rotterdam and Utrecht, 2003–2015	105
8.4	Unemployment in the major cities by ethnicity (the Netherlands)	106
9.1	Economic cycles and immigration waves: immigration and immigrant sedimentation (Grenoble)	123
10.1	Structural data of Berlin urban districts	141
11.1	Various problems identified in 'Districts with Special Development Needs' and corresponding intervention strategies (Germany)	151
13.1	Where London's new immigrants come from	169
15.1	Segregation in Belfast by community background	194
15.2	Policy costs of interfacing in Belfast	198
17.1	Renaming the streets of Sarajevo, 1994–2000	223
17.2	Postage stamps issued in Bosnia-Herzegovina	229
18.1	Foreign population in Greater Lisbon by continent and major representative country	236
19.1	Immigration by country of origin (Ireland)	244
19.2	Programme refugees in Ireland	245
19.3	Applications for asylum in Ireland	246
19.4	Decisions on asylum (Ireland)	246
19.5	Perceived weaknesses of direct provision as seen by welfare officers (Ireland)	249

Foreword

An announcement in the Berlin daily newspaper *Der Tagesspiegel* dated 4 May 2006: 'Yesterday morning in the subway a 24-year old man from the United Arab Emirates was spat upon, subjected to verbal racist abuse and kicked by two young women: "... f∗∗∗ foreigner... They'll never build a mosque in eastern Germany." Mustafa S. had previously drawn the two... women's attention to the ban on smoking (which is in force in all public transport contexts; authors' note).' In a report on another incident, the newspaper quotes in the same article: 'A 15-year old female told the police, ... (that she) had been kicked in the back by "Mediterranean types" – "Because you're a German woman". After this the three people fled.'

The present volume addresses a topic which is currently extremely controversial: it deals with questions of cultural inclusion. The authors look particularly at the question as to how cities might be able to contribute towards integrating immigrants and other cultural groups, what needs to be done, what lessons have been learned and what mistakes have been made. If we reflect that in not so many years' time in some of our European (large) cities the local or native population will be in the minority, then it is clear that the future picture of Europe will depend in no small degree on how successful the project of integration and inclusion can be. By comparison, the extreme alternatives are not so difficult to determine: ever more apocalyptic conditions – as was seen in Autumn 2005 in French cities; hostels for foreigners or refugees going up in flames, as was experienced in particular in the 1990s in Germany – or peace and discipline enforced by a police presence. Neither of these can surely be said to represent the European value system which has been so frequently appealed to in the last couple of years.

Admittedly, it is not clear what integration specifically means in the final analysis or how it can be brought about. In view of the weakness, perhaps the failure, of existing approaches on inclusion and integration of cultural groups, this discussion has been running full swing for a number of years – in public arenas, in politics, in official institutions – from local authorities or town councils right up to the European Commission – and in academic circles too. This discussion is not always conducted in a rational manner – a fact which should not surprise us, since people's ultimate individual and inherited ideas and values are being affected, perhaps being called into question. We 'native Europeans' are shocked by the vision that we are no longer the only Europeans who decide how Europe will look in the future. Did (and does) not from the outset the history of the European Union, of European integration, comprise struggling over the quite different value notions of the member states? And now the whole enterprise is going to be even more complicated and more diverse.

In such a situation controversies must arise. When all's said and done, two questions remain: How much difference can Europe bear? And what are those essentials, the indispensable values without which we cannot continue? At the point where tolerance in the face of difference is at a low level – for political and many other reasons – where fear over losing one's own identity prevails, at just this point we native-born Europeans are still trying to emerge from carrying out violent conflicts with one another – from the Balkans via the Basque country to Northern Ireland. Conflicts which remain smouldering, below the level of actual violence, are even more common.

Be this as it may. Cultural inclusion is quite definitely on the agenda. The contention that cities will bear a central role in this context surely does not need any special advocacy. It is here where 80 per cent of all Europeans live, it is here where difference and similarity are directly lived and experienced, it is here where inclusion and integration are on the test bed.

The idea behind this book derives from a symposium which was held in the European Academy of the Urban Environment (EA.UE) towards the end of 2004; with financial support from the European Commission, the Academy cooperated in this event with the School of Environmental Planning, Queen's University Belfast and the Urban Institute Ireland. The majority of the authors in this volume participated in the symposium. Some of the chapters are based on papers which were given during the conference; other chapters have been written entirely on a new basis. We would particularly wish to express our thanks to all the authors for their commitment. The editors would also like to acknowledge the contribution of Christoph Rau, former EA.UE project manager, and the encouragement in the production of the book of Victor Blease, former Chief Executive of the Northern Ireland Housing Executive.

We have decided to dedicate this book to Jenny Johnson of EA.UE. She has demonstrated great patience in dealing with both editors, has coordinated and monitored the genesis of the manuscript texts, has translated some chapters and read through all the texts for linguistic detail – often outside office hours. We would like to express our heartfelt thanks.

William J.V. Neill
Hanns-Uve Schwedler

Notes on the Contributors

Ingeborg Beer, urban sociologist, has her own agency with offices in Berlin and other towns in the Federal State of Brandenburg, addressing in research, consulting and mediation the topic area covered by 'Soziale Stadt' (Socially Integrative City programme). Her publications to date focus on the socially integrative city, reconstruction and urban design, and public participation.

Alev Deniz is a graduate in social sciences and has been employed as an urban neighbourhood manager in Berlin since 2005. The main focus of her activities is on furthering socio-cultural projects in the field of integration. Works published to date deal primarily with labour market and migration policy topics at national and international level.

Sten Engelstoft is associate professor at the Department of Geography, University of Copenhagen, Denmark; visiting research fellow (END) at the European Commission, associated with the EU FAST programme (Forecasting and Assessment in Science and Technology); research interests include urban geography, sustainable urban development, urban spatial politics and planning, and political geography.

Andreas Germershausen is employed with the Commissioner of the Berlin *Senat* for Integration and Migration as head of the department for integration policies. In this function he is coordinating initiatives for better access of migrants to education and vocational training and the development of employment strategies for minorities.

Sylvia Gordon is assistant director for development at Groundwork Northern Ireland, a leading-edge agency delivering community cohesion through environmental regeneration. In this capacity, the agency is instrumental in building partnerships with government departments, elected representatives and community activists.

Hartmut Häussermann currently holds the Chair of Urban and Regional Sociology at the Humboldt University of Berlin. He has published widely in book and periodical form on urban development and sociology, migration and poverty, changes in Germany post-1990, and is a member of several committees, expert groups and advisory bodies on issues related to the topic of this volume. He is head of the research project 'Divided Cities – Planning the Contested City: Policy Analysis and Implications of Reunification in Jerusalem and Berlin'.

Jean Hillier is professor of town and country planning, University of Newcastle, and director of the Global Urban Research Unit (GURU). Research interests centre on planning theory, planning and local government decision-making, and issues of social inclusion. Formerly professor of urban and regional studies, Curtin University, Australia; editor of *Planning Theory*, Sage. Recent books include *Shadows of Power: an Allegory of Prudence in Land Use Planning* (2002), and (ed. with Emma Rooksby) *Habitas: a Sense of Place* (2005, 2nd edition).

Iseult Honohan is senior lecturer, School of Politics and International Relations, University College Dublin. Current research projects include applications of civic republican political theory, and research into the normative implications of different kinds of interdependence; research interests include citizenship and immigration, social capital, the future of republicanism in Ireland; diversity and the politics of recognition.

Claude Jacquier is professor at the Institute for Political Studies in Grenoble and at the Institute for Urban Planning in Lyons; research director at CNRS (National Centre for Scientific Research), in charge of the *Villes et Solidarités* research team within Pacte, a research focus in the Grenoble universities; has managed European research programmes, such as *Quartiers en Crise* (Neighbourhoods in Crisis) 1989–95, Cost-Civitas (1995–2000) (Social and Spatial Changes in European Cities and Urban Governance) and participated in the Ugis programme (Urban Development, Urban Governance, Social Inclusion and Sustainability); research results in integrated development policies and urban governance implemented in Europe, North America and Africa.

Heidi Jakobsen is policy officer, based at the Brussels secretariat, dealing with social affairs for EUROCITIES, the network of major European cities.

Karen Keaveney is lecturer, School of Planning, Architecture and Civil Engineering, Queen's University Belfast. Her research interests are in housing and local planning, environment and culture.

Vanessa Maher is professor of cultural anthropology in the Faculty of Educational and Community Studies, University of Verona; research interests include migration and ethnicity, gender studies, urban anthropology, experience and transmission of knowledge, writing, memory and forgetting in societies with restricted literacy, oral literature (Maghreb) and the literature of migration, contemporary Islam, gender and development, maternal and infant mortality in Africa and the Middle East.

Mary McKee is director, Groundwork Northern Ireland, one of the major Groundwork Trusts in the United Kingdom, engaged in developing key projects in areas of high social and economic need in partnership with communities who have witnessed some of the worst of Northern Ireland's conflict.

Elizabeth Meehan recently retired from the post of Director, Institute of Governance, Public Policy and Social Research at Queen's University of Belfast. She is adjunct professor in the School of Politics and International Relations, University College Dublin, and honorary research associate at the Policy Institute, Trinity College Dublin. Research and publications cover: women and politics; European citizenship; citizenship and participation in the UK; constitutional change in the UK; and British–Irish relations in the context of the EU. She is a Director of the Northern Ireland 'think tank' Democratic Dialogue, and a member of the UK Home Office Advisory Board on Naturalization and Integration. In 2005 she was awarded a lifetime achievement award by the Political Studies Association for an 'outstanding contribution to the study of politics'.

Graça Moreira is assistant professor in the Faculty of Architecture at the Technical University of Lisbon (UTL); formerly lecturer in urban geography in the Faculty of Architecture; responsible for implementation of Digital Cities and Regions in the POSI programme (Information Society Operational Programme, 2001–2003); research interests include healthy cities and the geography of the night time city.

Janice Morphet is a member of the United Kingdom 'Modernizing Local Government' team and e-government advisor at the Office of the Deputy Prime Minister; honorary professor at the Bartlett School of Planning, University College London; former Chief Executive of Rutland Council; Professor and Head of Department at Birmingham Polytechnic. Recent books are *Understanding E Government: a Guide to Principles and Practice* (2004), and *Modernising Local Government* (2006).

Michael Murray is reader, School of Planning, Architecture and Civil Engineering, Queen's University Belfast; director of Strategic Planning Action Network, Queen's University Belfast, in collaboration with universities in France and Belgium. Research interests include strategic spatial planning, and multilevel governance and participatory processes in planning. He is a recent visiting scholar at Colorado State University. Books include *Partnership Governance in Northern Ireland: the Path to Peace* (et al., 1998), and *Participatory Governance* (with B. Murtagh, 2004).

Brendan Murtagh is reader, School of Planning, Architecture and Civil Engineering, Queen's University Belfast. Research interests include planning in contested cities and issues around housing segregation and the mediation of place. Recent books are *The Politics of Territory* (2002), *Participatory*

Governance (with M. Murray, 2004), and *Belfast: Segregation, Violence and the City* (with P. Shirlow, 2006).

William J.V. Neill is Professor of Spatial Planning at the University of Aberdeen, UK. He was formerly economic development planner with the Michigan Commerce Department, and is a member of the International Committee, Royal Town Planning Institute. Research interests revolve around issues of representation, identity and governance in the plural city. His latest books are *Urban Planning and Cultural Inclusion* (ed. with Hanns-Uve Schwedler, 2001), and *Urban Planning and Cultural Identity* (2004).

Günter Piening has been since June 2003 Commissioner of the Berlin *Senat* for Integration and Migration, after a similar position in the regional government of Saxony-Anhalt. Prior to this he was press spokesperson for the Bürgerbewegten-Fraktion in Magdeburg (Citizen's Active parliamentary party) – forerunner of the present party Bündnis 90/Die Grünen (*Alliance 90/the Greens*) – and he also jointly founded a self-help association for refugees. He has experience as a freelance journalist in Japan and in West Africa, as well as in China and South-East Asia.

Alma Pobric is senior lecturer/assistant professor, University of Sarajevo, and is currently completing a PhD at Kingston University London on 'Fertility and the Status of Women in Bosnia-Herzegovina'. She is the author of two textbooks for Bosnian schools: *Udzbenik geografie za VI razred osnovne skole* (2003), and *Radna sveskaza VI razred osnovne skole* (2003). Her Master's thesis was on 'Family planning, fertility and the status of women in Egypt' (1997). She is a contributor to *Atlas svijeta za osnovne I sredenje skole* (1998).

Hugo Priemus is dean of the Faculty of Technology, Policy and Management and professor in System Innovation Spatial Development at Delft University of Technology; scientific director of the Habiforum programme 'Innovative Land Use', also visiting professor in the Department of Urban Studies, University of Glasgow; managing director of OTB Research Institute for housing, urban and mobility studies, Delft University of Technology.

Declan Redmond is lecturer in the School of Geography, Planning and Environmental Policy, University College Dublin, and deputy Head of School. Principal research interests revolve around housing and planning; he has undertaken research on regeneration and community participation, is currently involved in projects investigating housing affordability; the role of private residents associations in the planning system; the participation of disadvantaged communities in the planning system and the role of entrepreneurial governance in urban change.

Guy M. Robinson holds the chair as Professor of Geography at Kingston University, London. He formerly worked at the universities of Oxford and Edinburgh. He is author of *Geographies of Agriculture* (2004), *Methods and Techniques in Human Geography* (1998) and *Conflict and Change in the Countryside* (1994).

Hanns-Uve Schwedler is managing director of the European Academy of the Urban Environment in Berlin. His personal publications include work on urban development questions, in particular dealing with socio-spatial segregation in the Middle East. In addition to acting as responsible editor for over fifty Academy publications, he is also co-author (with Bill Neill) of *Urban Planning and Cultural Inclusion* (2001), and (with Walter Bückmann and Yeong Heui Lee) of *Das Nachhaltigkeitsgebot der Agenda 21. Die Umsetzung ins Umwelt- und Planungsrecht* (The sustainability precept in Agenda 21. The transformation into environmental and planning law, 2002).

Peter Shirlow is senior lecturer in Human Geography at the University of Ulster. Research interests centre on the politics of identity, segregation in Northern Ireland and strategies of conflict amelioration. His books include *Who are the People? Protestantism, Unionism and Loyalism in Northern Ireland* (ed. with Mark McGovern, 1997), and *Belfast: Segration, Violence and the City* (with B. Murtagh, 2006).

Robin Wilson is director of think tank 'Democratic Dialogue' in Belfast which he founded in 1995; adviser on cultural diversity and intercultural dialogue for the Council of Europe; honorary senior research fellow and member of the board, Institute of Governance, Queen's University Belfast; co-leader of the Northern Ireland research team in the devolution monitoring project, coordinated by the Constitution Unit, University College London; frequent commentator in international print and broadcast media on Northern Ireland affairs and has published widely on nationalism, identity politics, European affairs and social exclusion.

1

Introduction: the Challenge of the Plural City

William J.V. Neill and Hanns-Uve Schwedler

The topic of cultural inclusion (and as a dialectical consequence exclusion) in the European city, the subject of this book,[1] is shot through with unavoidable controversy not only in public and political arenas but also in academia. Events such as the murder of Pim Fortuyn and Theo van Gogh in the Netherlands[2] and the violent street riots in many French cities in the autumn of 2005 when youths of mostly North African origin clashed with 'the power of the state',[3] have moved full square into European public consciousness issues of integration and disintegration, of conflict along ethnic-cultural lines, of segregation and of conflicting value systems. In Germany the wake-up call came earlier with the burning of refugee hostels in the 1990s.[4] The debate in Europe unfolds against a background of an alleged 'clash of civilizations' (Huntington, 1993) which has been arguably all too readily picked up and utilized in the United States (and not just since 9/11),[5] as a spectre of fear which percolates through the media and influences the tenor of public discussion. There is a dilemma here for theory which attempts to understand cultural difference and its social construction as a first step to its accommodation.

The dilemma of theories – comprehensible and instrumentalized or complex and politically irrelevant?

To be policy relevant theory risks imposing simplifications on complexity. Huntington (1993: 23) provides an example. He gets to the essence of his theory in an essay which precedes his famous and controversial book of 1996:

> . . . differences among civilizations are not only real; they are basic. Civilizations are differentiated from each other by history, language, culture, tradition and, most important, religion . . . the world is becoming a

1

smaller place. The interactions between peoples of different civilizations are increasing; these increasing interactions intensify civilization
consciousness and awareness of differences between civilizations and
commonalities within civilizations. North African immigration to France
generates hostility among Frenchmen . . . In conflicts between civilizations, the question is 'What are you?'[6] That is a given, that cannot
be changed. And as we know, from Bosnia to the Caucasus to the
Sudan, the wrong answer to that question can mean a bullet in the
head . . . Even more than ethnicity, religion discriminates sharply and
exclusively among people. A person can be half-French and half-Arab
and simultaneously even a citizen of two countries. It is more difficult to
be half-Catholic and half-Muslim.

Huntington's theory has been severely criticized. His efforts to compress
the majority of current conflicts into a theorem of cultural/ethnic/religious
differences seems too one-dimensional in explaining conflict, and thus
forced. In the words of one critic: 'Caution is to be advised with regard
to Huntington's global theory. It follows the virtue of simplicity at the
expense of truth and falsifies reality.'[7] It is doubtless due to this simplicity –
although Huntington expresses himself now increasingly in a more differentiated fashion – that his thesis has in the meantime become public and
political common 'knowledge' and has played an either orchestrating part
or provided a concealed between the lines media interpretation during the
recent controversies about the caricatures of the prophet Mohammed.
    It remains to Huntington's credit, however, that he made clear the fact
that in a world which is becoming ever smaller, due to rapid communication,
high levels of mobility, and globalization that the spatial borders between
'regions of civilizations' are becoming ever more blurred and pass through
our own countries and cities. This point of view is also to be found in
the work of the Syrian-born German political scientist Bassam Tibi, whose
book *Krieg der Kulturen* (*War of the Cultures*, 1995) put forward, even prior
to Huntington's book, similar reflections although being less bi-polar and
focusing more strongly on domestic cultural conflicts within countries. It
was Tibi who coined the term '*Leitkultur*' (the leading culture of the majority
in the host society) which has become a highly significant concept within
the German political debate over integration.[8] Tibi has undergone a similar
fate to that of Huntington. His concepts and theorems have been divorced
from their scholarly and empirical context and carried over into the public
domain in a crude manner and instrumentalized for political purposes.
    A 'pioneer' in scholarly discussion on ethnic-cultural conflicts, Frederik
Barth, suffered a different fate. His theoretical concepts were received enthu-
siastically in some scientific disciplines and are still cited (amongst others,
by some writers in the present volume); however, they have played little
part in political discussion. The relative complexity it seems, requiring a situational perspective on identity matters, does not translate well into political

Figure 1.1: Globalization and migration: the world is becoming a smaller place – Berlin

relevancy. Barth (1969) in the book *Ethnic Groups and Boundaries: the Social Organization of Cultural Difference* which he edited, points out that ethnic identity is not immutable having some essential essence but is potentially flexible and negotiable. Barth did not take identity differences for granted and subsequently consider how they affected social interaction in some crude way but, as Jenkins puts it, his approach was the reverse in seeking to understand how identity and difference are socially and contextually constructed.[9] Here Barth argued that group culture should not be seen as the continuation of some essential culture from a previous time but should be seen as the result of constant renegotiation over time of group identity and boundaries. Here the larger social and political context is important. In an oft quoted passage, as Barth stated, we can thus '... assume no simple one-to-one relationship between ethnic units and cultural similarities and differences. The features that are taken into account are not the sum of "objective" differences, but only those which the actors themselves regard as significant ... '[10]

Here power relations cannot be forgotten. As Barth demonstrated, some collectivities are in a stronger position to construct their identities and resist the imposition of identification by others and some are not so lucky. In throwing light on the endurance of ethnic identity over time and how new ethnic symbolic structures (and not those of traditional ethnic membership) can contextually emerge Barth provides an explanation for the fact that the optimistic views of 'nation' and of 'state building theories' have not proved to be true.[11]

If Barth provides some academic orientation to understanding the social construction of cultural difference a problem remains for European authors attempting to write about the inclusion of this difference in the European city. This is over and above the fact that complex social reality cannot be interrogated with theoretical concepts that lend themselves to slogan-eering or with one or two simple theorems seeking to resist rebuttal through attempts at falsification derivative of a Popperian critical rational approach. Every scholar or academic here, perhaps more so than in many other societal questions, is deep down a part of the subject matter being investigated. He or she is likely committed to one position or another and needs to be aware of this fact. Perhaps that is one reason for the caution shown in this volume. With only very few exceptions academics seem at the present time to be, if anything, more hesitant if they are required to generalize from their empirical findings up towards the level of theories. Academic discourse concerning questions of integration and non-integration, of segregation and socio-spatial integration is, in common with society's disagreement about it, currently in a phase of upheaval and uncertainty.

For the most part therefore, the present volume with the exception of Part 2, emphasizes less theoretical discourse on the subject matter and prefers to attempt to identify and present important aspects of political discussion and practice. The focus of the book remains, despite the foregoing comments on Barth, directed to inclusionary approaches to the accommodation of difference rather than the nature of difference in the first place, although this is a matter of emphasis rather than neglect. The adoption of case study approaches in Part 3 is not due to 'empirical arbitrariness'. On the contrary, it is due to the very fact that 'mega or metatheories' on cultural conflicts and on cultural inclusion have obviously failed and that our notions and intellectual approaches so far are approaching their limits of usefulness and that the situation in Europe is highly diverse. Cultural conflicts in the 'old continent' – and thus tasks involved in cultural inclusion – range from the disputes or conflict in the Balkans, via Northern Ireland right up to the controversies referred to at the beginning of this chapter revolving around immigration – to mention only the most obvious of the schisms. In particular the latter – immigration and the cultural plurality and diversity which this entails – characterize reality in all European countries and in nearly all the larger towns and cities.

This present academic uncertainty may cause some surprise, since after all questions of inclusion and exclusion, of socio-spatial segregation and disparities in cities have been subjected to academic investigation and discussion for at least the last 30 years[12] and such issues will play an even more important part in the future.

Segregation past and present

Cities which are divided and fragmented along ethnic and cultural lines are nothing new. The medieval European city had its Jewish quarter; whole societies, such as the despotic states in the Middle East during the Middle Ages and in the early modern period, were constructed on the basis of urban segregation and ethnic fragmentation. Whereas in the historical context of the Middle East this ethnic structuring had its conflict-regulating function and provided collective strength and social certainty, in the (modern) European context, segregation can often be seen as a spatial sign of societal fracture and marginalization. Many empirical studies provide evidence that spatial segregation along cultural and ethnic lines is overlaid by socio-economic factors.[13] Several of these studies also conclude that cultural quarters are the 'landing stage' for new immigrants, providing a sense of social security, familiarity, and ethnic and cultural networks. However, as Chapter 9 of this book argues many old certainties on spatial structure are disappearing. A major driver here lies in an increasingly neo-liberal economic policy context which has major momentum despite a hesitant path to economic re-regulation especially in Germany and France. The economic pressures are strong and the meteoric rise of the Asian economies has even caught the United States by surprise. In this context despite publication of the European Spatial Development Perspective in 1999, endorsing the notion of equitable polycentric development of the EU territory as a desirable guiding policy, it is likely that in the 21st century, Europe's cities will be fiscally squeezed and not all may fare equally in competitive success.

Häussermann (2001, 64), comments on the unsettling reality (but writing with slightly more hope in Chapter ?? of this book) of a growing spatial segregation of marginalized groups in major cities and associated discrimination and social exclusion resulting in a mutually reinforcing vicious circle of negative effects:

> The social development in western major cities – from Berlin to New York – has been for a number of years characterized by terms such as dualization and dichotomy . . . These are used to characterize a change in the social structure of major cities, which emerges from economic structural change, from de-nationalization of economic regulation and from decreasing welfare support . . . In the major cities, urban quarters or neighbourhoods are being created in which the 'superfluous members of society' are concentrated: marginalized local persons and discriminated immigrants . . .

As a result of these developments, cultural and ethnic quarters and specific areas of our cities (such as the inner city) are losing the functions as 'places of security' and as 'zones of transition' which they traditionally had in some European countries. And again, a whole theory – the approach of the Chicago School with its models of urban development – loses its capability to explain social and spatial patterns in our cities today.[14] In their book *Splintering Urbanism* Graham and Marvin (2001, 197), dealing with this complex reality, point out that geographical proximity within cities is no guarantee of meaningful relations or connections as places become bound up in global – local or 'glocalized' interactions. In a splintered local urbanism, with the use of modern technologies, globally distant places can be intimately connected and joined together by 'customized network spaces' (p. 101). The result is 'the fragmentation of the social and material fabric of cities' (p. 33). This hardly leaves room for the expectation that under present economic conditions and in a globalizing world with a multicultural society, integration will occur by itself. We are losing (as Häussermann argues) our 'traditional' regulation measures which involved in the past more generous compensatory policies and a path to social advancement thus off setting social exclusion. Quite simply social security and welfare systems are failing more and more with some kids growing up, as in many American cities, with the view that it is natural not to be part of the 'normal' society/economy.[15] New forms of integrative measures and instruments are needed. Several such approaches are described and discussed in this book. Without integration measures it may be that the riots with which French cities were confronted in Autumn 2005 will be only forerunners of the future reality in European cities. Already today in several European cities – such as some in the Netherlands or in Germany – people with a non-native background comprise more than one-third of the city's population.[16] This raises the issue of demographics.

Demographic change

It is obvious from Figure 1.2 that, with a few exceptions,[17] the foreign population in EU member states has increased to a significant degree within the last fifteen years. In nearly half of all EU member states, this proportion has at least doubled. In the case of the 'old' member states this is true for even more than half of the countries. In Spain the proportion of the foreign population has already increased by more than six-fold. On average, 8.7 per cent of European residents are of a different nationality than that of the country in which they are resident. The proportion of persons with a 'non-native background', that is, with a different cultural identity (see note 16) may well be even several per cent higher. Keeping in mind that immigrants tend to live in cities (concentrated in certain neighbourhoods), then the dimension

Figure 1.2: Foreign population in EU member states

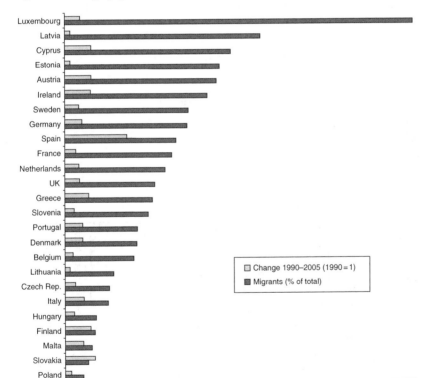

Source: Population Division of the Department of Economic and Social Affairs of the United Nations Secretariat, Trends in Total Migrant Stock: the 2004 Revision

of this as an urban issue and the necessity for integrative action becomes obvious.

This point is even more crucial when it is considered that in future Europe will be forced to rely on even more pronounced immigration for economic reasons than at present. According to UN prognoses,[18] as early as the year 2050, the average age of the population in Europe will be about 50 years, and therefore, approximately 10 years older than, for example, that of the USA. In a parallel process, the populations of many European cities are shrinking (and will continue to shrink – in some cases dramatically – without the necessary immigration), whereas in other economic regions, in particular in newly industrializing countries, but also in the USA, it is expected that populations and cities will continue to grow. Even allowing for an active immigration policy, the UN has calculated for Italy, for example, that the population will have declined by more than 20 per cent by 2050; by the year 2100, the population will be about half what it is now. Similar developments are expected for other European countries (Figure 1.3). Without necessary

Figure 1.3: European population change 2000–2100 (in %)

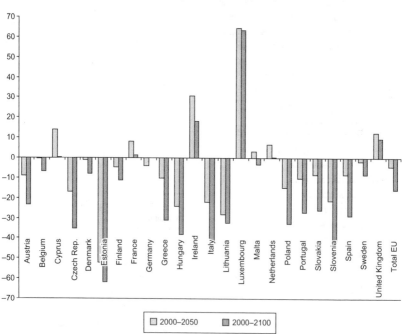

Source: United Nations Population Division (2004): World Population in 2100, ESA/P/WP.187 (New York: UN)

immigration, the decline will be even more dramatic. Europe is in danger, in other words, of falling behind other regions in the world in economic terms.

By 2010 it is predicted that there will already be shortages in the labour market in some of the EU member states.[19] Negative effects on labour markets and on the social system, on industry and on affluence will only be able to be compensated for or alleviated, by means of an active population policy in member states, in the first instance by means of immigration.

As a result of this process,[20] however, cultural and ethnic diversity will increase. The proportion of non-native inhabitants in Europe will probably be in the region of 30 to 40 per cent as early as the middle of this century (in some cities considerably above this figure). Between 2005 and 2050, the UN Population Division expects a net migration to Europe of between about 700,000 and 800,000 persons per year.[21] Challenges associated with integration will as a result increase continuously. This is true not only for those cities in which the majority of immigrants currently live and will live in the future. It is equally true for regions and for nation states. The challenge bears down especially on the European Union and its institutions, which by means of its policies and measures create the framework conditions for 'cultural inclusion in the European city' and on whose support – this is the argument used in Chapter 4 – European cities have to depend.

Migration and inclusion – on the way to a European approach?

While migration and cultural inclusion has been a topic of scientific research in Europe for at least 30 years, and a matter for urban action and programmes in some cities for about 15–20 years, it only came on to the EU political agenda within the last decade. Before this time, EU immigration policy focused very much either on asylum or on protecting external borders. When the Schengen Agreement was signed in 1985, internal borders – initially between a number of the 'core states' of the EU – were removed. At a later stage other EU member states joined the agreement along with a number of other countries. Associated with dispensing with these internal borders was, however, more severe (and more unified) control checks at external borders. The slogan of 'Fortress Europe' began to circulate.[22]

Faced with growing immigration and demographic change which is becoming ever more apparent since the Treaty of Amsterdam (1997), the realization has prevailed that migration into the EU is not simply a mere 'matter of common interest', the phrase which was still being used in the Maastricht Treaty dated 1992. Since 1991 the framework for a Community visa, inward migration and asylum policies have been in the process of development.

In the last few years the European Commission has issued a number of crucial documents dealing with migration and associated subjects, from which hints may be observed pointing towards linking migration, employment and social policies.[23] In its Green Paper on demographic change the European Commission (EC 2005, 6) summarizes the reasons that led to this possible policy shift:

> Europe is facing today unprecedented demographic change . . . This trend is even greater when just the total working age population (15–64 years) is considered: between 2005 and 2030, it is due to fall by 20.8 million . . . Immigration from outside the EU could help to mitigate the effects of the falling population . . . As stated in the recent Commission Green Paper (COM(2004) 811 final), ever larger migrant flows may be needed to meet the need for labour and safeguard Europe's prosperity.

In view of the fact that the 'mills' of Europe oft grind exceeding slow (especially when the member states believe that there are certain policy areas where the Commission has no right to be involved these being matters of national interest,[24] it would be rather simplistic to deduce from these relatively non-binding documents that in the future there will be a European integration and inclusion policy. It might be added, however, that in the light of demographic change, economic needs and cultural conflicts which are already manifest, there is no other alternative. It is therefore not surprising that other European institutions have recently also been dealing with these matters.

At the June 2005 Employment Council, EU ministers decided that there should be an EU level framework, setting out common principles, and identified as one major and unsolved issue the need for synchronization between immigration procedures and integration into society. On this basis, the Commission in December 2005 put forward a policy plan on legal migration, setting out action for the next four years. This plan focuses on legislative and non-legislative issues and tools (exchange of information and experience, for instance), on integration measures and on support for third countries (combating brain drain, professional and linguistic training and so on).

Other chapters of this book deal with further policy documents, considerations and approaches in European institutions and organizations (the chapters in part 1 and also Chapter ??). Rather than anticipating what is stated in these chapters, it can be summarized that there are steps afoot leading to the emergence of a more common approach to European migration and integration policy. It must be added that urban approaches towards cultural inclusion will, however, remain 'bloodless and without a backbone', if they are not embedded in a supportive political framework. The biggest challenge here will probably be, as Märker (2001, 6) puts it, to convince some member state governments and European citizens that Europe will need even more immigration in the future:

Obviously questions of inward migration in the majority of EU member states represent so high a level of social explosiveness that one can scarcely anticipate . . . any rational policy making process. Against the background of economic anxieties and fears of too much cultural demands being made

Figure 1.4: Passers-by? Place de la Bourse/Beursplein, Brussels, Spring 2006

of their (voting) public, European member state governments continue to have difficulty in accepting and articulating immigration policy facts.

Specifically in this light, the aim of this volume is to provide a barometer through various case studies of where a cultural inclusion agenda stands in a representative cross section of European cities. It also seeks to consider how such an agenda which is now pressing can be advanced. This may mean accepting what cannot be changed but it also entails facing up to what is needed – even if one does not like it and has to relinquish some dearly cherished ideas and points of view. The book considers what is happening, what works, what remains to be done, but also what is realistic. It gives an overview of present European policies and approaches (Part 1), considers some theoretical views on inclusion and dialogue (Part 2), gives a selective overview of what is happening in some of our countries and cities (Part 3) and tries to summarize and draw common threats from the various views presented in a conclusion (Part 4). Anticipating this it is fair to say that, while none of the authors reject the need for integration and inclusion, nevertheless, when it comes to the question of how and whom to include, differences appear. These are not only differences based on the specific reality and needs of a country, a city, a project. They are also very much linked to one essential, apparently simple question, which can be expressed in very simple words:

Who are we? Who do we want to be? And how much difference can Europe bear?

The answers to these questions have never been simple – at no time, in no society. The whole process of European integration was also about trying to find answers. The challenge in the Europe of today is, that we, the 'native Europeans' are not the only Europeans who need to provide and agree on those answers.

Notes

1. In actual fact this volume deals with integration in cities within the European Union. If Europe is referred to, in the majority of cases this means the EU (along with the present candidate countries and the regions in which they are located). This 'EU-centric' viewpoint may be justified in the sense that discussion about culture and inward migration takes place primarily in EU member states, that only in these countries are comparable efforts towards integration to be found, only here can common framework conditions and strategies be developed and – last but not least – these countries are at the present time and

in the foreseeable future the principal destination countries for immigration into Europe.

2. Pim Fortuyn, university teacher, writer and politician, was murdered on 6 May 2002 by a radical animal protectionist. Fortuyn was a declared opponent of Islam. Statements such as 'I am also in favour of a Cold War with Islam. I see Islam as an extraordinary threat, as a hostile society' or 'I think it is a backward culture . . . In any place where Islam holds sway, everything is simply awful' and his negative attitude towards a multicultural society led to some very vehement controversies in Netherlands public life (Eckardt 2003).

 The Netherlands film director Theo van Gogh was murdered on 2 November 2004 by an Amsterdam resident of Moroccan origin who was born and grew up in the Netherlands. Van Gogh had repeatedly criticized the multicultural society – both in print and in his films – in which the 'norms and values of western society' were not being defended vis-à-vis 'aggressive and backward Islam' (Frankfurter Allgemeine Sonntagszeitung issue dated 7 November 2004, p. 10). His documentary film *Submission* about Islamic misogyny was scripted by the Dutch MP Ayaan Hirsi Ali who has been the recipient of several fatwas (*Guardian*, issue dated 4 November 2004, 7).

3. What triggered the French disturbances in October and November 2005 were rumours about the deaths of two youths who were French inhabitants from immigrant families. Violence erupted amongst mainly young French youths of North African descent in a number of Paris urban districts (banlieues). These disturbances quickly spread throughout the country. In the end nearly half of the 100 regional authorities in France were affected (Roller 2006).

4. During the 1990s there were in Germany repeated attacks on refugees' hostels and immigrants' dwellings. The longest incident in time took place in August 1992 in Rostock, where for three nights – despite police protection – there were demonstrations in front of a refugee hostel and petrol bombs were thrown. In one of the most serious attacks on a dwelling house which was inhabited by two Turkish immigrant families, on 29 May 1993 five people were murdered in Sohlingen. (ZDF Politik und Gesellschaft (German Second TV channel, politics and society); http://www.zdf.de/ZDFde/inhalt/12/0,1872,1021900,00.html)

5. See for instance: Senghaas 1998.

6. i.e not any more: 'Which side are you on?

7. Müller 1998, 262; see also Senghaas 1998.

8. Tibi 1998.

9. Jenkins 1996, 100.

10. Barth 1969, 14.

11. Schwedler 1985.

12. In the United States research on ethnic segregation processes and socio-spatial dissimilarities has a much longer tradition. Whereas for example German geographers were dealing with formation of urban quarters in the Middle East and Asia – that is to say, with segregation as encountered by 'Others' – in America there was already an entire branch of research devoted to this topic. Based on Park's work there arose in the early 1950s the 'Chicago School' (of urban sociology), which addressed amongst other topics (spatial) questions relating to ethnic minorities, and whose representatives were the first to develop reliable statistical procedures to capture segregation (see for instance Duncan, Duncan 1955).

13. An overview can be found, for instance, in Siebel 2004. The results of several case studies and articles in this book are also in line with this view.

14. Friedrichs 1995; 1998. It is not quite certain, however, that these 'traditional' functions were present in all of our cities and in all countries. There is evidence from some of the chapters of this book (for instance, the studies of France and the Netherlands) that this was not the case.
15. For instance: Prager, Wieland 2005; OECD 2006.
16. It may be surprising to note that reliable and comparable statistical information on the proportion of non-native citizens in European cities is not available. However, if one reflects that in most national statistics naturalized immigrants are not listed separately, that in a number of member states (such as the Netherlands, France or the UK) people from former colonies (almost) automatically have nationality of that country and furthermore, if one reflects that in statistical information regarding demography in cities usually no account is taken of the fact that towns and cities do not abruptly end at administrative and census district areas, then the methodological problems – which can hardly be overcome – become clear. Any small-scale comparative study between European cities encounters these methodological limitations. In the case of Berlin, for instance, it is estimated that the number of inhabitants with an immigrant background is about one-quarter higher than official statistics state (see Chapter ??). Even the most ambitious approach to obtaining comparable data on European cities, the European Urban Audit project, delivers somewhat insufficient data in this field.
17. Exceptions concern some of the former Communist-ruled new EU member states, where in the process of political and economic transformation for instance citizens from the former Soviet Union returned to their home country or countries.
18. United Nations Population Division (2004): World Population in 2300, ESA/P/WP.187 (New York: UN).
19. EC 2005.
20. Not only will labour migration contribute towards a higher proportion of non-native inhabitants: poverty, violent conflicts, political oppression in some parts of the world will lead to increasing immigration pressures on Europe.
21. Population Division of the Department of Economic and Social Affairs of the United Nations Secretariat, Trends in Total Migrant Stock: The 2004 Revision. These estimates do not take into account the possibility that European Union member states – if only for economic reasons – will pursue a more active immigration policy than at present. There are currently indications that this is the case (see following section).
22. Märker 2001, 3.
23. See Sachverständigenrat für Zuwanderung und Integration 2004, 73ff (Federal Expert Group for Immigration and Integration).
24. This is frequently the case in immigration and integration questions; Märker 2001.

Part 1

Urban Mixing in a Changing Europe: Policy Context

2
Rethinking the Path to European Citizenship

Elizabeth Meehan

It may seem odd to include in a volume on *Migration and Cultural Inclusion in the European City* a chapter on citizenship on a political plane even further from the city than the local and state levels.

First, despite the hopes some had invested in the now stymied[1] Draft Constitutional Treaty as a kind of new contract between the European Union and the peoples of its member states, it is at the level of the city that there is the most debate about citizenship. According to Saloojee and van Heelsum, 'the post 1960s global cities are the loci of political and economic power' (2002, 151), making them 'magnets' that attract global migrants. 'Multicultural cities like Miami, Haifa, Brussels, Amsterdam, Montreal, and Toronto' are 'the sites of struggle over . . . rights, citizenship, the allocation of resources and political representation'. Focusing on the EU, Dunford and Hudson (1996, 5–12) also note a 'core of advanced city regions', including the 'global cities of London and Paris', which lie along 'a vital axis' from Greater London, through the Rhineland, south-eastern Germany and into Northern Italy. Secondly, and perversely, it is not cities, or, say, London's deprived boroughs and the 'dreary suburbs' of Paris, but rural areas and poorer regions that are the main focus of EU attention, through the Common Agricultural Policy and structural funding.[2]

However, EU citizenship is, indeed, relevant to the experiences of the socially and ethnically diverse range of people who inhabit cities. The very notion of citizenship originated in cities – the city state (see chapters by Honohan and Wilson in this volume). Moreover, as noted, many inhabitants of modern cities are migrants and it is the right to freedom of movement that is the root of EU citizenship[3] – albeit that in 'global cities' there are more migrants from outside the EU than there are other EU citizens.[4] As indicated later in this chapter, the comparative status of EU migrants and what are known as 'third country migrants', or third country nationals, is one of the main challenges to the notion of EU citizenship.

Moreover, while citizenship and nationality are not the same (see below, and Honohan in this volume), they are often used as synonyms. The fact that freedom of movement is the basis of European citizenship impinges on the elision in more complex ways than is acknowledged in the official dictum that European citizenship is complementary with and additional to national citizenship. In the west, the systematic denial of freedom of movement in the old South Africa and the Soviet Union and its periodic denial in the UK were often regarded as a clear violation of citizenship. Yet, in the EU, the full implications of migration and lawful residence or domicile as the criterion for participation have been avoided.[5]

The chapter opens with what policy makers had in mind in rethinking the path to European citizenship after constitutional reform and Enlargement. It then indicates the challenges to the achievement of a democratic European public sphere that includes both EU and non-EU migrants. A number of the challenges impinge upon the rival accounts of citizenship to be found in liberalism, civic republicanism and communitarianism. These categories are not exclusive. As Honohan shows, civic republicanism contributed to the development of liberal-democratic citizenship. But liberal-democratic citizenship as practised in recent centuries depends, not wholly successfully, on the prepolitical bonds or values and identities that are more usually associated with communitarianism. A reinfusion of civic republicanism into liberal-democratic citizenship, she suggests, could serve as a corrective; in effect, providing a form of citizenship more amenable to a collective life for people who do not necessarily share cultural or ethnic identities.

Since the Draft Constitutional Treaty[6] seeks to protect both representative and participatory democracy, it could be said to go some way towards that correction. And, indeed, the chapter goes on to draw attention to an attractive argument by Closa (1998) that a supranational political entity may be more capable than a nation state for the realization of democratic citizenship. But, such an actual outcome is far from inevitable. Indeed, the concluding section suggests that, even if the Draft Constitution were to be ratified, its version of liberal-democratic citizenship imbued with elements of civic republicanism will be weakened by member states which try to ride both horses of 'corrected liberalism' and communitarianism at the same time.[7]

What policy makers may have in mind for an evolving European citizenship

European citizenship is often seen as a modest version of liberal-democratic citizenship, as outlined by Honohan in this volume, focusing on individuals, involving openness, transparency, opportunities to participate, etc., and adding little to national citizenship.[8] Warleigh (2001, 23–4), however, draws attention to a debate about whether EU citizenship is 'thick' or 'thin'.

He suggests that what is in the treaties is, indeed, 'thin' but that 'understanding how formal entitlements are used in conjunction with other legislation (*acquis*[9]) generates a far more accurate view of the real value of EU citizenship which although less than revolutionary is far from a dead letter'.[10]

From the official point of view, EU citizenship should convey the rights and obligations that individually and collectively serve to create an open society in Europe that is free, fair, safe, sustainable and prosperous – a society that is so, and recognized to be so, because of integration. It is additional to and complements citizenship of a member state. It is grounded in the fundamental rights set out in the existing treaties and the Charter of Fundamental Rights, agreed in 2000 and incorporated into the signed, but unratified, Draft Constitutional Treaty.

The incorporation of the Charter was expected to provide a stronger link between the founding rights principles of previous treaties and to consolidate rights established under the *acquis*, thereby 'provid[ing] concrete substance to what it means to be a citizen of Europe' (personal communication to the author).[11] The new social contract to which the Treaty might have opened the way would, it was hoped, have added 'visible and worthwhile value' to peoples' lives. Moreover, the human rights basis of the EU fundamental principles required attention to be paid to the rights of non-EU citizens – legally residing third country nationals – through the bringing about of the idea of 'civic citizenship' (personal communication to the author).[12] Such an idea is consistent with part of an argument by Seglow (2005, 325) who reminds us that immigration is more than tourism. The 'right to be a permanent visitor' has moral implications that go beyond the 'right to visit' and beyond the familiar utilitarian justification for relatively open borders.

In anticipation of both enlargement and a new Constitutional Treaty, working parties were set up in the European Commission in 2003 to consider areas of work that would need to be developed. One of them dealt with freedom and European citizenship, as it was thought that, when new institutional and legal developments were completed, the focus of public attention would shift from the architecture of the Union to the expectations of its citizens and what it means to be European. With enlargement, this question of what it means, if anything, to be a European citizen would become more complex in the context of the even greater diversity arising from the inclusion of ten new member states. A number of areas for policy development in spheres related to being an EU citizen were identified: liberty, security, justice, wellbeing and civic participation. Together, they address policy fields matching a concept of citizenship that embodies a triad of civil, political and social rights. They also go beyond the Marshallian[13] triad by taking into account what was not on the agenda in Marshall's day. That is, the exercise of citizenship in a transnational public space defined as being based on human rights principles, ethnic or national diversity (in both the new public space and member states), as well as new social policy concerns.

On civil rights, the working party felt that more work was needed in developing a common area of civil[14] and criminal law and that the monitoring and enforcement of rights and obligations needed to be reinforced. New member states would require support to build their capacity to deliver equality and effective redress. The close link between the civil right, freedom of movement and EU social citizenship can be seen in the idea that, for the sake of mobility, high standards of education, training and life-long learning would need to be encouraged.

In the sphere of political rights, it was thought that access to knowledge and freedom of information needed to be re-examined. One of the ways that the Draft Treaty tackled this was through requiring meetings of the Council of Ministers to be public when proposed legislation was being considered and voted upon. Enhancing civic empowerment was considered necessary; for example, through the language used to explain initiatives and working with member states to ensure that citizens were aware of their rights.[15] The possibility was mooted of support for civil society organizations to facilitate civil dialogue at the European level, resting on the Draft Constitutional Treaty article on participatory democracy. The Draft Treaty, itself, introduces a new right of initiative through which a million signatories from across the Union could propose new legislation.

New thinking on social citizenship, including some of the post-Marshall concerns, addresses individual and collective wellbeing: good environmental protection and the promotion of sustainable development; consumer protection; an integrated approach to health policy; further action on social protection, employment, social inclusion and dialogue; and the fair treatment and integration of immigrants and minority groups. Specific actions were expected to be necessary in order to address inequalities within new member states and between them and older members.

An overarching idea was that the EU would develop further as a focal point for human rights, for both EU citizens and lawfully resident third-country nationals – and, indeed, the Draft Constitutional Treaty did propose to move beyond the Amsterdam Treaty.[16] The bulwark for the zone of freedom within the EU for citizens and lawful residents was also thought to need further attention to the management of illegal migration and the development of common asylum and immigration policies. More proactive approaches would also be needed to secure the physical safety of citizens and residents of the EU; in respect of crime and terrorism and other threats such as bio-terrorism, communicable diseases and maritime safety.

Challenges for the Commission and Council of Ministers

Even with ratification, formidable challenges would have lain ahead of the Commission and Council of Ministers in creating a renewed social contract between citizens and the EU. At the most basic level, despite diversity in notions of citizenship, many countries share similar trends in falling electoral participation rates and trust in national politicians. To the extent that there is apathy or alienation in national contexts, how would a level of governance beyond that succeed where its constituent states are failing? (but see note 10).

A second challenge lies in the fact that there is some evidence that, where citizens have engaged with the EU so far, it has been to protect rights previously secured at national level but which have become vulnerable because of pressures on national budgets and economies.[17] However, these pressures also affect member states as a collectivity and pressures on national systems have now become constraints on the model that originally characterized the EU – that is, that economic prosperity necessarily went hand-in-hand with social progress. This, combined with the uneven protection of different kinds of migrants, means that populations, particularly of global cities, experience new forms of exclusion and inequality which may now be too entrenched to be easily remedied. On the one hand, there are Leonard's (1998, 25–8) 'club class' Europeans who enjoy the 'open project' of a 'hybrid Europe in continuous cultural movement and renewal'.[18] Then there are the migrants who are not EU citizens, often 'scapegoated' by indigenous non-migrants who cannot enjoy the 'open project' and blame their situations on immigration and Europeanization. This leads to a third challenge; how to make real the aspirations of what used to be formulated as multiculturalism – now rethought as interculturalism (see Wilson in this volume).

The Amsterdam Treaty provides a basis for action to outlaw discrimination on grounds of, among other things, religion, race, and ethnicity. Multiculturalism or interculturalism is one approach to transcending negative freedom for members of different ethnic groups to achieve positive freedom for them to play an equal part in social, economic and political activities. Without this equality, the lives of three sets of minority ethnic groups are disadvantaged: EU citizens who are members of minority ethnic groups; lawfully resident nationals of non-EU countries; and potential new immigrants. Finding agreement on how to meet equality standards for them all is complicated by the diversity of approaches and outlooks in member states. Countries are distinguishable, by and large, by whether formal policy encourages 'diversity' or 'assimilation'. But there are differences within those countries.

For example, the UK adopted a multicultural approach (see Honohan and Wilson in this volume). And there was an outcry when a former Conservative Minister, Norman Tebbit, 'declared that one test of national loyalty might be to ask whether a person [primarily those of Indian or Pakistani origin] supported England at cricket'.[19] Now, in the UK, left-wing promoters of racial equality question multiculturalism as practised in Britain on the ground that it discourages the idea that citizens of different backgrounds should, and should be able to, inhabit shared public spaces (see Wilson in this volume on 'open-minded places'). In France, as seen in the *foulard* cases, a belief originating in 18th century radicalism has the same assimilationist consequences as Norman Tebbit's more right-wing outlook. And, equally, some in France have questioned the capacity of the 'one indivisible French Republic' to be a better buttress of liberty and equality than acknowledging diversity.[20]

In theory, it is current EU policy to extend to third country migrants the same rights as those accorded to EU citizens, be they of majority or minority ethnic communities. Some steps have been taken but, as Kostakopoulou (2001b, 182) points out, despite a rising sense that 'permanent visitors'[21] ought to have rights, third country nationals 'remain subjects rather than actors'. The notion of 'civic citizenship' could contribute to their becoming actors – and significantly so if it were to include political rights. The more fully-fledged human rights value base of EU policy (started in the Amsterdam Treaty and continued in the Draft Constitutional Treaty) will only be realized when the lived experience of minority ethnic groups within the EU is as secure as that of the majorities. This may be complicated by current policy and future developments over the management of external frontiers.

Even before the fatal attack on the Manhattan Twin Towers on 11 September 2001, the question of immigration was being 'securitized'.[22] That is to say, immigration was being regarded by member states, not as a matter of reasoned, if utilitarian, debate about economic and social factors, but as a matter of potential threat to political and cultural security; another sense of 'fortress Europe' – a matter for policing and surveillance rather than social policy. Conventional wisdom in many states and, it seems, at the EU level, is that general freedoms and ethnic integration depend upon confidence in the strength of perimeter controls. But when external frontiers are seen more as the means of keeping 'others' out than facilitating freedoms and equality within, non-Caucasian citizens and lawful residents travelling across internal boundaries are likely to experience difficulties. And, as noted, they may generally be treated with hostility by those against interculturalism and with a more communitarian outlook on citizenship.

A third challenge lies in new and applicant member states. As pointed out by Borneman and Fowler (1997, 491–3), the eastern Central European states sought to enter the EU on the basis of their ability to 'catch up' on the state model constructed in the west from the 17th century – after the Treaty of Westphalia – while, at the same time, having to recognize that those same western states are promoting supranational processes to which the sovereignty of the new states will have to be submitted. The conditions of their 'rebirth' mean that notions of citizenship are, or were, particularly closely linked to nation and state.

For example, Salecl (1994) notes that national movements in the constituent parts of the former Yugoslav republic built power by creating fantasies about the threat to the nation from 'others'. The construction of the new states was based on highly developed senses of national identity and on the idea that this is the proper basis for the organization of collective life. The former broader notion of 'Yugoslav' identity was displaced by a more 'primordial' ethnic identity.

The different histories in the twentieth century of the two parts of Europe also gave rise to different understandings of liberty and equality. In the period following the break-up of the Soviet empire, concepts of liberty and equality were more libertarian than those of the EU – even though the latter was beginning to move away from the model in which economic and social progress were thought to be inextricably linked. To the new states – except perhaps Slovenia – positive[23] notions of liberty and equality were discredited as being tantamount to communism. This can be seen in what has happened to the position of women at work and in political life and how this is viewed.[24] Even though the EU conceptions are less collective than they once were, social inclusion and gender equality, including mainstreaming, are central to EU notions of citizenship.

However, there are signs of change in the east. For example, the rebuilding of Croatia was carried out on the belief that Croatia could accommodate itself into the EU by state intervention, supported by inward investment, so long as it promoted a broader sense of identity. And it is reported about Slovenia that national borders are as permeable as any of those in the EU that used to be called 'frontier regions'.[25] Even so, as noted above, policy makers believe that special measures to support such changes are needed.

Despite the enormity of the challenge of such a large and complex diversity of identities, values, ideas and experiences, a case can be made for suggesting that the EU is, in principle, more likely to be able to rise to the occasion than states in the post-Westphalian form.

A supranational polity as more conducive than the nation state to democratic citizenship?

As noted, the liberal-democratic model of citizenship is associated with the development of the state after the Treaty of Westphalia. While this understanding may have come to seem 'natural', Heater (1990) demonstrates that the meaning of citizenship is contingent on history and social context. Even under the broad heading of 'liberal-democratic', some praxes might be more individualistic than others, have more obvious civic republican tinges of interdependence, appeal more strongly to a sense of 'fixed' community or identity, or vary in their emphases on the rights, duties and 'belonging' aspects of what it means to be a citizen.

What has been shared in the post-Westphalian states is a tendency – perhaps stronger amongst liberal-individualists than civic-republicans – to elide nationality and citizenship. Despite their synonymous use – not only colloquially, but also in much legislation – they are not the same. As Honohan (2004) has put it, when the citizen is contrasted with the non-national, it is a question of a status and the minimal legal right of co-citizens to be members of the same state. When the citizen is contrasted with the subject, it is a question of the practice of self-government, participation, attitudes, and behaviour. Histories of citizenship such as those of Heater demonstrate that some co-nationals, for example men and women, have not enjoyed the same rights of citizenship. Conversely, citizenship as a participatory practice can be, and has been, granted to co-residents who are not, or are no longer, co-nationals (through arrangements such as those surveyed in Gardner (1997), in the Commonwealth, and between Ireland and the UK).

The modern elision seems to arise because, following Westphalia, states engaged more strongly than before in nation building, dismantling feudal relationships of status and developing market-based contractual relations amongst men while retaining the older affective ties of the (patriarchal) family and social networks.[26] It came to be believed that it was only in the context of the nation state, now with clear borders and control over who crossed them, that all dimensions of citizenship could be realized. This began to be questioned in the more 'globalized' context of the late 20th century, especially and extensively by writers such as Held (1995) who argues that new theories are needed placing citizenship and democracy in a global-national-local paradigm and institutional framework.

Cosmopolitan approaches to citizenship are contested on the basis of the continuing pre-eminence of the state and, in particular, the nation state. Miller (1993), for example, reminds us that the demand made by citizens for physical and socio-economic security and rights are made on their states. Meeting these demands, through war time service, taxation, distribution and redistribution, depends on a sense of solidarity which gives legitimacy to such actions. Abstract principles of justice or constitutionalism may be too 'thin' (Honohan in this volume) to provide that solidarity. For Miller, the common bonds that make it possible can arise only through shared membership of a national political community.

But, as Honohan points out in this volume, this argument has been seriously weakened from within and without. On the one hand, she notes that a shared British identity did not prevent support for cuts in welfare spending under Margaret Thatcher. On the other, she draws attention to support for redistributive policies, such as EU structural funding, that transcend national boundaries. It could also be said that the assistance to Portugal to combat the raging fires of the summer of 2005 – the provision of specialized fire fighting equipment, including aircraft – was a very concrete expression of solidarity that reflected a sense of interdependence beyond state boundaries (personal communication to the author).[27]

Referring back to Amin (2001), the populations about whom he is concerned are, even when second or third generation migrants, either marginalized from 'mainstream membership' or concretely highlighted as the cause of the travails of the also marginalized members of the 'original' community. The clinging of those who feel dispossessed to the idea of citizenship as a 'fixed identity'[28] and a liberal re-evaluation of multiculturalism's apparently uncritical endorsement of all cultures and its neglect of the need for shared 'open-minded places' have combined to give rise to a 'reassertion of uniform national citizenship' (Honohan in this volume). But the communitarian basis of national citizenship cannot promote a democratic praxis in an ethnically diverse polity. Even if internally democratic, and promoting positive rather than negative freedom, communitarian models often seek to exclude others[29] and to promote communal self-determination and solidarity among those defined as included.[30] Moreover, as Honohan (this volume) points out, in taking the home and family as the model for the polity, communitarianism elides different kinds of 'recognition' – love, respect and solidarity – which are, in reality, appropriate to different kinds of relationships. Community models, she argues, presuppose intimacy or shared values which cannot easily be extended to diverse populations.

Going beyond negative arguments about what is wrong with a communitarian version of national citizenship, Closa (1998a; 1998b) makes a positive case that there is a greater prospect for democratic forms of citizenship in a supranational form of polity. He, too, sees a stumbling block in the dependence of national citizenship on bonds that were formed in a pre-democratic age and were affective rather than principled. A supranational site for citizenship is more promising precisely because it *cannot* rely on such bonds. Alternative, principled bonds encompass voting equality, effective participation, enlightened understanding, control of agendas and inclusiveness.[31] Weiler (1997a; 1997b), while departing from Closa on matters relating to nationality, a matter that will recur, provides practical examples of mechanisms necessary to a democratic European citizenship; a public space – supported by the new thinking on how to support civic dialogue – the possibility of a legislative ballot, some direct taxation and more extensive horizontal human rights, as appeared subsequently in the Draft Treaty.

Closa is, however, sceptical about the actual realization of democratic European citizenship because of his assessment of the condition of European civil society[32] and his judgement of the behaviour of the governments of member states – which, together, react on each other as in a vicious spiral. Weiler, too, notes the interaction of these two forces but argues the national identifications of people who nevertheless share some values cannot be circumvented. Closa expressed his scepticism before the Convention on the Future of Europe and the Draft Constitutional Treaty and is undoubtedly vindicated by the fate of the treaty at the hands of voters. Then, he suggested that the 'principled bonds' in the European public sphere were not strong enough to transform citizenship from an enhanced set of national and/or private rights into a means of transnational self-determination. And he thought that civil society in the EU was too weak to struggle[33] for anything different – without a willingness on the part of states themselves to agree to stop trying to maintain the impression that anxieties about national identities are well attended to in EU provisions.

Weiler (1997a, 508–09), noting the irresistibleness of nationality, argues the need for a combination of measures – not only those above relating to the transnational, but a concrete means of reassuring people about state-based competences. Closa, however, argues that, among other things, states must avoid seeking derogations and exemptions which 'offer shelter to communitarian understandings of the relationship between individuals and the state premised on nationality' (1998b, 431–2). And therein lies the rub. As Bellamy, Castiglione and Shaw (2006) point out, treatment of third country nationals in the EU cannot benefit from the supranationalist or federalist logic that enables 'privileged foreigners' (EU citizens living in another member state) to have the same rights. This is because the members of the EU have linked EU citizenship to a categorical border that is 'the sum of the nationalities of member states' – making it unlikely that they would agree to a 'civic citizenship' that included political rights for lawful non-EU residents.[34]

Conclusion: what can be done?

This chapter has indicated that there is some degree of consensus amongst proponents of liberal-democratic EU citizenship ('corrected' with a few elements of civic republicanism) about useful or desirable developments. The aspiration that the Draft Treaty, if ratified, would provide a clear statement about the relationship between the people and the polity chimes with Closa's call for 'the full constitutionalization of a European political status' (1998b, 431). Its ambition for human rights values to govern the lives of both citizens and lawful residents of other nationalities would have met some of Kostakopoulou's (2001) concerns about the legal and social, if not the political, interests of the latter. Other areas over which there is agreement about both what is desirable and possible include: better opportunities for direct, effective participation, not only to contribute to policy development (such as by support for civic associations), but also to influence outcomes;[35] greater openness or transparency; and stronger forms of redress.

It would not be unreasonable to think that there could be agreement over Weiler's call for a European public space and new thinking by officials about civic associations.[36] These are consistent with similar concerns voiced about national politics. Mouffe (1992), for example, in arguing against classical pluralism in which the state is viewed as neutral, has proposed that the state has a key role in structuring the public space to ensure that marginalized voices were heard on an equal basis. In the UK, New Labour's Modernizing Government Programme is replete with references to the need to include such voices.

More recently, Laclau and Mouffe (2001) have theorized the kind of dialogue that would occur in a democratic public space, and do so in a way that appears to resonate for a space that, being transnational, embodies an untidy mosaic of consensus and dissent. That is, they argue that it is necessary to move beyond the idea that antagonism can be removed when all voices are included in public dialogue to the recognition that 'struggles for power are a natural and democratic feature of democratic politics'. The prize is that, in a politics of 'conflictual consensus', the game is never a zero-sum one – a metaphor if ever there was one for the member states – so why not, too, for their nationals?

Hutton (2004) also talks about reconstructing the 'public sphere' – a restoration and modernization of the sense of public that attaches to, for example, the public footpath, or in cities, the public gallery, the public library – places that are shared, belong to all, regardless of how we live in the 'non-public' places and spaces. He crystallizes what he means by 'public' by noting that one would never talk about a 'state footpath'.[37] However, the state is not irrelevant as he, too, sees a role for it in working in partnership with voluntary and community associations to reconstruct the 'public' and to promote the safety, real and perceived, that is necessary to 'public places' being genuinely universal. As Wilson points out in this volume, the Council of Europe is engaged in such a project. The EU has played a recognized role in resolving territorial conflicts. It would be reasonable to think that, in partnership, the two bodies could do something to rectify the neglect of cities noted at the beginning of this chapter.

In conclusion, however, it is necessary to return to what is crucial but less readily the subject of agreement. Closa's calls for stronger reciprocity of rights, Kostakopoulou's (2001, 137) regret that domicile is not a criterion for the exercise of political rights and the contrary official hope for a 'civic citizenship' that would include immigrants bring us to the unresolved tension in EU citizenship. That is, between Honohan's 'minimal legal right of co-citizens to be members of same state' and 'the practice of self-government, participation, attitudes, and behaviour'.

Many EU member states have heterogeneous populations, because of imperial pasts or 'guest worker' traditions. So long as members of minority ethnic groups are naturalized, they, as nationals of member states, have, by definition, the status of European citizen and the concomitant rights.[38] However, such access to EU citizenship is haphazard. States retain the right to determine who are their nationals for the purposes of EU citizenship[39] and not all member states have the same rules about naturalization. Some systems are based principally on the doctrine of *ius sanguinis*, others on *ius solis* and others a mixture. Consequently, naturalization is a route that could provide equal treatment with EU citizens for some, but not all, nationals originating from third countries. But, while states remain tenacious in retaining prerogatives over (different) nationality rules, strains are beginning to show at the EU level.

On the one hand, the supranational Commission is meticulous in deferring to the primacy of member states over nationality and citizenship. The European Court of Justice, too, has maintained states' prerogative to determine matters relating to nationality. But the cases it has had to address demonstrate the difficulties of this allocation of competence. Once, such cases were mainly about the residence or employment rights of family members in 'mixed marriages'. In the 1990s, the question of the treatment of persons of dual nationality – of a member state and a non-member state – arose. In 1992, the Court upheld the exclusive right of states to determine nationality but also stated that this competence must be exercised consistently with Community law.[40] Kostakopoulou (2001a, 66–7) argues that this ruling was far from a challenge to the nationality competence of member states; it merely required that a person recognized as a national in one member state should be able to move without additional impediments imposed in another member state. But the fact that the problem arose is an indication of the difficulties of maintaining a *cordon sanitaire* around member states' nationality laws and the right to claim EU citizens' rights. Moreover, the *ius sanguinis* states have had to begin to adapt their naturalization laws. Closa exhorts states to show willingness to respond to 'spill over' pressures from employment, family status, mobility and so on, on to nationality laws. But the omens are not good – for that or for his plea to them not to 'shelter behind communitarian understandings of citizenship' (1998b, 431–2).

While the Convention leading to the Draft Constitutional Treaty was organized by the EU in an unusually open and participatory manner, the manner in which states engaged their citizens was not exemplary.[41] In countries where ratification required a referendum, the Draft Treaty was 'sold' as a victory for that national interest or, at least, as serving 'anxieties about national identities' by minimizing concessions to another set of national interests. The more successfully one country did that, the greater the difficulty for another. For example, the UK Prime Minister's efforts to reassure sceptical Britons is taken in France as a sign that the Treaty was too 'Anglo-Saxon' – leading to a paradoxical commonality in opposition between the French 'Left' and the British 'Right'.[42]

This does not bode well for any belief that, once legal and institutional reforms are completed, people will become concerned to tackle what it means to be European – at least, not through formal institutions. The apathy and alienation from formal politics, referred to earlier in this chapter, does not mean that people are uninterested in politics. Nor are they uninterested in Europe.[43] But their interest and even activism takes different forms – not least in those 'global cities' with which the chapter opened. If people are to turn their attention to what it means to be European, they are unlikely to do so through 'normal channels'. Therein lies a constitutional dilemma. As was seen in the 1960s and 1970s, the more the Commission tried to engage populations directly and the more the Court of Justice insisted that the legal order was one of peoples as much as of states, the more defensive of national prerogatives the member states became. They may have signed a Treaty that was something of a 'new social contract', and something of an intercultural one at that, but they failed – or chose not – to convince citizens that it was.

Notes

1. The peoples of France and the Netherlands voted 'no' in ratification referendums. These results in founding member states brought the ratification process to a halt while member states consider what, if anything, can be done to renew the process. Given the way that some member states and groups within them were presenting the Draft Treaty (see later in this chapter), the results were hardly surprising.
2. Begg 1998, 15; Leonard 1998, 54–5.
3. The original European Economic Community was founded on 'Four Freedoms'; freedom of movement of goods, services, capital and labour. In the early days, some had the idea that the last meant that employers had the freedom to move workers around. This was quickly scotched. The European Court of Justice ruled that the Treaty of Rome was not only a compact among states but also gave individuals rights. Its rulings on what counted as being a worker expanded the definition so greatly that those with the most minimal attachment to the labour market were construed as having the right to move to another member state. Freedom of movement for all citizens, as opposed to workers, was constitutionalized in the Maastricht Treaty, albeit with some conditions. See Meehan 1993 and Downs 2001.
4. Amin 2001, 285.
5. Kostakopoulou 2001a.
6. European Commission 2005.
7. Hilson (2006) discusses the argument that persons 'affected' by policy should have political rights – a case that does not depend on shared nationality. She argues, however, that the difficulty in getting member states to agree that this justified EU citizenship for their nationals indicates the hurdle that would have to be surmounted to get them to agree that the same logic applies to third country migrants.
8. Its formal provisions include: the rights of citizens living in a member state other than their own to vote and stand for election to municipal authorities and the European Parliament, and the right to be protected by the diplomatic and consular services of another member state when in a country outside the EU where their own state has no such representation (Maastricht). There are also rights relating to what may be expected in terms of redress – Ombudsman, and, in the Amsterdam Treaty, an entitlement to take EU institutions to the Court of

Justice over actions thought to infringe individual rights. The Amsterdam Treaty also allows the European Council to take action against a member state 'in serious and persistent breach' of rights.

9. The accumulated body of 'hard' and 'soft' law in a range of social and economic (employment) spheres associated with a modern version of a Marshallian concept of citizenship, as well as consumer protection, public health and the environment. The right to participation is augmented by how the EU does its business – for example, bringing about directives through social dialogue and the various consultation requirements relating to structural funding, the Committee of the Regions and the Economic and Social Council.

10. Moreover, according to Ladrech (1994, 69–74), the national rules governing citizens' rights have taken on an increasingly European character which impinges upon, without transforming, national prerogatives.

11. This was not an unreasonable assumption (though it should be noted that the Charter has been criticized for being justiciable only in respect of EU actions). Smith 1998 quotes Barnett's 1997 criticism of New Labour for bringing in 'the greatest constitutional reform for a century' but without 'a statement of principles', thus leaving 'the country with no clear idea' of what (the reform programme) means and where it is supposed to lead.

12. This is one of three ways in which lawful residents from outside the EU could acquire permanently the same rights as EU citizens. The other two are naturalization in the country of residence, or the breaking of the dependence of EU rights on nationality of a member state (see also later in the chapter). However, for 'civic citizenship' to mean more than 'denizenship' (Connolly, Day and Shaw, 2006), it would have to include political rights.

13. Marshall 1963; 1973 edn.

14. Of particular urgency is the question of the definitions of family partnerships and members because of the close links between these and freedom of movement rights. The Court of Justice had been confronting shifting ideas and practice on a case-by-case basis but, it was thought this needed to be tackled more systematically.

15. It was also thought that the smaller Commission, with its President elected by the Parliament (and Parliament being able to pass censure motions), could help to improve citizens' sense of influence over the appointment of the policy initiator and enforcer, making matters more clearly political and democratic even if not reducing alienation (personal communication to the author).

16. The Amsterdam Treaty made explicit that human rights were fundamental to EU values and adumbrated the possibility that the EU itself – as opposed to its individual member states – should become a signatory to the European Convention on Human Rights. This became a definite intention in the Draft Constitutional Treaty which, as noted, also incorporated the Charter of Fundamental Rights.

17. Closa 1995.

18. Amin 2001, 287.

19. Haseler 1996, 76; nor was this very tactful to Scotland, Wales and Northern Ireland! Something similar has, however, been proposed about the Europeanization of peoples' identities. Borneman and Fowler 1997, 508) propose that the extent of this should be explored by looking at human activities such as sport. In a different vein, they suggest that soccer is an archetypical example of Europeanization as, like the EU itself, it is 'an institutionalized system of aggressive yet cooperative competition among global, national and local entities'.

20. It should be noted that the practice of discrimination, irrespective of the prevalent model of ethnic 'integration' is not necessarily confined to relations between black and white EU citizens or lawful residents. In Northern Ireland, for example, there have been a significant number of attacks recently, not only on black people, but also on Portuguese, Poles and others from central and eastern central Europe.
21. See Seglow above.
22. Kostakopoulou 1998.
23. That is, in distinction to negative versions in which liberty means 'being left alone', not interfered with, and equality means no more than the removal of arbitrary impediments.
24. Galligan, Clavero, Sloat no date.
25. In the daily newspaper *Irish Times* of 6 April 2004.
26. Dahrendorf 1988; Pateman 1988.
27. This, of course, took place in the absence of the further Commission thinking, seen as entailed by a Constitutional Treaty, on the protection of the physical safety (see earlier in this chapter). In the same communication, the question was raised as to whether such solidarity would be forthcoming in a bigger crisis; for example over the sharing of vaccines and antiretroviral in an outbreak of avian influenza among humans. The point was made that this would be a powerful indication of solidarity but that, if it were not, it would dramatically demonstrate the weakness of EU citizenship, and would be comparable with what is being said or is shown by the fate of poor and black Americans in the wake of Hurricane Katrina.
28. Amin 2001, 287.
29. The more immigration policies are based on a state's history and culture, the closer they are to communitarianism, according to Seglow (2005, 321). While he proposes that communitarianism is antithetical to the right of free movement and lacks the normative authority to justify restrictions, he also rejects the argument for total openness, suggesting instead that policy should, to some extent, reflect history but, at the same time, both indigenous citizens and newcomers should be encouraged to think about the virtues of citizenship and international social justice. He also argues for multi-level cooperation over admissions (320–1, 328, 330).
30. Bellamy 2001, 65–7.
31. Taken by Closa from Dahl 1986.
32. See also contributors to Bellamy, Castiglione, Shaw, eds (2006) for evidence that supports Closa's doubts.
33. Accounts of the development of national citizenship often note that struggle from below is an important indicator of a real redistribution of power through the extension of rights – in distinction to privileges that are conferred from above without contestation. For example, see Turner 1990.
34. See note 7.
35. Weiler 1997a, 508–09, on legislative initiatives; the Draft Treaty on popular proposals for legislation.
36. 1997a; 1997b.
37. Though beyond the sphere of the city, it is common to refer to, for example, the *National* Gallery and *National* Library (often the repository of state papers).
38. See note 7.
39. For example, the people of the Isle of Man and the Channel Islands are not. Gibraltarians are, allowing them to move freely into Spain. But until a challenge

in the Court of Justice, they did not have the right to vote for a member of the European Parliament.

40. Mr Micheletti was Argentinian and Italian. The Spanish government, in refusing him leave to practise his profession in Spain, did not deny his Italian nationality, but held that, under Spanish law, his Argentinian nationality counted since that was where he habitually resided before coming to Spain.

41. Their divided approach was tackled in the European Parliament. The Chair of the Constitutional Affairs Committee, Jo Leinen MEP, questioned the Commission and Council about their intended communication strategies and, even, whether they were intending to facilitate a common approach. The Commissioner (then designate) for Institutional Affairs, Margot Wallström, made it plain that she felt it was for member states to bring ratification to a successful conclusion. And, indeed, she was right, in the sense that reaction in the UK to possible financial aid to run information campaigns was seen by opponents of the Draft as 'buying' a 'yes' vote. However, as Jo Leinen no doubt knew, it was predictable in 2004 that electorates would reject the Treaty. 'No' votes, or abstentions, in protest about not having been consulted on major EU affairs, were predicted in opinion polls (Neweuropeans Networks newsletter issue dated 15 November 2004).

42. Federal Trust News Letter issue dated April 2005.

43. Leonard 1998.

3
A Place for all our Citizens: the Council of Europe and Shared Cities

Robin Wilson

This chapter explores the lessons of the Council of Europe's work on 'shared cities', part of the Intercultural Dialogue and Conflict Prevention project carried out in the framework of the Council's Steering Committee for Culture. It is an amended version of a paper of the same name published by the Council in 2003.

The overall project had its origins in the wars of succession in former Yugoslavia and was stimulated by the '9/11' attacks in the United States. It became increasingly apparent that relationships between those perceiving themselves as belonging to different ethnic 'communities' represented a major – and potentially extremely violent – challenge, whether in terms of how neighbours could coexist in harmony or how enemy-images could be broken down between strangers across the globe.

The work was based on five city case studies conducted in 2002: Belfast[1] in Northern Ireland, Mitrovica[2] in Kosovo, Narva[3] in Estonia, Nicosia[4] in Cyprus and Uzhgorod[5] in Ukraine. These were presented and discussed at a round table organized by the Council of Europe in Frankfurt an der Oder in December that year. Unpublished, the authors are acknowledged as this chapter draws upon them.

It draws too on relevant Council of Europe material, such as the report of the Expert Colloquy on 'Dialogue serving intercultural and inter-religious communication' held in Strasbourg in October 2002. The Council of Europe project was sustained in 2003 and 2004 with Intercultural Forums held respectively in Sarajevo and Troina, Sicily. A major declaration on cultural diversity was agreed by member state culture ministers in Opatia, Croatia, in October 2003.[6]

By way of introduction, a contextualizing framework as to the nature of the city is offered for the subsequent empirical discussion. This also adduces evidence from cities outside the five cases, including Antwerp, where there has been xenophobic reaction to significant Muslim migration in recent decades. Responsibility for the content of the chapter rests with the author alone and any view expressed should not be assumed to reflect official positions of the Council of Europe.

The nature of the city

Eighty per cent of the population of contemporary Europe lives in cities.[7] But what is the city?

The noun 'city' and the related adjective 'civic' share the same Latin root in 'citizen' (*civis*), via the notion of citizenship (*civitas*). Aristotle made the connection between the individual and civic life in his comment 'that man is by nature a political animal, and a man that is by nature and not merely by fortune citiless is either low in the scale of humanity or above it'.[8]

It is the same root, too, as 'civilization'. From the Athens of the Greek *polis* to 1920s Berlin, the various 'golden ages' of civilization surveyed by Peter Hall (1999) are all 'urban' ages. For him, the 'global city' represents a 'creative milieu', which shows what the city can attain at its apogee.

But what makes a 'creative city'? Charles Landry argues that in a globalizing environment in which cities are competing for international attention, 'their cultural distinctiveness is perhaps the unique asset they have to offer the external world' (2003, 5). The associated positive images makes the city a magnet for investment, visitors, migrants – a magnet more powerful than other forces which might otherwise drain these physical, human and social resources away.

Key to that achievement is the outsider, *l'étranger, der Ausländer*, such as the Jew in Vienna before the First World War. As with Renaissance Florence, Elizabethan London or late 19th century Paris, the global city has sucked in creative forces. Of classical Athens, Hall writes: 'And it emerges that it was these outsiders, half inside the culture but half excluded from it, who were the true progenitors of the Athenian miracle' (1999, 21–2). Cultural creativity stems from inter rather than multiculturalism.

> Many social and cultural policies have aimed at multiculturalism, which means the strengthening of the separate cultural identities of ethnic minorities, which now have their own arts centres, schools, places of worship and social clubs. But multiculturalism can be problematic if there is little communication between cultures. We now need to move one stage further. Resources should now be directed more to intercultural projects which build bridges between the fragments, and produce something new out of the multicultural patchwork of our cities. Creativity may be encouraged by fragmentation, but not by marginalisation. Ethnic ghettoes are unlikely to contribute to solving the wider problems of cities.[9]

Bloomfield and Bianchini have sustained this train of thought. They give this definition of their interculturalist alternative: 'Interculturalism goes beyond equal opportunities and respect for existing cultural differences, to the plur-alist transformation of public space, institutions and civic culture. So it does not recognise cultural boundaries as fixed but in a state of flux and remaking' (2004, 12).

The architect Richard Rogers agrees. For him, '(T)he city is, first and fore-most, a meeting place for people.' At its best, it operates as 'a series of interconnected networks of places and spaces devoted to making the most of human interaction'.[10]

Similarly, for Ash Amin and Nigel Thrift, 'urban life is the irreducible product of mixture', a site of '*moments of encounter*', of 'unexpected juxtapos-itions' (2002, 3, 30, and 40). The challenge facing today's cities is to cement together through civic commitment an increasingly diverse citizenry. Those that succeed will indeed be dynamic magnets for the mobile and the cosmo-politan, where 'externalities associated with knowledge spillovers' act as 'engines of growth'.[11] Those that fail will be embittered places for those, often poor and excluded, trapped within them.

To turn this challenge around, managing ethnic diversity is largely an urban concern. For it is also in the city, where individuals find themselves cheek by jowl with the 'other', that violent intercommunal clashes take place.[12] Great violent tragedies of recent years, from the siege of Sarajevo to the attack on the World Trade Centre, have had multicultural cities at their heart. Yet it is here, too, that '*new forms of human sociality*, new modes of reciprocity'[13] can redefine 'community' in more flexible and contemporary ways. Yet Putnam (2003) has demonstrated a negative correlation between ethnic diversity and 'social capital' – the cohesion of a city as expressed in relationships of trust, agreed norms and vibrant networks. Los Angeles, for instance, scores very low on indices of social capital, such as confidence in government. Yet diversity is set only to increase and, as Putnam would argue, is basically 'healthy'.

So what is the answer? It may lie in Putnam's distinction (2000, 22–3) between 'bonding' and 'bridging' social capital. The former is intracom-munal, the latter intercommunal. Thus 'bridging social capital can generate broader identities and reciprocity, whereas bonding social capital bolsters our narrower selves', even leading to 'strong out-group antagonism'.

Bridging social capital, Putnam (2003) argues, is essential for democracy. A society that only has bonding social capital 'looks a lot like Belfast'. Putnam's contention dovetails with the argument of Varshney (2002, 281–2), in his study of Indian cities, that 'the key determinant of peace is *inter*communal civic life, not civic life *per se*'.

But how can these inter-ethnic relationships be stimulated? Rogers, following Walzer, argues that urban space can be organized in a 'single-minded' or 'open-minded' way. The former would comprise the conven-tional suburb, housing estate, industrial zone, car park or ring road. The latter would entail the busy square, the park, the lively street, the pavement café or the market. If the former favours an atomized, consumerist existence, ' "open-minded" places give us something in common: they bring diverse sections of society together and breed a sense of tolerance, awareness, identity and mutual respect' (1997, 9–10). Similarly, Lebon contends that 'public space turns cultural diversity into interculturality' (2002, 5).

Not automatically, however. Theoretically, public spaces can be colonized by one demographic group, and so shunned by others: city leaders will not thank planners who persuade them to invest in spaces that become vandalized and dominated by gangs of young men. Nor does contact, in itself, between individuals from different 'communities' necessarily lead to greater mutual understanding, associated as it can be with highly constrained and superficial engagements – as captured in the ironic phrase of the Irish poet Seamus Heaney: 'Whatever you say, say nothing.'

As Amin and Thrift express it, 'Cultural hybridization requires meaningful and repeated contact, the slow experience of working, being and living with others, and the everyday fusion of cultures in what we consume, what we see, where we travel, how we live, with whom we play, and so on' (2002, 137). This more demanding representation of the challenge points towards the importance of civic networks as conduits of repeated dialogue and supportive environments for exchanges in which body armour is willingly cast aside.

It cannot be assumed that such networks will arise spontaneously. Indeed, care is needed to ensure that well meaning policies of support for minority forms of cultural expression do not themselves inadvertently reproduce ghettoization.

Bauman (2001) has written of how the aspiration to reside in the warmth of 'community', where reflection is not necessary, homogeneity can be assumed and identity is taken for granted, is a tantalizing prospect. Yet individuals can only secure it by resigning their freedom. And he writes: ' "The really existing community" will be unlike their dreams – more like their opposite: it will add to their fears and insecurity instead of quashing them or putting them to rest. It will call for twenty-four hours a day vigilance and a daily sharpening of swords; for struggle, day in day out, to keep the aliens off the gates and to spy out and hunt down the turncoats in their own midst' (2001, 17). Ulrich Beck, in an essay on 'How neighbours become Jews', calls this the '*prison fallacy* of history' (1998, 138).

Today, the stresses of cultural diversity are compounded by the economic strains of modern urban life. Amid intensified global competition, employers are transferring risk to casualized, temporary and part-time employees. These changes are especially visible in the spatial concentrations of immigrants and ethnic minority communities in areas with deteriorating environmental conditions. Such environments are conducive to the scapegoating behaviour which Richard Wilkinson detects among subordinated individuals in 'dominance hierarchies' (2005, 224–8). Nevertheless, despite the difficulties, Amin and Thrift conclude: 'Our belief is that in order to encourage citizenship as an everyday practice, people need to experience negotiating diversity and difference ... Citizenship has to develop through its *practice* ...' (2002, 150).

Towards lessons for policy makers

Two ideal type models are 'assimilationism' and 'multiculturalism'. The former requires members of minorities to adapt to the norms of the dominant majority. The French, for example, only acknowledging citizens and refusing to recognize cultural diversity, have refused to ratify the Council of Europe Framework on the Rights of National Minorities. The latter poses no challenge to these norms either, but assumes that minorities pursue a separate (and equally unchanged) cultural identity. However, neither subordination nor separatism is a basis for comity in a diverse society, particularly in the context of the propinquity of a modern city. And so a third option has been increasingly canvassed: 'integrationism'. Integrationism is premised on a balance being struck between the pursuit of cultural diversity and the maintenance of a civic society. Where that balance is struck at any time is determined through intercultural dialogue, which it is hoped will change *all* participants over time.

This linking of cultural diversity and intercultural dialogue privileges the development of a culture of tolerance, assuming as this does the dignity of every citizen and his/her interdependence with others. Jürgen Habermas stresses that this is not 'a *one-way street* to cultural self-assertion by groups with their own collective identities'. Rather, 'the coexistence of different life forms as equals must not be allowed to prompt segregation. Instead, it requires the integration of all citizens – and their mutual recognition across cultural divisions as citizens – within the framework of a shared political culture' (2004, 17–18).

This demands in multi-ethnic societies a civic-cosmopolitan disposition, as a 'core value' of intercultural dialogue.[14] It implies a disposition towards 'hospitality' rather than 'hostility'[15] and a recognition that, in the contemporary world, identity is more a matter of politics and choice than fate.[16] What practical lessons then, within such a framework, can be suggested as to how cities can be shared, rather than segregated? The following observations are expanded in the rest of the chapter:

- Physical barriers are the most visible signs of inter-communal intolerance. Walls dividing populations dehumanize those on the 'other side', rendered strangers as a result. The task here is to contest the 'prison fallacy' of identity, by which an illusory 'security' is gained at the expense of individual freedom, in favour of the expansion of genuinely public space.
- In as far as cities consist of interconnected networks, *civic networks* are key antidotes to ethnic conflict. Interfaith and intercultural relations, as

well as secular cross-communal movements like trade unions, moderate ethnic identities and absorb the effect of ethnopolitical 'shocks'.

- Cities must not become balkanized into discrete 'communities' embracing antagonistic collective narratives of the past. Where populations are divided, the media and – more narrowly – museums have a critical role in challenging, rather than reproducing, stereotyped enemy images based on a selective reading of current affairs and the past, in which the 'self' is always victim.

- Symbols are of major import in the conduct of ethnic conflicts. The *arts* have the potential to explore the play of identity and social possibility in a manner that may help individuals appreciate better the multiplicity of their own identities and their inherent relatedness to the identities of others.

- Certitude in a complex and changing world is a dangerous thing, leading readily to intolerance. *Integrated education*, at all levels, not only brings individuals from different backgrounds together but at its best encourages them to reflect on their identities in a process of dialogue with one another. While this should begin in the nursery, it should embrace adults engaged in lifelong learning.

- In today's privatized lifestyle, the household is a major institution and the family a key factor in the socialization of young people. *Mixed marriages* need to be protected and supported, in the face of intercommunal tensions.

- A critical counterweight to ethnic tensions is the idea of a common civic pride. The city can then become like a giant atrium under which all its inhabitants can shelter. Engendering such pride requires the exercise of *civic leadership* rather than ethnopolitical entrepreneurship. It can motivate the previously uninvolved or disengaged to develop anew their relationship with civic life.

- Ethnic conflicts are often complicated by the fact that minorities are linked to larger 'communities' with which their members may have affinity on the other side of borders. They may thus come to be seen as Trojan horses, but can instead act as bridges across *porous borders* to other civilizations.

The remainder of this chapter fleshes out each of these themes in more detail. While their precise adaptation will depend on the concrete situation, the ideas themselves are of universal application.

Public space

Division can be manifested in physical form. Nicosia, like the rest of Cyprus, is divided by a 'buffer zone' between its Turkish and Cypriot parts. Tourist maps of the city on the respective sides present the area of the 'other' simply as a blank space, literally uncharted territory. This is associated with the 'homogenization' of the other, with no physical contact.[17] Such homogenization had internal as well as external effects. On the Greek-Cypriot side, it renders invisible Armenian, Maronite and more recent Asian minorities.

Mitrovica has a river bisecting its Serbian and Albanian populations. The bridge over the river – which could connect them – was in fact the site of intercommunal clashes following the recent war, with a group of self-appointed paramilitary 'bridge watchers' defending the Serbian minority against Albanian encroachment. Symptomatic of how the trajectory of cities can influence wider trends in the country as a whole, the division of Mitrovica has been seen as the basis for a wider *de facto* partition of northern Kosovo, linked to Serbia, from the predominantly Albanian and, increasingly, independence seeking south.

At the last count, Northern Ireland was officially recognized to have 37 'peace walls' and other physical barriers, 27 of them in Belfast.[18] George Orwell would doubtless turn in his grave at this 'Newspeak' euphemism. That these barriers should have proliferated – in response to sectarian clashes – during what was officially described as a 'peace process' is a sobering reminder that the philosophy 'high fences make good neighbours' is self-defeating as well as morally tendentious. It is precisely at these walls that intercommunal tensions tend to ignite, and there are thus frequent calls for them to be made even higher and wider. The fundamental problem is that they represent the ultimate dehumanization: why worry about throwing a missile if you cannot see the human being wounded on the other side? Bringing down walls – whether actual or in the head – requires the building of civic networks, a sentiment expressed in the Cantle report for the UK Home Office on the riots in northern English mill towns in 2001: 'We have been struck by the apparent success of those areas where funding has been used to build a coalition of interests and where there are firm expectations about working together for the good of that particular area. That can be contrasted with areas that have resourced many separate and distinct community interests, often for very similar purposes. These tend to reinforce cultural differences . . .' (2001, 37–8). The report argued that there should be a presumption against funding for distinct 'communities', in favour of cross communal 'themes'.

Civic networks

Varshney (2002) has argued that civic networks are the best antidote to intercommunal violence. In particular, while quotidian connections such as cross communal visits are helpful in this regard, it is 'associational' links that are most effective: business associations, trade unions, sports clubs, professional organizations and so on.

Varshney's work on Hindu–Muslim relations in India is similar to an independent 'peace enclaves' study in former Yugoslavia, carried out for the Council of Europe project. In each investigation pairs of cities, violent and peaceful, were selected for study.

From his research Varshney concludes: 'A multiethnic society with few interconnections across ethnic boundaries is very vulnerable to ethnic disorders and violence.' Of one of India's most riot-prone cities he writes: 'One can actually live one's entire life in Hyderabad's old city without spending more than a small amount of time with members of the other community' (2002, 15). This has powerful resonance with the Cantle report referred to above. In towns like Oldham, Bradford and Burnley, the review team were shocked to discover the extent to which 'many communities operate on the basis of a series of parallel lives'.[19] Similarly, in Mitrovica Serbs and ethnic Albanians live in 'parallel worlds'. More recently, the chair of the UK Commission for Racial Equality, Trevor Phillips, urged urban leaders to 'arrest the trend towards separate and competing ethnic fiefdoms within their city walls'.[20]

In an account which echoes Putnam's discussion of social capital, Varshney paints this picture of intercommunal civic associations in the peaceful southern Indian city of Calicut: ' . . . Calicut is a place of "joiners". Associations of all kinds – business, labour, professional, social, theatre, film, sports, art, reading – abound. From the ubiquitous trade associations to Lions' and Rotary Clubs, reading clubs, the head loaders' association, the rickshaw pullers' association, and even something like an art lovers' association, citizens of Calicut excel in joining clubs and associations.' And while there are religiously based organizations, as in cities marked by violence, 'what is distinctive is the extent of interreligious interaction in nondenominational organizations' (2002, 127).

It was the same story in Tuzla, in Bosnia-Herzegovina, in the early 1990s.[21] Traditions of interfaith and intercultural relations in the town, allied to the traditional solidarity of the labour movement, were able to protect Tuzla from the spreading flames of interethnic conflict.

If civic networks do not necessarily emerge spontaneously to counter potential 'shocks' to ethnically diverse cities, is the alternative to bring them about by coercion? Apart from the ethical issues this raises, the US experience of 'bussing' would suggest this is not feasible. But it is perfectly legitimate and practicable for civic authorities to 'broker' such networks, including by assisting civic actors and NGOs to establish them. One instance reported at the Council of Europe expert colloquy on intercultural and inter-religious dialogue was *Marseille-Espérance*.[22] Expressing the remarkable diversity of the city, this association brings together representatives from roughly 20 different faiths for meetings once or twice a month to discuss social or cultural issues or simply calendar clashes – a multireligious calendar is posted in places of worship. Every year, it also organizes an intercultural festival in the city's opera house and a debate, attended by thousands, on a subject with religious connotations, such as bioethics.

Media/museums

With black humour, the Belfast writer Glenn Patterson defines the meaning of 'community' in his native society as 'another word for side'. The anthropologist Neil Jarman, another resident of the city, has in more academic language criticized this 'essentialised sense of difference and otherness'. He writes: 'The notion of two communities, two cultures, two traditions, two identities or two tribes dominates perceptions, practices and processes. The effectively unknown "other" is always present to be invoked and confronted as a source of fear and threat rather than as something positive or as something to be engaged with and understood . . .' (2002, 17). Such 'imagined' communities (to borrow a phrase from Benedict Anderson's 1991 discussion of nationalism) are cemented by common narratives of the past which are mutually incompatible. Museums become critical institutions here in divided cities. In Nicosia stereotyped histories are reproduced by museums presenting a 'heroes and villains' view of the past. In Belfast, the Ulster Museum has sought to reach out to the citizenry as a whole. For example, an exhibition on the bicentennial of the rebellion by the republican but mainly Protestant led 'United Irishmen of 1798' provided a challenge to stereotyped views.

A usable past is essential if a common, civic vision of the future is to be elaborated. Here a steer is provided by Jean Petaux et al. Petaux argues that a path needs to be charted between 'collective amnesia', which makes a repeat of past tragedies possible as their lessons have not been learnt, and 'mnemonic obsession' (2002, 15), which rakes over past conflicts from one generation to the next. It is important to stress that it is by no means inevitable that historic enmities will automatically be sustained into the indefinite future. Essentialist talk of 'ancient hatreds',[23] rehearsed when those who had lived as neighbours in former Yugoslavia resorted to violence against each other, does not explain why long periods of interethnic peace are possible.

Indeed, the sociologist Rogers Brubaker (2002) argues that, left to themselves, the embers of ethnic hatred tend to burn out over time, as quotidian interests take over. In that – optimistic – sense, they have to be actively reproduced to be sustained. And, clearly, a major role is played here by the media – providing citizens, as they do, with information about events of which they have no direct experience and, more importantly, providing a frame of reference for how such events are understood. The 'peace enclaves' team, led by Vjeran Katunaric (2003), has explored to what degree headlines during the violence in ex-Yugoslavia were 'politically correct', 'neutral' or purveyed 'stereotypes'. Stereotypes are critical to reproducing the vicious circles by which human beings – those former neighbours – are reduced to mere emblems of the 'enemy' group. And the media are thus critical in the 'degenerate spirals of communication'[24] that bring horrific violence in their train. The researchers looked at Osijek in Croatia, a city that had been peaceful but became violent. They found that content analysis of the local *Voice of Slavonia* betrayed an associated shift towards stereotypical coverage, especially vis-à-vis political commentaries.

Belfast has two communally distinct morning newspapers, and lazy reporting – using as 'shorthand' ideologically loaded phrases like 'the unionist community' – helps reproduce divisions. Stereotypes, themselves the focus of the first Council of Europe Intercultural Forum,[25] always dissolve the individual into the – stigmatized – group. And here the individual artist has an important counter-role to play.

The arts

At the heart of the creative city must be the creative arts. And in as much as they allow of an exploration of the plastic against the fixed, the complex against the simple and the potential against the actual, they offer a medium outside conventional discourse for issues of interculturalism to be addressed.

Istvan Szabo's film *Sunshine*, for instance, portrays the lives of several generations of a Jewish family in Hungary, from the Austro-Hungarian empire through Nazism to Communism and its demise. Via the device of a succession of male characters all being played by Ralph Fiennes, there is seen in one figure the successive tensions of denial of Jewishness for purposes of assimilation, donning a chauvinistic Hungarian nationalism and the opportunistic embrace of Stalinism. The film invites viewers to see all these as dark aspects of what it means to be 'Hungarian' today. In short, the autonomy of the artist allows him or her – at least in principle – to stand back from and reflect upon taken for granted identities. The writer Amin Maalouf begins his book *On Identity*:

> How many times, since I left Lebanon in 1976 to live in France, have people asked me, with the best intentions in the world, whether I felt 'more French' or 'more Lebanese'? And I always give the same answer: 'Both!' I say that not in the interests of fairness or balance, but because any other answer would be a lie. What makes me myself rather than anyone else is the very fact that I am poised between two countries, two or three languages and several cultural traditions. It is precisely this that defines my identity. Would I exist more authentically if I cut off a part of myself?(2000, 3)

Civic leadership

Ethnopolitical entrepreneurs thrive where a civic culture is weak. Amid the decay of post-industrial northern England, the neo-fascist British National Party has secured pockets of support among the white *Lumpenproletariat*. The Cantle report found: 'Where a culture of blame was evident it appeared that community cohesion was going to be impossible to achieve. Where the local political leadership was either weak or divided, it left a vacuum which was then easy for extremist groups to move in and exploit' (2001, 17). Contrast this with Tuzla in the early 1990s: the former mayor tells how he and his colleagues from the town hall acted to insulate Tuzla against the war.[26] They knocked on every door in the multiethnic town to talk, and listen, to the citizens – with a view to keeping alive the tradition of trust in their political representatives.

One interesting idea is a declaration that political leaders in shared cities could embrace, ruling out the (ab)use of culture to divide communities for political ends.[27] Even if honoured more in the breach than the observance, this would be a valuable symbolic statement. A precedent can be found in the way the Commission for Racial Equality in Britain urged politicians to abjure playing the 'race card' in the 2001 elections.

Integrated education

In Nicosia, children on either side of the buffer zone go to schools where they are taught contrasting histories. Efforts to change this practice had met strong resistance from nationalists on either side. If in a conflict culture everything is polarized, with the self always the victim and the other always demonized, one response is obviously to start by depolarizing the youngsters. One of the great potential virtues of integrated education is that it can assist young people to resist the imposition of 'truth claims' in the name of religion or political dogma.[28] Interestingly, the experience of the 'foyer' project for young people in Bradford was that young people who mixed in this sort of environment did not favour monocultural or single faith schools.[29]

Research has been published on the long-term effects of integrated education on young people in Northern Ireland, with more than two decades having passed since the first cohorts entered the initial mixed schools.[30] And the evidence is encouraging: it is not so much that alumni develop a substantive, third identity, as against the two ethno-nationalist positions that face each other antagonistically across the sectarian divide. It is more that the former integrated students manifest, many years after leaving the school, a more tolerant 'approach' to identity than would otherwise be the case.

Religion is a particularly fraught subject in the school. A useful distinction can nevertheless be made between the teaching of religion as a subject and a faith.[31] The former would imply a need to focus particularly on an understanding of the religions of others, whereas the latter implies mere dogmatic inculcation of one's own.

Another important dimension in all schools is citizenship education. This is critical to socializing young people into a civic culture generally. It may also help them acquire the capacity, including the language, to develop as autonomous individuals, secure with a complex and evolving identity and tolerant of divergent identities. At best it can assist them to become effective civic actors in their own right, with an ability to reflect critically on themselves and to engage in dialogue with others – the network makers of tomorrow.

Mixed marriages

A civic attachment to place has a potential to bind individuals of different ethnic backgrounds. Uzhgorod, a Ukrainian city with perhaps more changes of jurisdiction than any other European place and with a large Hungarian minority population, seems bound by a civic sense of linkage to a common historical territory ('I come from here'). This is strengthened by support for mixed relationships. Mixed relationships have the potential to offer another avenue of socialization for young people, straddling communalist cultures and potentially questioning the associated historical narratives. There has been an implicit recognition of this 'threat' in Belfast, where 'loyalist' para-militaries have not just 'ethnically cleansed' Catholics from predominantly Protestant areas but also those in mixed marriages. In contrast, intercultur-alists are duty bound to protect and nurture mixed relationships. Again in Belfast, the housing authorities have conventionally reacted to intimidation by assisting the victim to leave the area, though this has been subject to legal challenge by one such victim. Yet this sends a clear moral signal to the perpetrator that intimidation pays, when it should be the other way around: the paramilitary should be punished by the authorities as a deterrent to similar behaviour by others. Interestingly, research on integrated education in Northern Ireland[32] shows not only an attitudinal but also a behavioural change: adults who have been to integrated schools are at least as likely to have a partner from the 'other side' as 'their own' – in sharp contrast to the strong pattern of endogamy in the region.

Porous borders

For cities in close proximity to borders, there is a special challenge: can they ensure that such borders represent a mere one dimensional line, rather than a three dimensional wall? And can minorities come to be seen as other than a Trojan horse?

In the Baltic states, this second problem represented a major difficulty as the three countries, occupied for decades by the Soviets, regained their inde-pendence. In that context, language requirements for citizenship exposed Russian speakers to discrimination. Here Narva, for example, is a predom-inantly Russian speaking city historically linked to Ivangorod. But it has been deposited by the collapse of the former USSR on the 'wrong' side of the Estonian – Russian border, marked by the River Narva. Cultural events which bring people from Narva and Ivangorod together provide reassurance to Estonia's Russophile minority in this region. Yet this is not at the expense of interculturalism: an 'Estonian House' has been opened in the city in 2002 to encourage Estonian and Russian speakers to meet and to assist young people in learning Estonian. Here there is a role for people who are at home in both cultures and who can thus build personal small bridges across cultural divides.

Conclusion

Any and all of the above recommendations can be taken forward by any municipal authority. Some institutions have made strenuous efforts: for example, more than 100 nationalities are found in the modest German town of Friedrichshafen, where minorities comprise between one in eight of the population. According to Margarita Kaufmann, the Mayor – who has also been involved with the Council of Europe project – the 'Foreigners' Advisory Council' in the town was replaced by an 'Integration Committee', which has enabled 'foreigners' to become 'citizens'. Apart from minority associations and local politicians, its members are drawn from the churches, the world of work, education and sport. It focuses on education (for example, integrating immigrant children into *Kindergarten* and school) and culture (such as organizing an annual intercultural festival) and is managed through five work teams. It is also conscious of the importance of public relations, so that the person in the street is made aware of the cultural richness of their town.

The Council of Europe's Congress of Local and Regional Authorities provides a pre-existing vehicle for cooperative endeavour and exchange of good practice. But one suggestion at the Frankfurt an der Oder seminar, for a more focused effort by a network of 'shared cities', may be worth pursuing: the idea of a network called 'Cities Overcoming Division in Europe' (CODE). The conclusions of the UK Urban Task Force here are of more general European application: 'To succeed, the urban environment of the future must foster and protect the diversity of its inhabitants while ensuring that all enjoy access to the range of services and activities which constitute the best of urban life. Without a commitment to social integration, our towns and cities will fail' (1999, 45). As citizens, the onus is on all Europeans to ensure that cities, a great bequest of centuries of civilization, do not.

Notes

1. Professor Tony Gallagher of Queen's University Belfast coauthored the Belfast case study with the present author.
2. Study by Yber Hysa and Dušan Janjić.
3. Study by Gulnara Roll.

4. Study by Maria Hadjipavlou.
5. Katarzyna Stoklosa.
6. Available at www.coe.int/T/E/Cultural_Co-operation/Culture/Action/Dialogue/ pub_DGIV_CULT_PREV%282004%293_OpatijaReport_E.PDF?L=E
7. Landry 2003, 8.
8. Cited in Hall 1999, 2.
9. Landry, Bianchini 1995, 25.
10. Urban Task Force 1999, 26 and 41.
11. Pinelli et al. 2004, 138.
12. Horowitz 2001, 381; Varshney 2002, 6.
13. Amin, Thrift 2002, 45.
14. Wilson: Solidarity among Strangers, in: EC (2004).
15. Amin 2004.
16. Keane 1998, 112.
17. There has been some easing with the opening of the 'green line' dividing the city.
18. Jarman 2005, 23.
19. Cantle 2001, 9.
20. The *Guardian* issue dated 23 September 2005.
21. Petaux et al. 2002, 11–12.
22. Etienne 2002, 6.
23. Glenny 1999, xxiv.
24. Giddens 1994, 243.
25. Bourquin et al. 2004.
26. Petaux et al. 2002, 12.
27. Petaux et al. 2002, 12.
28. Petaux et al. 2002, 35.
29. Cantle 2001, 16.
30. Montgomery et al. 2003.
31. Richardson as quoted in Petaux et al. 2002, 17.
32. Montgomery et al. 2003.

4
Setting an Agenda for Cultural Inclusion: the Work of EUROCITIES

Heidi Jakobsen

This chapter describes the ongoing work of the major European network of cities (EUROCITIES) to tackle the issues thrown up by migration and problems of integration in a rapidly changing demographic urban context. Following a brief history of the network and its organization, the point is made that it is cities that are in the front line of the integration challenge. The good governance principles, in this regard, adopted by the EUROCITIES Annual General Meeting in Porto on 28 November 2003 are reproduced followed by a summary of EUROCITIES' responses to subsequent EU discussion papers on economic migration and the development of a common EU level approach to integration. The chapter concludes with a brief discussion of the likely direction to be adopted by EUROCITIES with respect to these matters in the future.

EUROCITIES – the network of major European cities

EUROCITIES is the network of major European cities. Membership is open to democratically elected city governments with populations larger than 250 000, or for cities acting as regional centres or having an international dimension. Founded in 1986, the network currently brings together the local governments of 129 large cities in 32 European countries. The organization is financed by membership fees.

The network was established because cities were finding that they were not being consulted even when policies with a clear impact on urban areas were being developed at the European and national levels. The founding cities recognized the increased strength of a collective voice, and also realized that they had a lot to learn from one another. Despite the many differences in terms of history, culture and political structures cities basically face similar challenges. In pursuing its aims the network operates along three main lines of activity: *networking* – sharing and improving knowledge; *lobbying* – developing and influencing policies; and *campaigning* – raising public awareness.

The Annual General Meeting decides the overall direction of the network. EUROCITIES is governed by an Executive Committee composed of 12 cities that rotates on a three year basis. A Brussels-based secretariat takes care of the everyday running of the organization and is, together with the members, responsible for coordinating and initiating activities.

Work is undertaken within six thematic Forums[1] and around 40 working groups. Forums are chaired by a city and supported by a full time policy officer based in the secretariat. Forums meet three times a year to discuss relevant policy developments at the EU level, their impact on cities and possible joint reactions. The Forum meetings also provide a platform for networking, exchange and learning. The more detailed, technical work is undertaken within working groups that report to the relevant Forum. Working groups vary in mandate, size and composition.

EUROCITIES' work with migration and integration

EUROCITIES' work on migration and integration is undertaken within the Social Affairs Forum and the Working Group on Immigration and Integration. The overall objectives of this Forum are to fight poverty and social exclusion and to create equal opportunities for all. Migration and integration are thus addressed from an inclusion/equal opportunities perspective. As hosts to most migrants, cities are not only anxious to improve their own approach to these issues through exchange and learning, they are also increasingly active in influencing relevant policy developments at national and European levels.

Cities share experience through project work and more informal activities. Both the EUROCITIES Social Affairs Forum and the Working Group on Immigration and Integration provide platforms for this, supported by the secretariat that holds a co-coordinating function. The seriousness of cities' commitment to improving integration is well illustrated by 'EUROCITIES' contribution to good governance concerning the integration of immigrants and the reception of asylum seekers'.[2] This comprehensive charter, approved in November 2003, sets out common principles for cities in dealing with integration. It is considered in the following section of this chapter.

EUROCITIES' work is increasingly focusing on political lobbying. This is a direct result of the intensified co-operation at European level on migration and asylum policies and now also on integration policies, starting with the Tampere Process[3] and the Hague programme.[4] A set of recommendations on how to improve integration was compiled for national governments and EU institutions,[5] to accompany the Contribution to Good Governance. EUROCITIES members have furthermore developed joint responses to specific policy initiatives within the Hague Programme, notably on the development of a European level framework for legal migration[6] and the proposals for creating a common integration agenda.[7] EUROCITIES has also responded to smaller consultations and hearings and actively engages in dialogue with the EU institutions and other relevant actors in the field.

Links with the European Parliament, for example, have been strengthened through the alliance with the European Parliament Intergroup on Urban and Housing issues. This has made it easier to raise awareness of the urban dimension to migration and integration policies within the institution and to more efficiently influence Members of the European Parliament in their drafting of opinions in the field. Dialogue between decision makers from cities and the EU institutions has also been facilitated through the joint organization of thematic seminars attracting high level representatives of the institutions, including Commissioners. Furthermore, EUROCITIES works closely with the Committee of the Regions through a general co-operation agreement, and relations with the Commission services are good.

EUROCITIES is also actively trying to influence thinking around migration and integration through participation in, for example, the external advisory committee of IMISCOE,[8] and the advisory board of the Metropolis Project[9] as well as the steering committee of the European Policy Centre Programme on Multicultural Europe.[10] In addition, EUROCITIES is also continuously exploring relationships with NGOs and foundations active in this field.

Why this interest in immigration and integration?

It should come as no surprise that EUROCITIES is so heavily concerned with migration and integration. Cities have been – and continue to be – the main destination for both inter and intranational migration, and the majority of migrants – documented and undocumented – live in cities. Migration enriches societies but also challenges their functioning as new diversities and dividing lines are introduced. Cities are affected by migration in their capacity as service providers and as those politically responsible for social cohesion. Furthermore, as the government level closest to the citizens, cities are often left to explain and legitimize migration policies, an increasingly challenging task when integration seems to be failing.

In all EU Member States immigration and asylum policy is the affair of national governments, although the European Union is increasingly active in coordinating and harmonizing national legislation given the commitment of Member States to develop a common immigration and asylum system.[11] Implementation of legislation is delegated to national bodies (immigration services, the police and other legal authorities), while the task of providing immigrants and asylum seekers with support in their reception, settlement and integration is often left to local authorities.

In the majority of cities the financial and policy resources to adequately perform these public tasks are insufficient, and in some cities even non-existent. In some cases, the solutions found to pressing problems are therefore provisional and ad hoc. With the increasing number of immigrants and asylum seekers in recent years, cities have been faced with new, daily challenges in the management of urban society. Cities are aware that in order to successfully promote integration of immigrants in our societies and to guarantee access to social and other rights, the limitations of the welfare institutions in cities must be addressed, social policies and provisions must be strengthened and resources increased.

Policies to order and limit the entry of people from third countries, have added to the complications. Increasingly restrictive legislation regarding immigration and asylum is, for example, leaving some cities with a growing number of undocumented immigrants and refused residence and asylum claimants, cut off from any entitlement to provisions and therefore dependent on the assistance of charities and the informal economy for survival.

Part of the problem is definitely caused by the exclusion of local authorities from the development of policies. Unfortunately the important role that cities play, and the cost of their exclusion from policy development is unsatisfactorily reflected in national and European political discourse, and even more poorly recognized in policy making procedures. There are several reasons for this, nevertheless, the acceptance of the fact that migration policies have a significant urban dimension and that immigration and integration are intrinsically linked, is decisive in addressing the considerable challenges involved.

Cities' commitment to improving integration: 'EUROCITIES' contribution to good governance concerning the integration of immigrants and the reception of asylum seekers'

While continuing to lobby national governments and EU institutions in order to make sure that policy debates and initiatives reflect the reality and the pivotal role of local authorities, cities are also looking at how they themselves work towards improved management of migration and integration using the EUROCITIES' contribution to good governance concerning the reception of asylum seekers and the integration of immigrants as a basis.

In twelve points the charter, adopted in 2003, outlines both common general, and more specific principles relating to the delivery of key services. This involves:

- developing common principles for integration
- fostering opportunities for participation
- the adequate reception of newcomers
- a commitment to social cohesion and integration
- educational initiatives
- labour market policies
- health policies

- housing policies
- enhancement of social services
- respect for cultural identity and diversity
- concern for the eviction of refused asylum claimants, refugees and immigrants
- the monitoring and evaluating of progress.

This charter (reproduced as an annex) has been influential in the discussion leading to the EU Common Basic Principles on Integration considered in Chapter 20.

Making migration work

EUROCITIES' response to the EU Green Paper on Economic Migration

Increased global competition and demographic change has put the issue of migration and integration firmly back on policy agendas. The EU member states are currently developing joint strategies in order to meet these challenges, notably through the creation of a common framework for legal migration. Increased immigration is not only seen as a tool to develop the knowledge economy and improve competitiveness vis-à-vis countries like USA and China, it is also seen as part of the solution to the problem of Europe's ageing population.[12] Europe is ageing. Given the local implications of migration policies, EUROCITIES decided to take part in the debate at the European level and developed a response to the Green Paper on economic migration that was launched in May 2005.[13]

The aim of this Green Paper was to re-launch[14] a debate on an EU legislative framework for economic migration in order to develop a policy plan for legal migration. This would include admission procedures capable of responding to the fluctuating demands for migrant labour in the European labour market. The Green Paper is a technical – but highly political – document. It considers the degree of harmonization that should be aimed for, procedures that should be adopted for different categories of immigrants, rules concerning the migrant's family, and the rights that should be linked to the various types of work and/or residence permits.

A flawed discussion framework

In EUROCITIES' opinion, the Green Paper has major flaws even as a framework for discussion, because it completely overlooks the urban dimension and puts very little emphasis on the need for accompanying measures like integration strategies. Despite the highly technical nature of the document, the issue of implementation, competences and resources is not addressed at all. In line with this rather incomplete approach, the erroneous belief that common admission criteria can impact substantially on undocumented migration is also expressed. Furthermore, the perspective of the migrant seems rather absent, something which is illustrated by the limited reference to international Treaties and conventions on workers rights, for example.

As one member state after another comes to realize that previous or current integration strategies are at best incomplete, it is becoming all too clear that future migration policies need to be accompanied by integration measures, and existing initiatives need to be revised and improved. They must, as outlined in 'EUROCITIES' contribution to good governance . . . ', be multi-dimensional and cover measures in a multitude of areas. They must be developed with the cooperation of all levels of government, and with the involvement of the main stakeholders including the migrants themselves.

Furthermore, it is important to recognize that migration policies are a sensitive issue and that there might be popular opposition to them. It can be difficult for people to understand and accept that even countries that have relatively high levels of unemployment would want to open up for economic migration. In addition, socio-political changes and expressions of violent radicalization seem to have led to a growth of racism and xenophobia, and diminishing support for migration in cities. As the relationship between newcomers and the host society tends to be more emotional than rational, it is important to address these issues in a serious manner. National governments should set aside resources to explain to the public the complexity of policies in this area and to help cities counteract today's negative mood.

It is thus important to stress that the development of a strategy for economic migration can not and should not replace the training of the existing migrant workforce. Priority must be given to using the untapped and often undervalued potential of those already present on the national and EU labour markets, EU citizens as well as third country nationals and undocumented migrants. EUROCITIES therefore urges the European Commission and national governments to pay more attention to the migrants already living in our societies – and particularly the young – who are more often poor and unemployed than other groups, possibly as a result of discrimination.

Undocumented migrants

Experience shows that stricter or more structured admission regulations do not automatically lead to a reduction in illegal migration, but simply push it to take on new forms. Regardless of the quality and reach of migration policies, as long as there are conflicts and poverty in the world, illegal migration will continue. Therefore, governments should focus on dealing with the root causes of migration or at least accept undocumented migrants as a fact.

Illegal migration represents a special challenge to cities. Local governments have, for example an obligation to care for all citizens including undocumented migrants when it comes to, for example, healthcare provision and education for children. Illegal migration also has several negative effects on cities in terms of crime and insecurity and even, in some recent cases, the spreading of diseases. Undocumented migrants also face dangers and abuse in terms of exploitation in the labour and housing markets. EUROCITIES stresses that these migrants must be better protected and cities equipped to deal with challenges related to illegal migration in a constructive and decent way.

EUROCITIES regrets that the perspective of the migrant is largely absent in the Green Paper. The paper refers mainly to win–win situations for sending and receiving countries, without reference to the perspective of the migrant worker and this person's family, his or her rights, needs and wishes. To make the EU an attractive destination for immigrants, the new immigration system should not replicate the old 'guest worker system' but rather facilitate reunification, this being a basic human right. In a system meant to encourage migration to Europe, migrants cannot be expected to stay only as long as they are 'needed' and that without their families. EUROCITIES, furthermore, believes in the importance of attributing social and political citizenship rights to long-term resident migrants and their families. In Eurocities view, migration should – as far as possible – be to the benefit to all parties involved and be based on internationally recognized norms and values.

EUROCITIES calls upon member states and the EU to explicitly acknowledge that all international and European instruments on human rights apply to migrant workers, regardless of their legal status. EUROCITIES furthermore defends the principle of equal rights and obligations for all with regard to the labour market and the need to fight against exploitation, employment segregation and abuse of any kind, in terms of salary, working hours, conditions of work and contracts. EUROCITIES sees the need to prevent and eliminate illegal and clandestine work, and to protect legal immigrants as well as the undocumented from exploitation.

Who will eventually finance and coordinate the implementation of new migration policies and their accompanying activities? This is an important concern for cities as they are often responsible for implementing these policies at the same time as most of them are currently experiencing cuts in their budgets. Though it is impossible to foresee all possible implications of policy initiatives, one can predict certain scenarios through basic impact assessments prior to taking policy decisions and therefore allocate necessary resources and competences to those managing migration policies. Before a decision is taken on new policies on economic migration, EUROCITIES proposes a Europe-wide mapping exercise of local responsibilities, competences, and resources combined with an impact assessment of the effects of the various policy proposals on cities.

EUROCITIES' response to the EU Communication on a Common Agenda for Integration

Integration remains a national competence. At the same time, the cooperation between member states is intensifying as awareness of the importance and complexity of integration is growing. Since the initiation of the Tampere Process,[15] a network of national contact points on integration[16] has been established, the European Council has invited the Commission to present annual reports on migration and integration,[17] a communication on the link between immigration, integration and employment has been launched[18] and a first edition of a handbook presenting good practises and recommendations in the field of integration published.[19] Furthermore, in November 2004 a set of Common Basic Principles for Integration were agreed in the first informal meeting of ministers responsible for integration. These principles are reproduced in Chapter 20 of this book.

The European Commission Communication 'A Common Agenda for Integration, Framework for integration of Third Country Nationals in the European Union'[20] responds to the invitation from the European Council to establish a coherent European level framework for integration based on the common principles. The communication sets out concrete proposals for implementing these principles in the member states, accompanied by a series of support mechanisms including the establishment of a European Fund for Integration, a Commission hosted website for the collections of integration practices and a European Forum for Integration.

EUROCITIES welcomes the attempt to establish a European framework for integration, believing that it can contribute to the development of sustainable integration through improving governance and by facilitating exchange and learning as well as research, monitoring and evaluation. As the effective integration of immigrants cannot, in EUROCITIES opinion, be achieved without the proper and active involvement of cities, the relative success of the framework depends on the degree to which it manages to reflect the urban dimension.

Achieving sustainable integration

In order to achieve sustainable integration, holistic, multi-dimensional strategies must be developed at all levels of government. As outlined in 'EUROCITIES' Contribution to Good Governance ... ',[21] these policies must cover a wide range of issues, promoting social, economic, cultural and civic participation as well as social cohesion. They should include awareness-raising initiatives targeting both newcomers and the receiving society, as well as anti-discrimination measures. These must be developed through structured dialogue with all levels of government and all spheres of governance, including representatives of immigrants and ethnic minorities. Furthermore these strategies must be based on impact assessment and therefore accompanied by adequate resources and necessary competences allocated to those public authorities that will be responsible for their implementation. Finally, in order to ensure constant improvement, these must be followed-up with comprehensive monitoring and evaluation.

Improving governance

Good governance, based on informed decision making and impact assessments forms part of the sustainable development concept; the guiding principle for European level co-operation. Establishing structures to facilitate dialogue between government levels and other stakeholders is central in this respect, as this will eventually contribute to better decisions, transparency and ownership. Although improving, the current European level co-operation on integration is weak in terms of systematically involving local government. EUROCITIES hopes that the development of a more tangible common framework for integration results in the development of structures and processes that can remedy this.

Member states, through their National Contact Points for Integration (NCPs), can play a decisive role in this respect. The NCPs should actively seek the advice of local authorities and transfer local knowledge and expertise to the European level. In addition, reference groups could be established around each NCP, with the participation of representatives of local and regional authorities, social partners and relevant NGOs including those representing migrants. Establishing advisory platforms on all governance levels should also be considered. These platforms could provide valuable input to policy development. It is essential, however, that these platforms are connected vertically.

At the European level, the Commission can play a significant role in supporting the development of governance structures and in creating a meeting place for central actors. In this respect, the possible composition and mandate of an integration forum and a migrant's platform[22] should be further explored. It is particularly important to give the migrants themselves a forum for debate.

A framework for consultation with large cities and their associations in Europe should also be established in order for them to communicate the issues concerned and the impact of European policy at local level. The latter could be achieved by means of a sectoral dialogue in the field of integration, under the umbrella of the Territorial Dialogue between the Commission and the European and national associations of Local and Regional Authorities.[23] The annual meeting of integration ministers should become institutionalized.

Furthermore, the European Commission can work towards ensuring improved and continuous co-operation between relevant Directorates General on the complex issues of migration and integration and to make mainstream integration an objective of all policies and processes at the European level, linked in particular to the European Inclusion Strategy, the European Employment Strategy and the Growth and Jobs (Lisbon) Strategy.

Facilitating exchange and learning

Despite the many differences between countries in terms of migration history, political and administrative structures, government levels and other stakeholders have a lot to learn from each other in terms of how to support integration. This is well illustrated through the attention given to the Handbook on Integration, and the fact that the INTI programme[24] has been very popular among stakeholders. In principle, the financing and co-ordinating of these kinds of activities at the European level has a clear added value.

Reflecting the learning needs of local government throughout all learning processes and initiatives as well as funding tools at European level is an obvious necessity. In order to improve services and address practical challenges in new and effective ways, exchange of experience between cities is essential. EUROCITIES functions as a platform for these kinds of exchanges, but has no resources to do this in a systematic and consistent way. EUROCITIES therefore hopes that new initiatives will help alleviate this problem.

EUROCITIES is therefore convinced that cities should be more systematically involved in developing future editions of the Handbook on integration as well as in shaping the proposed Integration Internet Website, as this would undoubtedly increase awareness and usefulness for the potential main end-users. Regarding the website, cities are eager to assist in defining criteria for what constitutes good practice as well as in developing a presentation format that maximizes comparability and transferability. A network like EUROCITIES has the capacity to co-ordinate input from member cities both regarding the development of the handbook and the website, as well as to mobilize politicians and practitioners if and when called for.

EUROCITIES furthermore believes that the Integration Fund should have an easily accessible urban strand devoted to supporting local initiatives. Such a strand should support exchanges on all relevant actions including awareness-raising initiatives, and should focus in particular on initiatives addressing the needs of immigrants and refugees in terms of education, training and employment. Given the complex and multidimensional nature of integration policies, the goal of integration ought to be mainstreamed as an objective in all European funding programmes.

Arguably the single most efficient investment in facilitating exchange and learning processes, however, would be the funding of the implementation and monitoring of action based on 'EUROCITIES contribution to good governance . . .'. Considering the large membership of EUROCITIES and the key role cities play in implementing integration strategies as well as in delivering services and building partnerships at the local level, the impact would be considerable. In addition, it could possibly provide examples for the website and the Handbook.

Monitoring, evaluation and research

Monitoring, evaluation and research are essential to the constant improvement of policies. With the European Commission well placed to facilitate European level actions in these areas, there is, here again, obvious added value in European level intervention. If we are to build a clearer under-standing of both the intended and unforeseen effects of policies in the various member states, then a greater emphasis on comparative research, the development of common indicators, statistics, monitoring and analyses, is required.

Indeed most aspects of migration and integration remain hazy. Target groups for integration measures must be more carefully defined, and quant-itative and qualitative indicators still require clarity. Meanwhile a clear common definition of 'integration' itself is yet to be developed. Though a consensus may be impossible, more thinking and debate around how we conceptualize integration, is certainly not. It is hoped that in this respect, this book has a contribution to make.

Tools for the systematic monitoring and evaluation of action need to be established. The Annual report on migration and integration should be revitalized[25] and further developed into a comprehensive monitoring tool for use across the European Union. Adapting the report to better reflect the urban dimension would be key to its improvement. Most migrants live in cities; measuring migration and integration trends at national level is too superficial and fails to provide information on local level realities. Policies are implemented at city level – regardless of where they are made – and their effects are experienced by the local population. The relative value and usefulness of the annual report would be further enhanced if its terminology were defined more clearly and if its basis lay on common indicators.

Finally, research networks like IMISCOE, financed by the Commission, could and should be tasked with developing indicators and definitions, but also with undertaking comparative, in-depth studies of specific sectors like education and employment. This would be helpful for policy makers and practitioners at all levels.

Conclusions

There is no sign that the focus on integration is diminishing. Efforts to reform European economies in order to face challenges related to global competi-tion and ageing have created a political demand for increased immigration to Europe. It is recognized too that integration as such can be instrumental in avoiding a waste of human resources. Recent violent expressions of radic-alization, like the London and Madrid bombings and the murder of the Dutch film-maker van Gogh, have also led to an increased focus on conflicts arising along cultural/religious lines and on issues related to Islam.

The challenge of realizing integration is complicated by the lack of consensus over its meaning. There seems to be common agreement, however, that integration does not equal assimilation and that it is in principle a two-way process involving both the receiving society and the newcomer. The fact that immigrants under-perform in the education system and in the labour market is possibly due to discrimination from the side of the host community, for example. Society's fragmentation and permanent state of change represent yet another obstacle to integration. Perhaps, then, it makes more sense to discuss whether societies, rather than individuals, are integrated or not.

Regardless of how integration is defined, cities will continue to be at the forefront of the action. As hosts to the majority of migrants – whatever their legal status – cities are hugely affected by immigration. They are service providers and are politically responsible for social cohesion. City administrations most often take a pragmatic approach when they are left to deal with the challenges that result from successful or less successful immigration, asylum and integration strategies, often shaped at other government levels. They look for ways to ensure access to healthcare also for undocumented migrants and rejected asylum seekers for example, or set up neighbourhood dialogues on Islam in order to fight prejudice and increase mutual understanding and tolerance.[26]

Migration and integration issues will no doubt continue to be central to EUROCITIES for the foreseeable future. Members' desire to improve service delivery and other relevant integration measures is substantial, and there is growing awareness of the urgent need to find a voice in the European level debates that are currently shaping new migration and integration policies. As a membership organization focusing on lobbying, networking and learning as well as campaigning, EUROCITIES will continue to function as a platform for learning and project development as well as a co-ordinator of political activities.

In this respect, EUROCITIES will continue to actively participate in European level discourse on migration and integration by producing policy statements, participating in hearings, consultations and meetings in order to raise awareness of the urban impact of immigration and integration policies. In doing this, EUROCITIES will continue to develop relations with the EU institutions, like the European Parliament Intergroup on Urban and Housing issues, the Committee of the Regions and the Commission services, and will continue to pursue opportunities to work in alliance with other actors like migrant organizations and foundations.

A more concrete, future priority for the organization would be to find ways to implement and monitor action based on 'EUROCITIES' Contribution to Good Governance Concerning the Integration of Immigrants and Reception of Asylum Seekers'.[27] This could take the form of campaigns or exchange projects focusing on service delivery, or on concepts promoting dialogue and active citizenship, for example. Funding cross-border urban action would be extremely valuable because it would provide learning examples also for widely accessible tools like the Handbook on integration and the planned Integration Internet Website.[28]

Migration is a reality. So how can we maximize the advantage for everyone concerned? Multidimensional integration strategies targeting both the newcomers and the receiving society are a must. Luckily, the realization appears to be growing. The main challenge now is the development of sensible integration strategies. EUROCITIES strongly believes that the only sustainable way to do this is through structured dialogue with the main implementers and stakeholders; namely local authorities and immigrants themselves. Cities on their side are more than ready to make their contribution.

Notes

1. The Forums on Culture, Economic Development, Environment, Knowledge Society, Mobility, and Social Affairs, respectively.
2. The 'EUROCITIES' contribution to good governance concerning the integration of immigrants and reception of asylum seekers' can be downloaded at: www.eurocities.org/main.php
3. Member States agreed in the Tampere European Council (1999) to develop a common immigration and asylum system.
4. The Hague Programme (COM(2005) 184), May, 2005.
5. 'Immigration and Integration at the local level. Political recommendations to national governments and EU institutions', approved in EUROCITIES Annual General Meeting in November 2003, can be downloaded at: www.eurocities. org/main.php
6. Green paper on an EU approach to managing economic migration (COM(2004) 811, 11.1.2005.
7. A Common Agenda for Integration, Framework for integration of Third Country Nationals in the European Union COM(2005)389, 1.9. 2005.
8. IMISCOE (International Migration Integration Social Cohesion) is a network of excellence established by 19 European research institutes and sponsored under the Sixth Framework Programme, by the European Commission's DG Research.
9. The Metropolis Project is an international forum for research and policy on migration, diversity and changing cities. (The International Metropolis Project is a set of co-ordinated activities carried out by a membership of research and policy organizations who share a vision of strengthened immigration policy by means of applied academic research.)
10. European Policy Centre is a Brussels based, independent, not-for-profit think tank, committed to forwarding European integration.
11. As set out at the Tampere European Council (1999).
12. Green Paper 'Confronting demographic change: a new solidarity between the generations', COM(2005)94, March 2005.
13. Green Paper on an EU approach to managing economic migration (COM(2004) 811, 11.1.2005.
14. In 2001 the European Commission adopted a proposal for a directive dealing with 'the conditions of entry and residence of third-country nationals with the purpose of paid employment or self-employed economic activities', which was refused by the European Council.
15. Through which Member States agreed to establish a common area of asylum and immigration.

16. The Justice and Home Affairs Council of October 2002 requested that the Commission establish a network of national contact points on integration.
17. 'First Annual Report on Migration and Integration', COM(2004) 508, 16.7. 2004.
18. Immigration, Integration and Employment, COM(2003) 336, 3.6.2003.
19. 'Handbook on Integration for Policy Makers and Practitioners', November 2004: http://ec.europa.eu/comm/justice_home/funding/doc/Handbook%20Integration.pdf
20. 'A Common Agenda for Integration, Framework for integration of Third Country Nationals in the European Union', COM(2005) 389, 1.9. 2005.
21. Presented earlier in this chapter.
22. In the Communication 'A Common Agenda for Integration, Framework for Integration of Third Country Nationals in the European Union', COM(2005) 389, 1.9. 2005, both a European Integration Forum and Migrants Platform are suggested.
23. Introduced as a response to the White Paper 'European Governance', COM(2001)428, (25.7. 2001).
24. INTI (Integration of Third Country Nationals) is an EU funding programme for actions promoting the integration in the EU member states of people who are not citizens of the EU.
25. There have been no more annual reports since the 'First Annual Report on Migration and Integration', COM(2004) 508, 16.7. 2004.
26. During 2004–2005, the City of Rotterdam organized a series of neighbourhood dialogues on Islam. http://eumc.eu.int/eumc/index.php?fuseaction=content.dsp_cat_content&catid=43a17e680d287&contentid=43a27ee689b4c
27. As outlined earlier in this chapter.
28. Read more in 'A Common Agenda for Integration, Framework for integration of Third Country Nationals in the European Union', COM(2005) 389, 1.9. 2005.

Part 2

Evolving Ideas of Citizenship: Theoretical Perspectives

5
Civic Republicanism and the Multicultural City
Iseult Honohan

Two disparate inclinations in contemporary cities have the joint effect of distracting people from their increasing interdependence: on the one hand, they seek to identify with distinctive cultural communities and, on the other hand, they search for individual independence. In this chapter the conditions for equal citizenship in the context of modern cultural diversity will be addressed. Common citizenship has been proposed as a counter to the fragmenting pressures of modern economies and societies that liberalism has not been able to address adequately. However, both what common citizenship entails and what it requires of people are variously understood, often in ways that are oppressive to minorities. It is argued that the republican conception of citizenship may offer something with regard to dealing with difference in the modern city. On this view, citizenship allows realizing freedom and the common good in a political community of those who are interdependent.

Common citizenship: tolerating, celebrating or retreating from cultural difference?

Theoretical responses to increased cultural diversity have ranged along a spectrum from the dominant liberal approach of tolerating difference in the private sphere while maintaining a neutral or secular public sphere, to the multiculturalist 'celebration of difference', often thought to imply 'recognition' or establishment of the values and practices of all cultures in public life. The theoretical and practical difficulties which policies associated with the latter approach have encountered have led to a certain 'retreat' from multiculturalism of this sort, less – it must be said – in the direction of a liberal neutrality than towards a reassertion of the idea of uniform citizenship.[1] There seems to be a new demand for national or cultural commonality among citizens – based, for example, on arguments that it is a precondition for popular support for redistributive welfare measures, or that civil security requires it. In the context of increasing migration, this view has given rise to proposals for more stringent policies on admission and requirements of cultural assimilation as a condition of citizenship, and less willingness to accommodate cultural difference in social and educational policies. If there is a renewed emphasis on the importance of common citizenship, however, there are very diverse views as to its essential basis.

On one hand, certain liberals see agreement on principles of justice or constitutional arrangements as a sufficient framework for common citizenship.[2] Critics argue that these principles are liable to be too thin to motivate citizens, have to rely on pre-political commitments for support, and thus also become too substantial to be really inclusive. On the other hand, more communitarian views (for example, in many post-communist states) ground political unity and policy in a pre-political sense of belonging, whether in terms of ethnicity, culture or history. Such approaches draw on emotional commitments to the nation, or to a particular historical or local embodiment of more universal values such as freedom, that are inherently exclusive.

The assumption that cultural identity is necessary or sufficient to create political solidarity has been criticized as both empirically unfounded and normatively undesirable.[3] In practice, a common sense of ethnicity, culture or history is not enough to guarantee political community or support for redistributive policies. A shared British identity did not prevent widespread toleration and support for cuts in welfare spending in Britain under Mrs Thatcher in the 1980s. Similarly, notwithstanding shared ethnicity, tensions exist between citizens of the old 'East' and 'West' Germany. Those who share an identity or a sense of belonging to the nation are not necessarily prepared to support one another or to contribute to the common good. Attempts to impose cultural identity are likely to be both unjust and counterproductive.

The obverse of this is that it may not be cultural difference *per se* that causes conflict. The experience of Northern Ireland suggests that it does not arise from cultural difference in itself (as cultural differences between Protestant and Catholic, however strongly they may be experienced, may seem to outsiders to focus on a limited range of aspects of life). On one view, the problem arises not so much from the fact that people are different, but that some differences are made salient, become entrenched and act as a block to communication. As Arendt puts it (1958, 53), then people are 'isolated in their own experience, which does not cease to be singular if the same experience is multiplied innumerable times'.

So if common citizenship is not best understood as a matter either of adherence to constitutional principles or of cultural identity, how should it be understood?

Rooting citizenship in interdependence: civic republicanism

The republican approach to citizenship sees it in terms of the ineluctable interdependence of human beings. Accepting common citizenship is a matter of acknowledging this, and engaging with those with whom one is, at least initially, involuntarily interdependent in a subjection to common institutions and authority. The question that politics has to address is what kind of freedom is possible in the light of this interdependence, and how it may be realized. Freedom is understood as a political achievement, rather than a natural possession of individuals. It is inherently fragile, requiring both a strong legal framework to prevent domination and the civic engagement of citizens in supporting the common goods they share alongside their separate and often conflicting interests. Citizenship thus entails responsibilities as well as rights; what self-governing citizens achieve is the chance to exercise some collective direction over their lives, rather than complete self-sufficiency. Since common interests are easier to overlook, and therefore more vulnerable than individual interests, corruption – that is pursuing individual or sectional interests at the expense of the common good – is identified, along with domination, as the crucial political problem. Freedom requires political equality and two dimensions of engaged or active citizenship: 'public spirit', traditionally termed 'civic virtue', and 'political participation' in determining what is in the common good.

This tradition took shape in early modern European 'city-states', but with the development of the sovereign nation state, by the nineteenth century it was largely sidelined by liberalism, nationalism and socialism. It may be relevant again, if, as many believe, the nation can no longer unproblematically be the unit of self-government, being both too large for self-government and too small to deal with problems of the global environment and security.

Rather than opposing liberalism's central value of freedom, republicanism is an older tradition that has contributed to its development in the past, with a distinctive centre of gravity within a cluster of values of liberty, participation in self-government and solidarity. Its emphasis on the political construction of community distinguishes it from the nationalist and communitarian focus on 'pre-political' shared values or identity among citizens. It may also represent a useful corrective to the prevailing account of liberalism, with its emphasis on legal rights and safeguards and a narrow account of freedom as the absence of interference. This neo-liberal view sees the principal threat to freedom as coming from government, and freedom as promoted if government activity is reduced to the minimum, by privatizing and deregulating, paring down or contracting out public services and, above all, cutting taxation and increasing individual discretionary income. But this is too limited an account; it overlooks threats to freedom that do not come from the state, but from individuals or groups that can exercise arbitrary or unaccountable power, such as established elites in religious or cultural communities, corporations who endanger the health of their workers and consumers, and media cartels who control the news available to the public. It also overlooks the economic and social conditions necessary for the exercise of freedom and equal citizenship, and the ways in which, even in the close coexistence of cities, the privileged can displace their costs on others. As Markell (2003, 22) puts it, 'structures of subordination organise the human world in ways that make it possible for certain people to enjoy an imperfect simulation of the invulnerability they desire, leaving others to bear a disproportionate share of the costs and burdens in social life.'

There has been much discussion of the problem of political apathy, measured in decline in voter turn-out in almost all democracies today. This reflects a widespread feeling of powerlessness and alienation from politics, from a sense that citizenship lacks depth and meaning, that significant questions are either not publicly debated, or that people's voices are not heard. The republican valuation of participation in politics calls for more opportunities and structured public spaces for ordinary people to contribute to political decisions – not just to express individual or sectional interests more effectively, but to encourage deliberation about the common interests shared by otherwise diverse citizens. As Pitkin (1981, 344) puts it, 'what distinguishes public life is the potential for decisions to be made . . . actually by the community collectively, through participatory public action and in the common interest. . . . the possibility of a shared collective, deliberate, active intervention in our fate, in what otherwise would be the by-product of private decisions.' While it is true, as Madison noted, that 'the room will not hold all', critics of such expanded participation as impractical due to numbers or competence overlook the possibilities of multi-level institutions for participation from local and regional to trans-national levels: citizens' juries, deliberative polling, participatory budgets. The point of this is not to make participation compulsory, but to offer more opportunities for people to have a say in things that affect them directly, to take account of the common good, and to elicit more deliberative engagement with other viewpoints when they do participate.

Civic republicanism and cultural difference

When it comes to dealing with cultural difference, civic republicanism, in emphasizing engagement among citizens, has resources to develop a more nuanced approach than either liberal neutrality or multicultural recognition. On this view, it may be argued, the idea of equal citizenship requires two dimensions of recognition, even if it is not possible or desirable to recognize all cultures simultaneously in the sense of celebration or public establishment.

The fact that participation in given structures and contexts is relatively easier and more difficult for different kinds of citizens has to be taken into account. So, if there is to be equal citizenship, it is necessary to 'acknowledge the specificity' of different kinds of citizens and the burdens and costs they suffer in existing forms and norms of civic participation, and to offer some compensatory support. Precisely what is required is a matter of deliberation in particular cases, but policies supported on these grounds have included child care provisions for parents; access for the disabled; special language rights for minority groups in their interactions with government, education provisions, procedures and funding to increase minority participation in politics; some kinds of special representation; consultation bodies; exemptions from legal requirements where these are not strictly universally required. The point is that, on this dimension, the republican solution is concerned to grant recognition to citizens themselves 'in' their identities, rather than 'of' their identities *per se*.

Equal citizenship also requires that all citizens can have a chance to be heard. This means it is necessary further to 'authorize the voices' of those who are different – that is, to see them as contributors to the common, over-arching public realm, and not just to let them live separately in their own way. Instead of merely tolerating practices, this means giving public space for citizens to voice their deepest concerns, and giving a serious hearing to claims to influence public debates and public culture. It follows from the deliberative nature of politics that republican recognition of citizens requires taking the voices of others seriously as well as allowing them to speak. Ways of giving previously excluded viewpoints institutional authorization of this kind may involve state-sponsored subsidy for political organization; guaranteeing representation; creating specific representative bodies for federal, regional, city or neighbourhood self-government. But, unlike some contemporary models of consultation or consociational government (which might satisfy the requirements of acknowledgement above), it is not enough for these to remain insulated from the wider political culture, they need at some level to be integrated into a wider political forum where a broad spectrum of views encounter one another. The other side of this dimension of recognition is that groups cannot claim a right to remain entirely isolated from the rest of society and to insulate themselves (and their children) entirely from encountering ideas which differ from their fundamental values.

Yet this is not to argue that it is necessary to 'establish' publicly or to set beyond criticism all practices, viewpoints and values according to a third and strongest (in the sense of most demanding) dimension of recognition. To begin with it, is often not possible simultaneously to recognize in this sense the values of opposing groups of, for example, fundamentalist Protestants and gays and lesbians, secularists and religious groups. For gay marriage is either recognized or not; religious education is either supported or left to private initiative. It is in the nature of politics that, on some issues, only one perspective can be embodied in policy, and it cannot be assumed that it is possible to achieve consensus among all groups. This is a reflection of the ineluctably agonal nature of politics, where conflict is a reality to be acknowledged. Yet these people must still live together and can create (or fail to create) a common future.

In any case people gain a certain recognition when they are given an open-minded hearing, when their viewpoints are authorized and heard through institutional provisions and esteem initiatives. Those who have had a say in a fair procedure are more likely to identify with the institutions and other participants. The good of a serious hearing for all may be more attainable than the equal recognition of all cultural practices.

Some degree of basic agreement is no doubt a prerequisite for political interaction; but one should not exaggerate the extent of uniformity of beliefs and values necessary for a political community. Functioning modern societies are not commonality-based wholes, but loosely co-ordinated patchworks. Their coherence derives from convergent and common interests, habits and inertia as much as from actively shared values or identity. Over time, even conflicts over values appear to have an integrating function.[4]

Thus, while civic republicans believe that citizens need to be committed to the common good they share, citizenship requires, not conformity to a specific model or similarity, but engagement at different levels and between different perspectives and cultures. The public space of such politics could be envisaged as one 'where people are with others and neither for nor against them'.[5] The substance of republican politics is based on interdependence rather than commonality, created in deliberation, not prepolitically, emerges in multiple publics to which all can contribute and is not definitive, but open to change.

This requires a public realm that fosters interaction, and calls for a civic education – for majority as well as minority citizens – that emphasizes interdependence (rather than commonality or difference), that instils what might be called civic self-restraint, and encourages openness to deliberation with others.[6] While the need for involvement and communication suggests developing smaller-scale public spaces at local levels, increasing interdependence suggests the need for higher level forums.

Acknowledging a shared fate and future can come to be the basis of a kind of political community. 'That sense of sharing a common fate may often be enough to motivate support for policies which aim at the common good without there needing to be a deeper sense of belonging together, which a shared national identity would involve.'[7] As Arendt again puts it, the sort of solidarity that might be aspired to is neither love nor tolerance, but a certain kind of respect – a 'friendship without intimacy or closeness; . . . a regard for the person from the distance which the space of the world puts between us, and this regard is independent of qualities which we may admire or achievements which we may esteem' (1958, 218). The republic may be a community of 'civic solidarity', that is, an involuntarily instituted, and relatively distant relation of citizens, marked by equality, diversity, and relative distance, but growing through reiterated interaction and practices.

'The feelings of friendship and solidarity result precisely from the extension of our moral and political imagination . . . through the actual confrontation in public life with the point of view of those who are otherwise strangers to us, but who become known to us through their public presence as voices we have to take into account.'[8]

In rooting citizenship in the interdependence and mutual vulnerability of those who share a common fate and future, a republican account of citizenship is at least potentially more open than those based on common ethnicity or culture, even a liberal nationality which may evolve over time. All entail a sharper boundary between those who share a nationality and those who do not.

From a republican perspective, it is justifiable to require immigrants to learn the language of their adopted country as an essential means of communicating and deliberating with their fellow citizens; but this need not exclude providing education and public services through minority languages as well. Immigrants may also be expected to be prepared to engage with the citizens of their adopted country and to make some adjustment to its ways in a spirit of give and take. But it is less clear that they should have to adopt 'British' (or 'Irish') 'norms of acceptance' for example, just because these norms are British and so on. If immigrants should make the attempt to adapt to their adopted country, it is not so much because they are 'last in', but because they need to make their future together with other citizens, and not just to coexist with them.

Civic republicanism and the city

The idea of self-governing citizenship originated first in the city state. But this assumed a small, self-sufficient society with face to face interaction between citizens, who, as Aristotle argues, must know one another in order to be able to bring each other to account. Building a wall around the Peloponnese will not create a city. For the Roman republican, Cicero, what binds the citizens are the many things they share in common:

> There are several degrees of fellowship among men. To move from one that is unlimited, next there is a closer one of the same race, tribe and tongue, through which men are bound strongly to one another; more intimate still is that of the same city; citizens have many things in common: temples, porticoes, and roads, laws and legal rights, law courts and political elections, and besides these acquaintances and companionship and those business and commercial transactions that many of them make with many others.[9]

Modern civic republican theory first crystallized in Italian city states where the classical idea of free self-governing citizens was rearticulated, most notably by Machiavelli. There, too, common cultural identity could be taken more or less for granted, not only because of the small size of these states, but also because the narrow definition of citizenship excluded women and all those outside a tightly drawn circle. Since then liberal-democratic citizenship has become much more extensive, including populations widely dispersed across territories as well as previously excluded categories of people. The locus of self-government has been transferred to the level of the sovereign nation state. But it has become so by making citizenship weaker and thinner. In most states now, citizens are no longer expected to participate actively beyond voting, or by doing service, military or otherwise, let alone holding office.

The contemporary city cannot be self-sufficient in the way that Aristotle describes; it exists within the nation state, where citizens are united in imaginary community, and it is less encompassing. It is easier to leave, or to inhabit in a partial way, departing to the suburbs or beyond, living in or making regular passage through only one or a few city quarters, or communicating with and looking to another city or country to which one dreams of going home. This can strengthen the illusion of self-sufficiency – that we choose particular spaces and move among like-minded people, living in communities of choice. The modern city is understood as a space of difference, disconnection and anonymity.

Some theorists – both liberal and more radical[10] – have embraced this understanding of the city as the model of modern citizenship, not expecting citizens to be engaged with one another as people who share a common fate, but only to accept one another as strangers who must live together.

But the distance between city dwellers can be exaggerated. For example, even in the big city, as Pettit argues, we are concerned about what others make of us:

> The anonymity of modern society is often exaggerated. While we may each lack a name on the street of a big city, that namelessness is quite consistent with being well-known in a range of the interlocking circles that fill the space of the modern world. Some of these circles will be small of radius, like the circles of friendship and workplace and sports associations; others will be of larger compass, like the circles of the extended family, the professional association or the e-mail network. (1997, 228)

Living together in cities calls for more solidarity and active participation of citizens than liberals have tended to acknowledge – to deal with the many aspects of urban life that are not easily dealt with by coercive legislation, but need the active civility or solidarity of citizens who do not know each other personally. Analysis of city life highlights the interdependencies among those who are different, but whose lives are affected by their vulnerability to one another, not just from the proximity of neighbours, but from the sharing of a common public space.

This then calls for many forums to allow different kinds of participation, but also for electoral areas and representative bodies that transcend particular areas to include the whole of a city and the interdependent hinterland of extended suburbs.[11]

Republicanism and cultural diversity in practice: the Irish experience

It should be noted that in practice republicans have dealt with cultural diversity in different ways. Traditionally, the French republican model comes close to liberal neutrality, allowing diversity in the private sphere while insisting on a neutral public sphere, and constitutes an ideology with clear implications for economic, social and education policies.

By contrast, since the nineteenth century, Irish republicanism has been associated mainly with national independence and the military means to achieve this, and has not been understood as a neutralist ideology. Indeed, for half a century after its independence in 1922, the Irish government took a strong communitarian form, influenced by an authoritarian version of Catholicism, which, for example, gave a special constitutional status to the Church, organized education along religious lines and expressed many Catholic moral doctrines in law. The republicanism of De Valera aimed to realize not a politically determined common good based on deliberative participation, but a pre-politically defined vision of the good for society which was shaped by cultural nationalism and a powerful institutional church.

A gradual process of change has led not so much towards neutralist liberalism or a French-style secular republicanism as towards a pragmatic pluralism with a strong underlying framework of 'banal' nationalism.[12] Thus, though the state had for long great difficulty in supporting non-religious schools, recently it has quite readily sponsored Muslim elementary schools that parallel those of other religions. There have been no controversies over mosque building, but those that have been built have accepted local conditions (and do not sound the muezzin, though Catholic churches and RTE's public broadcasting stations still ring the Angelus bells). Thus, the Republic of Ireland has been marked by a pragmatic and largely unreflective openness to compromise but with strong assumptions of uniformity. Foreigners who lived in Ireland in the past experienced tolerance combined with an unspoken expectation that they would assimilate or conform in certain areas of behaviour.

Further changes have occurred in the context of a reversal from net emigration to net immigration in the 1990s. Initially many immigrants were returning emigrants or had Irish connections, but now a broad range of other cultures are represented, particularly from the new EU member states of eastern Europe and the Baltic; Africa, especially Nigeria – and, on a more temporary basis, students or workers on work permits from China and the Philippines. The recent and rapid nature of this reversal makes it difficult to give a systematic analysis of the social integration of the new immigrants.

In Greater Dublin, containing almost half the Republic's population, new immigrants have begun to constitute residential and commercial clusters in some inner city and less expensive housing areas, though without any clear evidence of systematic segregation. The impact of immigrants has been most remarked upon in the transformation of the character of the main Dublin street market and revitalization of dwindling Protestant congregations (and some cricket clubs). There has been an increased incidence of racist behaviour, focused initially on asylum seekers, but increasingly affecting anyone perceived as a foreigner. Even here there is room for ambivalence; when a young Nigerian failed asylum seeker was repatriated, despite his being enrolled for the School Leaving Certificate, a wave of protest by school friends, teachers and the public brought about his return. But many issues of cultural difference that have been contentious elsewhere have yet to arise in public debate. While the refusal of hospital doctors to perform male circumcision became an issue after the death of a baby in a kitchen table operation, whether female circumcision is taking place in Ireland has not become a widely discussed issue. The generally limited reflection on cultural difference was illustrated again when the Somalian musician, Youssou N'Dour was due to play in Dublin in a large music venue and public house on the first day of Ramadan; some members of his orchestra objected to playing under these conditions, so it was agreed just at the last moment not to sell alcohol during the performance.

This might seem to suggest that Irish republicanism may offer a way of accommodating cultural and particularly religious difference more easily than a country such as France which has a clearly secularist republican tradition (and some Jews and Muslims have in the past said that they preferred to live in a country where religion was taken seriously). It is not long since there were three Jewish members of the *Dáil*[13] in a country with a Jewish population of less than two thousand. But the rise in low-level racism suggests that it could equally well reflect a lack of awareness of cultural difference, which could become more problematical in the future. It should be pointed out that, even with its rapid growth to over 17,000, the population of Muslims, for example, is still very small. Many issues have yet to arise.

Finally, the conception of citizenship in Ireland has undergone significant changes whose direction is not yet clear. While Irishness has long been understood primarily in ethnic and cultural terms, at another level there was also a certain tacit identification of Irishness with living on the island. Thus, those born in England even to Irish parents are not popularly considered Irish, even if they return to live in Ireland (unless they represent Ireland in soccer). Likewise, when Mary McAleese first ran for President in 1997, there were those who thought her an unsuitable candidate because she was born and educated in Northern Ireland (though a Catholic or 'nationalist'). The Good Friday Agreement led to the constitutional guarantee of citizenship to all born on the island, in what was greeted by some as an inclusive gesture.

But in 2004, citizenship by *ius soli* was restricted by legislation requiring three years prior parental residence. The overall effect of this may be to reconstrue Irishness in more ethnic and cultural terms than civic terms, in which citizens are those who share a common fate.

Conclusion

In the republican view outlined here, a political community is composed of people who do not necessarily share a common culture, but who find themselves together. They share a wide range of interrelated interdependencies framed by the political institutions to which they are subject and have some possibility of collectively shaping their future. This grounds membership in the interdependence and mutual vulnerability of people who share a common fate. It requires not just the toleration of private difference, but political engagement in public space between citizens of different cultures.

Addressing the implications of a civic republican perspective for multicultural cities, three points emerge. First, cultural minorities need to have the basis for equal participation – which may require resources, guaranteed representation, special rights and exemptions – so that they do not have to bear costs greater than other citizens. Second, citizens of different cultures should be able to appear in their identities, and have their voices heard, in order to engage as equals in deliberation with other citizens in the public realm. Finally, there must also be provision for cross-cultural political interaction and engagement. This means that, rather than being composed of fragmented enclaves, the city constitutes a common public space between citizens. The point of 'thinking about the things that unite us rather than divide us' is not to reinforce commonality but to promote engagement.

Notes

1. Goodhart, 'Discomfort of strangers', *Guardian*, Tuesday 24 February, 2004; Joppke 2004.
2. Habermas 1995; Ingram 1996.
3. Bader 2001; Abizadeh 2002.
4. Bader 2001.
5. Arendt 1958, 160.
6. Honohan 2005.
7. Mason 2000, 134.
8. Benhabib 1988, 47.
9. Cicero, *On Duties*.
10. Such as, for example, Young 1990.
11. Baubock 2003.
12. Billig 1995.
13. The Irish Parliament.

6
Multiethnicity and the Negotiation of Place

Jean Hillier

The urban is a site where the tensions of multiethnic and multicultural diversity are manifest; where people seek certainty and security through an institutional legislative structure of governance designed to care for them in their everyday worlds. Dynamic interactions take place around the symbolic representation of difference; interactions which are translated into specific, tangible outcomes directly affecting the lives of inhabitants.

As flows of human migration cross the world and Indigenous peoples continue to claim their rights, this chapter emphasizes micro-scale issues of spatial planning which increasingly engage a necessity of accommodating difference in negotiations of place as people struggle to co-exist in shared spaces; to live together differently.[1]

There are few 'more-different' ways of being than those of Indigenous Australians and the descendants of the European invaders. Yet in urban locations throughout Australia these ways intrinsically interrelate. The 'urban' locale, as both a geographical location and the socio-spatial institutions within it, is a site through which important struggles for cultural recognition take place.[2] The chapter seeks to reveal the 'multiply scaled workings'[3] of power relations and struggles by means of a case example which typifies the tensions between Indigenous and whitefella[4] negotiation of shared space: the regulation of land and land uses.

The underlying themes of this story have relevance for multiethnic citizenship in Europe as people struggle over what Castree (2004, 136) terms 'differential geographies': the right to make their own places. The role of law and legislation is highlighted as this gives the legal basis for claims and counter-claims of sovereignty and of rights and also for inclusion in and exclusion from processes of place-making.

Concentration is on the tensions between Aboriginal customary law and Australian state law. Law is often regarded as a set of neutral, disembodied principles and abstract values. It is, however, determined by 'the character of those processes that make, interpret, and enforce law'.[5] With regard to processes of place-making, its characteristics may be cultural, political, or even arbitrary desire or whim. Law itself is thus a process, full of limits and exclusions. Yet, as will be argued, the Aboriginal desire for multiplicity offers us an opportunity to recognize that legal 'norms' cannot be an entirely closed system. They may be resisted and transgressed to 'open up all kinds of "undisciplined" and "multiple" possibilities'.[6]

As Howitt (2001, 272) ironically points out, Australia has widely been seen to exemplify 'a mature, humane and tolerant multicultural society, (with) innovative policies of indigenous recognition, multiculturalism and social welfare'. However, the forward strides taken by the Mabo judgement[7] and the 1993 Native Title Act have often been challenged and transgressed by the farming, mining and development industries encouraged by populist politicians at State and Commonwealth levels. Amendments to the Act by the incoming Liberal (conservative) administration have restricted the rights available to Aboriginal peoples and mean that land use must be formalized in what has become a 'field of complex technical legal argument that often leaves indigenous people on the sidelines'.[8]

In the following section, selected points in the story of the bridge at Kumarangk (Hindmarsh Island) in South Australia are revisited in order to illustrate the tensions which exist in negotiations over land use when practices of state law come into contact with 'the other' of Indigenous customary law. Recognizing that as a non-Indigenous outsider the author can but present a gross oversimplification of extremely complex events and positions, the focus is placed on the privileging of colonial, rational, documented, adversarial systems of land and land use-related law over Indigenous, oral, spiritual knowledges and the state law's capacity to reinterpret Aboriginal women's subjectivity.

The argument examines how the processes of place-making regulated by law in the 'hands' of the Australian state(s) serve to monopolize the violence that is transformed into legitimate force[9] to reify the asymmetries in the abilities of individuals and social groups to define and realize their needs. It is demonstrated how land-use related practices further marginalize Indigenous communities, and Indigenous women in particular, silencing and excluding them and their knowledges.

Though originating in the particular context of Australia, the implications of this case example are international. Wider possibilities for culturally inclusive place-negotiation and place-making are therefore explored. Attention is turned to the work of Jürgen Habermas, who has looked to juridical and communicative strategies in his attempts to overcome theoretically apparent incompatibilities between particularistic ethical claims made on behalf of a particular way of life or conception of the good and universal moral claims made on behalf of conceptions of justice and human rights.[10] An attempt is than made to move 'beyond Habermas' to consider the work of Leonie Sandercock, and in conclusion the question is posed of whether instead of tinkering with the process so that multiethnic groups 'fit' the system, why not either transgress its limits or change the system itself?

Speaking of the unspeakable

Like Allan Pred (2004, 147), the author seeks to '(re)fuse the prPeAsSeTnt', to demonstrate how the past and present interweave in processes of place-making and how such processes are riddled with the unspeakable. The Kumarangk case exemplifies the tensions between the 'rationalized', legalized space of the state[11] and the 'irrational', mythical space of an Indigenous community. It brings to the surface 'issues of knowledge and who is deemed to possess it; of power and how it is used; . . . of process; . . . of land and property rights'[12] and of tensions between Indigenous customary law and non-Indigenous Australian state law.

Australian state law embodies an obsessive philosophical and cultural search for certainty and stability. It 'privileges knowledge based on schematisation, isolation, and decontextualization over knowledge grounded in experience and context'.[13] But law cannot escape culture. Law is a cultural construct, based, in Australia, on the principle of *terra nullius* and the unspeakable presence of Indigenous peoples at the time of European invasion and colonization.

Kumarangk could be regarded as a 'heterotopia':[14] a sacred place to Ngarrindjeri women; the deviant, abject 'other side' of the spatially and temporally ordered spaces and places of the South Australian land-use and juridical systems. The places of Kumarangk serve to articulate resistance to the external and the dominant.

The story of Kumarangk runs from the initial planning application and permission for construction of stage 1 of a marina resort in the early 1980s to the opening of the Hindmarsh Island Bridge in March 2000, and approval of the management plan for resort stages 4 and beyond in November 2001. Kumarangk developed into a major national conflict less about planning practice *per se*, but about money, power and Aboriginality, involving several legal actions, bankruptcies, a Federal Royal Commission, major government reports (one of which was declared invalid following a change in regime) and a Shadow Ministerial resignation.[15] At the forefront of attention, largely due to media sensationalization, was the claim that details of so-called 'secret Ngarrindjeri women's business' were fabricated, in order to prevent construction of Hindmarsh Island Bridge.

Legal processes of place-making typically work through 'isolation, division, separation and fixity'.[16] Stories must be deconstructed and reconstructed to fit given frames. But the Ngarrindjeri women's stories do not fit the frames. They are the excluded Other. Their stories of respect for ancestors, of feelings for a land alive with meaning, of a world where the living and the dead, the human and the non-human interact cannot be simply assimilated into Western notions. The gendered temporal knowledge of Ngarrindjeri women presents a problem for the claimed neutrality of law-based systems grounded in Anglo colonization which reduce an Indigenous world to Anglo-Australian universality. As such, they ignore Ngarrindjeri histories and experiences passed down orally through generations which have structured their lives and meanings: a 'rich, vital world within which the living and the dead constantly interact'.[17]

In indigenous Aboriginal cultures, orally-transmitted, gender-segregated knowledges create and enact cultural experiences. Moreover, Aboriginal people are often reluctant to share their knowledge with whitefella bureaucrats who embody some 200 years of imperialist oppression and abuse. In the Kumarangk case, because the knowledge concerns women's bodies, birthing rites and even abortions, it is understandable that Ngarrindjeri women would not share this knowledge with other Ngarrindjeri women, much less with Ngarrindjeri men and whitefella institutions. Ngarrindjeri women elders' knowledges and laws are often gender, kin and even within-kin specific. Hence the pejorative term coined by the media of 'secret women's business'. The land use and juridical systems demanded to know the precise and 'authentic' (that is, in written record) nature of the Ngarrindjeri women's sacred knowledge in terms of potential desecration of a 'significant' site, in order to prevent construction of the Hindmarsh Island Bridge. The systems simply could not cope with absence. Into this gap came politically engineered accusations that the women were fabricating memories and stories in order to frustrate development.

The decision to build the bridge maintains the colonization of Ngarrindjeri women. The Kumarangk decision represents a victory for a fixed and normalized conceptualization of Indigeneity over an historical, gendered Ngarrindjeri trajectory. Lack of fixed, verifiable documentary evidence for spiritual beliefs provides rationalized foundations for appropriating the Kumarangk land. Lack of 'proof' renders the Ngarrindjeri women's knowledge as silent. In 'fact' it is 'fabricated'. It is less than silent – it is a pack of lies. The women become 'unfit' to speak in the panoptic gaze of the state legal system. The Kumarangk case illustrates two paths of rights in conflict: whitefella planning and legal systems, and Indigenous ways of being. They represent two conflicting systems of 'truth': historical truth or material truth versus Indigenous narrative truth. Despite a decision by the Australian Federal Court some six years later, in 2001, which vindicated the Ngarrindjeri women's stance, whitefella systems generally continue to overpower Indigenous ways of being.

Habermasian analysis: the power of mediatization

Jürgen Habermas attempts to anchor juridical systems in the substance of socio-cultural material realities in what Burgess (1997) terms an 'evolutionary' approach to reconstructing the link between cultural substance and legal form. Habermas argues that regulations are historical products, motivated as much by expediency as by moral absolutism or rational principle.[18]

Habermas argues that a democratic society must be able both to know and to steer itself. As March and Low (2004) explain, to 'know' itself, a society must understand its challenges and the options available and aim to plan using rational, inclusive and empowering argument. To 'steer' itself, a society must have the capacity to take action to deal with the challenges it faces in knowing itself. Habermas (1996a, 35) argues that mediatization is the key blockage to democratic knowing and steering. He admits that attempts to reach consensual communicative agreement are fraught with problems as societies are riddled by spheres of strategic or mediatized interaction. Media include money, law and power.

In his earlier work, Habermas (1987) suggests that legislation plays a vital role in coordinating action and integrating society; provided that it is accepted as legitimate. Habermas (1996a) begins to resolve the tension between ideal and empirical validity, and between legitimacy and enforcement, by attempting to ground the juridical nature of rights in the broader perspective of a discourse principle, itself understood in terms of a moral universalism.[19] The distinction between 'facticity' (facts) and 'validity' (norms) underpins the logic of the argument. Habermas includes in the category of facticity those ideas such as the 'possivity' and certainty of law, its institutional connections and coercive enforcement. Validity is associated with law's ideal legitimacy and rational acceptability.[20] Habermas believes that there is a communicative path between facts and norms, in which those subject to law can at the same time understand themselves as authors of that law (1996, 120); that is, lawmaking and its implementation become democratically inclusive. Habermas (1996, 150) advocates that citizens' communicative power should be the source of legitimate law.

Habermas (1996, 56) regards law as a 'hinge between system and lifeworld'. In his idealized democratic process, the production of legitimate law connects the 'communicative power' of citizens' public sphere discussion with the 'administrative power' that operates within the administrative system.[21] Legal systems in reality, however, impede the very discursive democratic mechanisms which they theoretically 'hinge'. Legal perspectives are increasingly formulated as rationally defensible universal principles that are decreasingly grounded in wider socio-cultural values. Processes of reaching mutual understanding tend to be bypassed and individuals and groups are faced with the choice of either obeying or conforming to the system rules or suffering sanctions. Mediatized law is based on instrumental logic and resists free and open debate. It becomes a block, rather than a hinge, reducing forms of knowing to standardized 'facts' or stereotypical 'labels'.

Consideration of Habermasian steering media locates structural power relations in intersubjective and material institutional relations (March, 2004).

Can these Habermasian concepts then help to establish a foundation for more democratic, inclusive planning-related decisions? If, as Habermas (1998, xvi) contends, 'the internal relation between the rule of law and popular sovereignty calls for a proceduralist model of deliberative democracy in which all political decision making, from constitutional amendments to the drafting and enactment of legislation, is bound to discursive processes of a political public sphere', is it likely that legal systems will actually integrate communicative principles through which communities can themselves establish the norms upon which laws and rights can be founded?

There are inherent paradoxical questions here as to whether justice is synonymous with equality of right. For example, if justice is universalized, can it then recognize and protect difference? Or would a more contextualized approach to justice fall into the trap of relativism?

Habermas (2000, 48) writes: 'the entwining of the two different pragmatic roles played by the Janus-faced concept of truth in action-contexts . . . can explain why a justification successful in a local context points in favour of a context-independent truth of the justified belief'. So, truth, for Habermas, is two-faced. On one hand, he suggests that truth is at play within a specific local 'action-context', such as the various decision arenas in instances of place negotiation. Ideally, Habermas demands that these arenas operate through procedures of communicative rationality (mutual understanding, reciprocity, consensus formation, etc.), or what he terms 'an ideal practice of argumentation' (1999, 15). However, as media reports of place-exclusion and oppression indicate on a daily basis, practices are often far from 'ideal'.

The second aspect of Habermas' 'Janus-faced concept of truth' is context independence. Habermas writes that 'in order to distinguish between true and false statements I make reference to the judgments of others – in fact to the judgments of all others with whom I could ever hold a dialogue (among whom I counterfactually include all the dialogue partners I could find if my life history were coextensive with the history of man[*sic*]kind'.[22] Potentially this statement has something to offer Indigenous Australians and minority ethnic peoples whose dialogic conversations include their ancestors and global diasporas. Communicative actors, in this regard, have a capacity for unconditional truth which is 'defendable on the basis of good reasons . . . At any time and against anybody'.[23]

Habermas (2001, 117) suggests that constitution (or place) making be treated as a discursive situation in which private rights are justified and legitimized through democratic public deliberation. 'Neither public nor private autonomy is given priority over the other, ensuring that the ideals of stability and legitimacy, facticity and validity, are brought into a working balance',[24] theoretically ensuring that the system of rights is blind 'neither to unequal social conditions nor to cultural differences'.[25]

The 'open-ended discursive process' of construction of law and place making theoretically fosters a civic bond of patriotism to a shared polity as a 'sense of belonging arises out of identifying with a set of institutions, practices and laws, which in turn reflect the will of citizens as its authors'.[26] However, is this likely in contexts where very different ways of being are involved? It seems that there is a tension between the two faces of Janus here. Can a notion of truth be *both* pragmatically context-dependent and universally context-transcendent? Or is such a notion idealized and unrealistic as some authors suggest?[27] As will be demonstrated below, the mediatizing power of vested interests is strong and power plays often reduce opportunities for inclusive, democratic and deliberative opinion and will formation.

However, on the 'plus' side one can list comprehensiveness, the idea of communicative power and the location of basic democratic processes outside formal institutions of governance in the political public sphere and in civil-social associations, combined with the legitimating role of democratic procedure in a material social reality.[28] These aspects could be attractive if made to work. The basic idea of respect, for instance, is one that is central to cross-cultural ways of being.

Beyond Habermas

Habermas himself accepts the counterfactual idealization of his 'reconstructive legal theory' (1996, 462) and suggests that fair bargaining and compromise may be appropriate.[29] It is easy to criticize Habermas' theorizing, and many have done so.[30] Here only three key criticisms will be rehearsed.

Firstly, Habermas' theory is highly abstract. He describes the sorts of rights that people must accord each other if they are to establish themselves as a legitimate community with and through the medium of law.[31] At such a level of abstraction, harmony becomes simple. It is when one attempts to think through Habermas' ideas institutionally and empirically that the harmony breaks down and the inescapable tension between facticity and validity, between facts and norms becomes apparent.

Secondly, Habermas focuses once again on communicative action, with his acceptance of instrumental action and the strategies of bargaining and compromise appearing as an afterthought.[32] If Habermas' theorizing is to form any sort of basis for moving forward, then it must take account of the less-than-rational empirical realities of antagonism.[33] Most place negotiations, especially those involving groups with deep-seated value differences, are not, and cannot be, based on a Habermasian communicatively rational, consensual outcome. It is argued here that conflicting differences between groups' conceptions of the 'good' are not negatives to be eliminated, but rather diverse values to be recognized.[34]

Finally, in essence, a Habermasian-inspired 'solution' does little, if anything, to resolve the postcolonial condition of Indigenous people and the circumstances of in-migrant minority ethnic populations. Land use decision makers 'are sometimes confronted with values incommensurable with modernist planning and the modernist project which it serves, a planning which privatises "development" and in which exchange value usually triumphs over use value'.[35] Overlaying a Habermasian communicative 'template' without reading the contextual institutional dynamics will be unlikely to achieve a shift in power to benefit minority ethnic groups. If the desires and needs of such people are to be met, there is a need to fully comprehend the deep-rooted core of these desires, which, as Porter (2004) and Sandercock (2004a; 2004b) suggest, may be a desire for sovereignty and rights rather than for more superficial inclusion and participation.[36]

Sandercock (2004b, 121) suggests that the state 'rules of the game' cannot be 'done away with', and that Indigenous and minority ethnic people must, therefore, work within state-based systems to find 'strategic moments of opportunity' when radical revisions to 'rules' (both written and unwritten) are possible. People are constituents of states, whether they like it or not. Ivison (2002, 141) suggests that such dichotomies of 'location' should be challenged to enable the claims of those subject to '*concurrent and simultaneous* multiple affiliations' (emphasis in original), such as the Ngarrindjeri women who are both citizens of the wider Australian state[37] and also members of a specific, internally differentiated ethnic community.

Ivison (2002) believes that negotiated debate on the nature of Aboriginal knowledge and more explicit guidance on the admission of 'evidence' need to be worked out between those with knowledge and experience of Indigenous and non-Indigenous systems of law. Such discussions may promote innovative modes of 'transformative accommodation'[38] which may include the possibility of 'reversal points',[39] whereby the option of appealing to an Indigenous adjudicator is provided if the appellants are dissatisfied with state processes. However, Ivison's and others' ideas of 'postcolonial liberalism' still talk about 'accommodating' Indigenous peoples and submitting 'evidence' to what remains essentially a whitefella-dominated, western legal system. This is also true in Europe where discussions about the Roma have tended to concern how 'they' can 'fit into' 'our' systems of planning, schooling, housing, etc.[40] Re-visions and reconceptualizations need to go further than this. The rules of the game require changing more radically.

Sandercock (2003a, 152) proposes seven policy directions to achieve her 'multicultural project' of spatial planning and the negotiation of place working for 'greater social and environmental justice, and supporting culturally pluralist ways of living together' (2003a, 158). These directions include 'sensitivity training' and the development of appropriate multicultural policies, through new conceptualizations of citizenship, to a need to understand and work with the underlying emotions behind ethnic and other forms of urban conflict.[41]

However, as Gunder (2004, 6) indicates, whilst many world cities are constituted by multiethnicity, what is lacking is its acceptance as a dominant discourse whereby diverse groups and cultures are actively given equal voice and legitimacy. Even if planning practice were to become more multiethnic, any achievement would be largely negated by the dominant social reality of the western city as fundamentally an economics-driven, male-gendered, Caucasian-led environment where 'others' are seen as strangers[42] and threats.

Planning practice cannot deliver a utopian harmonious and secure future. Moreover, 'the fantasy of a utopian harmonious social world can only be sustained if all the persisting disorders can be attributed to an alien intruder... a certain particularity which cannot be assimilated, but instead must be eliminated'.[43] As Gunder (2004, 10) points out, we need an outsider for the dialogical character of an identity to occur: 'we are *x*, we are not *y*'. Difference becomes necessary for our fantasies of harmony and also to provide the scapegoat on which to pin the failure of that fantasy.[44]

It is necessary to take care, as spatial planning academics and practi-tioners, that 'multiculturalism' as such does not become merely our 'neutral universal' definition, with us defining what is 'good' for the multiethnic Other, even though the Other may not share the definition or wish for it in practice. Zizek (2000, 316) argues that multiculturalism is a phenomenon of western upper middle-class identity politics, willing only to accommodate a 'filtered Other' which conforms to dominant liberal-capitalist standards.[45] 'We' profess support for multiculturalism, 'we' like Indian and Chinese food and pride ourselves in seeking the most 'authentic' restaurants, but 'we' are prepared to accept 'them' only on our terms.[46] With regard to spatial planning practice, this might translate into no flat-roofed houses, no inner courtyard-style homes facing high blank walls to the street, no extensions for temple or shrine rooms, and so on. Planning officers become privileged 'judges' of multiethnicity, remote from that on which they pass judgement.

Would Habermasian communicative arguments help us here? Could some context-independent 'difference-centred universalism' of multiculturalism be sufficiently flexible in local action-contexts of communicative ration-ality to meet the needs and wants of a wide range of cultural groups? Or would the likely outcome be more of a 'colonising process... where minor variations of superficial difference may be legitimated in the name of multiculturalism while at the same time important, but perceived aberrant cultural differences are vanquished'?[47] Such practice tends to overgeneralize superficial differences, glossing over the unspeakable and ascribing stereo-typed unified wholeness to cultures, rather than recognizing and respecting the multiplicity of differences and counter-cultures which comprise cultural forms. Difference cannot be negated by reason. It is irreducible to consensus.[48]

Is it the objective to constrict ethnic and cultural differences to become mere objects of urban management, a question of 'what about we hold another cultural festival?'[49] Is such 'difference-centred multiculturalism' merely a tokenistic ' "gift" of the powerful to the weak' which simply serves to confront the weak with a double bind, in which 'to refuse the gift is to lose; to accept the gift is to lose'.[50]

Do we want a planning of 'mosaic multiculturalism', allowing cultural groups effectively to author their own planning regulations in areas where cultural difference is held to make similar treatment unfair?[51] Or are we prepared to address the logic of oppressive mechanisms within the institution of planning practice, to transgress and potentially to change the system itself?

Conclusions: reconceptualizing rules

Ethnicity and culture are performative practices, as are spatial planning and place making. As such, they are verbs rather than nouns: active, dynamic and transformative. An example from South Australia has been cited in an attempt to question and unsettle the conceptual preconditions which underlie place making and negotiation; to turn negative into positive in which the limit is not a 'fixed point of arrival but rather a fluid point of departure'.[52]

Legal decision systems of place making require the establishment of boundaries between what something is and what it is not: true/false, us/them, order/chaos, rational/irrational. Such a binary, 'Eurocentric' view of 'fact' and 'knowledge' is imperialist, self-legitimating rather than self-reflexive, displacing and hystericizing 'other' minority ethnic knowledges. In Australia and elsewhere, there is a need for Indigenous and minority ethnic knowledges and laws, not only to challenge and unsettle, but to reconfigure the knowledge-power nexus constructed in mainstream decision making. Simply acknowledging the existence of multiple knowledges will not suffice. As Howitt and Suchet-Pearson (2003, 565) state: 'the ontologies of other peoples need to be understood and engaged with in active partnerships in the construction of knowledge (and power)'.

The author would suggest more radical transgression than do either Sandercock or Ivison. Such approaches are doomed to liberalist conformism as their working through the symbolic could be anticipated to produce new signifiers or 'labels' (such as multicultural) which would effectively reshape peoples' knowledges and laws in limited terms whilst continuing to 'accommodate' them within the given order. In this way, 'other' ways of being and knowing would continue to be engulfed and neutralized. Their roles in shaping rules would be simply formal, rather than politically consequential.

It is necessary, then, to have the courage to think through the constitution of mainstream laws and regulations, to interrogate their presuppositions, to recognize that we live in what Jean-Luc Nancy (1990) calls an 'inoperative community', a shared space of 'mutual transgression without fusion', a 'between-space of co-appearance'.[53] This is not mosaic multiculturalism, nor is it a 'Hegelian framework of dialectical interdependence and mutual consumption of self and other'.[54] If we as spatial planners really want to move towards a multiethnic society, where place making is negotiated and inclusive, then transformation cannot only be concerned with 'them', the 'others'; it must also dislocate the position and rupture the prerogative of 'us'.

Sandercock (2003a, 132) suggests that 'we might consider overhauling the planning system, either by revising legislation, or challenging it in the courts or appeal tribunals, testing whether it is consistent with, say, anti-discrimination legislation, or espoused multicultural policies.' (An ethical judicialism perhaps?) But without overhauling the system in which the courts, appeal tribunals and legislation themselves are established and operate, it is doubtful whether much can be achieved. It is necessary to 'dare to break the rules', as Sandercock (2003a) advocates, to ask what forms of governance and legal systems of place making may be appropriate. If legal systems (including planning law) are to mirror 'the multifaceted identities that populate a political order',[55] then they will inevitably open up virtually impossible problems of interpretation, reflecting – rather than transcending – competing principles and a multiplicity of identities, needs and desires. This does not imply that one should not try to change the systems, however, but it will not be a comfortable ride.

In the current conjuncture of the first decade of the 21st century, as ethnic, and especially religious, differences seem to become more polarized, perhaps informality offers a way forward. Several examples exist of individuals and small groups working informally to negotiate spaces of common ground across core differences. In Northern Ireland, Gusty Spence, a para-military Protestant loyalist imprisoned for the murder of a Catholic, came to espouse the cause of local reconciliation between the two traditions and led the way for informally based dialogue and cooperation amongst the prison community.[56] Similarly, during the Regional Forest Agreement (RFA) dispute over logging old-growth trees in Western Australia, local people, including environmentalists, business leaders and wives of timber workers, worked together informally to negotiate settlement of the often-violent dispute.[57]

Permezel and Duffy's (2003) example of the Greater Dandenong Council[58] in Melbourne, Australia, also demonstrates that under certain conditions, in the less formal sphere of social relations of the community that cultural issues and debates can 'edge into' the Council's institutional structures, defining programmes and activities which meet local residents' needs and aspirations 'according to their frameworks and understanding of the issues'.[59] In Greater Dandenong, 'relatively "easy" symbolic nods to cultural difference . . . created their own momentum' (2003, 6), to reach a point where the only way forward for the Council was to deliver far more tangible institutional change.

Greater Dandenong provides a classic example of the immanence of what Negri (1999, 25) terms 'constituent power' as a 'productive source of rights and juridical arrangement that refuses to close . . . in the face of . . . attempts to fix it in a final form'. Despite the complexities of constituent power, it does not lose sight of the singularities which comprise diversity. Arguably, this is a core strength, as is its embracing of changeability, disunion and antagonisms, in an opening up of cracks in the closed categories of thought which govern legal, social and political systems. In the cracks of the system lies the potential for its transgression and transformation.

Yet how would the above resolve this inherent paradox of contextualism and universalism? As Osborne (2003, 529) demonstrates, 'neither side of the dichotomy will quite do'. He advocates a 'contextualism of the universal'. Does this imply a sort of 'interculturally constituted common culture'[60] of spatial planning and place making? Does this mean a Habermasian two-tier structure, with Gunder's 'fantasy-scenario' neutral universalism of formally produced motherhood statements as relatively empty signifiers at the top, and local interpretations having either powers of subsidiarity or informal negotiability beneath?

Informal 'shadow negotiations'[61] may be fragile. In the Northern Ireland and Western Australian examples above, the informal negotiations faced considerable opposition from group 'spokespersons' and officials with higher media profiles, who felt a need to score points and posture politically and whose purposes were not suited by negotiation.

Nevertheless, negotiations in the shadows of power could enable people to build relationships across deep differences, to establish credibility for the values and ideas of marginalized ethnic groups and to lay groundwork for developing elements of tolerance[62] and respect. Mutual respect can help to domesticate antagonism to 'agonism' in which people recognize the boundaries of what is and is not possible.

There is evidence, for example, that Indigenous groups in Australia are increasingly negotiating issues of access to land directly with developers, mining and other companies, rather than going through formal government systems, in circumstances where actors have vested interests in achieving outcomes.[63] This is the key point in this chapter. Where groups 'need' to achieve an outcome in order to proceed (for example, building a road, mining and so on), there is a stimulus to negotiate. Although the various actors might not like or respect each other, they engage informally in a transaction of enlightened self-interest or a coalition of convenience in which a compromise is negotiated and then taken into formal decision arenas as a fait accompli.[64]

The difference between transactions of enlightened self-interest and the Spence and RFA examples is that in the latter, there were powerful vested interests in maintaining conflict. If multiethnic and other deep-seated conflicts of difference are to become agonistic, rather than destructively antagonistic, preciousness about past structures and inertia will need to rupture. However, if the atmosphere can remain creative, perhaps non-representational[65] forms of law and planning may yet emerge, bringing 'something into being, which did not exist before, and which was not given, not even as a cognition or imagination'.[66]

Notes

1. Healey 1997.
2. Permezel, Duffy 2003, 21.
3. Pred 2004.
4. Whitefella or wadjela is an Indigenous term for a non-Indigenous person.
5. Komesar 2001, 3.
6. Threadgold 1999, 371.
7. In 1991 the Australian High Court ruled that Australia had not been an 'empty place' (*terra nullius*) populated by inferior savages no better than animals, but that Indigenous Australians possessed systems of property rights and law which must be recognized and respected by Australian Common (state) law (Bartlett, 1993).
8. Howitt 2001, 265.
9. Blomley 2003, 121.
10. Benhabib 2002, 40.
11. I use the term 'state law' to refer to governmental legislative decisions. In Australia, State/Territory and Federal Parliaments have legislative juridical powers.
12. Sandercock 2004a, 95.
13. Shamir 2001, 136.
14. Foucault 1967.
15. Bell 1998; Simons 2003.
16. Shamir 2001, 136.
17. Bell 1998, 37.
18. Osborne 2003, 524.
19. Osborne 2003, 524.
20. Baxter 2002a, 240.
21. Baxter 2002b.
22. Cited in McCarthy 1978, 299.
23. Habermas 2000, 46.
24. Payrow Shabani 2004; 203.
25. Habermas 1998, 208.
26. Payrow Shabani 2004, 204.
27. Such as Rorty 2000; Porter, Porter 2003.
28. Baxter 2002a, 340.
29. See Hillier 2002.
30. With regard to criticism of Habermas' juridical theorizing, see Baxter (2002a; 2002b) and Komesar (2001) in particular.
31. Baxter 2002a, 257.
32. Baxter 2002b, 551.
33. Hillier 2002; 2003; Pløger 2001; 2004.
34. Hillier 2003.
35. Sandercock 2004a, 119.

36. See Castree (2004) for discussion of Indigenous rights and the relational construction of place, and Tully 1999; 2000) for the example of the Canadian Charter of Rights (1982) and practices of law making involving the right to dissent and the duty to listen to dissenting voices.
37. NB: Indigenous people were 'granted' citizenship only in 1967 and included in Census data from 1971.
38. Shachar 2001.
39. Ivison 2002.
40. See for instance, Amin 2004.
41. Sandercock 2003b, 322.
42. Sandercock 2003a; 2005.
43. Stavrakakis 1999, 108.
44. See also Zizek 1999, 216; 2004, 158–9.
45. For example not eating dogs, no female circumcision, no multiple wives, no suttee, etc.
46. See Ghassan Hage (1998) for an excellent account of such realities in Australia.
47. Gunder 2004, 11.
48. Hillier 2002; 2003; Mouffe 2000.
49. Permezel, Duffy 2003.
50. Wallerstein 1991, 171 & 199.
51. Such an approach tends to treat cultures as 'homogeneous, holistic, cleanly-bounded, encompassing, and incommensurable' (Peritz 2004, 271).
52. Stanley 1996, 52.
53. Dallmayr 1997, 182.
54. Braidotti 2002, 14.
55. Chambers 2004, 159.
56. Garland 2001; Hillier 2002.
57. Hillier 2002.
58. The local government area of Greater Dandenong has 60% of its residents of non-English speaking background (Permezel, Duffy 2003, 6).
59. Permezel, Duffy 2003, 5.
60. Parekh 2000, 220–1.
61. Hillier 2002.
62. Thompson 2005.
63. Hillier 2002.
64. Rubin 1991, 4; Fenger, Klok 2001.
65. Thrift 2004.
66. Arendt 1977, 151.

7

Participatory Citizenship through Cultural Dialogue

Brendan Murtagh, Michael Murray and Karen Keaveney

Urban spaces have become more differentiated and contested, in response to technological change, globalization and social restructuring. Atkinson and Flint make the point that racial, economic and gender contests are not confined to highly ethnicized settings but increasingly characterize late capitalist cities where 'various defended territories exist' to mitigate the effects of fear, insecurity and ultimately difference (2004, 876). The normative response saw urban planning repositioned around communicative participatory processes, which encouraged dialogic understanding between different stakeholders with an interest in the use and development of land.[1] This chapter looks at the potential of this form of Collaborative Planning to guide meaningful action in dealing with the spatial expressions of cultural difference and territorial conflicts that increasingly take on an unpredictable and violent character.

The analysis suggests that there are important weaknesses in the approach, especially when applied outside the largely Anglo-Saxon contexts within which it was developed and empirically tested. Yiftachel (2001) Gunder (2003) and others have highlighted the significance of power contests in ethnicized settings, which are simply not reducible to consensual management, agreement or finite resolution. Agonistic strategies, in which 'strife' between interests is valued, need to be better understood as a guide to both thinking and methodology in contested land use environments. The chapter reviews Equity, Diversity and Interdependence (EDI) as a model of agonistic practice, in which attention is drawn to the needs of marginalized 'Others' in local development. Critical reflection, skilled intervention and challenges to planning systems premised on efficiency and order, are some of the components of the approach. Whilst it has been developed and applied in the particular circumstances of Northern Ireland, the analysis concludes by suggesting its wider applicability in planning and by highlighting the need to acknowledge difference in education and practice in order to handle pluralism in more open and realistic ways.

Collaborative planning

Communicative theorists argue that different modes of reasoning and systems of meaning have equivalent status in debate, and the task for planners is to develop strategies for collective action through interaction and dialogue.[2] Here, language is vital and in spatial planning practice, the priority is to establish a process of interactive collective reasoning or discourse which, in turn, involves a degree of collaboration, trust and reciprocity.[3] "In the end, what we take to be true and right, will lie in the power of the better argument articulated in specific socio-cultural contexts."[4]

Booher and Innes (2002) developed this approach emphasizing what they termed 'network power', which 'emerges from communication and collaboration among individuals, public and private agencies, and businesses in a society. Network power emerges as diverse participants in a network focus on a common task and develop shared meanings and common heuristics that guide their action' (2002, 225). Success will be guaranteed when Diversity, Interdependence and Authentic Dialogue – DIAD – are present in specific situational contexts:

> Interdependence among the participants is the source of energy as it brings agents together and holds them in this system. Authentic dialogue is the genetic code, providing structure within which agents can process their diversity and interdependence ... Diversity is the hallmark of the informational age. The wide range of life experiences, interests, values, knowledge and resources in society is a challenge for planning and the efforts to produce agreements and collective action. (2002, 227)

For planning to be mobilized as a dialogical process it needed a new methodology in which 'information' 'influences by becoming embedded in understandings, practices and institutions, rather than being used as evidence'.[5] However, the central criticism of communicative planning is its approach to power relations and the DIAD model makes little reference to how diversity and interdependence relate to 'inequity' within society and the identification of interests that are encouraged to discourse with one another. Yiftachel, for instance, made the point that collaborative planning focuses on a 'critical commentary about planning' rather than a 'societal critique of planning'. The emphasis should not concentrate on the conduct of planners and their practices but rather on the broader power structures and 'legitimization dynamics within which public agencies often act' (2001, 253). Similarly, Tewdwr-Jones and Allmendinger (1998) pointed out that different interests have different access to information and can mobilize and interpret knowledge in vastly differing ways, especially within and between place bounded communities.

Agonism and strife

Flyvbjerg (1998), Hillier (2003), Pløger (2004) and Gunder (2003) all criticized Collaborative Planning for its preoccupation with consensus, rationality and order:

> This seeking of certainty and the avoidance of conflict that this entails – harmony – is at best an unrealisable fantasy, an unfulfillable desire for security and modernity, and one that has considerable costs in its continuous unsuccessful implementation.[6]

These costs include the exclusion of the marginalized 'Other', ethnic minorities, women and resource-poor people, living at the edges of society, whose rights and entitlements are obscured by processes aimed at control and normalization through the use of a plan, which forms a rigid consensus of the future. Flyvbjerg made the point that Habermasian theory lacks an ethic for respect for the 'Other', particularly in matters of gender, race, sexuality and ethnicity. He was especially critical of 'detached' structures that give the illusion of engagement and called for 'devices that acknowledge and account for the working of power and for passionate engagement of stakeholders who care deeply about the issues at hand' (Flyvbjerg 2002: 364). Based on the work of Foucault (1991), Flyvbjerg called for a 'genealogy' of planning in which 'lost' or 'disqualified' fragments of knowledge become important strategies of resistance to power and state rationality. He argued that

> the goal is to problematize planning by exposing dubious social, political and administrative practices. The goal is to bring it about that planners and politicians no longer know what to do, so that the practices and discourses that up until then have seemed to go without questioning become problematic, difficult and even dangerous to those involved. (2001, 191)

For Hillier (2003 and in this volume), 'agonism' is the real game, by which she means competing claims and objectives, discourses and values constantly at play in a struggle for and against the issue, plan or proposals on offer. Democratic struggles are inter-subjective, multi-linguistic, continuous, complex, non replicable and tactical. She relies on Lacan to critique the utopian and idealistic aspirations of collaboration:

> The ideas of complete information, a harmonious society and of consensus are the Lacanian impossible 'Real' of utopian dreams rather than actual lived reality. (2003, 45)

Lacan suggested that consensus formation is illusory, that argumentation and conflict are at the heart of social progress and that there is a gap between this reality and the 'Real'.[7] This gap is referred to in Lacanian terms as the 'lack'. The lack expressed in Northern Ireland, for instance, is evident between the professionally produced renditions of Belfast as a normal, outward looking and even progressive city and the 'dark side of difference' expressed in the reality of physical peace lines needed to separate Catholic and Protestant communities.[8] Lacanian theory suggests that it is vital to recognize the inevitable 'lack' between, on the one hand, frictional social reality derivative of the 'Real' and associated unrealistic aspirations for consensus and, on the other hand, the 'Real' itself, a dimension of experience not open to full articulation and constituted through void and trauma. The reality of planning should not devalue or ignore the 'Real' but rather engage it as an aspect of collaboration and competition in the pursuit of social advancement. Ultimately, 'it can help planners to recognize the symptoms of irreducible conflict and rather than forge ahead with intended strategies of revolutionary consensus-formation, to think through strategies aimed at settlement.'[9] However, what these strategies might be, how they are developed and applied and whether they hold value in deeply ethnicized and violently expressed contests over land, remain undeveloped in planning theory and methodology.

Flyvbjerg (2004) has, however, suggested a framework in which planners need to turn their attention to the basic question of who gains and who loses, and by which mechanisms of power (2004, 290). In this, planning processes and methods should do dialogue with a polyphony of voices (2004, 295). Conflicts will always be involved in such 'politics-laden communication'.[10] Pløger draws a distinction between antagonism and agonism using the concept of 'strife'. Strife is the 'expressive form of agonism, and essential to disputes about words said and written and therefore to meaning, schemes of significance, interpretations and discourses in play' (2004, 75). The problems created by agonism cannot be made to disappear by laws but provoke new ways of thinking about power, conflicts and 'how to make strife the constitutive centre of planning' (2004, 75). Local empowerment strategies that strengthen citizens' consciousness around decision making, defining the sites of power and working politically, form part of the delivery of a strife agenda. Thus, Mouffe (1999) highlights the central challenge for planning in ethnicized settings, as being to transform antagonism into agonism between potential adversaries. For this shift to happen, there needs to be a move away from static liberal forms of governance to empowerment:

> The wish to empower local citizens politically within the heterogeneous, multicultural and individualized city makes it more difficult to govern through rules and predetermined goals and programmes, because the political space of action will depend more on the ability to include and legitimate multiple voices and demands.[11]

Strife and localities

Pløger (2004) defines five dimensions to agonism in local community planning, and these are illustrated in Table 7.1. First, he identifies the tension between elected representatives and community leaders vying for legitimacy and attention from 'their' community, decision makers and those with resources in private or public markets. The development of an active civic society in the political vacuum of Northern Ireland, for example, created competition with elected representatives, whose authority and legitimacy was especially threatened by the flow of money and resources to the voluntary and community sector as an arena viewed, by government, at least, as progressive and secular.[12] Second, he found that petty power structures and competition consumed the energies of activists over questions of leadership and control of the local development agenda. In highly ethnicized settings this can take on a distinctive edge, especially where power is narrowly structured around paramilitaries and extremist politics. The 'reality' of Belfast is that paramilitaries, heavily involved in criminal activity, immutably sectarian and irrational apart from their own corrupt greed, act as powerful gatekeepers who can decide: if there will be any discourse; the

Table 7.1: Strife in community settings

No.	Type of strife	Development challenges
1	Between citizens and politicians	This is encapsulated in the debate between civic and representative forms of democracy, especially in tribal territories.
2	Challenge the representation of the most active citizens	This arises when politicians, municipal authorities, community groups or individuals make counteractive local alliances in order to usurp or question the legitimacy of local leaders and critical voices.
3	Internal conflicts between different community groups or individuals	In this case inter and intracommunity rivalries, competition for support and questions about the authenticity of the plans and priorities retard effective empowerment strategies.
4	Citizens are in conflict with formal tenant or community groups	Here, the formal sector, in the form of NGOs or residents/community groups is disconnected from the constituency they purport to represent.
5	People follow their own self-interest against the interests of the wider community	Community representatives actively try to hinder individual citizens from gaining influence by, for instance, mobilizing political contacts, withholding information and controlling the agenda of meetings and fora.

Source: based on Pløger 2004.

nature of the relationship; who is allowed to talk and who are they allowed to talk to; when it takes place; under what rules; and even what the outcome will be.[13] The chapters by Shirlow and Gordon/McKee in this book draw attention to the struggle to create and maintain delicate relationships across Northern Ireland's particular ethno-religious divide and the self-destructive, parasitic influence of local warlords. That discursive strategies might identify, explain and expose these hidden (and often open) routines might provide an insight into progressive practice and conflict transformation. The hypo-crisies of local elected representatives, denial by the statutory sector, and impotence of policing around these forms of 'strife', underscore the nature of power in participatory processes in ethnically contested places.

Third, intracommunity and intercommunity rivalries fracture any sense of coherent empowerment and action by local people. Shirlow and Murtagh (2004) showed how the formal NGO sector working in a republican area of North Belfast failed to connect to the local community who were either unaware or disinterested in their work which was often seen as self-indulgent and irrelevant. Finally, Ploeger suggested that elites may work in their own self-interest against the interests of the local community. The question for this book is the extent to which this complex 'strife' can be unpacked, challenged and made productive in local development. This is especially the case in highly ethnicized settings where socio-spatial layers and injustices further stretch the competencies of professional planners.

Ethnicity, citizenship and planning

In ethnic and religious conflicts, ideas around land, power and inclusivity take on sharper relief and perhaps unsurprisingly, it is from this perspective that some of the most important criticisms of collaborative planning base their arguments. Yiftachel pointed out that the liberal democratic tradition of planning is historically and professionally centred on rationality and technical competencies:

> Western planning ideas thus found their way to many deeply divided societies, where ethnic groups have often had a long history of struggles over land control and where local political systems were far from the Western version of liberal democracy. The introduction of Anglo-Saxon planning ideas to these fundamentally different societies has created a set of problems and contradictions. (1995, 125)

These problems and contradictions relate primarily to the normative stance adopted by planners in particular contexts. Fenster (1996) identified three roles for planners in these situations:

1. The first is the 'Assimilation' model where planners, together with other policy interests, attempt to progressively integrate ethnic groups based on equality of citizenship rights and the reduction of difference over time.
2. A 'Pluralist' model recognizes the distinctiveness of ethnic identity and celebrates rather than curtails difference. In this case, ethnicity and citizenship rights are complementary rather than competitive.
3. In the third model the planner adopts a 'Discriminatory' stance. Discrimination arises when ethnic groups are treated differently from the majority in similar situations suggesting that their citizenship rights are not being met. Discrimination is also encountered when minorities are treated similarly in different situations, that is 'when their unique ethnic needs are not taken into consideration in policies and planning schemes, and they are not permitted to retain their uniqueness in the society as a whole.' (1996, 414)

In reviewing these scenarios and the discursive possibilities that flow from them, Fenster concluded that:

Each of the models can be applied to the processes of social change, and allow for varying degrees of assimilation, while preserving ethnic uniqueness where possible. They permit the recognition of and respect for diversity. (1996, 415)

Discursive planning in doing this is not a procedural task bringing interests to an unattainable consensus – impossible in Lacanian terms – but rather is a framework to identify and understand difference and for seeking out the potential space for interests to come together to create change. Allmendinger and Gunder point to an obstacle in the form of 'master signifiers' in tribal societies. Here 'master signifiers' become more pronounced and defended. They are the key words of belief that capture and label our characteristics, principles and values (2005, 101). They help us to explain prejudice and fear of the other, especially where there are no shared signifiers or mechanisms for discussing each group's particular point of conviction. The task is 'not to privilege one "side" over another but, instead, look for the historical and normative basis to each perspective and their associated ontologies and epistemologies...' (2005, 106). 'Equity, Diversity and Interdependence' as an approach is not the total answer to that task, but it does offer some insights into the 'construction of positions', the real and fantasized qualities of the respective claims and the scope for supportive discourses in local circumstances.

Equity, Diversity and Interdependence

Equity, Diversity and Interdependence (EDI) provides a model for learning about how organizations understand diversity, evaluate its implications for their work and deliver their programmes in more creative and credible ways. EDI emerged from the work of Eyben, Morrow and Wilson (1997) and their innovative research on community relations and policy making in Northern Ireland. It was especially influential in directing the Belfast based Community Relations Council (CRC), which is the NGO with primary responsibility for tackling sectarianism and promoting good relations between religions in this region. Its 'Strategic Plan 1998–2001' defined the terms accordingly:

- 'Equity' is a commitment at all levels within society to ensuring equality of access to resources, structures, and decision making processes and to the adoption of actions to secure and maintain these objectives. Equity is about achieving equal opportunities and fairness in redressing inequalities.
- 'Diversity' can be seen in the ever-changing variety of community and individual experiences. Respect for diversity affirms the existence, recognition, understanding and tolerance of difference, whether expressed through religious, ethnic, political or gender background. Diversity is about being free to shape and articulate identities as well as acknowledging and valuing difference.
- 'Interdependence' requires recognition by different interest or identity groups of their obligations and commitments to others and of the interconnectedness of individual and community experiences and ambitions leading to the development of a society that is at once cohesive and diverse. Interdependence is concerned with building better relationships and trust. (1998, 1)

CRC took the view that 'civil society depends on a shared discourse which recognises and affirms differences, but allows these to exist in constructive relationships with each other.' For this to happen, 'initiatives at all levels must be able to integrate these principles into their work in appropriate ways' (1998, 6). Eyben et al. (1997) pointed out that community relations activity in Belfast has traditionally focused on interpersonal and intergroup encounters at the community level rather than on embracing government bodies and institutional stakeholders. In particular, they emphasize the need to move beyond the procedural rationality of legal equality compliance to engage the 'reality' of difference in institutional contexts. A report in 2000 challenged the urban planning profession in Belfast to take the lead in bringing planning for cultural pluralism into the mainstream of urban management practice.[14] Morrow et al. (2003) describe this challenge and the necessary response accordingly:

Rather than coercive legislation, which requires conformity with preordained legislative outcomes, the requirement is for measures which support the development of a culture of learning and development, which encourages innovation and commitment in pursuit of an agreed vision and values. The key measure of success in such policy is in the growth of new capacity to deal with difficult but real problems rather than the absence of surface difficulties which leaves underlying issues untouched. (2003, 180)

EDI has, therefore, a wider relevance for the discussion of exclusionary processes and reaches across the mosaic of public, private, community and voluntary bodies that comprise contemporary governance. On the basis that the elements become core values in that governance, it has the capacity to foster good relations within organizations and between organizations and their constituencies.

The EDI model has been applied in a range of local development and institutional settings.[15] Murray and Murtagh (2004), for instance, high-lighted the value of understanding the extent and nature of exclusion among multiple constituencies in a largely rural environment via the working of Rural Community Network.[16] Here, the starting point was an attempt to map and understand interests marginal to or excluded from mainstream policy discourses (2003). Using participatory quantitative and qualitative research, connections – and differences – were established between, for instance, older people, racial minorities and women in specific situations. The shared experiences and understandings of this cluster of interests drew attention to the lack of regard for their distinctive and shared needs, not just in the language and aims of 'official' policies, but also within the advocacy priorities and programmes established by the NGO sector. The research showed that agricul-tural restructuring differentially affected their sense of self-worth, productive value and status within rural society. Their particular need for services, support, acknowledgement and inclusion in everyday routines were missed in the campaign agendas of active groups working in the rural arena. RCN, it can be said, adopted a purposeful strategy, which has a clear commitment to targeting a specific set of marginal interests, building their concerns into mainstream local development programmes and acting as their advocate with policy makers and politicians (2005). Here, the approach may be charac-terized as 'predicated on ongoing agonistic debate motivated by a constant critical resistance to totalising power'[17] and the importance of reflection on the value base and ethics of the organization's work as highlighted in the methodology of EDI. In particular, the approach drew attention to micro-community conflicts and the dynamics of 'strife' outlined in Pløger's analysis. Dialogue that seeks to challenge cultural difference and build alliances among common publics is the key to local working in these contexts.

Figure 7.1 highlights the implications of the approach for critical discursive practice. It suggests that there are a number of normative possibilities open to organizations in order to engage what Heikkila (2001) refers to as the

Figure 7.1: Equity, diversity and interdependence: the planner as resolver

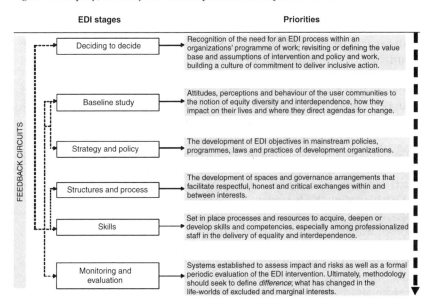

'multiple oppressions' expressed by disadvantaged communities. First, there needs to be organizational commitment to the nature of the task, the relevance of the agenda to the mainstream policy and interrogation of institutional values and assumptions. In EDI, baselining conditions should display a commitment to understanding and mapping equity relationships in given problem (and spatial) settings. Equity is primarily concerned with making connections and in Pløger's terms, 'placing power at the core of the analysis'.

Murtagh (2004) showed that despite the legislative weight behind equality of opportunity and Targeting Social Need policies in Northern Ireland, there is comparatively limited evidence of its delivery in the practice of planners, urban managers or housing officials. Here, professional values and routines dominated policy discourses with the deployment of technical language premised on efficiency and order holding sway. Figure 7.1 suggests that challenging the skills base of professionals located in critical positions in bureaucratic settings is an essential strategy in achieving this commitment 'to decide'. Likewise, there are implications for the whole area of knowledge production, especially by the university providers of professional courses, in areas such as planning, urban management or housing management. Here, respective professional institutes value generic skills which have the potential to marginalize more substantive debates about the distributive effects of policies and laws, how to analyse and understand difference and how to negotiate and manage a range of interests, not just those concerned with the property economy.[18] As Gunder argues:

> Alternative structures for planning education have been proposed: curricula in which traditional, multicultural, ecological, and design skill literacies constitute ethical inquiry... This is a perspective focused on the student's adoption of identification-defining signifiers and their supporting but contestable planning discourses – what shapes the fledgling planner's ego-ideal into being that of a planner. (2004, 309)

Understanding and evaluating the connections that explain the nature and effect of difference requires a distinctive set of methodological lenses in which participatory research, open space approaches and more penetrative data gathering methods would be prioritized. Clearly, strategies that build equity, respect distinctive cultural claims but which challenge the manipulation of difference and construct durable interdependencies are crucial to the development of a more ethically sensitive planning profession.

In ethnicized settings, where violent territorial conflicts characterize the local discourse, the challenge is to urgently explore the potential for conflict transformation:

> Since we cannot eliminate antagonism, we need to domesticate it to a condition of agonism in which passion is mobilized constructively (rather than destructively) towards the promotion of democratic decisions that are partly consensual, but which also respectfully accept irresolvable disagreements.[19]

Reeves (2005) argued that the planners need to be more diversity conscious in training, development plan processes and consultative methods. Her review argues that we must take a more serious view of the way in which land use policy can help to integrate all the relevant interests and agencies involved in the development of divided places. 'Spatial planning' moves beyond the narrow regulatory definition of the discipline to embrace a wider understanding of people, place and diversity, and within this framework Reeves offers an alternative vision for planning:

- 'Planning' that takes into account the needs of numerous different people;
- 'Planning' that takes a rights based approach and incorporates a duty to promote equality of opportunity;
- 'Planning' that engages people in a participatory way as equals rather than a passive target groups simply to be consulted; and
- 'Planning' that takes the social dimension of sustainable development as seriously as the environmental and economic dimensions.

Similarly, arenas that allow discussion, mediation, disagreement, agreement and resolution will challenge formal consultation processes and in particular, state-led participatory practice. Arrangements that provide space and crucially time for interests to develop and define their priorities, with technical support and facilitation, can help to move the governance debate beyond representation to more meaningful action. Ultimately, the quality of decision making will depend, in part, on the quality of the arenas for discussion, their legitimacy among stakeholders and the avoidance of the coercive agreement that has often characterized some partnership experiences in the past.[20] Finally, there also needs to be robust systems to evaluate the progress that initiatives make on the quality of life of the target groups, restructuring of conflict and the broader conditions described in the baseline analysis. In short, everyone must be capable of showing what the difference has been.

Conclusions

Equity, Diversity and Interdependence is clearly not the complete answer to the contradictions faced by planners in divided places. It was developed and applied in particular circumstances and needs further empirical testing and refinement before it is capable of guiding practice in technical and professional disciplines such as planning. However, it does highlight the need for models, methods and guidance in the creation of cultural dialogue in 'tribal territories'. The idealism of collaboration and the anarchy of some alternatives provide little value in divided societies, where territory is so violently contested. Recognizing and valuing disputes (not ignoring or displacing them) hold, at least, the promise of a more grounded debate about the possibilities open for planners and planning.

By focusing on inequality and injustice, the approach tries to weave a narrative about inclusion and diversity in particular situations. Focus on power and capacity for conflict transformation need to be central in the development of radical methodology in ethnically and racially divided societies in particular. What is perhaps surprising in a Northern Ireland context is the paucity of models aimed at guiding practice, challenging professional norms or mounting alternative strategies for peace building in the region. One contribution that this book can make is to offer validation or to reject approaches and techniques to management of diversity in a range of socio-spatial environments. This is an important task in assembling, evaluating and disseminating case studies of place that can help to tool up planners and related disciplines in conflict management.

This body of knowledge also has the potential to challenge planning education and professional development. The influential 'Egan Review of Skills' in Britain[21] highlighted the importance of generic competencies to guide practice in a range of spatial planning environments. However, there is little in the analysis about understanding inequality, respect for diversity or building alliances in explicitly 'agonistic' settings. Planning educators and custodians of professional values need to take on board the realities of spatial contests and not the fantasy of the model adaptable, technically competent planner producing imagined consensual worlds. What this book might offer is concrete examples of the value of this type of thinking, and some of the costs of ignoring or devaluing contestations in an increasingly fractured world.

Notes

1. Healey 1997.
2. Healey 1997 53.
3. Habermas 1987.
4. Healey 1997, 54.
5. Innes 1998, 52.
6. Gunder 2003, 239.
7. Hillier 2003.
8. Neill 2004.
9. Hillier 2003, 54.
10. Pløger 2001, 226.
11. Pløger 2004, 77.
12. Hughes et al. 1998.
13. Shirlow, Murtagh 2006.
14. Neill 2000.
15. Morrow et al. 2003.
16. RCN, the region's largest NGO working in advocacy and local development issues.
17. Gunder 2003, 280.
18. Kitchen et al. 2004.
19. Hillier 2003, 42.
20. Shirlow, Murtagh 2004.
21. ODPM 2004.

Part 3

Governance and the Accommodation of Difference: City Profiles in a Cold Climate

8
The Dutch Approach to Planning for Multiculturalism post Fortuyn

Hugo Priemus

The Netherlands has traditionally promoted a multicultural approach to urban renewal.[1] For several decades, national and local governments were reconciled to the fact that immigrants from Turkey, Morocco, Surinam and elsewhere were becoming concentrated in a number of less popular urban neighbourhoods – until the 2002 national elections, when a new political party calling itself the Pim Fortuyn List (LPF – Lijst Pim Fortuyn) with its charismatic leader, Pim Fortuyn, burst onto the scene. Fortuyn had published a book entitled *The Shambles of the Purple Coalition*, which challenged the policies of the coalition government in the Netherlands.[2] Fortuyn's popularity soared in the opinion polls, but on 6 May 2002, just a few days before the election, he was shot dead. His LPF party became the second largest party in Parliament, closely behind the Christian Democrats (CDA). The social democrats suffered the greatest losses.

One of the explanations mooted for Pim Fortuyn's political success was his ability to voice the deep displeasure experienced by many Dutch residents in a number of urban neighbourhoods, who felt marginalized by the unrelenting influx of immigrants. What once were the ethnic minorities in their neighbourhoods had become ethnic majorities, and many people felt threatened.

Fortuyn put most of the blame on the social democrats for the lack of safety and the poor quality of life in many urban neighbourhoods, in which Dutch national and ethnic minority groups usually lived without any real contact. He portrayed Islam as a 'backward religion', demanding that immigrants adapt to the Dutch democratic system and dominant Dutch norms and values. Fortuyn's approach was often dismissed by his opponents as xenophobic, but, however, this description is inappropriate. Indeed, several candidates on the LPF list were of foreign origin, albeit fully integrated citizens and fluent Dutch speakers.

In 2002, the LPF entered the centre-right coalition alongside the Christian Democrats and Conservatives to form the Balkenende I government.[3] This coalition was unsuccessful, mainly because of internal quarrelling. The Dutch had to go back to the polling stations as soon as 2003, where they punished the LPF severely, allowing the social democrats to regain all the ground they had lost. The Christian Democrats were again the largest party and opted for a new centre-right coalition,[4] which formed the Balkenende II government. Meanwhile, the social democrats, under their new leading candidate Wouter Bos, had rediscovered the old city districts, and attempted – with success – to restore the trust of the electorate that it lost in 2002.

This sudden shift in the political balance in the Netherlands has sparked many differences of opinion on planning for multiculturalism and urban renewal. This chapter starts by explaining the dominant approach pre Fortuyn (next section), then addresses the Fortuyn approach as pursued in Rotterdam by the LPF city alderman Marco Pastors (following section). Finally, the emerging compromise between the pre and post-Fortuyn approaches is outlined.

Planning for multiculturalism pre Fortuyn

Development towards a multicultural society took shape most clearly in the four major cities of the Netherlands.

The final column in Table 8.1 represents the combined figures for all four big cities in The Netherlands, which are known as the G4. However, it would be more appropriate in this context to speak of a G3, since the proportion of 'Dutch national' residents is far greater in Utrecht (69.0 per cent) than in the other three cities (51.9–56.3 per cent). Among these G3 cities, the similarities are more significant than any differences, although Rotterdam has a higher proportion of residents with an Antillean or Turkish background and rather fewer Moroccans.

Table 8.1: Population of the four major cities by ethnicity (as at 1 January 2003; %)

Country of origin/ background	Amsterdam	Rotterdam	The Hague	Utrecht	Four largest cities: G4
Surinam	9.8	8.7	9.6	2.6	8.5
Antilles	1.7	3.4	2.3	0.9	2.2
Turkey	5.0	7.3	6.4	4.5	5.9
Morocco	8.3	5.7	4.8	8.5	6.8
Other ethnic minority	23.4	21.7	20.6	14.4	21.1
Dutch (national)	51.9	53.1	56.3	69.0	55.4

Source: Priemus (2004).

In 1997, the Centre for Research and Statistics[5] conducted a comparative study of urban migrants, including those locating in Rotterdam and those moving out of the city. The study revealed little difference between the two groups in terms of education and qualifications. Those moving into the city were slightly less likely to be in paid employment, often being students. They were also more likely to be in a lower income bracket, while leavers had a higher income. This pattern is hardly surprising given that Rotterdam is a university city and home to several colleges of further education.

Between 1999 and 2002, the number of people locating in Rotterdam slightly exceeded the number moving away. In fact, the net population increase was attributable to an influx from overseas, while the growth in numbers of people moving between the city and the surrounding region was negative (Table 8.2).

If this pattern continues, the proportion of non-western foreign nationals living in Rotterdam will exceed 50 per cent soon after 2015.[6] In Amsterdam, this milestone will be passed not much later (Table 8.3). No corresponding figures are available for The Hague. The key question here is whether, and to what extent, the largely well-integrated second and third generation immigrants will still be regarded (or will regard themselves) as 'foreign'.

Table 8.4 shows Rotterdam's somewhat higher level of unemployment than the other major cities. Moreover, the difference in employment

Table 8.2: Migration between Rotterdam and the region, the rest of the Netherlands and overseas, 1999–2002 (averaged by year)

	entering	leaving	balance
Rotterdam urban region	6,632	11,143	−4,512
Province of South Holland	5,773	5,928	−155
The Netherlands	8,581	7,600	981
Overseas	8,804	3,077	5,728
Total	29,790	27,747	2,043

Source: Priemus (2004).

Table 8.3: Proportion of non-western ethnic minorities in Amsterdam, Rotterdam and Utrecht, 2003–2015 (%)

	Amsterdam	Rotterdam	Utrecht
2003	38.4	38.7	24.1
2010	42.3	45.5	25.4
2015	44.9	49.7	26.9

Source: Priemus (2004).

Table 8.4: Unemployment in the major cities by ethnicity (in % of potential working population), 2001

	Amsterdam	Rotterdam	The Hague	Utrecht
ethnic minorities	6	11	6	6
Dutch nationals	4	4	2	3
average	4	6	3	3

Source: Priemus (2004).

participation between ethnic minorities and Dutch nationals is greater in Rotterdam, where the unemployment rate for ethnic groups is 11 per cent, than in the other cities, where the corresponding figure is 6 per cent. However, the figures in Table 8.4 indicate also that 89 per cent of the Rotterdam ethnic population are actually in paid employment, so that there can be no justification for saying that all non-western immigrants live in poverty or lack prospects.

It goes without saying that, also pre Fortuyn, different attitudes existed in the Netherlands on how to deal with a multicultural society. Nevertheless, a dominant approach started to form, with the following characteristics:

- *cultural relativism*: there was recognition that many foreign groups had their own culture, and widespread tolerance existed towards these different cultures. It was acceptable to follow these foreign cultures, and furthermore, activities with an ethnic background would sometimes be subsidized by the national or local government;
- *tolerance*: it was deemed 'politically incorrect' to level critical generalizations at particular cultures or migrant communities, although it was clear that the number of criminal activities and violations of the law was much higher among Turkish and Moroccan young people than among Dutch national young people;
- *prospect of integration*: the outlook on the future was generally very optimistic: ultimately, Dutch national and ethnic minority groups would integrate with few problems;
- *naivety*: the authorities were deaf and blind to numerous empirically demonstrable facts.

The fact that the majority of Turkish and Moroccan men, after living for a very considerable time in the Netherlands, sought their brides in their home country escaped almost everyone's attention. The fact that lack of safety on the street was far worse in some neighbourhoods with a high ethnic minority population than elsewhere was usually not stated out loud.

What Dutch themselves often labelled 'tolerance' appeared in practice to have more to do with a denial of facts and problems, while ignoring the feelings and perceptions of both Dutch national and ethnic minority city dwellers.

Around the turn of the century, urban renewal shifted from pre-war to post-war city neighbourhoods, where much property is owned by housing associations. These neighbourhoods are characterized by many relatively inexpensive and small medium-rise and high-rise flats, and a market share of between 80 per cent and 100 per cent of social rented housing. The new urban renewal approach involved redifferentiating the housing stock to increase the proportion under owner-occupation, with more high-value and one-family dwellings with a garden. Clearly, the idea was that greater differentiation of the housing stock would lead to a 'more balanced population' of the neighbourhood, in other words a mix of low, middle and higher incomes and a mix of different cultures and ethnicities.

Planning for multiculturalism according to Fortuyn

'Rotterdam pushes forward. On the path to becoming a city in balance, Rotterdam Municipal Executive'[7] is the title of the policy memorandum published by the coalition municipal council of Rotterdam.[8] This municipal policy memorandum identified in 2003 the number of immigrants, and more in particular the rate at which it was rising, as a major problem for the city. The first policy priority is to close the municipal borders to immigrants from poor countries, which are labelled as 'disadvantaged'. These groups should be stopped at the national borders. Once they have been through the legal procedures, have gained positive status and permission to stay in the Netherlands, then the villages and small towns in the regions around Rotterdam are expected to absorb these poor immigrants.

A second policy priority is the formation of committees to operate a positive selection policy, in order to keep the unemployed and low-income households out of urban problem neighbourhoods. The endurance of the residents of these neighbourhoods has been tested to the limit. The households that should be admitted are not the poor ones, but those with good prospects and with a medium or high income. However, this is in breach of the Housing Act, which states that housing associations' main public task is to serve households that cannot find their own way in the housing market. Their task, therefore, is to give priority to, not to refuse, low income households.

The urban housing policy is formulated in terms of income, unemployment and disadvantage. The Rotterdam policy memorandum argues: 'Skin colour is not the problem, but the problem does have a colour . . . ' It is clear that the municipal administration sees not only a low income or unemployment as a problem, but also and especially a different skin colour and a different culture.

Figure 8.1: Street cartoons: The Hague

A striking fact is that the national Housing Ministry creates an opportunity, albeit temporarily and on a small scale, to use the Housing Allocation Act[9] as a way of refusing applications for housing in problem estates and neighbourhoods from candidates who have a low household income or are unemployed. This policy, which has been adopted not only in Rotterdam but also in other cities such as Nijmegen and Dordrecht, is highly controversial.

The policy goals of current urban renewal and housing policy in Rotterdam are:

- to attract and retain 'desirable' residents in problem (or potential problem) neighbourhoods;
- to better manage the influx of less prosperous groups into the region, city and neighbourhood;
- to distribute the less prosperous groups more effectively across the city, region and country as a whole, not as an objective in itself, but as a result of the overall approach.

Evaluation of current new urban renewal and housing policies in Rotterdam

It cannot be denied that the large cities in the Netherlands have many problems. Safety is a major concern, as is the social integration of immigrants in many (too many) urban neighbourhoods. This is particularly true in a number of areas in Rotterdam. Anyone reading the Rotterdam Municipal Executive's policy document with an open mind, even if its diagnosis is accepted, will nevertheless be astounded at the plethora of measures presented – intensified policies, binding agreements, positive selection policy and other expressions of faith in measures that are only one step away from racial discrimination. Social engineering is considered possible and desirable. At the very least, the document represents a policy 'overkill'. A number of critical remarks can be made, based on an assessment of the policy document.

Words not deeds

The policy document is an example of management by speech. It evinces a great confidence in the feasibility and desirability of social engineering, in other words of 'repairing' society. Notably, it will fall to other organizations to bring this about, ranging from the Ministry of Housing, the Ministry of Immigration and Integration, the regional authority, the other local authorities in the region, housing associations and private landlords, to the police, welfare organizations and other societal institutions. The City of Rotterdam itself is stimulating others to make 'agreements', preferably of a binding nature, and to monitor performance. It will do remarkably little itself. This will greatly simplify the buck-passing process later on: if the policy fails to get off the ground, or simply does not work, others can be conveniently blamed.

Social engineering

The policy document places a surprisingly great emphasis on the 'repairability' of society, which is the idea that problems which have developed can be readily reversed. Dotted throughout the document can be read how the 'desirable' residents will be 'tied' to the city and the neighbourhood. In the case of young graduates, it would appear that they are to be 'tied' for life – the document uses the word 'permanently'. The influx of less desirable groups, which, it must be remembered, are very sizeable, will be deflected without the need for border controls. Rotterdam officials, it seems, are able to tell at a glance whether a person is 'desirable' or 'undesirable', and whether they enjoy good future prospects or are total no-hopers. Even if you have never been convicted of a criminal offence, your legal status in Rotterdam remains very uncertain. You can be branded as having 'poor prospects', as 'undesirable', and made to take part in a 'positive lottery', the outcome of which is likely to be anything but positive for you. It is extremely unclear what legal foundation will be found for such far-reaching decisions. It is certainly not to be found in the Housing Allocation Act, and the current government has no plans for introducing any legislative basis of this kind. It is equally unclear whether a person will be able to challenge his 'undesirable' label in the courts. If so, the judicial system would do well to prepare for an unprecedented caseload.

The policy document is also remarkably confident that means to combat 'illegality' exist. Illegality is seen as a large part of the problem, and its eradication a large part of the solution. Estimates put the number of illegal immigrants in Rotterdam at anywhere between ten thousand and fifteen thousand. However, under the policy proposals, many activities that are currently legal will become illegal. In other words, by definition illegality will increase rather than decrease.

From fewer rules to more rules

One of the main points of the current Netherlands government programme is an intention to reduce government intervention and the volume of rules and regulations. The Rotterdam Municipal Executive does not wish to join in this game, however. It will introduce yet more rules and yet more criteria for entry in the Population Register. These criteria relate to variables that change so rapidly that keeping them up to date is impossible, and which will serve to clog up the databases in no time. The policy document includes countless other new rules and 'intensification' of existing ones.

The requirement of 'household income at twenty per cent above the minimum wage' seems simple enough, but what exactly constitutes a household? Who is living with whom? This is particularly difficult for either the government or a housing association to ascertain without invading people's privacy. Moreover, the document states that the minimum income requirement should be subject to some flexibility. Anyone who registers as a student will automatically be regarded as 'having good prospects', even though some 50 per cent of students never graduate. It seems likely that 'flexibility' will apply mostly to Dutch and white home-seekers. The policy document is full of generalizations, whereas real life involves variation, differentiation and dynamics.

Ethnicity and prospects

Close analysis of the document reveals that it almost totally focuses on ethnicity, despite claims that the policy it proposes centres on 'future prospects', or lack thereof. The document and the policy itself limp along on these two incompatible concepts. It is possible to deduce that the perceived problem is really one of ethnicity, but the document does not dare to state this outright.

At one point, the document acknowledges that immigrants often represent the most enterprising section of the donor (home) community. This is a point not to be overlooked. International migration is a real problem for donor countries. Migration to Europe has been ongoing for several decades, and may be regarded as an unstoppable dynamic process, succinctly analysed in Russell King's book *Mass migration in Europe: the Legacy and the Future* (1993). Migrants have arrived in Europe from Asia, Africa and South America, attracted by better opportunities for personal and economic development, levelling-out of natural population growth and rising average age of the population. Another factor is progress in global communication technology. International migration into Europe represents a useful and fruitful counter-balance to population ageing and economic and demographic stagnation in Europe. Moreover, several international treaties oblige civilized countries to accept genuine political refugees. The European Union has not even begun to formulate any joint asylum or migration policy, and has not implemented any additional controls at the external borders. There is simply no coordination of policy between the member states, which renders implementation of a national asylum and immigration policy well nigh impossible, not least because EU internal borders are now almost fully open. Of course, the same applies within the Netherlands, where one can cross municipal or provincial boundaries 'without let or hindrance'.

Anyone examining the statistics will soon realize that many of the immigrants in the Netherlands actually enjoy extremely good prospects, in both economic and social terms. They are prepared to enter the employment market by taking on jobs that most Dutch people would consider beneath their dignity. Yet immigrants with a low starting wage are demonized in the Rotterdam policy document. In fact, this is a clear case of discrimination. They will remain the 'poor black sheep' well into the second or third generation.

Overvaluation of databases as an administrative weapon

The policy document sets great store by linking various databases, deployment of case workers and introduction of registration and prevention systems in the battle against illegality and social impoverishment. However, linking databases will not automatically reveal illegality. The document ignores many developments already implemented at national level for creating valid data registration and improving administrative systems.[10] The Rotterdam document underestimates the need for agreements at a national level as well as staffing and financial consequences. It grossly overestimates the opportunities that databases will offer in tackling illegality.

Trivialization of the consequences in terms of enforcement

Throughout the document, policy is 'intensified' and new measures added, yet costs and staffing requirements for the colossal enforcement operation that this will entail are consistently brushed aside. At present, there is capacity in Rotterdam to offer integration training to just 5,600 people, while some 60,000 established immigrants are proposed to be offered these courses. Higher demands are placed on the immigrants themselves, including command of the Dutch language, a knowledge of the Netherlands and its culture, paid employment and officially recognized accommodation. Those responsible for providing courses, employment and accommodation cannot hope to meet the demand in a month of Sundays. The document signally fails to state who is to be responsible for enforcement efforts or what administrative organization is to be set up. The proposed policy quite simply cannot be implemented. Moreover, it is in stark contrast to the current government's cost-cutting policy, which has already severely eroded the housing allowances system, the investment budget for urban renewal and the social component of the Major Cities Policy.

Structural problems are ignored

The problems facing Rotterdam, its outlying region and the Zuidvleugel[11] as a whole have been recognized for many years and are well documented. First of all, the economic structure of this part of the country is weak. True enough, the Port of Rotterdam established new records for the volume of freight processed in 2003 and 2004, but this does not greatly benefit the region. The local 'value added' is negligible. Development of the knowledge-intensive business services sector has long lagged behind that in cities further north. The policy document has very little to say on this subject.

Secondly, the quality of much of Rotterdam's housing stock is very poor, as is the residential environment. The Municipal Executive's Vision Statement on Housing (2003) insists that quality must be improved: as indeed it must, but it will take years, if not decades. While Rotterdam's housing and employment markets remain so weak, it will be impossible to solve the problems by excluding low income groups. In fact, there is a very great risk that this measure in the long run will merely increase the vacancy rate in sections of the housing stock, because the exclusion policy (if it were successful) would not lead to any additional influx of higher income residents.

Misunderstanding of the role of the housing associations

The Municipal Executive policy document calls upon housing associations to exclude households with an income lower than 120 per cent of the statutory minimum, and to give preferential treatment to those with higher incomes. This is totally inconsistent with the content and intent of the 1992 Housing Allocation Act and the Decree on the Management of the Social Housing Rental Sector, which oblige housing associations to give priority to lower income groups. Rotterdam is not exempt from this legislation. Nevertheless, it is appropriate for housing associations to offer rented and owner-occupied accommodation in the mid-price sector as well, in order to attract and retain households with an above-average income in the city and the neighbourhood. This is one of the fundamental measures of current government policy for promoting urban renewal.

The near future of planning for multiculturalism

The Rotterdam policy document has met with a positive response from media commentators and many in the profession. The author's assessment is, by and large, negative. Problems are defined in an extremely partisan manner, and then transformed into an unwise, unworkable and, frankly, unpleasant policy that opens wide the door to discrimination, although the Rotterdam Municipal Executive strenuously denies that this is the intention. So what is the solution? How can the degeneration of some urban districts be halted and reversed? How can the poor standard of housing and the poor quality of life in parts of the city be improved? What can be done about the ongoing selective migration to and from the city?

The solution is not to be found in new policy or new instruments, but in eradicating the enormous 'implementation gap' in the pursuit of existing policy. A workable alternative was put forward many years ago in the form of the government's Major Cities Policy, with its interrelated physical, social and economic pillars (to which a public safety pillar might usefully be added). Further to this policy, the Ministry of Housing, Spatial Planning and the Environment[12] published a well formulated policy document on urban renewal in 1997. Both the Major Cities Policy and its urban renewal counterpart are relatively recent. They are intended as structural policy for the longer term. The successive ministers responsible for the Major Cities Policy have all been from the social-liberal party. It is surely unwise to give the portfolio for such a vital area of policy to just one, rather small, political party in government after government, which can only undermine support among the larger parties.[13] The current budgetary cutbacks affecting the Major Cities Policy will be disastrous to cities such as Rotterdam.

Within the national programme for strengthening the economic structure,[14] urban renewal was recognized by previous governments, notably those led by Wim Kok, as a strategic policy area: after infrastructure, it received the greatest financing amount from the Economic Structure Fund. The programme itself has been derailed by a paralysing combination of dwindling resources and increasing demands.

Since Wim Kok's departure from office in 2002, national governments have systematically underestimated the significance of the Major Cities Policy and of urban renewal. A reappraisal of the field is now required in order to address the quality of life issues facing the cities. In many cases, emergence of a successful business services sector has helped to promote the process. Nevertheless, a long-term policy involving local authorities and the relevant ministries is required if the problems are to be resolved and opportunities seized. The extent of the problems in Amsterdam, Rotterdam and The Hague is, of course, greater than in the other 27 Netherlands towns and cities directly involved in the Major Cities Policy.

If Rotterdam is compared to Amsterdam, the differences are not to be found in terms of the number of ethnic minority residents or in immigration. Rather, the differences are in the political ambitions of one party,[15] the legacy in this city of the murdered politician Pim Fortuyn and, above all, in major differences in economic structure. This is why another existing

Figure 8.2: Living together in the Netherlands

policy approach is so important to Rotterdam, which was formulated many years ago but is not mentioned in the Rotterdam latest policy document.[16] Reference is being made to economic revitalization of the Zuidvleugel as a whole. In 1997, a Zuidvleugel Administrative Platform was set up to achieve greater coordination and cohesion between a number of strategic investment projects and to promote their implementation. The strengthening of the economic structure in this region is recognized as being of particular strategic importance.[17]

There is growing discomfort within the civic society of the Netherlands concerning generalizations about Muslims or certain ethnic minority groups. There is growing awareness of the large range of opinions, behaviour and possibly values within both immigrant and national groups. The welfare state, legal systems, language and values are all now stressed more than in the recent past, and immigrants are coming under increasing pressure to learn the Dutch language, familiarize themselves with social and economic institutions and obey Dutch laws. Separation of church and state is being pursued with renewed vigour. Cultural relativism has made way for a self-aware – sometimes self-satisfied – sense of superiority about the Dutch democratic system, culture and welfare state. At the same time, there is growing awareness that immigration from distant countries for economic or humanitarian and political reasons is a structural phenomenon all over Europe.[18] A revaluation of the need for more communication and interaction between population groups can be observed. A zero-tolerance policy by the police is becoming more popular, to be adopted vis-à-vis both immigrant and national groups. New urban renewal is being targeted increasingly on social climbers in urban neighbourhoods (both with a Dutch and a foreign background), to enable these residents to make their housing 'career' within the neighbourhood, should they wish to do so, and to strengthen social capital in the city.[19]

Conclusions and recommendations

What Netherlands towns and cities need for the coming years is not the new policy unveiled by the 'Rotterdam pushes forward' document, but continuation and implementation of four existing policy lines, each of which should serve to strengthen the others:

1. Intensification and de-bureaucratization of the Major Cities Policy and that covering urban renewal;[20]
2. Intensification of efforts to strengthen the economic structure and the joint planning policy for the Zuidvleugel;[21]
3. Intensification of the public safety policy and efforts to reduce crime and crime-related issues in and around Rotterdam;[22]

4. Regionalization of housing policies, with construction, demolition, restructuring, sales and purchase, and allocation organized and coordinated on a regional basis. Local authorities other than Rotterdam and Schiedam must be able to offer a greater number of social housing units. However, because the Rotterdam region beyond the Rotterdam–Schiedam–Vlaardingen–Maassluis agglomeration has only limited housing stock available, it is inappropriate to expect miracles of a regional policy.

It is important that these policy areas are not subject to further budgetary restrictions. Intensification is required, as is patience and a long-term view. And immigration policy? Here too, the path set out by the second Kok government should be followed and the new Foreign Nationals (Immigration) Act must be applied consistently. The Dutch presidency of the European Union in 2004 offered an excellent opportunity to place joint European immigration and asylum policy on the agenda. Unfortunately the chance was not taken.

Notes

1. Priemus, Smid 1995; Priemus 1995.
2. The joint conservative (VVD), social-liberal (D66) and social democrat (PvdA – Partij van de Arbeid) parties.
3. In 2002 Balkenende formed a new government, in the wake of the resignation of Prime Minister Wim Kok. This cabinet is known as Balkenende I. This government (including the LPF party of the murdered politician Pim Fortuyn) fell after just 86 days in office. After elections in 2003 Balkenende formed his second cabinet Balkenende II with VVD D66.
4. Of CDA, VVD and D66.
5. Centrum voor Onderzoek en Statistiek, COS.
6. This was predicted in: Priemus 1993.
7. Stedelijk beleid in balans; gemeente Rotterdam 2003.
8. CDA, VVD and Leefbaar Rotterdam, the Rotterdam political movement led by Fortuyn that gained an electoral victory some months before the national elections of 2002.
9. Huisvestingswet, Housing Allocation Act, 1992.
10. Examples include a database of all residential properties in the country and the BSIK Geo-information programme.
11. The south-western 'rim' of the Netherlands.
12. VROM, Housing, Spatial Planning and the Environment Ministry.
13. VVD, CDA, PvdA.
14. ICES.
15. Leefbaar Rotterdam.
16. Gemeente Rotterdam 2003.
17. Provincie Zuid-Holland et al. 1999; Adviescommissie Zuidvleugel 2000; Bestuurlijk Platform Zuidvleugel 2003.
18. King 1993.

19. Putnam 1993; 2000.
20. The process to be led by the Rotterdam Municipal Executive, and the four relevant national ministries: Interior; Housing, Spatial Planning and the Environment; Economic Affairs; and Agriculture, Nature Management & Food Quality.
21. Province of South Holland, City of Rotterdam, City of The Hague and their respective regional authorities.
22. City of Rotterdam, Ministry of Justice, Ministry of the Interior, the police, probation service and crime prevention organizations.

9

Being and Living Together in French Cities: a Conflict-ridden Path Paved with Euphemisms[1]

Claude Jacquier

One of the main problems concerning urbanism in France (and perhaps elsewhere) is to achieve a clear and unprejudiced debate on what cities consist of today and what their future is. The problem lies in the fact that paradigms and concepts generally used to describe urban reality need to undergo a root-and-branch transformation. The urban world is practically upside down and back to front. Where do centres lie? Where are edges to be found? Where are the frontiers that traditionally separated the interior from the outside and thus provided the basis for political power?[2] Nowadays frontiers run through cities and metropolises, balkanize them and distribute their inhabitants as a function of their geographical, social and cultural origins. What is the meaning of all this? What makes sense? How can we put a name to all this? To name means surely to attach reality to a certain mental and symbolical existence, to its representation, because we can only really discuss representations.[3]

These profound mutations force us to reconsider what it means 'to be and to live together'[4] in cities, a question that has perhaps never carried such political weight as it does today! To be and to live together assumes cooperative processes among city dwellers, but these people are ever more diverse in their origins, their cultures, their references, their projects and their visions of the future. Consequently, they conflict with one another. In a world that highlights and glorifies individual success, their life paths are no longer focused on a shared objective.

It is not easy to accept this, and the very idea of conflictual relationships among social groups (the archaic class struggle) is no longer politically correct. This is why one hears more and more euphemisms to ignore or make a travesty of this conflictual reality and make it quite simply acceptable. Official documents are riddled with such euphemisms; the media swallow these whole and regurgitate them slavishly; elected representatives and professional staff use them to build an apparent consensus; researchers tear their hair out in their attempts to decipher these mutant representations.

Henceforth, partnership is the only acceptable perspective if we are to build 'living and being togetherness'. Conflict has no place in a naive vision of cooperation.

Perhaps all these euphemisms are a way of coming to terms with – or of ignoring – conflicts and thus reality. While these euphemisms create difficulties for researchers, they cause even greater ones for the places, people and institutions who make up these urban areas: how can one exist and be socially recognized when one does not have a name that is socially and publicly recognizable by all?

To name is a fundamental act, which states the place and the role that a person has in a society and which confers existence. The author's hypothesis for explaining the eruptions of Autumn 2005 is that the problems encountered by certain groups in French cities are not merely a function of their economic, social and residential situation, but also and possibly fundamentally a function of their inability to position themselves in the representational structure because they do not benefit from a name.

Some French definitions: a huge heritage

In France it is difficult to name the groups among those whose presence arises from immigration. Here, for example, the notion of community, like that of a minority, is not recognized in public and cannot be used to designate a part of the population. The French Republic, *La République*, is one and indivisible and the French people consists exclusively of individuals who are born and who remain free and with the same rights. The only grounds for distinctions between individuals within the population are those of nationality.[5]

In other words, on the one hand there are French people and, on the other hand, foreigners. Consequently, in the public arena as far as the French are concerned their origins are totally irrelevant. There are three ways of becoming French, namely by birth (*jus soli*) or 'by blood' (*jus sanguinis*), and by naturalization (i.e. the choice and request of French citizenship). Once a person has become French, in theory, the only relevant data is that of their ID card. It is not only politically incorrect but also illegal to point out a person's geographical, ethnic or religious origin.

This is the legal side of matters. Of course in reality things are not like that; between the ideal world of the Republican triptych of liberty, equality and brotherhood (*liberté, égalité, fraternité*) and the real world, with its everyday references to all the features that go to make up a person, there is a gulf with all the possible behavioural deviances on both sides of the exchange. For example French-born children of foreign parents (French citizens by *jus soli*) have a great deal of difficulty in being recognized as such because of their name, their physical appearance or even because of their postal address.

The situation in terms of citizens' rights has grown more complicated recently. All French nationals, and they alone, have the right to vote and to stand for election. The Maastricht and Amsterdam treaties extended the right to vote, in local and European elections, to residents from other EU countries, but with restrictions that a person had to have spent a certain time in France; they could not stand for mayor, nor be or designate what are known as the *grands électeurs* responsible for electing *sénateurs dépositaires de la souveraineté nationale*.[6] In the French case, therefore, European directives have thus created three types of political being, which saps the fundamental principles of citizenship/nationality. There now are French people who have full civil rights, EU foreign residents who have limited civil rights and other, non-EU foreigners who have no political rights at all, even though, because of France's colonial heritage, they have unstintingly contributed to French wealth and have spilt their blood in French wars to pay for the rights that go with French citizenship.

The current French position of refusing to make political room for communities and minorities goes back to the construction of citizenship and society in the republican framework.[7] At the end of the 18th century, the revolutionary process was a paroxysm in the struggle of the rising bourgeoisie, against the aristocratic sectors (nobles and clergy) and the privileges denounced by the list of grievances (*cahiers de doléances*), and in favour of freedom and individual rights. The Revolution marks the seizure of full power by the industrial and trading classes but also by professional people such as lawyers, doctors, teachers and the great thinkers of the Enlightenment.

It is above all the triumph of individual rights over collective, community rights which go along with calling into question power and intermediaries controlled by the aristocrats. The principle is thus the following: between the individual citizen and the State there must no longer be any intermediary body to act as an obstacle.

This principle is incorporated in the Le Chapelier law of 1791 which runs as follows: 'There are no more guilds and corporations in the State; there is now only the particular interest of each individual and the general interest. No one may incite citizens to take up an intermediate interest, to separate the public good by a spirit of group interest.' This law was a law for liberty inasmuch as it attacked the shackles of the guilds, as they then were, with respect to freedom to work and trade. From this it was extrapolated to cover any form of intermediary representation and to present such as an attack on the unity of the nation; thus a deep reticence arose with respect not only to organized minorities and communities but also any type of association. Parishes, in particular, the primary form of local organization, were closely monitored. In these fields it proved necessary to wait for over a century before local authorities, professional bodies, trade-unions and associations were fully recognized.

The second historical era to be considered is that of colonization. Colonization followed on from a period of violent domination of certain African people by a number of European countries particularly with the development of the trade triangle. The trade triangle involved the 'exportation' of black slaves to the West Indies. In the example of France it was a case of – beyond commerce – projecting on to the world the principles of the Enlightenment and the universal values for which it was a vector. This was a civilizing mission continuing the glorious dream of exporting the Revolution to the whole of Europe. It was the work of a merchant and industrial bourgeoisie, but also stemmed from what would nowadays be referred to as modern technocracy avidly seeking our new frontiers to test out its new knowledge. The colonization process was not supported by the public and successive governments had to continually generate propaganda in order for it to be accepted. There are numerous immigrants today who are descended from the populations of these colonies; some of those who have arrived from the last tatters of this colonial empire (the West Indies, Guyana, Reunion, and Mayotte) are French citizens and full members of the European Union.

With the exception of Algeria, French colonization was not based on settlement, and this is perhaps the most characteristic feature of the relationships between these countries and France. Unlike other old French 'possessions', Algeria was militarily subdued. It was then occupied and settled.

Algeria was the only French possession to have been integrated administratively into France. It was divided up into three *départements*, but Algerians were not granted full French citizenship. Unlike what happened in other possessions,[8] the decolonization process was very violent, involving a war of liberation that lasted over seven years. This war has for long been referred to under the euphemism of the Algerian incident (*les évènements d'Algérie*) and its horrific nature has been as it were bottled up beneath a love–hate relationship. More than 40 years later, bottled-up sentiments have come back to haunt French society. Similar remarks may be made about slavery, the slave trade and poorly implemented colonization and decolonization.

The third historical development was the emancipation of politics with respect to the Church and the separation of the Church and the State. This process officially came to an end with the 1905 law affirming the nonreligious nature of the French state and politics. Religion is a private matter, and France became one of the few countries in the world where government is not in the name of God. Neither the head of state, the president nor the prime minister, or indeed any political authority, swear allegiance in the name of God or on the Bible. This separation between God and Caesar has been accepted by the main faiths including Judaism, Catholicism and the Reformed Church. It can give rise to problems with Islam, which does not separate political and religious matters. This is the case inasmuch as Islam finds it difficult to play the role of a negotiator with political authorities.

An indivisible diversity in France and in Grenoble

Faced with this, traditional institutions responsible for initiation into society are running into substantial difficulties. This is felt most acutely in primary schools where teachers have been referred to as the 'black hussars' of the Republic.

Over the last few years generations emerging from immigration flows – basically French – find themselves out of kilter. Moreover, these generations are beginning to hark back to a past that is often long gone, and to demand explanations (such as equating slavery and colonization with crimes against humanity, creation of organizations seeking identity such as the so-called movement of the *indigènes de la République* and so on). The question of the Islamic veil is more a function of this search for identity and an explosion of hitherto bottled-up feelings than a persecuted religious practice. The events of Autumn 2005 (riots, emotion) can also very largely be put down to this fundamental movement, which reached a paroxysm with the death of two youths pursued by the police and were also stoked up by the comments of a government minister which were not merely clumsy: referring to young people of immigrant origin in some neighbourhoods as 'scum', and that these same neighbourhoods needed industrial cleansing with high-pressure hoses. Heavy-duty escalation of security measures is far more profitable electorally than finding a real answer to the problem.

In brief, it was relatively easy to achieve living and being together in a France that had merely to cope with immigrant workers or, even easier, political refugees. Today the problem lies in the fact that no longer are flows of relatively docile immigrants to be dealt with, whether people who have turned up to fill a job or who are politically highly aware and well integrated. Now society is facing the difficulties caused by the reality that the offspring of these migrants are confronted with because of the social liabilities of the circumstances created for their parents and grandparents. The new generations find these to be simply unbearable. It is worthwhile pointing out that the French riots were not the work of foreigners or of recent immigrants: they were the reaction of young French people who happened to be the inheritors of the grim colonial past of Sub-Saharan or North Africa – particularly Algeria – and the slavery of the West Indies. These are young French citizens who stand side by side with the rest of this abandoned portion of society, who find it difficult to cope with globalization and the free circulation of ideas, capital, good and services and are set alongside the closely observed men and women in the street if they originate from the poorer regions of the world.

Euphemisms are not much use against the emergence of bottled-up emotion.

The situation in Grenoble

When Grenoble is compared with the situation on the scale of France as a whole, it can be seen that Grenoble is a city marked by immigration. This is much more the case than might be supposed from data allowing only for those who do not have French nationality. Grenoble as such is growing only in terms of foreign residents.

In general, and for France as a whole, statistical data downplays the effects of migration flows on the population structure since it includes only foreigners. In fact, as was seen earlier, minorities, communities and people of immigrant extraction are not distinguished.

This under-estimation is greater in cities and particularly in a town like Grenoble which has been an immigration 'sink' since the middle of the 19th century. Immigrants came first of all from other areas of France such as Savoy (which was not then part of France) and especially from Italy. In more recent years immigrants have arrived from almost all the source countries and from former French colonies.

These migration flows corresponded to the economic development that has characterized Grenoble over the years. One feature of the town is that it lies in a region that suffered from many drawbacks in the 19th century. Agricultural resources were poor, there were no minerals or coal, the location was an enclave formed by the surrounding mountains; the town was a military strong point designed to discourage the powerful nearby Austrian empire. The economic history of Grenoble from the early 19th century was marked by the need to cope with handicaps and deploy what would now be referred to as a knowledge-based economy. Over this period 40-year economic cycles can therefore be identified, with a complete regeneration of the export-oriented base economy (see Table 9.1).

Table 9.1: Economic cycles and immigration waves: immigration and immigrant sedimentation

1840	glove manufacture	rural immigrants
		Savoy
		Northern and Southern Italy
1880	water power	Italy
	mechanical engineering	Switzerland
1920	electricity	Italy, Armenia
	metallurgy	Poland, Russia
	chemical engineering	Algeria
1960	nuclear research	Northern Europe and North America
	information technologies	Spain, Portugal
	construction	Algeria, returning French expatriates
2000	bio and nano-technologies	Europe, America, Asia
	services	Africa, Turkey, Eastern Europe

All these changes arose from the need to get beyond stumbling blocks, especially of transport barriers and the small size of the local market, by emphasizing high value-added production. This development was not driven by market forces alone. It was heavily subsidized by public sector investment (research and training). Evolution was constantly based on influxes of migrant labour, both highly and poorly qualified. Other migrants arrived for reasons which had nothing to do with international variations in economic potential. Examples are afforded by the socio-political tensions in certain countries such as Armenia and Russia in the 1920s, and Spain and Italy in the 1930s.

Euphemisms 1 – urban structure: recognizing complexity

As can be seen, the migration phenomenon is not a recent one in Grenoble – as elsewhere. It may be said that throughout history French and European cities have been modelled by migration flows, both national and international emigration and immigration. It may in fact be said that sedentary living is more recent and less widespread than migration, and indeed nomadism. Yet sedentary living seems to be viewed in a more positive light. Until recently, the migrant and the nomad were not seen as a threat to local society and cities.

Moreover, the concept of immigrant often has negative connotations whereas that of emigrants is generally perceived more positively, except perhaps at the time of the French Revolution when the word was used to refer to French aristocrats who had joined the anti-revolutionary European coalition (*émigrés*).

Lastly, the concepts of immigration and immigrant denote especially those who have come to undertake low-prestige positions, particularly jobs that French people no longer want. The concept is rarely used when talking about those of higher social rank coming from countries with the same standard of living. In a nutshell, an Algerian is an immigrant, but an Englishman, an American, a German or a Swede who comes to France for a high-prestige position is most definitely not thought of as an immigrant.

These third-world immigrants are sometimes referred to by a range of euphemisms. They are exploited but it is said that they are 'welcomed' and the land to which they go is a 'land of welcome'. In Germany they are known as guest workers (*Gastarbeiter*). They are guests and society is their guest-house.

The spatial expression of social fragmentation

As time goes on, changes in the economic foundation and in immigration flows have led to new urbanized areas appearing in response to both public and private sector and socio-political coalition initiatives. All these factors interact and contribute to this mutual spatial jostling. It is not easy to represent the spatial distribution of this constellation of urban areas, given the range of possible situations and the difficulty of defining the

Figure 9.1: The writing on the wall: protest on the Petit Bard estate in Montpellier, August 2004 (photo Jean Michel Mart, © maxppp)

hierarchy one is trying to depict. In fact this hierarchy is a subjective one, showing symbolic positioning and sometimes ideological prejudice. At this time when the spatial and social fragmentation of cities has greatly increased, the dominant approach seems to be to occupy the more highly valued areas of a city, whatever the cost, while contributing as little as possible to necessary metropolitan solidarity.

In France in the 1950s and 1960s, some of the historic neighbourhoods that had been settled by southern Europeans (usually Italians, Spaniards and Portuguese) resisted the arrival of new migrants, mainly from North Africa. Often these immigrants live side by side with ageing French people, thus creating neighbourhoods that are socially highly convoluted.

Though there are no ghettos of the poor nor are there ghettos of the rich such as are seen in some North American towns or in some cities in developing countries, a growing fragmentation of cities and a radical transformation of their traditional topology (centre–edge and urban–rural) can nevertheless be perceived.

First of all, urban fragmentation and social deprivation themes have often traditionally been connected to the dialectic between the centres and the outskirts of cities. Over time, the concept of the urban fringe has become less and less clear. Today its urban topological meaning is less used than its symbolic one.

Over time, in France and in European countries, the content of this notion has changed greatly and it has been used in many different ways. Designations such as suburbs, inner and outer suburbs, outskirts and *banlieues* do have meaning in Europe; they have a historical reality and a contemporary reality with the phenomenon of urban sprawl developing more or less along the lines of the United States, but the situation varies greatly from one city to another.[9] The periphery has expanded enormously over the last half-century. It is composite in its functions, its activities and in its architectural form. This is particularly the case in the oldest areas ('inner suburbs'), consisting of highly diverse neighbourhoods (suburbs, factory towns, high-rise estates, low-rise estates, and so on), inhabited by heterogeneous groups of people, because these are also places of urban fragmentation and social segregation.

Moreover, the edges of cities are not necessarily deprived places. Urban peripheries are areas where both the adding of value and blight can be seen. This makes them potential catchment areas for a great range of people, including, notably, the more underprivileged. Thus, peripheries of cities are, like most city centres, urban and social mosaics, and it is not easy to analyse their configuration over Europe as a whole. Obviously it is difficult to represent this mosaic by a single and simple model.

Research undertaken in Europe over recent years has shown that 'stigmatized areas' exhibit great diversity in their location and in their morphology. The use of a single term such as *banlieues* to describe this urban reality hides the fact that these areas vary a great deal. They range from old districts in city centres, suburbs or working class districts developed in the 19th century, through factory towns or factory company towns, high-rise complexes built in the post-war period, to more recent low-rise habitats or, as in the south of Europe, shanty towns or zones of unstable or spontaneous occupation.[10]

In its stigmatized form, the concept of the 'edge' of the city (where the poorest can live) must not be reduced to its topological dimension (a far away place). French, European and world urban reality show that these relegated or 'assigned to residence' areas can also actually be located in the city centre. Just as it is possible to imagine a 'peripheral centrality', one may think in terms of a 'central periphery'. Such considerations reorient the research perspective. Fragmentation in European cities is far from being homogeneous, and deprived areas are sometimes located on sociological rather than geographical fringes. To arrive at a satisfactory comparative approach, it is necessary to show how French cities have had a range of possibilities for generating, in space and time, both 'elective settlements' and 'forced residences'.

This change in the meaning of the term 'periphery' is visualized in the model of spatial migration patterns (Figures 9.2–9.4). It leads to a new approach to the concept of border. Borders are no longer materialized by fortifications, by the 'pale' around the city or by the limits of a military buffer

Figure 9.2: The French fragmentation process 1945–1975

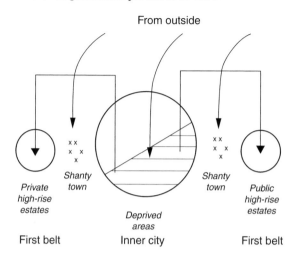

Figure 9.3: The French fragmentation process 1975–1995

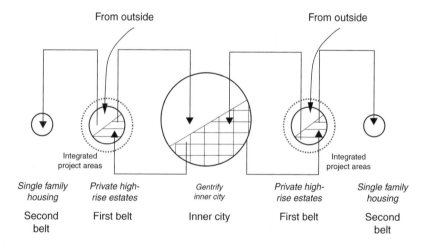

zone between the city and its inhabitants and other powers or menacing people out in the wilds with 'neither hearth, nor home'. Nowadays this concept corresponds less to an external limit (the topological meaning of periphery) than to a range of fractures, discontinuities or 'hinges' disseminated over urban territories. The entrance to a territory occurs less and less at its edge (access by seaports and custom posts on traditional borders). Rather does it take place increasingly via its core, through cities, generally via railway stations and airports. Thus the political border is now actually

Figure 9.4: The French fragmentation process 1995–present

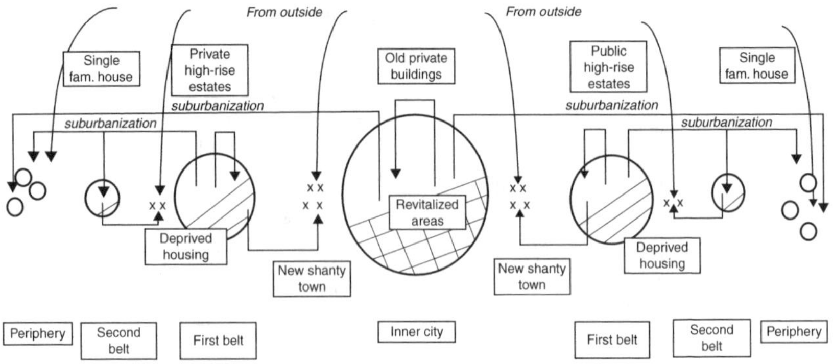

within the core of metropolitan areas. It is these latter-day harbours that provide direct access to urbanized areas.

Borders are also to be found within the core of fragmented cities. These are physical borders between urban areas and social groups. 'Gated communities' or 'rich ghettos' are not a phenomenon specific to the USA. They can also be observed in Third World countries, and also in France, in an American guise, but in a more subtle way, through the balkanization of metropolitan areas, arising from the refusal of the richest neighbourhoods to show financial solidarity with others.

Finally, the 'metropolitan-archipelagos'[11] resulting from this fragmentation of urban space question, in a way, the ancestral ways of regulating human violence which have been established for centuries in western cities. As Hobbes (1982) explained, pacification in our societies was built historically in relation to an outside world (foreign countries, infidels, enemies). To escape from the war of all against all, people had to accept a contract defining a space inside of which they agreed to renounce mutual violence in order to benefit from the safety provided by the authorities (a king, a government) in exchange for this sacrifice. But what is becoming of this concept when, the stakes having been redistributed over vast expanses of territory, this distinction between inside and outside is no longer clear? Western cities are at once the focus of the world and its impoverished periphery. Are they becoming 'city peripheries', which have broken with the fundamental principles of democratic societies?[12]

Euphemisms 2 – neighbourhoods and populations: the need for new governance

It is a fact: minorities and communities do exist in France and they occupy identifiable areas of the city, even though they are not as clearly demarcated as in, say, American ghettos. The place that they occupy in society and in spatial terms has no expression in the official public and political arena. So how can these groups and the areas they occupy within a city be accurately represented?

For example, people do not know how to designate the 'deprived areas' where these minorities and communities live. How can these places be accurately named within the framework of public policy? In France, within the framework of ad hoc policies, the areas are officially referred to as sensitive neighbourhoods (*quartiers sensibles*). Clearly, these areas are not in any way special when it comes to 'sensitivity' or 'affection'. They are increasingly referred to quite simply as neighbourhoods (*les quartiers*). This says a great deal about the force of the stigmatization process at work: it has succeeded in converting a common noun into a proper noun!

Analogously, people do not know how to designate young persons who are children of the immigration process. There are of course a whole range of slang terms, usually pejorative words that are actually illegal under anti-racism laws. Despite the fact that they are clearly all French citizens, these juveniles are or feel themselves to be so marginalized that they consider this citizenship barely worth the paper it is written on. This distinction that works back to front – like the *verlan*[13] that they speak – has been fully taken on board by the politicians. They can use descriptions that the young people themselves use. For instance, young French people of Algerian extraction refer to themselves as *Beurs*.[14] As a euphemism following on from the areas they inhabit, they are assigned to the category youth from neighbourhoods (*jeunes des quartiers*); this is an anodyne and politically correct label that everyone understands and which sticks to them like glue.

What policies are needed for these people and these places?

Generally speaking and whatever their spatial position in the city, these symbolical 'fringe' areas are not very highly thought of, a consequence of very stereotyped diagnoses.[15] These diagnoses are frequently partial (a census of negative features: unemployment, poverty, drop-out rates, criminality and so on) and thus generally overlook the real potential.

These 'partial' diagnoses can often be linked to top-down policies, programmes and projects. Due to the fact that these top-down programmes are often implemented to deal with city evils using a corrective and curative approach, such partial diagnoses do not really come as a surprise. In fact, the problem of these neighbourhoods and their inhabitants is that they are perceived to be a handicap, an urban and social pathos, a lack of something, which has to be balanced by bringing in missing positive elements in order to get them back into the mainstream of city life. The aim of such programmes is to make these areas 'like the others' or to recreate conditions which in the past made them residential neighbourhoods of choice. Thus, terms describing these programmes often use the prefix 're-' (such as *re*habilitation, *re*generation, *re*covery, *re*newal, *re*vitalization), a prefix which indicates a return to the origins, to a former *re*markable state – the quality of which is often actually a myth. For example, this is the case with the alleged social and cultural diversity of cities in the past, the mixed use and user friendliness of old towns or the discrete charm of the old city, which overlooks the violence reigning between social classes.

These diagnoses seldom highlight the potential of these territories and their layout for bringing forth a new urbanity. This is not because of some conspiracy of silence but, because usually these resources are usually incongruous with the values, standards and reference frames of overly top-down political programmes. An example among many others: the cultural diversity of immigrants is not viewed as a resource in societies that are aligned along a single dominant cultural standard. However, from time immemorial, city development has been built precisely on the expression, if not the recognition, of this cultural diversity and potential. In fact diagnoses that are more closely aligned with this essential recognition are often those elaborated within the framework of locally spawned projects – bottom-up approaches – because such diagnoses are very often an integral part of the development strategy being implemented.

Thus the challenge for France (and indeed for Europe) is not to substitute some mythical past for the reality of today, but to exploit existing potential by reinforcing synergies between different parts of the city, places and people to build the desirable but difficult to achieve 'being and living together'.[16] Obviously, we have to think about what urban development today could be, not by returning to some mythical past, but by an anthropological discovery of that part of the city that is unknown or ignored. At the very least we must instil an anthropological dimension into all the various disciplines (economics, architecture, town planning, sociology, political science) which have to explain what urban reality is or could be.

As destinations for immigration flows coming from all over the place, French and European cities are increasingly tending to become areas where communities are juxtaposed. While it is not possible in Europe, except perhaps in England, to identify ghettos in the American sense of the word, it is clear that borders are appearing between social groups, marginalizing people and among them immigrants. Mapping these borders is, however, not easy and, in any case, cannot be reduced to that of districts where these foreigners are over-represented. These borders overlap others – particularly that corresponding to gender, a border less recognizable than the preceding one, although its position on the urban map is growing clearer with the increase in single-parent households with a woman at the head.[17]

With regard to these questions of 'new urban peripheries' another explanation needs to be put forward in order to explain the need for the emergence of new urban policies and governance. The urban fragmentation phenomenon experienced by European cities is appearing in parallel with the shift from an extensive urbanization period to a period of recombining already urbanized territories. We have moved from 'making the city' (at the time of the urbanization boom) to 'making the best of the city'.[18] 'Making the city' was characterized by a 'productivist' intervention on 'virgin' sites (massive urbanization of inner urban belts), using urban planning projects which almost completely ignored the pre-existing characteristics and complexity of the areas concerned. On the other hand, 'making the best of the city' is characterized by a reconquest of former urbanized space (rehabilitation, requalification, urban renewal, regeneration). This process has to come to terms with areas and the people and institutions already present there. At the same time, this urban reconquest has to take into account the components of urban territories, their cultural and social capital, their 'atmosphere' in a Marshallian sense[19] and to allow for simultaneous, sometimes complementary but also sometimes antagonistic acts of a range of participants. Urban governance is the arrangements of participants and stakeholders, some of whom are completely new, in a sort of 'conflicting coproduction' process[20] regulated in new ways by both the public and private sectors.

New urban policies and governance approaches need changes in the political and administrative organizations of the central government and local authorities as well as in the other public and private partners involved in the process. These integrated urban policies are a way of introducing and managing these changes and sometimes of implementing the almost impossible reforms of the bureaucratic systems which have proliferated to regulate the multiple issues within contemporary urban societies.

These necessary political and administrative reforms are linked to three kinds of changes – territorial coordination, subsidiarity and jointed-up governance:[21]

- The first change concerns a shift from a traditional spatial fragmentation of cities (the political balkanization of urban space) to territorial cooperation between local authorities (inter-parish cooperation). This is the oldest from of cooperation. It began at the end of the 19th century, and is implemented on a sectoral basis (water supply, electricity, sanitation, public local transport, and so on). This cooperation concerns political bodies in particular and involves power sharing and sometimes a transfer and an abandonment of power from local authorities to a super-parish level. It is not an easy process and this cooperation is not without conflicts of interest, especially among local elected representatives. It also involves cooperation between a range of public- and private-sector agents acting within these areas (public–private partnerships).
- The second change started in the 1960s with the shift from a hierarchical organization (top-down approach) to vertical cooperation emphasizing decentralization and subsidiarity (contractual and multilevel approaches). Like the territorial cooperation mentioned above, this type of cooperation

is implemented on a sectoral basis and its aim is to reallocate political power amongst the various levels of authority (between central government and local authorities: subsidiarity). It is not an easy process to implement and the cooperation required for power redistribution is a source of major conflicts among elected representatives and administrators.

- Things are very different with respect to the third type of cooperation. The change here is linked to a shift from hermetically partitioned policies to transversal cooperation (partnership, inter-ministerial and interdepartmental cooperation, networks of public policies). In most countries it was launched in the 1970s when it became necessary to manage more global urban approaches (e.g. the revitalization of city centres) and to find ways for regulating new forms of urban and social pathos (*les nouveaux pauvres*, increased rates of interethnic conflict, cultural crises, crises in representative systems). In each country this cooperation is considered to be a critical key change. In fact, there is a big difference between this sort of cooperation and the two others. Unlike the others, this horizontal cooperation is expected and wanted by the powers that be. Nevertheless, due to the fact that it is an attempt to coordinate and to hybridize sectoral based policies, this cooperation stimulates resistance from people working in these different sectors. Horizontal cooperation does not lead to conflicts between elected representatives but it is a confrontation between ways of thinking and doing, between professional cultures and organizations, sometimes between routines and lobbies. It does not merely require an abandonment of power; it needs root-and-branch changes in professional behaviour and in organizations. That takes time, sometimes a generation along a sort of path dependency and it requires anticipation of changes on the part of training systems.

These shifts from old urban policies to new ones, as well as from government to governance are not glitch-free. It is not just a matter of substituting new ways for old. It is partly the result of a recombination of new management styles (like public–private partnership) with the old, administrative one. This is called for by the manifest necessity of allowing for the full complexity of urban reality, hitherto ignored, and which manifests itself in all sorts of malfunctioning of modern urban society. In fact, over and above being a possible solution to new urban challenges, integrated urban policies and governance are a way of regulating the actions of multiple participants within an area in the face of problems that are beyond traditional solutions. These approaches lay stress on the problems to be solved (most of them new) whilst simultaneously constituting a way of responding to these problems rather than being a ready made solution. In technical terms we are really talking about the issue of reducing transaction costs among participants, while realizing that this cost reduction cannot be imposed, even by official authorities who have the legal armoury and the legitimate powers of coercion to do so.[22] This transformation cannot be decreed from the upper echelons even though the role of official authorities in this transformation is an important one.

Euphemisms 3 – physical solutions are not enough

Minorities and communities hold centre stage in these new French urban policies. The areas targeted by these urban policies are very largely inhabited by 'non-EU' immigrants or people of immigrant extraction. One could even go so far as to say that one of the reasons behind launching and periodically reactivating these sorts of policies is their presence. The *évènements* of autumn 2005 in French cities have again brought these issues back to centre stage on the political agenda whilst, only recently – just before these upheavals – we were wondering if such policies were still required. So much so, in fact, that some of the financing for these polices had been cancelled – the portion concerning its social dimension. The so-called French *politique de la ville* has not only eliminated this aspect but has transferred effort purely to the physical, bricks-and-mortar aspect of these areas: emphasis over the last three years has been laid purely on demolishing them, as though their architectural and physical planning dimension was pathogenic indeed criminogenic. As if demolishing buildings and moving people elsewhere could solve social problems. A technocratic euphemism!

The very name *politique de la ville* has also left merely implicit the need to coordinate and reform sectoral public policies, which have been blamed for many of the problems faced by the people and areas in question. Are we looking at the failure of a policy or the failure of the traditional bodies and institutions responsible for promoting being and living together, those who must imperatively lay down laws (political instances), promulgate them (educational system), apply them (judicial system) and ensure that they are complied with (police). The lack of political courage and professional, cultural, and often bureaucratic, backsliding within these institutions have, in practice, severely weakened a policy that was not political enough, not manipulative enough behind its mask of euphemisms.

Conclusions

The fragmentation in French as well as in European cities and their fringe areas is not merely a research topic for social scientists and a challenge for those who draw up public policies or who elaborate new approaches to urban governance. It is also an opportunity to better understand the nature of the changes that are taking place concerning the whole community, that is to say places, people and institutions. Because of the diversity of urban situations, cities offer a generous and varied laboratory within which to compare the changes which affect the organization of urban areas as well as the government system they have adopted in the past.

The inversion of a longstanding urbanization movement (deceleration of population growth, spreading out of cities to their remotest hinterlands) has apparently opened up a new age for urban development, one that is happening within borders which are no longer clear-cut, borders that have in fact been turned inside out.

In parallel, the decline of nation states and the shift of power to large institutions and firms have put cities fairly and squarely in the front line when it comes to regulating both the old and new contradictions of economies and societies. It is for this reason that there is a need for new urban governance and new skills. Cities are responsible, in particular, for the living and being together of groups who are not necessarily for evermore diverse but who believe themselves to be so. We see the exaggeration of group identity, growing individualism, the constant exacerbation of the 'me' phenomenon, the creation of 'personal languages', which is a contradiction since language is, after all, first and foremost, a medium for exchange. And all this has to be organized over areas whose contours are becoming fuzzier and fuzzier. 'The limits of my language mean the limits of my world.'[23]

These two transformations, i.e. the splitting asunder of cities into city-archipelagos together with the sudden appearance of cities as new governance systems, challenges what was and is still the foundation of French and European societies, namely a being and a living together, a common good built on the basis of democratic principles for which cities were to some extent the cradle. What rewriting of these democratic principles will emerge from this endless social and spatial fragmentation and this networking governance policy? Perhaps the answer lies on the fringes and borders of cities, and within these new peripheral territories running along the new frontiers that criss-cross today's cities and where migrants dwell. We need to dare to move beyond Euphemisms

Notes

1. Translation from French to English: James Faulkner Brougham.
2. Hobbes 1982.
3. As Heisenberg put it: physics is not about reality, it is about what we can say about reality (note from translator).
4. Arendt 1958.
5. And, following much debate on the risks of 'communitization', those of gender. Unlike certain other European languages, French does not have a neutral gender: both written and spoken French constantly use masculine and feminine nouns. Notwithstanding this, reference is made to the rights of *man* and of the citizen, a formula that has not been feminized, since in this case, the word 'man' refers

to human beings whatever their sex may be. In a way the word 'man' is a sort of euphemism that designates both men and women.

6. Elections to the upper house of Parliament, the Sénat, are indirect. The electors (called 'grand électeurs') are local elected representatives.

7. This may seem paradoxical, but it is reasonably rational even though it is not eminently practicable in fact. We are talking about the passage from gemeinschaft (community) to gesellschaft (society). Durkheim 1991; Simmel 1999; Tonnies 1946.

8. An exception to this is French Indochina, but for other reasons.

9. Indovina 1987.

10. Vranken 2004; Jacquier 2004.

11. Veltz 1996.

12. Viveret 1993.

13. *Verlan* (l'envers) may be rendered in English by *versin* (*inverse* inverted).

14. Beurs is a reformulation in verlan that began with the word Arabe, which became *Rebeu*, and subsequently Beurs.

15. The categories used to capture the social reality of these areas are not particularly useful; this is especially the case when socio-economic classifications are used because many of the inhabitants of these areas fall through the interstices of the measuring device since they are excluded from economic activity.
Morris, Carstairs 1991; Cheshire, Carbonaro, Hay 1986; Flynn 1986.

16. Arendt 1958.

17. Korpi 2000.

18. Certeau 1980.

19. Marshall 1920.

20. See Perroux 1991 and his 'struggle-cooperation'.

21. Jacquier 2004.

22. Weber 1959.

23. Wittgenstein 1951.

10
Berlin: Urban, Social and Ethnic Integration – an Urban Policy Challenge

Ingeborg Beer, Alev Deniz and Hanns-Uve Schwedler

Berlin's present urban policy is faced with the challenge of shaping social cohesion in urban society under difficult conditions caused by transformation from an industrial to a knowledge society, by socio-spatial and ethno-spatial polarization and limited financial scope. Since the unification of the city, Berlin has been confronted with the decline of 220,000 industrial jobs. The industrial and economic deterioration in particular affected Berlin's non-German inhabitants, which comprise 13.4 per cent of the total population. While the overall unemployment rate is about 18.5 per cent, currently more than 44 per cent of non-German inhabitants are jobless. Related to this economic decline and social marginalization process was the spatial decline of several neighbourhoods where affected persons are concentrated. In 1999, the Berlin *Senat* started a programme for disadvantaged neighbourhoods, that is urban areas with high unemployment rates and high proportion of welfare benefit recipients, with problematic physical and social infrastructure and, in most cases, a high to very high proportion of non-German residents. This programme entitled 'Urban Districts with special development needs – the Socially Integrative City' (*die soziale Stadt*, see Chapter 11), which was launched jointly by the Federal Government and *Länder* in 1999, is not only operated in Berlin, but also in other *Länder* and cities, as the most important instrument in order to mitigate spatial and social decline, to counter ethnic and social marginalization and segregation. In Berlin it is accompanied by the city's integration plan dated 2005, with its central theme of 'promoting diversity and strengthening cohesion'.

Berlin's urban interface: ethnic, socio-economic and spatial factors

Immigration to Berlin – an overview

Outlining the history of immigration to Berlin up to German unification means it is necessary to distinguish between migration to the western and to the eastern parts of the city:

- immigration to West Berlin started in the 1960s with the recruitment of so-called 'guest workers' (*Gastarbeiter*) who mainly came from Turkey and Yugoslavia. Up to the point when recruitment was halted in 1974, the proportion of foreigners rose from 1 per cent in 1960 to 9 per cent. During the 1980s the western part of the city became a preferred location for asylum seekers and refugees from all over the world.
- East Berlin also hosted refugees, but only in small numbers. The majority of the migrants were contract workers from socialist states such as Vietnam, Angola, Mozambique, Cuba and Poland. Many of them left the country after reunification.

Though migration took place to West as well as to East Berlin, the effects are hardly comparable: While non-Germans contributed some 15 per cent to the overall population of the western parts in 1989 the corresponding figure for East Berlin was only 1.6 per cent.[1]

After reunification, immigration naturally affected both parts of the city. During the 1990s migrants from eastern Europe predominated. Among them were labour migrants as well as refugees, but also a considerable number of 'resettlers' (*Aussiedler*) who are 'ethnic Germans' and whose ancestors had in some cases been living in the countries of the former Soviet Union for centuries. Although they have a different cultural background, most of these migrants were naturalized immediately, while many of the guest workers of the 1960s and early 70s had acquired only resident status. Approximately two-thirds of the 126,000 persons to whom German citizenship was granted between 1991 and 2004 were either 'ethnic Germans' or others who have the right to naturalization (*'Anspruchs-Einbürgerungen'*).

All these different migration phases and patterns contributed to Berlin's demographic situation of today. While the proportion of non-Germans was 9.9 per cent of the total population of the united city in 1991, in 2004 13.4 per cent of the 3.39 million inhabitants were of non-German origin. In addition there are about 100,000 citizens who are naturalized, but nevertheless have a non-German, a 'migrant' background.[2] These latter are not included in Figure 10.1 which gives an overview of the composition of the non-German population.

The Turkish community – and to a certain degree Arabic speaking minorities – is the only community that affects the urban structure to visible

Figure 10.1: Composition of Berlin's non-German population in 2005

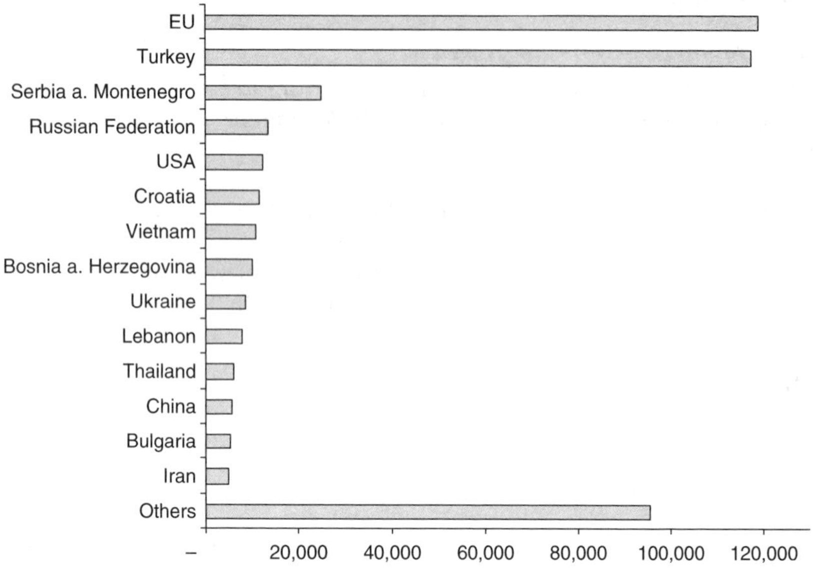

Source: Statistisches Landesamt Berlin, 2006

extent. Not only do Turks form the largest single foreign community in Berlin, they also have the longest tradition of immigration to the city. Their early residential patterns still affect spatial distribution patterns, not only of their own community but of other non-Germans too.

Residential patterns and segregation

In the early 1960s immigrants were concentrated in old working class districts which had been scheduled for urban renewal and where many former German inhabitants had moved to other residential areas. Many of these dwellings were standing empty, and urban decision makers assumed that labour migrants would return to their home countries after a couple of years – an illusion that was not only common for German politicians and planners, but also for other European decision makers. This view affected German political and public discussion on migration and integration until the end of the 1990s.[3] Thus immigrants were limited to settling only in certain areas, such as in the urban districts of Kreuzberg and Wedding – either by political measures, or due to the fact that landlords let apartments to foreigners mainly in these areas.[4] The present segregation patterns which are summarized in Map 10.1 on urban district level, are based on these early formal and informal 'policies'. The concentration of non-Germans developed during the 1960s has remained stable until now. This is not only the result of residential patterns and needs of new immigrants, who look for familiarity, security and ethnic networks, and of immigrants of the second generation – with limited access to participation and economic and social benefits of the society (see next section)[5] – but also a result of the change in urban renewal policy, which stopped demolishing buildings and began to renew and maintain existing old housing stock without relocating sitting inhabitants, who were in certain neighbourhoods Turks or other non-German nationalities, due to the residential policy of the 1960s.

This concentration and segregation process was aggravated and expanded in the 1990s. Whereas prior to German reunification it was difficult for non-Germans to rent an apartment in social (subsidized) housing estates, due to increasing numbers of vacant apartments and the fall in price levels on the housing market[6] after 1989, these residents had an opportunity to move into these areas. As a consequence additional 'foreign' neighbourhoods came into existence on the map of Berlin. In addition, 'ethnic Germans' who had 'returned' from the former Soviet Union were settled in specific areas such as Marzahn-Nord. As a result, several 'neighbourhoods' (census districts to be taken as statistical spatial/physical units of size) have a non-German population of 35–55 per cent – a fact that is not reflected in Map 10.1, which only shows the distribution at urban district level. Many of these census areas are defined by the Socially Integrative City programme as 'urban districts with special development needs' – not only because of the high proportion of non-Germans, but mainly due to socio-economic conditions (Map 10.1).

Socio-economic situation

Originally immigrants were employed in manufacturing industries, in the building and construction sector. Although there is a tendency amongst those who stayed in Germany for some time to shift into the service sector or to become self-employed,[7] the proportion employed in manufacturing industries is still considerably higher than that of Germans. Approximately one in four foreigners holds a job in a factory.[8] Thus non-Germans were over-proportionally affected by the economic decline which Berlin has been facing since the early 1990s. The unemployment rate amongst non-Germans amounted to 44.2 per cent at the beginning of 2006. Nearly every second foreigner is without a job and dependent on welfare payments. As a consequence, the income level of non-Germans is considerably lower than that of Germans. While 72 per cent of migrants have an income of below 1100 € per month, the same applies only for 49 per cent of the German population. On the other hand, 28 per cent of Germans earn more than 1500 € per month, whereas only 14 per cent of foreigners do so.

Table 10.1 provides an overview of uneven socio-spatial distribution in Berlin. A more close and detailed breakdown would enable these socio-spatial disparities to be seen even more distinctly. In actual fact, the social data

Map 10.1: Non-German population and urban neighbourhood management

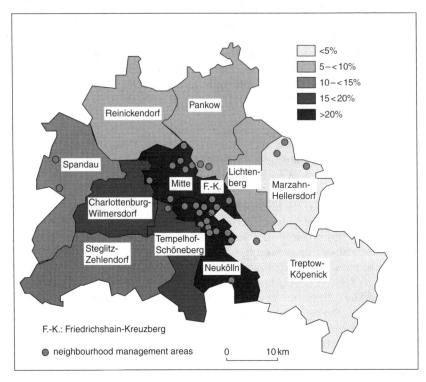

Source: Statistisches Landesamt Berlin (http://www.statistik-berlin.de); Senate Department of Urban Development, Berlin (http://www.stadtentwicklung.berlin.de/wohnen/quartiersmanagement/index.shtml); (adapted by the authors)

which are here outlined are, in the urban neighbourhood management areas indicated in Map 10.1, significantly higher/lower than the average values for the urban districts which are given in Table 10.1.

In connection with unemployment and low (often social benefit) income levels, those affected have less opportunities in education and to participate in other societal spheres. Thus for example the OECD studies have repeatedly stressed that in Germany – to an extent not present in scarcely any other (developed) country – educational attainments are dependent on social status.[9] In fact, immigrants and other students of low social status have worse school examination results and often leave school without any examination or qualifications at all. This severely influences their future chances for societal participation as well as in the labour market.

As these 'problematic groups' are concentrated in certain areas, due to the reasons outlined above, socio-spatial decline in these neighbourhoods

Table 10.1: Structural data of Berlin urban districts (2004)

	Total population	Non-Germans (% of total)	Non-German pupils (% of total pupils)	Average monthly income per household (€)	Welfare recipients (% of total population)
Mitte	320,800	27.2	39.2	1275	13.2
Friedrichshain-Kreuzberg	258,500	22.6	32.4	1200	13
Pankow	350,500	6.0	4.3	1400	5.2
Charlottenburg-Wilmerdorf	314,700	16.9	19.2	1625	5.9
Spandau	225,700	12.4	12.0	1500	9.7
Steglitz-Zehlendorf	288,500	9.4	10.5	1800	4
Tempelhof-Schöneberg	334,400	15.1	19.4	1500	6.9
Neukölln	305,700	21.8	30.4	1325	14.3
Treptow-Köpenick	234,700	3.4	3.1	1600	4.3
Marzahn-Hellersdorf	251,400	3.6	2.8	1550	7.3
Lichtenberg	257,500	8.1	8.7	1475	6
Reinickendorf	245,500	9.0	11.0	1700	7.6

Source: Statistisches Landesamt Berlin

was as it were programmed by economic development in Berlin since the early 1990s.

Social urban development and urban neighbourhood management in Berlin

In view of this socio-spatial downwards spiral in several neighbourhoods in Berlin, in 1999 the Berlin city government (*Senat*) initiated initially in a pilot phase the socially integrative city programme. The objectives were to stabilize and to promote development in urban areas or districts with particular urban development needs. This category of particular development need was identified in a district or area where a number of the urban development factors listed below were to be found concurrently:

- urban design, construction and ecological deficits,
- infrastructure deficits,
- economic stagnation at a low level,
- rapid decline in economic activity,
- uneven development in the resident population,
- high levels of unemployment,
- high level of dependence on social welfare payments,
- high proportion of non-Germans, especially in the case of children and young people,
- high levels of mobility (moving away, in particular in the case of families, those in (regular) employment and higher income households),
- increasing social and cultural segregation and exclusion,
- increasing criminality in public places.

Initially in Berlin 15 urban neighbourhood areas[10] were identified, where local neighbourhood activities were undertaken by neighbourhood management (teams – *Quartiersmanager*). Berlin City Government has since this date subjected the integrative neighbourhood management process to an evaluation. The decision was taken to further elaborate the neighbourhood management process in accordance with the evaluation process recommendations and to continue the process up to the end of 2006. At the present time the neighbourhood management system is undergoing reorientation, so that the process can be adjusted to the socio-spatial developments in the city and also to incorporate the lessons learnt during the first phase.

Two interdepartmental approaches and instruments are making a special contribution in this respect: the Federal programme entitled 'Urban districts with special development needs – the Socially Integrative City' (*die soziale Stadt*), and Berlin's 2005 integration plan. In combination, these programmes are designed to contribute to reducing socio-spatial disparities and creating equal opportunities for people from different cultural, social and religious backgrounds.

Figure 10.2: Neighbourhood management area 'Kottbusser Tor'

Differentiated approaches towards providing support: intervention, prevention, consolidation

Thirty-three areas of varying size have been identified in Berlin today as being in particular need of (urban) development and action at present. These areas exhibit a concentration and combination of economic, social and cultural problems. Areas containing many old buildings in the western inner city districts and large housing estates in the north-east have been particularly affected by downward spirals. As these areas require a differentiated approach, Berlin has opted for a strategic 'triad', namely 'intervention' in especially disadvantaged areas, 'prevention' in districts with 'strong partners' (housing companies or associations, churches, ethnic associations, charitable organizations), and 'consolidation' in places where stability has already been achieved. The road to urban integration and self-supporting structures can thus vary in length.

Key strategic instrument: neighbourhood management

The aim of urban neighbourhood management is to create sustainable and effective district structures for the built environment and for residents by means of intermediate agencies. Residents should be empowered to look after their own interests. Actors and integrative bodies, such as schools or enterprises, are assisted in 'working together' to make progress with urban district development. To this end, integrated action plans are compiled, numerous projects developed and committees established to promote participation in designing the process and in decision making. All of these elements are based on the potential of 'the district and its people', but must also create access to 'interdistrict' systems: in secondary schools, all the possible economic and administrative agencies, and in political bodies.

Need-based action: a wide range of neighbourhood projects

Numerous projects are being developed – primarily by the agencies rather than the residents – in the key action areas of 'school and education', 'the economy and employment', and 'the urban neighbourhood and coexistence'. Complicated application procedures and bureaucratic obstacles make it difficult for residents actively to implement their own ideas. Many 'shortcomings' have become evident, some of which can be attributed to political omissions (language acquisition among school students, structural defects in school buildings) or seen as tasks for economic actors (training of apprentices). Urban, social and ethnic integration requires 'top-down support' at the socio-spatial level from other policy departments and a local perspective that takes greater account of ethnic diversity. Three key action areas clearly illustrate this point:

Increasing the integrative functions of schools, focusing on education and further education

While many schools become focal points of district life with the assistance of urban neighbourhood management, they struggle to fulfil their true key function of achieving integration into the labour market and society. Great significance is attached to improving language skills and providing assistance with homework, and yet sustainable effects also depend on small class sizes, improved access to the secondary school system and innovative responses in ethnically segregated schools. These are all tasks for education policy.

Supporting the local economy and creating links to the economy and employment

The hands of urban neighbourhood management are also largely tied as regards boosting the local and social economy. Numerous projects are dedicated to improving 'access' to the labour market. Residents are encouraged to take school leaving examinations as mature students, social competences are promoted, and apprenticeships and work experience placements are found. The local economy receives 'stimuli' from business incubation centres and networks of enterprises. However, Berlin's dwindling potential for economic integration means that there is no real answer to the question of how urban district residents can successfully achieve equal participation in economic development in the long term. Furthermore, skills remain unutilized due to legal restrictions (refugees), and there is still no consistent orientation towards qualified professions within the knowledge society.

Promoting tolerant coexistence and enhancing lively neighbourhoods

A wide range of grassroots activities are being organized in urban neighbourhoods to promote cross cultural coexistence and acceptance of different social and ethnic groups. These include interfaith dialogues, projects in public spaces (tree-planting programmes, gardens), festivals and training for facilitators. However, focusing solely on the disadvantaged 'immigrant' target group will not suffice – cross sectional strategies are still largely in their infancy.

Local responsibility: new participatory structures

Immigrant participation is a central issue for newly-established decision making bodies such as the Neighbourhood Councils (*Quartiersrat*). These fora enable local institutions, associations and residents to participate in decisions on allocation of grants and selection of projects (see Figure 10.3). Neighbourhood Council participants are primarily residents with high levels of professional and cultural integration. Thus, the challenge is to also make opportunities and possibilities for participation available to residents with more limited language skills and very low levels of social integration – both immigrants and non-immigrants. Structural exclusion from opportunities

Figure 10.3: Composition of (new) Neighbourhood Councils

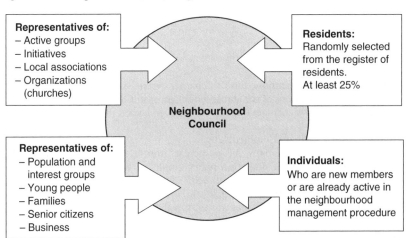

Source: Senate Department of Urban Development, Berlin (adapted by the authors)

for political participation (the right to vote) constitutes an obstacle for non-Germans, and results in the paradoxical situation that while 'public participation' is compulsorily required of immigrants, important elements of citizen status simultaneously remain denied to them.

Conclusions: integration into the socially integrative city, between vision and reality

Although improvements can be achieved and participation increased at the local neighbourhood level, three main issues will undoubtedly play a crucial role in the future. Firstly, continual adjustment of the flows from 'bottom-up' and 'top-down', and secondly, on the spot strategies that take greater account of the multitude of ethnic groups and social strata. Finally, progress will only be made in striking a better socio-spatial balance if steps are taken to promote this balance within urban districts and are also adopted in interdistrict systems. Doubts remain as to whether local and state actors involved possess the requisite capacities to solve problems caused by socio-economic processes or federal policies (asylum policy, labour market policy, drug policy) at the urban district level. The cohesion of urban society and equal opportunities for the many and varied social and ethnic groups pose a challenge to the urban districts and to the entire city of Berlin. In this respect the German capital, as may be seen in another chapter of this book (Chapter 4), is by no means standing alone. Cohesion in urban societies and equal opportunities are Europe wide challenges. On their own and without the support of European and national institutions our cities will probably not be able to cope with such challenges.

Notes

1. All statistical figures mentioned in this chapter derive – unless stated otherwise – from various publications of the Statistisches Landesamt Berlin (regional statistical office) (http://www.statistik-berlin.de). For an overview on migration to Berlin see Gesemann 2001.
2. Häussermann, Kapphan, Gerometta 2005.
3. Several influential politicians, in particular from the Christian Democratic (CDU) Party, rejected the migration policy employed by the former 'red–green' coalition – which ruled Germany until 2005 – by stating that Germany is not and will not become a country of immigration (*Einwanderungsland*). The necessity for wide-ranging integration measures was thus neglected. This attitude has changed, however, since the new 'large' coalition of Social (SPD) and Christian Democrats (CDU/CSU) came to power in Autumn 2005.
4. Häussermann, Kapphan, Gerometta 2005; see also: Müller 2001.
5. See for instance: Schwedler 1985.

6. Berlin had a net population loss of up to 30,000 annually at the end of the 1990/beginning of 2000, not only due to economic decline, but also due to a tendency of middle class families to move out to surrounding areas of Berlin. In addition, because of euphoric growth expectations in the early 1990s, many new housing estates were planned and built, thus putting additional pressure on the housing market (Schwedler 2001).
7. Müller 2001.
8. Häussermann, Kapphan, Gerometta 2005.
9. OECD 2004.
10. As early as the pilot phase (1999–2002, extended until 2004), two additional urban neighbourhood areas were included.

11
The Socially Integrative City: Results of the Interim Evaluation of a German Programme[1]

Hartmut Häussermann

When the Federal red–green coalition government took office in 1998, a new urban policy programme was adopted in the same year: 'neighbourhoods with special development needs – the socially integrative city (*Soziale Stadt*)'. The programme targets neighbourhoods with high proportions of unemployed and financially disadvantaged residents – who also frequently come from migrant backgrounds. The programme was a joint decision by the federal government and *Länder* (German states) aimed at countering 'social polarization' in cities and preventing districts from being 'left out' of the city's general development. The increasing level of segregation in cities has complex causes, which can only be combated effectively using an integrated set of measures related to labour market policy, as well as education, social, family, youth and immigrant policy, and also urban planning and housing policy. Map 11.1 gives an overview of German towns and cities participating in 2002 in the Socially Integrative City programme ('*Soziale Stadt*').

The programme was inspired by similar agendas in France and Great Britain, which were already in operation. In Germany, a fundamental controversy exists between the national and federal levels. Many federal states believe that the federal government should have no involvement whatsoever in urban development issues, and were correspondingly reticent at the beginning of the programme. However, the programme has since become established, and has even been included as a permanent statutory task in the Federal Building Code *(Baugesetzbuch)*. Paragraph §171e states: 'The Socially Integrative City's urban development measures are measures to stabilize and improve local areas disadvantaged by social inequalities, or other parts of the municipal area with special development needs. Social inequalities exist particularly in areas experiencing significant disadvantage due to the composition and economic situation of their residents.' A clear reference is made here to neighbourhood effects, although no preliminary

Map 11.1: Towns and cities participating in the programme '*Soziale Stadt*' (2002)

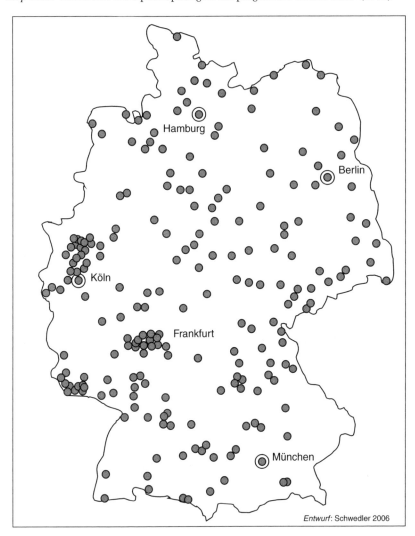

Entwurf: Schwedler 2006

Source: IFS 2004, 58.

academic work was done to provide a theoretical analysis of the problems and determine the measures. For this reason, the programme is being implemented in very different ways in the different federal states. There are also highly divergent ideas at the local level on what the programme should achieve, with some placing a special emphasis on combating poverty, and others prioritizing neighbourhood improvement.

The Socially Integrative City programme is a form of urban development regeneration, but it accounts for a relatively small share of funding when compared to classic urban renewal, protection of buildings of historical interest and urban reconstruction programmes. However, the programme's primary target is not to increase investment, but instead to change the economic and social development of neighbourhoods 'with special development needs'. The programme thus has a dual purpose:

- it formulates urban development policy goals for parts of cities in which the social repercussions of deindustrialization and the labour market crisis are particularly prevalent,
- while also seeking to develop an exemplary new form of policy, namely cooperative control which involves state and private institutional actors along with citizens and public administration.

Decentralized decision-making processes are to open up avenues for development supported at the 'grassroots' level, which interlink residents, businesses, welfare organizations, initiatives of all kinds and public authorities.

Selected evaluation results

Identifying problems and setting precise goals

The programme is a form of urban regeneration but is following the tradition of classic urban renewal. In practice, the Socially Integrative City programme continues to adhere substantially to the tradition of construction-oriented urban renewal. For this reason, descriptions of urban development problems and construction measures frequently continue to play a central role in defining neighbourhood strategy, even though the programme's philosophy requires a much more complex approach to be taken, an approach which involves and interlinks a wide range of actors and integrates their contributions. Table 11.1 summarizes various problems identified and intervention strategies found in cities.

An interim evaluation showed that many municipalities still have considerable difficulties and little experience in addressing these problems. In general, greater precision is required when identifying problems and outlining goals for the individual programme areas. This is also a prerequisite for creating a progress monitoring method. Unambiguous goals and methods for monitoring them necessitate a realistic view of the programme's possibilities and limitations, in order to avoid disappointing expectations, which inevitably result in setbacks to district policy and its political support.

Table 11.1: Various problems identified in 'Districts with Special Development Needs' and corresponding intervention strategies

Problems identified ('inequalities')	Causes	Intervention strategy/measures
'downward spiral', slums created reduced opportunities in life, social inequality	inequalities in the built environment, lack of investment poverty, unemployment, low level of education; inadequate German language skills; family problems	urban renewal, renew and extend infrastructure, promote investment labour market, education and social policy measures; strengthening the local economy
spatial concentration of disadvantaged sections of the population experiencing discrimination results in a situation that reinforces, increases and intensifies social problems; stigmatization and neglect of the neighbourhood	involuntary segregation of disadvantaged sections of the population; urban development and social situation prevent social mixing; disinvestment	strengthen community and local economy; careful urban renewal and modernization of housing; steer allocation of public housing; improve access by disadvantaged groups to housing; counteract polarization in urban development

Segregation and interneighbourhood links

Segregation in German cities was reduced after the Second World War in comparison to the pre-war period. This was due to:

- increasing real incomes and a growing demand for labour;
- the expansion of the social security system;
- construction of public housing, which resulted in tenancy-controlled housing being spread throughout cities;
- the landlord and tenant law, which combats displacement of tenants through rent increases;
- the housing benefit system, which reduces the rental burden;
- programmes for 'careful' renewal of inner city areas containing old building stock, in conjunction with Berlin urban preservation goals;
- support for acquisition of ownership by the occupying tenant.

The current increase in segregation is being caused by changes to many of these factors. The substantial reduction in funding for construction of public rental housing, and rapid decrease in existing public housing stocks due to the expiry of commitments and privatization, have resulted in negative external effects on social integration.

To combat urban polarization effectively and sustainably, action programmes for individual neighbourhoods must take much greater account than has been the case until now of developments in a city as a whole. This is because 'polarization' within a city cannot be counteracted only in areas in which it is especially visible. An 'end-of-the-pipe' strategy will ultimately be unsuccessful. Failure to take into account developments in the city as a whole creates a risk that problems will either remain unsolved or will simply be shifted to another neighbourhood. Until now, however, most local action programmes have been clearly characterized by 'tunnel vision', with their gaze fixed only on the individual neighbourhood. As the causes of segregation and 'disadvantaged' communities are also to be found in other political and economic developments, an appropriate policy is needed that integrates all of the political and administrative levels and sectors.

Integrating departments

Given that the urban district development goals outlined in the programme clearly go beyond what can be achieved through investment in the built environment, the attempt to establish inter-departmental cooperation and area-related pooling of resources is both logical and appropriate. However, at the national level attempts made at the beginning of the programme to encourage other federal departments to become actively involved have so far failed to be successful. Following the launch of initiatives, commitments to programme-related cooperation once again declined. Only the Federal Ministry of Family Affairs, Senior Citizens, Women and Youth has taken clear account of the Socially Integrative City programme in its own programmes – and evaluation has shown such participation to be very important and highly conducive to achieving the objectives. Should it prove impossible to revive and increase interdepartmental cooperation, this 'lead programme' is in danger of becoming merely a tool for narrow urban development, and will ultimately turn out to be just another conventional departmental programme, despite its specified goals.

Once the goals of the programme have been reformulated and potential contributions of other departments have been more precisely described, a new attempt should be made at federal level to foster increased interdepartmental cooperation in urban neighbourhood development. Coalitions must be formed that correspond to the goals to be prioritized. Special efforts should be made to acquire participation of education, social affairs, domestic affairs and economics/employment departments.

Increased departmental integration should not be limited to provision of additional funding by individual departments, as departmental integration involves more than pooling resources. Policies of individual departments create important framework conditions for neighbourhood development. The relevant decisions currently take too little account of their impact on city and neighbourhood development (such as in the field of labour policy).

Pooling resources

Pooling resources is a strategic approach adopted by the programme. However, this approach is considered extremely difficult to implement, even though the need for focused inter-departmental action and pooling resources has been recognized at political level. The vertical structure of specialist administrations, with the federal level at the top, followed by the *Land* and *Bezirk* (administrative region) levels of government, and then local government authorities, remains a defining characteristic and makes pooling resources difficult.

At the state level, prerequisites and conditions for assistance under the relevant specialist programmes must be better tailored to the circumstances in disadvantaged areas and to the Socially Integrative City programme. Some states (North Rhine-Westphalia, Hamburg, Berlin, Bremen, and also Hesse up to 2004) have therefore set up parallel programmes to supplement the Socially Integrative City, in which non-investment projects are eligible for aid. This remains the exception rather than the rule, however, and a great deal of uncertainty exists at municipal level as to how the pooling of resources can actually be achieved.

Area selection and integrated action plans

The practical selection of the areas reflects continuing uncertainties about linking different dimensions of problems in disadvantaged urban communities, and analytical tools which are often inadequate. Selection often tended to be made intuitively, based on knowledge and experience of local conditions. Data depicting special problems in neighbourhoods was either completely non-existent or was not compiled systematically. Though this did not result in 'wrong' areas being selected, nevertheless, more objective bases need to be established for selecting areas, identifying problems and action plans, in order to enhance the programme in the future. This is especially important in major cities, as it enables trends to be recognized that may result in emergence of neighbourhoods with special development needs. Guided intervention at an early stage could potentially be more successful and effective in these cases than in those where problems have already become substantially entrenched (a preventive or early warning function).

Minimum requirements to be met when applying to be included in the programme should be:

- analysis of the city's overall development and definition of the area's functions in this context,
- analysis of social and physical environment-related aspects (problems) of neighbourhood development,
- account of the area's likely development were it not to be included in the programme,

- description of potential and actors to be reached through the integrated action programme,
- transparent and comprehensible ideas on the future development of the district.

In many cases, there is little consistency between the reasons for selecting the areas, the stated goals and the projects implemented in practice. This is another reason for developing quality standards for the integrated action plans.

Involving external actors

The Socially Integrative City programme aims to have actors outside the administration play a major role in decision making processes and in implementing the programme at municipal and area level. The results of the interim evaluation show that this goal is already being achieved to a large extent. Good progress has been made in networking organizations in the neighbourhood, and this is one of the tangible improvements launched by the programme. Organized neighbourhood actors play an important role in decision making processes in community development in many cities. Participation by external actors can generally be seen as an important programme focus, which utilizes the resources of the organizations and institutions in the district in line with neighbourhood development goals.

However, levels of participation vary between individual groups. Housing companies and schools have clearly been successfully involved in the implementation of the programme on the whole, although this involvement is not always related to the core area of their activities. However, involving organizations from the economic sector, as well as youth, culture, social and migrant organizations, should be further advanced.

Area-level effects

As in the federal state (*Länder*) evaluation studies, it was practically impossible to make quantitative statements on the effect of the Socially Integrative City agenda in the programme areas within the framework of an interim Federal evaluation. This is due both to the early stage of implementation and the lack of valid data on development in the areas. It is thus only possible to speak in terms of trends.

No positive economic or labour market changes appear to have occurred yet in the vast majority of the programme areas; the situation has in fact often deteriorated in terms of poverty and unemployment. However, positive changes have been noted in many neighbourhoods as regards the built environment and urban development, condition and cleanliness of public spaces, and the range of social facilities and options for children and young people. Improved neighbourhood relations or increasing identification with the district have also been seen in at least some of the areas, and the programme has created a 'sense of awakening' in many areas.

The empirical studies conducted for the interim evaluation indicate the following temporary conclusions:

- the Socially Integrative City programme has usually almost no impact on the economic situation in the programme areas and on residents' opportunities in the labour market. Dominant developments outside the area, such as general economic and labour market trends, cannot be neutralized at district level;
- however, the Socially Integrative City programme can certainly have a positive impact on the built environment and urban development in the neighbourhoods. This also applies to social infrastructure (range of social facilities, options for children and young people) in the relevant urban districts;
- the Socially Integrative City programme can also have a positive effect on the overall cooperative atmosphere in the area and identification with neighbourhood development;
- the Socially Integrative City programme appears also to be able to have a positive impact on such aspects as the quality of coexistence in the area and the feeling of safety in public places. Effects of this type are being primarily observed in programme areas located in larger cities.

Future fields of activity: education, integration of immigrants, local economy

Both the interim evaluation and federal state level evaluations demonstrated that three issues have until now not been playing, or have been unable to play, the practical role in the Socially Integrative City programme that they should in fact be having in urban district development. These fields of activity are education, integration of immigrants, local economy and employment. What all three fields have in common is that potential approaches and the prospects of success of neighbourhood policy are especially dependent on external developments and on the framework set by the federal level and federal state level.

Education

Although efforts are being made in most of the programme areas to involve schools more intensively in neighbourhood development – and results show high levels of participation by schools as 'external actors' – plans so far to include schools in other aspects of neighbourhood development have been rare. However, the situation in schools is often a reason for education-oriented families to move away. This is true both for inhabitants of German origin as well as those with a 'migrant background'. Furthermore, improving the level of education of future generations in problem-plagued districts plays a key role in neutralizing negative effects in the neighbourhood. It is not solely a matter of improving conventional educational achievement, but instead of encouraging schools increasingly to assume certain surrogate family functions, in order to break the strong link that still exists between scholastic success and the parents' level of education. Educational qualifications are a lifelong ticket to better opportunities, especially for the children of immigrants. This task cannot be achieved solely by improving a specific policy (school policy in this case), as it is a complex issue that is interconnected to other areas of life. Indeed, the neighbourhood must be the field of activity in this case, and improving educational outcomes must be a top priority in the next phase of the programme.

Neighbourhood management should encourage cooperation, promote interfacing and networking. However, the necessary prerequisites must first be met by the schools. Communalization and autonomy are conditions for boosting the local significance of schools. Schools must open themselves up to the neighbourhood, and the neighbourhood must support the schools. This can only be achieved if a reliable and cooperative relationship exists between the educational authorities and local government policy: a desideratum that has – quite possibly – never yet been realized anywhere.

Integration of immigrants

The integration of immigrants is one of the most pressing problems in society and for the position of neighbourhoods within the urban structure. This also applies to eastern German cities which, despite having experienced only low levels of migration until now, will be particularly dependent on immigrants for their future development.

In many large western German cities, 40–50 per cent of residents under the age of 40 will be from a 'migrant background' within the next three decades, and yet the Federal Republic of Germany still lacks clear ideas as to how cities with large numbers of immigrants could or should be organized. All cities have seen the emergence of areas segregated along ethnic lines. Coexistence between local inhabitants who have suffered from the structural changes and immigrants, of whom a very high proportion are also unemployed or receive social transfer payments, has had problematic consequences, and is one of the fields of activity most often mentioned in neighbourhood policy. Many ideas, good intentions and even projects exist, however, they remain largely symbolic in character, given the tasks that must be addressed. Neighbourhood managers still lack the tools and resources needed to organize effective integration efforts.

The attitude towards the formation of 'immigrant districts' seems largely unclear. While this is generally considered to be highly problematic, and support exists for 'desegregation', no one knows how this should be achieved. Another unanswered question is how the social integration functions currently performed by 'ethnic colonies' could subsequently be replaced. Urban policy must make a fundamental choice of direction, namely whether to strive for cooperative relations with ethnic organizations in segregated areas or, conversely, strive to end this segregation.

Local economy and employment

The publications on the Socially Integrative City programme ascribe a great deal of importance to the goal of strengthening the local economy. However, it has been difficult to ascertain exactly what is meant by this, and how this goal is to be achieved. Districts have different concepts of this goal: reducing unemployment, promoting local businesses or establishing new enterprises, or creating local economic cycles (local exchange trading systems, cooperatives, and so on). When neighbourhood managers make reducing unemployment their goal, partly to avoid being accused of ignoring 'people's most important problems', they inevitably end up confronted with an insurmountable discrepancy between the possible courses of action and the goals of the action, that is, caught in an 'instrumental trap'.

Despite effective cooperation between local employment agencies and neighbourhood management in some areas, targeted implementation of labour policy measures in places with the highest unemployment density has proved largely unsuccessful until now. In fact, funding cuts and the federal government's new labour policy orientation have actually resulted in a decline in the number of job creation measures being implemented in disadvantaged districts and in cancellation of some social projects financed by ABM (job creation schemes).

Given that people are increasingly living and working in different places nowadays, there is also no point in focusing labour policy efforts on projects to introduce job creation measures in areas for the benefit of the residents. Area-based job creation measures for residents can be especially valuable, however, if the measures target groups of residents (particularly older unemployed persons) whose opportunities for integration into the wider labour market are almost nil, or are combined with other tools to create a set of measures aiming to achieve integration into the mainstream labour market in the medium term.

A realistic perspective has been adopted on the future significance of the 'local economy' field of activity within the Socially Integrative City programme. In many programme areas, local economic structures have become so weak (or never actually existed) that neighbourhood development does not provide any jump start for genuine economic revival in the areas. The primary focus in this situation is to ensure that the resident population has local access to consumer goods and services of all kinds. In this context, promoting local business, and especially the 'ethnic economy', plays a key role in stabilizing neighbourhoods.

In the field of local economy and labour policy, the Socially Integrative City programme is not, however, primarily focused on creating new forms of promotion for enterprises, emerging small businesses and the unemployed. Most cities already have enough institutions and agencies specialized in this field. The neighbourhoods' initial focus should thus be to draw the attention of local actors engaged in promoting the economy and labour market to the problems, but primarily to the potential, in the urban communities, their residents and their businesses. It is then useful to network the different tools and institutions. Socially Integrative City funds can also be used to improve the infrastructure needs of local enterprises in part of the areas.

Conclusion

The findings of the interim evaluation have shown that the relationship between the Socially Integrative City programme and other urban programmes requires clarification. In general, the programme should be organized much more as a 'learning programme' than has been the case until now. The federal level, federal state level and municipalities should agree to institutionalize the following tools in a permanent process of reflection and monitoring:

- more precise analysis of problems on the basis of data at the beginning of the programme;
- continuous monitoring and reporting according to a standardized format that also facilitates comparisons among cities; definition of more specific objectives, which also allows for progress control, would be an important foundation for political support for the programme in the medium term;
- nationwide evaluation by independent experts should be arranged at regular intervals in the most important urban development fields and problems, in line with existing common practice in the areas of family, economic and social policy. This would also increase public awareness of urban policy in general.

The Socially Integrative City programme is an urban policy innovation. It takes a new approach to tackling social and spatial problems of neighbourhood development which could otherwise result in growing inequalities becoming entrenched and which pose an increasing danger to social integration in cities. It is thus decidedly forward-looking. However, its innovative qualities must receive greater political support. The institutions involved must be even better prepared to implement the programme and be equipped with appropriate tools for doing so.

Note

1. This chapter summarizes selected results and aspects of an interim evaluation of the programme 'Soziale Stadt'. The author has been responsible for part of this evaluation (IFS 2004).

12
Paradigm Shift: the Experience of Berlin's Commissioner for Integration and Migration
Günter Piening and Andreas Germershausen

Due to Germany's federal structure, the legal framework for integration policy is defined by the federal government, whereas its implementation is within the responsibility of individual federal states. This chapter examines how a state government, i.e. the *Senat* of Berlin, can shape integration policy for the metropolis of Berlin.

New perspectives at national level

Among other things, the origin of current integration problems can be seen in the irresolute attitude towards migration and integration policies displayed for decades by the federal government. Even though since the end of the Second World War, immigrants were taken in and also actively recruited, the paradigm – according to which Germany is not an immigration country – was adhered to for a long time. Hence, no agreement and common political view was sought about what integration and integration policy should or could be. Particularly the educational system failed to react adequately as was revealed by the first PISA study.[1]

This policy changed with the reform of the German citizenship law in 1998, followed by the entry into force of the Immigration Act on 1 January 2005. With this legislation, Germany's 'red–green'[2] coalition government installed a new regulatory framework for migration and integration, and moved away from the paradigm of a non-immigration society. The drafting of an anti-discrimination law also played some part in this process. Even though legislation on this issue has not yet been adopted, the federal government supported adoption of the respective EU directives in 2000.

Immigration history: composition of the immigrant population in Germany

To understand the history of migration, it has to be kept in mind that, until 1989, migration to Germany, in the main, meant migration to West

Germany (FRG). Even though East Germany (GDR) had contract workers as well, they originated from other socialist countries, came for a limited period of time and in small numbers only. Besides this, the GDR government was very strict about their return at the end of the contract period. Consequently no major immigrant community could develop.

Since the Second World War, the FRG has always been an immigration country. In addition to immigration of ethnic Germans after their displacement from eastern Europe and other regions of the former Soviet Union, and the large numbers of refugees from the GDR before the Berlin Wall was built in 1961, the federal government started to recruit guest workers for the booming economy in the mid-1950s. This recruitment was halted at the time of the oil crisis in 1973. However, immigration continued in the form of reuniting families split up under the previous system. In addition, recruitment of contract workers was continued – though in smaller numbers than under the 'guest worker' scheme.

Since the late 1970s, immigration of asylum seekers increased considerably. Over the years, respective federal governments limited the right to asylum in several steps. But many refugees who were not recognized as having a right to asylum were able to stay in the FRG as de facto refugees.

Global changes and the fall of the Berlin Wall in 1989 brought an increase in the number of immigrants. In the 1990s, these were mainly asylum seekers, ethnic Germans and civil war refugees from former Yugoslavia.

Immigrant population in Berlin

Berlin as a city is characterized by immigration. Various immigration phases and groups have added up to a complex and fragmented immigrant population. The total number of migrants is estimated to be 600,000 persons, among them approximately 450,000 foreigners, i.e. those with a non-German passport. However, the number of immigrants has stagnated since the mid-1990s. Given a total population of some 3.3 million, one in eight Berlin inhabitants (13.5 per cent) is not of German nationality. Also, those who came into the country in the 1960s and 70s under the 'guest worker' scheme are frequently categorized as immigrants. Many of them did not acquire German citizenship – in part due to an old-fashioned citizenship law. The vast majority of these immigrants have, however, secure legal residence status.

A distinguishing feature of the demographic structure of Berlin is the uneven spatial distribution of immigrants in the city: whereas in central districts such as Mitte (28 per cent), Kreuzberg-Friedrichshain (23.2 per cent) and Neukoelln (21.9 per cent), one in four citizens is of non-German nationality, the proportion is markedly below 5 per cent in the outskirts such as Marzahn (4.2 per cent) and Treptow-Köpenick (3.7 per cent). The largest immigrant communities originate from Turkey and central and eastern

Europe. In 2004, most people of non-German nationality came from Turkey (118,732), while migrants from the former Yugoslavia represented the second largest group (51,519) followed by citizens from Poland (35,842).[3]

Integration problems

A large proportion of the immigrants came to Berlin without any long-term perspective. This is particularly true for the generation of 'guest workers' who were employed in jobs requiring only low qualifications. Not only did German institutions and firms have short-term recruitment in mind, most guest workers, too, planned to stay for the duration of their contracts and then intended to return to their home countries. Asylum seekers were issued temporary residence permits but only for the term of their asylum application. Civil war refugees from the succession states of the former Yugoslav Republic were invariably granted temporary protection status only.

Many members of the latter two groups lived in Berlin for many years without secure legal residence status. As a rule, this meant limited access to professional training and employment, and dependency on public fund transfer payments.

This exclusion from qualification measures and employment, as well as employment in low-skilled jobs, are considered to be the main reasons for integration deficits in some of the immigrant population. Since many immigrants had jobs in the manufacturing industry, they were hit in disproportionately high numbers by the deindustrialization of Berlin which set in after the political events of 1989. As tax and other subsidy benefits – granted by the national government when the city was still divided – were cut back, many companies closed down production lines or even whole factories in Berlin. Consequently, the number of low-skilled jobs, for which the labour migrants had once been recruited, was reduced considerably. A growing number of immigrants, especially those with low qualifications, found themselves cut off from work, and the labour market lost its function as the main motor of integration. The remaining integration instruments and structures proved to be unable to counterbalance the effects of this rapid economic change. The resulting problems and conflicts accumulated primarily in the central districts.

The unemployment rate of foreigners[4] in Berlin is 46.1 per cent (as of June 2005) and is thus more than double that of the total population (20.8 per cent). The result is increasing impoverishment of parts of the immigrant population. In addition, there is a worrying gap between the educational qualifications of children with a migration background and other children of the same age; hence it is to be feared that the next generation, too, will have less opportunities in the future.

Integration policy in Berlin

The Office of the Commissioner for Integration and Migration, a public body and part of the Berlin *Senat* administrative authorities, was set up in 1981 (then entitled Commissioner for Foreigners' Affairs) in reaction to social tensions that occurred in central (West Berlin) districts at the time. At about the same time, too, politicians began to realize that part of the immigrant population would not return to their home countries but would stay permanently in Berlin.

Figure 12.1: Living together in Berlin

Right from the beginning, it was one of the most important tasks of the Commissioner to advise the *Senat* in matters of integration policy, at that time defined as policy with respect to foreigners. The Commissioner also acted as ombudsperson for immigrants, offered them legal advice, informed the Berlin public about immigration issues and reasons for immigration and represented the interests of immigrants vis-à-vis the *Senat*. Also, as early as the 1980s, the Commissioner supported some immigrant self-help organizations. In the beginning, the activities of such organizations were geared only to the interests of their own group of origin. Over the past 20 years, however, some successful immigrant organizations have developed into representatives of the whole immigrant population and are accepted by the *Senat* of Berlin as partners in matters of integration.

Reorientation of integration policy in Berlin

In contrast to the situation before 1998, German politicians nowadays widely accept the objective of integrating new immigrants into society. It is implicitly recognized that immigrants will stay permanently in Germany and will make up a growing part of the German population in the long term.

Hence, there is broad consensus among democratic parties in being critical of the former policy of not defining integration targets, as was pursued since recruitment of the first 'guest workers'. Generally speaking, this policy is perceived today as muddling through, according to the needs of the labour market at the time. However, there is no agreement so far between the democratic parties, concerning to what extent, to what segments of the labour market, and to what levels of qualification new immigration should be restricted.

In the interests of rapid integration, the current Immigration Act offers ways and means to further individual integration of new immigrants as well as – at least to a certain extent – of immigrants who have been living in Germany for some time. This includes German language courses as well as a general introduction to German law, history and culture. The agency responsible for the implementation of the Act[5] is working at the present time on a comprehensive integration programme. At the same time, the expectations of, and demands on, immigrants are also increasing: they need to prove their readiness to integrate – for which their German language capacity is seen as the main indicator. Immigrants are to encourage their children to obtain qualifications in occupational fields where there is labour shortage. On the other hand, keeping alive their own traditions and mother tongue is ranked lower in priority.

The legislation mentioned above – i.e. citizenship law and Immigration Act – provides the cornerstones of this new orientation. On this basis, social and political actors are addressing immigrants with new expectations concerning integration, and the role of the players in integration policy is changing accordingly.

The integration concept of the *Senat* of Berlin

This new orientation in integration policy requires redefinition of the role of the Commissioner for Integration and Migration. Today, the task can no longer be to represent the interests of immigrants vis-à-vis the city government and administration. Participation is the key term. This means that immigrants need to articulate their own interests. They have to be involved in a democratic process which aims to reach a common understanding of integration objectives, recognized by all citizens as the foundation for living together in a city characterized by immigration and by the diversity of its population. In this context, the Commissioner sees his role more as a coordinator and manager or facilitator of negotiation processes in which immigrants participate through their own organizations and bodies, together with political and administrative representatives.

The new role of the Commissioner for Integration is reflected by Berlin's integration concept adopted by the *Senat* in August 2005. Its key function is to provide a framework for numerous individual measures by government departments, for instance in schools, in vocational qualification and the employment sector. This will be monitored in order to verify to what extent set targets have been implemented. Thus integration policy is acknowledged as a task of high priority to be included in all policy fields and *Senat* departments.

In its concept, the *Senat* of Berlin defines integration as follows:

> In general terms, integration is the opposite of segregation or exclusion. Applied to concrete life situations integration means that individuals or entire groups have equal opportunities to participate in social life and articulate their interests, and are protected from individual or collective exclusion. Basically, integration policy is about creating equal opportunities.
>
> But integration is not to be misunderstood as complete adaptation or assimilation to existing conditions. Quite the contrary, integration is a constituent element of urban life and thus a process involving both the immigrants and the receiving society. Integration is a process spanning across generations, drawing in all groups of the population and all fields of social life. Consequently, integration is a task for politicians and citizens alike.
>
> It is part of the integration process to come to an agreement about joint integration targets and core values recognized by all citizens as the basis for living together in diversity.This understanding rests on the constitution and the core values it specifies: fundamental rights, democracy, the rule of law and separation of powers. Hence the dialogue between institutions of the receiving society and those of the immigrants (immigrant organisations and other forms of representation) plays a major role. (*Senat* of Berlin 2005, 6–7; author's translation)

Against this background, the concept outlines four dimensions of integration policy:

- social and economic integration: this dimension comprises equal opportunities with regard to access to the key social institutions of the labour market, training market, educational system; plus integration into the social space;
- legal integration: this dimension comprises the opportunity for political participation through becoming active in political parties or bodies, associations and trade unions. It also means access to a secure residence status, acquisition of citizenship, exercizing the associated rights as well as entitlement to state transfer payments and health care services;
- cultural and social integration: this dimension first and foremost comprises acquisition of the language of the receiving society. Besides, it stands for factors such as sense of belonging to the receiving society and to one's own group of origin, the process of identity formation and the prospects opened up by it. Also to be mentioned here are social activities (leisure time, voluntary work) and integration into more informal networks;
- intercultural opening up of the receiving society: this includes an open, accepting, democratic attitude of the receiving society towards immigrants and intercultural opening of administrative and educational institutions. (*Senat* of Berlin 2005, 7)

These dimensions form the framework of Berlin's new integration policy. It is crucial that the framework was agreed upon by the government of the federal state, the *Senat* of Berlin. On that basis, the policy paper offers a direction for mainstreaming integration policy as a general task, which needs to be followed up by all *Senat* departments with regard to policy fields such as employment and self-employment as entrepreneurs, education and vocational training as well as urban development.

It is essential that challenges and deficits of integration should not be 'argued away'. They need to be analysed and addressed by policy strategies in the respective departments. Most specifically, such problems arise due to the significantly lower employment rates, and in the context of the school system, where immigrants, generally speaking, are less successful than the overall population. Along with high unemployment figures, deficits in urban development are to be observed in some districts of the city.

At present, the *Senat* of Berlin is about to initiate a monitoring process with the aim of evaluating these effects, to identify which policies by the relevant departments bear upon individual population segments. In this way, monitoring is directly related to implementation of the integration concept.

A crucial issue in this process is the participation of immigrants. In that regard, two features referred to above will be re-addressed: the large number of immigrants with no German passport, and the existence of a number of relatively strong immigrant organizations which have emerged over the last 20 years. Despite the fact that the *Senat* of Berlin favours naturalization for long term residents of foreign origin, these persons are currently still excluded from national and regional elections and thus from fundamental democratic representation. Representatives from immigrant NGOs are therefore seen as spokespersons of the immigrant population. In that context, two bodies are in particular noteworthy, both of which were founded within the last three years:

These are the Migration Council which represents immigrant non-governmental organizations, and secondly, the Advisory Council for Integration and Migration which has a secretariat in the Office of the Commissioner for Integration. Immigrant organizations are represented in this Council, along with representatives of the *Senat*, particularly the heads of departments having a major impact with regard to integration issues, such as the regional ministries for the interior, for social affairs, for education, for economic affairs, labour and women, for urban development, for justice and for culture. Six delegates from different immigrant communities are members. They were delegated by larger immigrant organizations, and thus have the mandate to represent Berlin's overall immigrant population, rather than their individual NGO or ethnic group. The Advisory Council is the main instrument and body with which to encourage the immigrant population to participate in the implementation process of the integration concept.

Shaping the process of immigration and integration will be one of the major concerns for the future. There is a broad consensus[6] that the city needs a vigorous immigration policy to activate its potential for worldwide exchange, to enrich and strengthen its culture, science and economy through the experiences of others, and to empower people and their capacity for intercultural dialogue. The internal and external strengths of Berlin will depend considerably on the extent to which it can develop further as a city of immigration.

Notes

1. OECD Programme for International Student Assessment, first survey 2000.
2. Social Democrat with Alliance90/Greens.
3. A comprehensive survey of the development of Berlin as a city of immigration is to be found in the data report published by the Commissioner of the Berlin Senat for Integration and Migration: Ohliger and Raiser 2005.
4. Source: Federal Agency of Labour, regional section for Berlin-Brandenburg. The subdivision into the categories 'foreigners' and 'Germans' no longer reflects adequately the social reality of Berlin as an immigration city. Nevertheless, the labour agency office differentiates its data according to nationality only.
5. BAMF, Federal Office for Migration and Refugees (http://www.bamf.de).
6. Reissert at al. 2001; OECD 2003; Berlin House of Representatives (Abgeordnetenhaus von Berlin) 2001.

13
Embracing Multiculturalism: the Case of London

Janice Morphet

The challenge of multiculturalism in Europe's cities has become the opening challenge of this century. The break with colonial ties, the opening of eastern European states and the labour requirements of an ageing society have all generated a different structure in city societies which will have a major significance in history. If the twentieth century saw Europe as an exporter of its people to the United States, Australia and South Africa, the twenty-first century is seeing that position reversed. Rather than creating ethnic diversity in other continents, Europe's major cities are now the hosts of multiculturalism.

London, like a number of European cities, has experienced these changes in migration patterns. Like other cities, race has been a defining characteristic for over fifty years, when public services recruited people from the Caribbean to become London's nurses and run its public transport. Other world events also brought new economic migrants from Commonwealth countries – the wars in Cyprus in the mid-1950s, the separation in Cyprus in the 1970s, the expulsion of Ugandan Asians, and the creation of a travelling generation from Australia in the 1990s. London grew as a financial centre, attracting to it those working for major international companies and those who worked in the industries alongside the financial sector. London became a place of refuge against war such as in Croatia or West Africa, a place of return when Hong Kong was handed back to China and a good place to get a job at any time. Finally, the entry of new member states into the European Union in 2004 has brought a new and growing group to London[1] and this group now accounts for the first growth in London's white population since 1991.[2] Since 1991, most of London's electoral wards have seen a growth in their diversity and none have seen a decrease, whilst, in 2001, 29 per cent of London's population belonged to the Black and Minority Ethnic BME group, which in turn represented 46 per cent of the BME population of England and Wales in 2001.[3]

London has also had many difficulties in adjusting to this new and growing cultural mix. Many Afro-Caribbean migrants to London found that it was difficult to obtain somewhere decent to live and that jobs were not always equally open to black people. Prejudice was high and its manifestations were shown on film and in popular TV programmes. In the 1980s, there were high levels of racial tension amongst young Afro-Caribbeans in London that manifest itself through the Brixton riots – not dissimilar to events in Paris in late 2005. There were similar events involving young people from Asian born families in Bradford and Oldham, but the responses in London have not been of the same kind. London has also accepted in-migrants with a variety of legal status, and until recently there has been no overt discussion about assimilation as part of British citizenship.

Thus the experience of Londoners and their children has been one of multiculturalism. Many areas of London have schools where over 100 languages are spoken. In London, over 300 languages are used. In fact it may be this diverse range of peoples which has reduced the potential for racial tension rather than increased it as frequently such episodes arise between two dominant cultural groups in one area. London has therefore accepted its multiculturalism as a way of life, its schools and cultures have adapted to a wide range of communities living within its boundaries. In some areas, particular cultural groups cluster but not to the exclusion of others, being described as 'magnet' areas rather than monocultural enclaves.[4]

The extent of London's multiculturalism and recognition of its benefits to the city as a whole were seen in the city's bid to stage the 2012 Olympics. It was the city's multicultural diversity which was seen to be its strength and a key component in its ability to welcome athletes from across the world. The second main component of this bid was seen to be the involvement of a multicultural group of children, not only in 2012 but directly in their appeal to the Olympic Committee in Singapore in July 2005. London's faith in its own ability to mobilize its multicultural legacy was seen not only in the winning bid but in the sad rollcall of victims of the 7 July bombings where the majority of victims were from across the world.

Places can offer security, support and familiarity. If English is not your first language, then moving to a place where others have come before you from the same country or even the same village – as was the case for many Bangladeshis coming to the London borough of Tower Hamlets – can provide the bridge from the old to the new. Those coming to cities have always followed these pathways and sought familiar cultural settings. Now that migrants arrive from a wider range of origins it creates a more diverse set of 'transferred' home locations in the new city, as Table 13.1 demonstrates.

Table 13.1: Where London's new immigrants come from

Country	Increase since 1990	Magnet areas
Nigeria	33,000	Southwark
S. America	42,000	Vauxhall/Tooting
Bangladesh	28,000	Poplar
Sri Lanka	24,000	Wembley
ex-Yugoslavia	22,500	Tottenham
Pakistan	22,000	Walthamstow
Hong Kong	22,000	Mill Hill
India	21,000	Barnet
S. Africa	20,000	Wimbledon/Putney
Turkey	18,600	Haringey
Australia	18,000	Earl's Court
France	17,000	Kensington/Hyde Park
Zimbabwe	16,000	East End
USA	12,000	Highgate/Golders Green
former USSR	10,000	Stepney/West Ham
Caribbean	9,400	Vauxhall/Tooting/Battersea
Sierra Leone	9,300	Southwark
Kenya	9,300	Greenford
New Zealand	9,000	Brondesbury
Italy	8,700	Chelsea/Hyde Park
Portugal	8,500	Vauxhall
China	6,700	Harrow/Barnet
Greece	5,000	Holborn/Chelsea
Sweden	5,000	Richmond
Cyprus	1,000	Enfield

Source: bbc.co.uk/born abroad.

Strategic policy approaches to the development of multicultural community cohesion

London has been the place in which the UK's strategic approaches to developing and supporting cultural cohesion have been established and developed. The first responses to the adverse effects on the life chances of those coming to London were first established in the Urban Programme in 1968.[5] Developed as a response to Enoch Powell's 'Rivers of Blood' speech, this first version of the Urban Programme was put in to support young learners directly through extra assistance in schools. In the 1970s, the government's Inner Area Studies were established to provide action research in investigating ways of reducing city inner area poverty, with the borough of Lambeth as London's study area. This led to the second wave of the Urban Programme, launched in 1978, which supported wider scale direct community development programmes in inner city areas including

Lambeth, Islington and Hackney with significant programme and partnership funds for five years. The Brixton riots, again in Lambeth in the early 1980s, were investigated in the 1986 Scarman report which began the understanding of what was later to be known – from the report investigating Steven Lawrence's death in Lewisham – as 'institutionalised racism' in the police and some other public services.[6]

The latest spur to consider how to improve multicultural approaches nationally have arisen as a result of the riots in the northern half of England in 2001.[7] These riots and those in 2005 in Birmingham have primarily been between two dominant groups in the same area – white and Asian origin in the north, and between those of Afro-Caribbean and Asian descent in Birmingham. The successive waves of inward migration in London now make this polarity a much rarer occurrence. However, local government approaches to community cohesion have become more urgent since these riots and after the London bombings. Further specific initiatives have been launched, but a more fundamental overhaul of English local government and of how it can respond to its immediate challenges has been set in train, and London is at the forefront of these processes.[8]

After a period of what has been seen as a centralizing agenda for local governance, the ten-year review of local government entitled local:vision,[9] has drawn upon the principles of 'new localism'[10] to create an emergent 'tight/loose' approach to local government for the future. In the case of some services, the public expect a national standard of delivery and do not want to see a 'post code' lottery for the delivery of basic education for children or access to prescription drugs. At the same time, the 'choice' agenda is promoting the extension of citizen choice in public services which can only be delivered in a system which supports differentiation. The development of 'Local Area Agreements' (LAAs),[11] between local partners from three sectors – private, public and voluntary – is drawing together common programmes for a finer grain delivery of services appropriate to locality and needs within local authority areas. These LAAs work on the principle of agreed priorities and objectives and in some cases the pooling of public funds. London local authorities have been amongst the leaders in piloting these new approaches.

These more recent initiatives sit alongside some which have been promoted since the introduction of the 'modernized local government' programme. This has been as part of the post-1997 approach, associated with the return of a Labour government after a primarily 'Thatcherite' period, to community leadership and locally focused working, which has included a number of different initiatives to encourage local governance at a sub-local authority level. These initiatives have built on existing activities but have been enhanced over time. The first is the opportunity for town and parish councils to further develop in terms of their roles and responsibilities. The second has been the enhanced role that can be played by neighbourhood renewal and Neighbourhood Development Companies (NDCs) which can operate in areas which are the most deprived, whether they are in urban or rural areas, although their work is primarily focused on urban areas where deprivation is seen to be at the most concentrated. The third initiative has emerged from the Local Government Act 2000, following which local councils are now able to deliver services in sub-areas which are within their administrative boundaries and to give responsibility for this delivery to the councillors and community representatives of each of these sub-areas. Although these initiatives arise from separate provenances and have differing foci, one of the key issues for the future is how they may be brought together into a more coherent sub-local authority model, which would be similar to the arrangement of local government in France for example.[12] With new localism, all of these approaches provide a legitimizing basis for working at the lowest appropriate level – in some ways a rebranded principle of subsidiarity.

Responding to the variety of forms of multiculturalism in England's communities, 'new localism' is primarily drawn from the United States as a policy vehicle.[13] In England, the emergence of 'new localism', with the New Local Government Network as its main proponent, has started a considerable debate on appropriate levels of governance. This has been accelerated by civil disturbances where racial tension was seen to be a root cause of community dissatisfaction. In July 2005, the Government published 'Together we can'[14] as a key policy initiative of the new government following the 2005 general election. This sought both to reinforce the role of partnerships, multiculturalism and democratic engagement. The urgency of this agenda has been increased since the London bombings in July 2005.

In addition to the New Local Government Network, other agencies have also been reviewing ways in which more localized working would be more beneficial. The Audit Commission, in their 2004 study 'People, Places and Prosperity', demonstrates that the continuing separation of streams of funding and objectives serve to undermine 'joined up' working at the local level, and that this is still having a deleterious effect on communities. They found that the promotion of economic, social and environmental 'well being', which since 2000 local authorities have a duty to promote, was more likely to be successful where national and local priorities are 'fully aligned and where local partners achieve coherence in establishing their priorities and targets' (2004, 2). The continuing number of partnership arrangements and funding streams which still exist are seen to hamper delivery at the local level, a finding which is supported by other research.[15] These partnerships seem to be primarily engaged in attracting short term project funding which renders mainstreaming and long term planning for change difficult as it is seen to be undertaken as a separate activity from day to day delivery. However, the Audit Commission does not suggest that the partnerships, including Local Strategic Partnerships which cover every local authority area in England, should be replaced by another vehicle. Rather, they should be strengthened to become the focus of LAAs and they should be the basis of a contract with central government through a Local Public Service Board.

The government has responded to the Audit Commission's proposals with two approaches. The first is the publication of 'Local Area Agreements: a prospectus',[16] and the second is an invitation to contribute to the consideration of 'the future of local government: developing a 10 year vision'.[17] In the ministerial foreword to the prospectus, LAAs are described as representing 'a radical new approach to improve coordination between central government and local authorities and their partners, working through the Local Strategic Partnership' (2004, 5). The key components remain much the same as in earlier partnership working and are stated as:

- simplified funding for safer and stronger communities
- strengthened Local Public Service agreements
- strengthened national strategy for neighbourhood renewal
- a stronger role for government offices; and
- pilot Local Area Agreements (2004, 7).

LAAs are proposed to have a series of key themes around specific groups and communities which are already identified in the jointly agreed priorities for local and central government.[18] These will be included in three 'blocks' – children and young people, safer and stronger communities and healthier communities and older people – which are to be negotiated separately and brought together into a single LAA. These have been joined by regeneration as a further block subsequently. The more developmental features proposed also include a 'single pot' for funding in a locality with no barriers between different public sector budgets and funding streams, with greater flexibility in order to address local needs. The second is to further rationalize separate locally based funding initiatives which run in parallel to bring these into the LAA. The proposals for implementation are that all English local authorities have LAAs by 2008, with pilots to be followed with more mainstream implementation. The effectiveness of delivery is seen to be assessed in a number of ways, including publication of Local Area Profiles,[19] developed by the Audit Commission and other forms of local performance management.[20]

Thus it is clear that the concept of 'new localism' is continuing to develop; some argue that it is being diluted as a result. There are also those who see 'new localism' as a means of helping to serve primarily central government ends through the localization of services which are currently centrally delivered,[21] although this does not necessarily mean that the outcome would not be beneficial. The results from the government review of the most appropriate scale for each service to be delivered may serve the public better and be much cheaper to operate.[22] There are other parts of governance which are being accused of either paying lip service to 'new localism' through LAAs or establishing their own version of it through local police or health boards which in effect would create an even stronger direct relationship between the centre and the locality, without necessarily divesting any central power.

Local approaches to multicultural spatial policy in London

The legacy of London government following abolition in 1987 of the Greater London Council, GLC, had been a major item on the political agenda in 1997. There was an expectation that the Labour Government would in some way reverse what was seen as one of the most political acts undertaken by Prime Minister Margaret Thatcher, the abolition of the GLC. It had both symbolic and practical consequences. At a symbolic level, the removal of London government was seen as a price that was being paid for the active development of political voice at subnational level. There were also wider implications for the relationship between the central state and the rest of the country, if London, one of the world's largest and most important cities, did not have its own governance structures. This was seen as an outward sign of the movement to complete state centralism. The ability of London to take any strategic action without any specific governance layer was also seen to be a difficulty. It would always be difficult for thirty-three individual and strong London boroughs with their own political leadership to promote London on the world stage with a single voice. The structure seemed to be too disparate and thus too risky for this kind of investment. This was seen to be an issue when London wished to promote its case to government, and externally on the world stage such as the capture of major sporting events such as the Olympics. The coordinating role within London for the period from 1987 was held by the London Office of the relevant central government department, the Department of the Environment DoE, as it then was, and subsequently the Government Office for London following its establishment in 1994, reinforcing central control.

Changes in London's governance following the 1997 general election, as part of a long promised devolved governance settlement, exhibited a shift away from London being viewed as a political problem to a realization that London remains critical to the UK economy as a whole, and that the complexity of its governance was hampering the progress it was able to make in making that contribution.[23] London governance has been changed in fundamental ways at regular periods since 1837,[24] and the new arrangements implemented in 2000 – following the 1999 London referendum – to have a mayor, is another stage in this history. The new and directly elected Mayor of London and the new Greater London Authority GLA, elected by both direct election to fourteen geographically based seats and by proportional representation for eleven London wide seats, remains a different governance structure to any other part of the UK.[25] The Mayor of London has executive responsibility for four bodies – the police, fire and rescue, Transport for London TfL and regeneration through the London Development Agency, with all four bodies being held to account through the GLA. The members of the Assembly have three clear powers: over the budget, over staffing and their power of general scrutiny.

The work of the first four years of mayoral government in London has resulted in the adoption of some innovative policies, such as introduction of congestion charging, whilst some policy processes such as the Spatial Plan for London have also been undertaken much more quickly than was the case in the past. At the same time, the Mayor has developed a working relationship with the Association of London Government and the Government Office for London, which had its powers substantially reduced at the time of the Mayor's election. The government of London is still viewed as a work in progress, with further proposals for additional mayoral powers published in 2005.[26] The boroughs see the Mayor's position as contestable in some areas, including his major policy priorities, and this relationship will need to mature over time.

Promoting localism as a means of supporting multiculturalism in London

The utilization of the 'new localism' principle in London has been no different from elsewhere. London has its range of sub-regions – such as the Central London partnership, the West London Alliance – and it is piloting some of the first Local Area Agreements for more joined up local public services, involving for example the London Borough of Hammersmith and Fulham, and the London Borough of Greenwich. These will sit alongside new proposals for neighbourhood policing and other area based initiatives for crime reduction and antisocial exclusion policies. In what may be seen as a counter trend to new localism, the Mayor of London has proposed that the 32 London boroughs, together with the City of London, should be combined into larger more efficient units in a replication of the process which last occurred in London in 1965. These units could be based on the developing subregions within London. However, if London government moves on to a subregional scale, then this might suggest that the neighbourhood approaches of 'new localism' could be even more necessary than now, as public administration and democratic representation may become more remote. The proposals remain at a preproposal stage at present, but if they do go forward they would echo similar trends in Wales and Scotland which both obtained their devolved powers at the same time as London. They also sit within the revised debate on the application of the principle of governmental subsidiarity in the European Union which is led by the Committee of the Regions CoR.[27]

The use of localist principles also helps to support practical differentiation of policies and implementation approaches – a philosophy of 'keep it local' is being seen as a means of dealing with localized problems in housing areas and communities – where solutions go with the grain of microcultures as the means of being effective.[28] Thus taking a more programmed approach within an overall framework of an LAA is seen as a means of both identifying the challenges of under performance or lower life chances in each community, and then utilizing locally determined and appropriate solutions for action. This is seen to be a key component of helping all London's citizens to fulfil their economic potential, for example.[29]

This is the approach which has been developed from the lessons learned for the large scale redevelopment which happened in London Docklands from 1980 onwards. In this redevelopment programme, a centralized team was set up by central government and led by a civil servant who created new development but did not always manage to generate new communities, at least initially. Later development delivery within the creation of new development in Docklands, to the east of the Isle of Dogs, concentrated more on attracting a more balanced approach to development rather than monosectoral places. The second major phase of regeneration to the east of London, the Thames Gateway, has learned some of these lessons and is seeking to generate communities through local initiatives within the defined area, and the development delivery is being managed in smaller areas which make up the whole.

Development of the Olympic proposals which were at the heart of the successful bid put together both the achievement of Docklands and the lessons learned.[30] They demonstrated that major infrastructure works could be implemented in time to meet the requirements of 2012, but that also the legacy would be a place which could function within an existing urban fabric. Many previous Olympic Games facilities have been developed on the urban periphery, leaving them as monuments after the event, frequently used as major sporting venues but without real integration into the existing city. The London Olympic proposals took an opposite view. It promoted the theme of London: the World in One City.[31] Olympic athletes would be part of an integrated place within a city where all their home communities were already represented. This both utilizes the benefits of multiculturalism, accepts it as a strength of the city and was seen to be at the heart of the proposals. This was further highlighted by the use of well-known locations for Olympic venues – Wimbledon and Horse Guards Parade – which are already recognized across the world as well as being part of the existing urban fabric. The Olympic bid also strongly made its case on the basis of mass participation in sport in the community, with sport being seen as a cultural frame of reference to which people could relate beyond race, class, gender or religion. The main new location of the Olympics, Stratford in the London Borough of Newham, to the north of Docklands, is one of the most multicultural places in London, with a majority population having either been born outside the UK or from families coming from other parts of the world.[32] Indeed, Newham has nine of the ten most diverse electoral wards in London.[33]

At local level, the planning for Olympic delivery in the London Borough of Newham is utilizing new planning frameworks which were introduced in 2004 in the Planning and Compensation Act. Within these, the Local Development Scheme[34] has to work within the Community Strategy which is also the basis for LAAs. For the first time, the Spatial Plan is now being linked directly with the action programme for the whole area, and with the cross sectoral Local Strategic Partnership.

Conclusions

The emergence of London as the world's leading multicultural city has been one of the key discoveries of 2005, which was brought to prominence by the successful Olympic bid on 6 July and the four London bombings on 7 July. Ironically, both events reinforced the same message: London is a place of people from all parts of the world who now regard it as their home whilst maintaining ties to their own culture. This diversity is now seen as a strength and as a means of reducing racial tension, and where tension exists it tends to be in areas of London which remain monocultural or bi-cultural rather than multicultural. This is reinforced by the finding that the London bombers who grew up in London were living in outer London boroughs, Enfield and Harrow, to the north of London, which were seen to be more racially divided.

Whilst London's employment base now fully represents its diverse population, there is still evidence that life chances for some groups remains much lower. In a longitudinal study,[35] it was found that those from minority ethnic backgrounds were more likely to suffer unemployment than their white British counterparts and this was particularly true of Caribbeans. The study also found that 'for some minority groups (Caribbeans, Black Africans, Indians and Chinese and other) children with working class parents are more likely to end up in professional/managerial class families than white British people from the same origins'.[36]

The events in July 2005 held up a mirror to British society and London's character. Before the Olympic success and the London bombs, multiculturalism was seen to be an ambivalent issue and its extent was not fully understood in parts of the country which are primarily monocultural, such as the south west and north east regions. Up to this point, people had seen biculturalism as the main manifestation of multiculturalism and this had been most recently associated with tensions and segregation in the riots in the northern cities.[37] The scale of multiculturalism, demonstrated through the origins of the victims, their families and those who helped them, brought about a profound change in the understanding of the dignity and strength that multiculturalism can bring to a city. There were some obvious comparisons made with New York and '9/11', and former Mayor Giuliani's presence in London on 7 July – having travelled there from Harrogate in Yorkshire, close to the starting point of three of the July 2005 bombers on the preceding day – is one of those coincidences which these events throw up. Yet New York has always understood itself as a melting pot and its main links with London, as two great cities, have been primarily through their roles as major financial centres, which again was reinforced by the destruction of the World Trade Center. What the world learned in the Olympic process and from the London bombings was that its conception of London had to change. London's multiculturalism is now setting it apart from other places as it steps into new territory for the future.

Although evidence shows that discrimination exists amongst some groups and that life changes in health and education have to improve, London has also shown that it has reached a different place compared with many other cities in Europe which are not grappling with biculturalism and multiculturalism in new ways. Much of this reluctance to change has been caused by a sense that this is a transitory rather than a permanent process. Yet migration from new member states into longer standing EU member states is causing some tensions, particularly where unemployment is high. In other places, new migrants are helping to meet labour shortages of a declining workforce, which is creating a major demographic wave of change across Europe in the period to 2020. Some tensions, for example in Germany, are caused by the potential change in status of longstanding guest workers, who have never been allowed citizenship even if born in Germany, should Turkey be invited to join the European Union. In France, civil disturbances and major fire tragedies involving black communities in 2005 have caused a rethink on citizenship and the nature of life chances in these groups.

In many ways, London's experience of multiculturalism and the tension it can generate has been gained over a fifty year period. London has had serious disturbances related to race issues from 1958 onwards. London does not proffer solutions, but the experiences of July 2005 will be a turning point in the city's history when it was first appreciated that its multiculturalism was its strength.

Notes

1. Institute for Public Policy Research IPPR 2005.
2. GLA 2005a.
3. GLA 2005a.
4. IPPR 2005; Pimlott, Rao 2002.
5. Lawless 1986.
6. McPherson 1999.

7. Cantle 2001.
8. Miliband 2005; ODPM 2005.
9. ODPM 2004.
10. Corry Stoker 2003; Morphet 2006.
11. ODPM 2004.
12. Le Gales, Mawson 1994.
13. Alesina, Spolaore 2003; HMT 2004.
14. HMG 2005.
15. Buck 2002.
16. ODPM 2004.
17. ODPM 2004a.
18. Central Local Partnership agenda and minutes, 4 December 2000, www.lga.gov.uk/agenda.
19. Audit Commission 2005.
20. ODPM 2005b.
21. Cross (2004) 'Public domain', 12 August 2004, Online *Guardian* newspaper.
22. HMT 2004b; National prosperity, local choice and civic engagement, Sir Michael Lyons, 2006 report of the Lyons Inquiry London, www.lyonsinquiry.org.uk.
23. Walker 2002.
24. Travers 2004.
25. Corry 2003.
26. ODPM 2005b.
27. P. Woolas (2005), speech to EU second conference on subsidiarity, 29 November.
28. Pimlott, Rao 2001.
29. GLA 2005.
30. Newham 2005b.
31. http://www.london2012.org/en/city/onecity/
32. Newham 2005a.
33. GLA 2005a.
34. Newham 2005b.
35. Platt 2005.
36. Platt 2005.
37. Ritchie 2002; Cantle 2001.

14
Immigration to Italy: National Policies and Local Strategies in Verona and Turin

Vanessa Maher

This chapter presents case studies from the Italian cities of Verona and Turin. It highlights the importance of local strategies in meeting the special problems which contemporary urban environments pose to their inhabitants. These problems are frequently related to the scale and pace of contemporary immigration from non-European and eastern European countries. There are many factors involved, which new methodological approaches in anthropology may help to elucidate. A summary will be given, in the light of anthropological research, of the use and perception of space in Veronetta (Verona) and in the Turin neighbourhoods (*quartieri*) of San Salvario and Porta Palazzo. Here, at neighbourhood level, spontaneous 'committees' of Italian residents (citizens' committees) have called for municipal intervention to deal with disorder, which is attributed to immigrant activities and cultural habits. The very existence of such citizens' committees in many Italian cities and the 'ethnic' language they use suggest a lack of institutional channels for influencing living conditions. It is argued that cultural diversity, which should be a significant theme of the political debate, is not given in its consequences, but is wrapped up at local level with the use and nature of shared space: how this is handled in local strategies matters – and here an anthropologist may have a unique contribution to offer.

Immigration to Italy

The immigrant population in Italy has increased in leaps and bounds over the last thirty years to reach its present total of 2.6 million, around 5 per cent of the total population, with 'irregular' immigrants estimated at another 200,000 or more. They come from approximately 150 different countries, and about half of them are women, many on their own. The migration of women to Italy has many causes but is also a response to an intense local demand for domestic labour and help with the aged, reflecting the structure of gender relations, family organization and the labour market in Italy.

Ten nationalities now account for 75 per cent of the total immigrant population, an indication of increasing stability; one-third of these immigrants are from eastern Europe.[1] The distribution and concentration of immigrants from different countries varies from region to region and from city to city.[2]

Although the scale and rate of recent immigration have alarmed many Italians, several factors have forced governments and citizens to face the inevitable. Among these are: a segmentation of the labour market, such that 'immigrants do the jobs which Italians no longer want to do', the low birth rate combined with high life expectancy and the prospect of a pension crisis, and finally, an industrial boom (now waning) in the north-east, bringing in its wake a lively demand for immigrant labour. It is estimated that nearly 30 per cent of the labour market in Italy consists of 'irregular' immigrants or *'clandestini'*, particularly among small enterprises, which avoid paying taxes and social insurance for their employees. The real demand for immigrant labour, and indeed the presence of many immigrants, is thus masked by the informal economy, making a realistic estimate of immigration figures impossible. Two laws, the Martelli law of 1989, and the Napolitano-Turco law of 1998, attempted to provide a legal framework for immigration and integration policies, and several interim measures have been passed to enable illegal immigrants to acquire legal status, the last dating to 1996. Nevertheless, illegal immigrants overall are in a weak position to resist being sucked into rackets, such as prostitution or drug dealing. The right-wing Bossi-Fini law of 2002–03 aimed to reverse the trend towards stability and settlement, by reducing the quotas of long-term permits in favour of seasonal permits, requiring immigrants to renew 'long-term' permits every two years, while also making it more difficult to obtain entry permits for relatives. Legislators in successive governments since 1989 have in fact, in the main, concentrated on stemming the influx of new immigrants and expelling *'clandestini'*, with scarce attention to the question of integration. In the press and in public opinion the impression has been created that the main task facing the country is to contain a threat.[3] Illegal immigrants and those applying for political asylum – seldom granted – are held for identification in one of fourteen Temporary Detention Centres (*Centri di Permanenza Temporanea*) in prison-like conditions.[4] Recently, the Home Affairs minister decreed that such centres were to be built in every province, which could mean more than a hundred new centres.

Citizenship for immigrants appears to be a long way off

Following T.H. Marshall,[5] a distinction will be made between political, civil and social aspects of citizenship. Concerning political aspects, Italians acquire citizenship by descent, according to the *jus sanguinis*, or by marriage, and the procedures for naturalization are long, tortuous and rarely successful. However, children of Italian emigrants living in other countries are eligible for citizenship, and indeed have the facility to vote, until the third descending generation. All proposals to admit immigrants to the electorate have come to nothing. Immigrants living in Italy cannot even vote in local elections, though this is under debate in several cities, including Turin.

Concerning the civil and social aspects of citizenship, although the 1998 law recognized fundamental social rights for foreigners (health, education, lodging) and full civil rights for regular residents, implementation of such rights tends to depend on action by various agencies at local level. On matters such as housing and the sharing of space, immigrants in urban neighbourhoods are often inevitably in competition with natives.

Cultural difference and stereotypes

The notion of cultural difference is ambiguous. How are the 'boundaries' between cultures to be defined, and who is to define them? Which differences are to be considered important?[6] Laura Maritano's recent anthropological study of stereotyping and attitudes towards immigration in the Turin municipality of San Salvario is subtitled 'An obsession with cultural difference'. She points out that well-educated interviewees who had joined the citizens' committee identified immigrants first in terms of 'them' (*stranieri, extracomunitari*) and 'us', then in terms of nationality, with which they associated cultural and behavioural stereotypes, ranked in a moral hierarchy. The characteristics attributed to different groups were treated as fixed and naturalized. A typical comment would be:

> We are not angry with the Somalis and the Chinese. I have always explicitly complained about the Nigerians and not about all the immigrants. The Albanians, for example, go to tea in people's homes and drug and rob them. How can we feel sorry for them?

The newcomers were described in terms of their different families, living habits, food and religious observances.[7] Suggestions for the incorporation of this judgmental 'recognition of cultural difference' into national policy have been advanced by a Catholic dignitary, Cardinal Biffi, who has suggested that Muslim immigrants should not be admitted to Italy, because they are culturally incompatible with Italians. However, most Muslim immigrants have no more 'cultural' problems than Buddhists, Sikhs or Christians who are of many different denominations and countries of origin.

Many anthropologists have deplored the indiscriminate use of the term 'culture', whose heuristic value has been undermined by its adoption as a political slogan. Lila Abu-Lughod claims that the Western use of the culture concept has distanced and rendered 'others' the populations studied by anthropologists.[8] It ignores the ambiguity and manipulation of norms by actors in different situations and the fuzzy cultural interconnectedness of groups sharing space.[9] During a sophisticated debate on ethnicity in the 1960s and 70s, Frederik Barth (1969, 13) pointed out that ethnic boundaries were generated by (fluctuating) social and political relations and not in a simple way by cultural difference. He warned that although ethnic categories might refer to cultural difference, it was not the sum of 'objective' traits which counted, but only those which the actors themselves considered as being significant.[10] Abner Cohen (1974) also usefully put forward an instrumental theory of ethnicity, according to which, in a competitive social context, an appeal to common identity, however defined, served to mobilize interest groups for political ends, in the absence of institutional channels for achieving them. Cultural difference is only one of ethnicity's arguments.[11] Finally, contributing to this debate, Philip and Iona Mayer observe that ethnic identification does not imply common collective behaviour but can be associated with a wide range of personal choices.[12] Closer to the present, Gerd Baumann (1994), in a fascinating study of Southall in West London (a borough where people of Punjabi, Caribbean, English and Irish descent have been living for decades), points out that the municipal administration and the heterogeneous local population have different ways of using the notion of 'community'. He identifies a 'dominant' and a 'demotic' strategic discourse: the former is used by the media, the politicians and the local authorities. It equates 'community' 'identity' and 'culture' to produce 'otherness', by way of simple concepts, in such a way as to confirm institutional objectives. The 'demotic' discourse consists of the images and communicative strategies used by individual residents to respond in a flexible way to changing situations and relationships.[13] To a certain extent, the administration produces communities separated by cultural difference, whereas the local inhabitants see their relationships in much more fluid and circumstantial terms. In other words, cities as lived sites of experience can be 'fuzzy' places.

Fuzzy places – case studies in the micro-management of conflict: Turin and Verona

In 2003, a research group called 'fuzzy places', comprising three anthropologists and two cognitive psychologists, was established in the Department of Psychology and Cultural Anthropology of the University of Verona. A first task was to compare different approaches to problems of spatial perception. For the anthropologists, the way the physical world was evaluated depended on socially constructed perceptions. For the psychologists, humans need physical props – 'affordances', perceptible to the various senses – to set off different kinds of space, in order to 'perceive' boundaries.[14] The anthropological side of the research agenda concerned the use or non-use of physical space (itineraries, crossing, visiting, waiting, avoidance behaviour) by individuals and social categories (defined by gender, generation, social class, geographical provenance); the 'habitus' (learnt practices of the physical and cultural environment) of the social actors; and collective and individual representations of space. The psychologists were interested in application to empirical findings of their research on the perceptual organization of margins in outside space: streets, squares, pavements and buildings. Their idea that some margins and spaces are perceptually 'fuzzy' (ambiguous or difficult to set off from others) and others were 'crisp' or unambiguous, turned out to be useful to the anthropologists in analysing contradictory or overlapping representations and uses of space in the city by different categories of people. In contrast to this approach, official representations of space tend to represent it as neutral, as if there were no cultural rules for its use. Informal processes of social segregation by gender, class or ethnicity, however, mark space in a qualitative way. At the same time, kinds of space define the people who frequent them.[15] Diverse and competing representations – what Filip de Boeck[16] has called 'the invisible city' – give meaning to places, cities and urban areas, shaping the world of empirical interactions. The hypothesis proposed was that it was this affective city and the issues of symbolism wrapped up in it that lay at the root of the rise of citizen's committees and their protests concerning the presence and activities of immigrants in their neighbourhoods. But as Shields puts it: ' . . . if desire is the impulse which founds society, how can we grasp the emotional and affective city (a sort of perspective from the grass-roots) rather than concentrate on the rational and planned city (seen from the Town Hall)'.[17] As has been pointed out above, official representations of the city, such as town plans, are static, freezing social processes. On the one hand, such images prevent the scientist from grasping flows and mixing of people, information and goods, which involve negotiation over the use of space. On the other hand they cancel the 'chronotopographic' aspect of the city, the way in which memory and the temporal aspects of living influence the spatial aspects. Further, official representations treat space as 'public', ignoring domestic space, that prototype of inhabited space, shared by several generations. Ignoring domestic space means it is easy to overlook the fact that it may extend into the street. Historical accounts of Verona describe women sitting outside to chat with neighbours and craftsmen working in the street where they also met their customers, as late as the 1950s. Nowadays, roaring traffic inhibits this kind of use of the street, and neighbours have less to do with each other. However, the 'figura' or social 'persona' – an intimate aspect of the person – is constructed in interaction with others in public situations and especially in the street, not without consequences in the Verona of today. The margin between the domestic and the public, between work and social life, between inside and outside is a 'fuzzy' one.

Veronetta

In 2004, adopting the view that places have to be understood as fuzzy, fieldwork began in Veronetta, a neighbourhood of Verona. In the remainder of this chapter some preliminary findings are presented and compared to corresponding research in Turin.

To begin with, 'microenvironments' were selected for participant observation, but also as 'points of view' on the neighbourhood: an old people's home, a Nigerian shop, a bar where Albanian students meet, a hostel for the homeless and a new women's intercultural association.[18]

Veronetta is close to the centre of the city, with some fine buildings, many churches and a pleasant position between the hill and the winding River Adige, whose canals formerly provided energy and outlets for numerous textile factories and saw mills. After a devastating flood at the end of the nineteenth century, the canals were earthed in, and the neighbourhood began a slow process of decline. Today, Veronetta has a settled population of around 10,000 people, a third of them over 60 years old (compared to 18 per cent overall in the city of Verona), an immigrant population of around 17 per cent, and many students, who are temporary residents with a high turnover.

While this type of demographic pattern is often associated in the press with a crime problem, the police regard Veronetta as a 'quiet neighbourhood' with no serious tensions. In fact evidence suggests that immigrants are more likely to be victims of crime and exploitation than its perpetrators. Yet the cry likewise for 'security' is uttered by the citizens' committee, in common with dozens of others throughout the country. The conclusion is that this has more to do with observance or non observance of symbolic boundaries than with crime. While in most cases people live parallel lives of non-relation to other groups (albeit with some contact in an intercultural centre, and through special initiatives in the old people's home) and xenophobic behaviour is not much in evidence, it is the use of public space that still causes tensions. The main street and some side-streets are lined with shops, many of them run by Nigerians, Moroccans, Sri Lankans and Chinese, and there is a small open air market on several days a week. Immigrants, especially men, socialize in the main street, particularly in the evening. This male use of public space turns Veronetta into a place where women, in particular, feel ill at ease. The approach in Veronetta to what is a conflict over appropriate relations to the symbolic appropriation of space, unfortunately, remains one of laissez-faire. In an interview, the neo-liberal comment was even expressed by one Verona official that ultimately gentrification, property speculation and rising rents would solve the problem, forcing immigrants out. In contrast to this laissez-faire approach, the Turin municipality, prompted by angry citizens' committees, was forced to experiment with a policy of 'urban governance' or 'active management' whose outcome seems to have been positive.

Turin: the neighbourhoods of San Salvario and Porta Palazzo

There are about 100,000 immigrants in the province of Turin and 50,000 in the municipality, of whom 25 per cent are Romanian, 25 per cent Moroccan, 15 per cent Albanian, 8 per cent Chinese and 8 per cent Peruvian (data for 2004). A paper produced for the Institute for Economic and Political Research on the Piedmont region (*IRES Piemonte*) offers a detailed analysis of the local authority response to perceived 'urban crisis' in the neighbourhoods of San Salvario and Porta Palazzo.[19] Both neighbourhoods are close to the centre of the city, having had older buildings abandoned by the local population.

In Porta Palazzo, there had been protests by dozens of citizens' committees since the early 1990s, complaining that local people needed to be defended against 'delinquents', often identified with immigrants. This neighbourhood is near the cathedral, the royal palace and the prefecture. It is dominated by a vast square, where the main open-air and covered markets are held, frequented by 40,000 people a day. Immigrants have taken on much of the heavy work in the market and have gradually opened their own stalls and shops. At the time of the 'urban crisis' (1995–2000), they lived in particularly dilapidated and overcrowded houses, rented at outrageous prices. Various kinds of illicit activities went on in the neighbourhood and fights were common, especially among immigrants.

San Salvario is a neighbourhood of solid mid-nineteenth and early twentieth century buildings, sometimes slightly run-down, surrounding a popular open-air market. Immigrants, many of them illegal, comprise about 20 per cent, and older people (over 60) roughly 30 per cent of a population of 40,000. Immigrants are concentrated in relatively few buildings, and during the 1990s were actively resented by some of their Italian neighbours. Enshrined in Italian civil law, it must be remembered, is the notion that certain kinds of behaviour (for example prostitution) are tolerable if they do not create a 'public scandal'. The visibility of immigrants, and the fact that activities previously shrouded in mystery were carried on in the street, seemed to cause considerable concern.

In 1995, the local parish priest claimed in a press interview that the situation in the neighbourhood was explosive. With hindsight, his decisive outburst can be seen as having prodded the municipality into taking decisive action in time in both neighbourhoods. Substantial funds were subsequently earmarked for physical refurbishment and in the course of five or six years both San Salvario and Porta Palazzo were transformed. Gardens were enclosed to discourage pushers and prostitutes, lighting was improved and parking patrols introduced. But most important and far reaching in San Salvario was the building of an underground parking area and a permanent covered structure for the market. In Porta Palazzo, construction of an underground through-pass to siphon off traffic from the market, conversion of

Figure 14.1: Semiotic mosaic: San Salvario

a large part of the neighbourhood into an attractive pedestrian area with shops and cafés, building a Turkish Bath and an Intercultural Centre were the central elements.

The research indicates that the perception surrounding these developments in the realm of the 'affective' city has been all important in ameliorating intercultural tension. Formulating events in terms of 'crisp' and 'fuzzy' spatial perceptions, the following interpretation is advanced. Invasion of the neighbourhoods by traffic and supermarkets coincided with changes in work patterns and the decline of small local businesses. The 'dislocation' of many firms to countries where labour costs are lower, the crisis of the 'work ethic', and disruption of traditional social networks in the city resulted in the fragmentation of society and identities, such that the established social means for taking part in public life (parishes, political parties, trade unions) appeared to lose relevance. An office set up to collect complaints registered as many tensions between Italian neighbours as vis-à-vis the immigrants who had become their scapegoats. The ex-industrial workers in Turin, many of whom felt that they had assured the future of their children by emigrating North and working for many years in a hostile social climate, viewed the industrial decline of the city, exemplified in the crisis of Fiat Industries, with a kind of bewilderment. At the same time, they were filled with dismay at the predicament of many immigrants, who worked in dangerous, underpaid and polluting jobs, lived in crowded, insalubrious flats, being prey to old and new mafias and soliciting on the streets. It is, writes Melossi, as if Italians were overcome with disappointment for the way in which their dreams of emancipation, democracy and social order had been shattered.[20] The plight of the immigrants threw back to Italians – and indeed to many immigrants themselves – an image of their neighbourhood which frustrated their aspirations to social mobility and respectability. The once sharp divide, which protected the familiar neighbourhood near home with its work and social routines from the area given over to traffic and strangers, had fallen away. The confusion between different kinds of space gave rise to images of disorder, contamination and danger, quickly blamed on the highly visible immigrants. The measures taken by the municipal authorities restored 'crispness' to the distinction between kinds of space, by providing perceptual props or 'affordances', moving the noise of traffic and promiscuity of markets away from the quiet, familiar area. Controls on rents, sales licences and prostitution emphasized the distinction between legal and illegal activities and reduced overcrowding. Thus the familiar, protective environment could be seen to include both Italians and immigrants. The question of whether people could share space depended on much more than 'shared culture'. Technical assistance offered to small enterprises helped them to envisage a more modern horizon – even a European one – rather than feel left behind in an outdated time and place. The decisive action of the municipal authorities dampened, it is contended, the fuse of xenophobia and helped identify underlying causes of social tensions. In general terms, the measures taken in Turin redrew normative boundaries and restored order, as opposed to a strategy of governing disorder. Turin is considered a 'tough' city because of the unfriendly attitudes of sectors of the population, but its administration and many of its citizens have invested great efforts in providing social rights for newcomers and for their children, emphasizing the need to renovate notions of citizenship rather than accent cultural difference.[21] Mention may be made of cultural mediation work and that of Intercultural Centres in this context.

Intercultural Centres and cultural mediation

Local authorities in Italy tend to refer to 'communities' when discussing the presence of people of different origin in their cities. Some have attempted to institute Immigrant Consultative Committees made up of the 'representatives' of the different 'communities', but these have proved ineffectual because their legitimacy has been contested by the people they were supposed to represent. Informal advocacy, practised by educated immigrants on behalf of bewildered newcomers – and not only those of their own nationality – was the norm for many years. The former helped the latter to find their feet in the new environment and make their way through the intricate labyrinth of bureaucratic procedures.

Verona's immigrant population arrived more recently than that of Turin, at a time when there was a 'centre-right' administration. For years, the fate of immigrants was thus left to voluntary associations and religious charities, often dealing with immigrant associations consisting of people of a single nationality. This tended to enhance the importance of cultural difference. For example, a football tournament which pitted 'national' teams against others caused considerable tension. The current 'centre-left' administration, however, has focused considerable attention on immigration and Intercultural Centres, including an Intercultural Centre for Women established in 2004, and has put more emphasis on integration and cultural mediation, a practice common in Turin since the early 1990s. Turin, in fact, was one of the earliest provinces to invest in the training of cultural mediators, usually with European Social Fund financing, and to employ them to facilitate communication between immigrants and social, health, judicial and educational services. It is clear that this support helps immigrants to exercise social and even civil rights which might otherwise remain a dead letter. The fact that many courses provided were promoted by intercultural associations has been important for the way the profession and its practice has developed in Turin, with a minimal emphasis on 'cultural difference' and a deliberate policy of avoiding 'ethnic compacting'.

The intercultural approach and the number and variety of links between immigrants and Italians in Turin are significant achievements which go a long way towards compensating for a generally harsh environment. A cultural mediator, for example, might not necessarily work with immigrants of his or her own nationality or even religious or linguistic group. This approach is not common to all Italian cities. In Milan, which has been governed for some years by an administration with strong 'Lega Nord' elements, associations emphasize the need for cultural mediators to help immigrants of their own area of origin and language, and encourage them to 'build up' their 'communities' so that the latter will find their 'own voice'.

Conclusion: reterritorialization within a context of common citizenship

New forms of association, therefore, both 'ethnic' and intercultural, have been built up over the years from heterogeneous beginnings, as a response to the difficulties of life as an immigrant and the need for communication and help, not always forthcoming from the host society. Transnational networks,[22] which link immigrants to people in their countries of origin, both facilitate emigration and help people survive in the new country. Moroccans, for example, of whom there are about 10,000 in Turin, come from many different regions but above all from Casablanca and Khouribga, where whole neighbourhoods have been 'Italianized'. Capello points to the role of Porta Palazzo as a place to meet, a '*suq*', for exchanging news on jobs and home networks and keeping in touch, for constructing 'closeness', '*qaraba*'. It is a socially and symbolically structured space and it needs to be understood as such.[23] Quite often, religious forms and congregations of migrants are different from the ones at home.[24] But for many immigrants, the rhythm of periodic meetings, the exchange of help and information and the guidance of religious leaders create a shared symbolic place to which they can 'belong'.

This process of religious and social mapping is called in this chapter 'reterritorialization', because the network of contacts structures the city and gives its meaning. To the extent that discrimination, disadvantage and lack of communication with Italians create social distance, these meanings divide migrants from Italians.

The research described here on African and Middle Eastern immigration to Turin has revealed, not surprisingly, that those people who speak one or more European languages, who have somewhere stable to live and a job, include in their social networks more Italians and people of other countries than people from their home country. In contrast, those who do not learn Italian (especially women in domestic service, whatever their degree of education) or have housing and work difficulties, tend to frequent only their own compatriots.

At the administrative level, the emphasis on 'cultural difference', not on citizenship, common humanity and the possibility of mutual comprehension, may lend itself to support of segregationist policies, inhibiting the development of daily relations of friendship and civic collaboration among people of different experience.

Attention to spatial perception offers a methodological aid to living together in difference. Spatial perception and practice are structured to a certain extent by cultural categories, but also by the cognitive capacities, physiological and psychological needs common to all human beings. The recognition of these two dimensions may be a precondition for negotiation of norms for sharing common space and collaborative relationships. Local administration (and not the police) must assume responsibility for material intervention in situations of conflict, but any measure will be seen as ineffective and authoritarian without prior research and mediation carried out by experienced and independent researchers and investigators to establish the real causes. In other words, policies to encourage cultural inclusion must respect the specificities of place.

Notes

1. Barrucci, Liberti 2004, 28.
2. Romania, Morocco, Albania, Ukraine, People's Republic of China, Philippines, Poland, Tunisia, Senegal, Peru, India and Ecuador. Cestim: analysis of police data, Questura di Verona, 12–2003.
3. Colombo, Sciortino 2004.
4. Rahola 2003.
5. Marshall 1963.
6. See, for example, MacDonald 1993.
7. Maritano 2002.
8. Abu-Lughod 1991.
9. For a discussion, see: Hannerz 1980.
10. Barth 1969, 13.
11. Cohen 1974.
12. Mayer, Mayer 1980.
13. Baumann 1994.
14. Gibson 1979.
15. Ardener 1993.
16. De Boeck 2004. See also: Feld, Basso 1996.
17. Shields 1996.
18. Anthropologists: Vanessa Maher, Francesco Ronzon, Daniela Marchese, psychologists: Ugo Savardi, Ivana Bianchi. Research grants were awarded to: Rossella Cevese, Marialuisa Magagnotti, Sabaudin Varvarica. The project was financed with funds from the *Ateneo di Verona*, awarded to V. Maher in 2003 and 2004. An account of this research, including an Italian variant of this chapter, was published in *Dipav Quaderni*, 14/15 2005, Luoghi e pratiche sociali fra antropologia e psicologia, 1–117.
19. Allasino, Bobbio, Neri 2000; IRES Piemonte has undertaken or sponsored a large number of important research projects on immigration since 1989, covering the viewpoints of the immigrants, of the local population, a comparison of policies of local authorities in Turin and Lyons. See Maher 1996.
20. Melossi, Silverman 2004, 10.
21. Commissione per le politiche di integrazione degli immigrati 2001.
22. Glick, Schiller, Basch, Szanton-Blanc 1992.
23. Capello 2003.
24. The policies of single communes vary enormously, showing that the immigrant has no 'right' to a place of worship.

15
Fearing to Speak: Segregation and the Divided City of Belfast

Peter Shirlow

The civil unrest in France in 2005 included a series of riots and other forms of violent clashes between groups of youths composed of Muslim immigrants from North African backgrounds and French citizens including those from non-immigrant backgrounds and the French police. The riots occurred simultaneously in various poor suburbs of large cities, and most of the violence included the burning of cars and public buildings as well as stone throwing and petrol bombings. The riots in France as well as recent riots in the north of England in 2003 all indicated that there remain sections of society who feel alienated and cut off from the mainstream of civic, cultural and political life. In each instance, the marginalization of such groups is based upon some form of segregation whether it is racial, social or in most instances a combination of both. Segregation and the consequences of that separation in the production of violence are crucial determinants in evaluating the causes and meaning of such city-wide division. Such divisions whether they be in Paris, Belfast or Nicosia are a constant reminder of the failure of the modernist project and the consequential and negative diversity of the post-modern landscape.

Negative diversity in Belfast

A crucial problem in relation to conflict transformation in Northern Ireland is that sections of the two main communities wish to remain physically, culturally and politically apart. Such physical detachment is linked to disapproving attitudes and hostility towards the 'other' community and what is deemed to be appropriate versus inappropriate 'ways of life'. As with racism and other exclusivist renditions of identity, much of this hostility is reproduced around a mixture of fear, misunderstanding and the stereotyping of the 'other' ethno-sectarian group. Some senses of fear have been predicated upon the disruptive practice of violence and the desire to harm and intimidate across the ethno-sectarian divide.[1]

It is evident that segregation and the interfacing of community life have also disrupted the creation of shared values, opinions and cultural codes. Segregation and the desire to promote cultural and political uniqueness within place also has the capacity to silence those who wish to promote alternative discourses based upon stimulating shared living and the de-escalation of sectarian consciousness. Despite several years of tentative peace building and related political initiatives the control of territory – especially within socially deprived environments – remains linked to narratives of community devotion and ideological practice.[2]

A social narrative of territorial belonging and ownership is central in the explanation and indeed logic of identity construction within Northern Ireland. Within the Belfast context violence and the search for security – especially during the 1970s – furthered physical separation and encouraged place-centred renditions of community that were themselves tied to actively resisting an ethnic/ideological 'other'. It is important to note that ethno-sectarian segregation – whether in Belfast, Mostar or Jerusalem – is more than simply a separation of people. Separation is the instrument through which animosity and the reproduction of mistrust and division are manifested. It is crucially important to note that, although segregation in Belfast is generally linked to religious affiliation, religion is an insignificant part of what is essentially a constitutional conflict.

In Northern Ireland, the ability of paramilitary groups to create the cognition for 'counter-hegemony' was tied to the ideological control of certain places.[3] The symbolically coded identification and political control of places such as 'South Armagh', 'Ardoyne' and 'the Shankill' have been the most important determinant in the reproduction of both Irish republicanism and Ulster loyalism. But the creation of ethno-sectarian enclaves has not simply been posited around a desire to create 'places' within which the community-based 'self' gains a sense of security. In addition, the promotion of residential segregation regulates ethno-sectarian violence via a range of complex spatial devices. These include the narratives of 'protection', marching, schooling and the enactment of violence.

Such narratives and realities are in themselves inter-linked devices in the whole reproduction of violence and conflict. It is in this sense that the disquisition, which shapes ethno-sectarianism in Belfast, is interpreted through what are essentially 'lived experiences'. In particular, the violent defence of terrains of material reference and the perception that communally defined boundaries are, or could be, altered by the inward migration of an ethno-sectarian 'other' means that a reactive consciousness is not solely reproduced through ideology itself, but also in physical and spatial terms.[4] The objectifying instrument of violence has throughout Belfast's history produced cultural practices, symbolic understandings and the sanctification of conflictual enactment in place. Belfast is separated by both physical and mental constructions and composed of sites within which enmity between

Catholic and Protestant communities is ever present, as is fear and the avoidance of the ethnic 'other'.[5]

However, as argued by Shirlow (2003), much work on residential segregation tends to overplay the simple cataloguing of people and ignores the nature of political heterogeneity within ethno-sectarian groups. This chapter argues that ethno-sectarian identities are complicated by the existence, within segregated communities, of populations which are non-sectarian. Many individuals in fact repudiate symbolic representations and discursive hegemonies that are tied to sectarianized discourses. The existence of those who do not assent to sectarianized modes of living and loyalty indicates that ethno-sectarian boundaries are less fixed than has been assumed. Crucial to the interpretation of conflict transformation in Northern Ireland is the argument that the reasons for ethno-sectarian separation are not merely framed by the poor intercommunity relationships but also by the fact that non-sectarians are rarely prepared to challenge 'community' based renditions. In crude terms they are afraid to talk out due to intracommunity based threats.

Unfortunately the construction of sectarianized affiliation casts those who do not accept a repetitive ethno-sectarian discourse as deviant and treacherous. Evidently, the implied deterritorialization needed in order to shift Northern Irish society toward more agreed and agreeable forms of political ownership and consensus building remains difficult and incomplete.

Segregated spaces

It is difficult to gauge the exact level of segregation within Belfast for several reasons. Firstly, segregation is relative and is understood via various interpretations. Some places are more segregated than others, and within such places there are active practices which aim to maintain a form of community dominance. Mixed places are obviously less physically segregated but citizens living in shared environments may maintain a dependence upon institutions and sites that are chosen via ethno-sectarian attachment. Examples include schools, sports clubs and various leisure and consumption sites. In effect, mixing does not mean that the residents of such places integrate around the same series of cultural and social practices.

There is also a suggestion that as socially mobile Catholics move into mixed middle-income communities there is a tendency for some Protestants to move out. Whether there is any validity in such a suggestion is unproven but it is evident that many private housing arenas within the city have been moving towards more significant shares of Catholics.[6] These shifts in the ethno-sectarian composition of the private housing market are based less upon a desire to create mixed communities and more upon the emergence of a socially and increasing spatially mobile Catholic community.[7]

Secondly, the spatial units that are used to construct census boundaries are altered on each occasion that a census is undertaken. Therefore, without available data, it is impossible to link each census together to determine how and in what ways the religious demography of places has altered. Finally, census based data may suggest that an output area is mixed, even though it is evident that such units contain populations living within different parts of the spatial unit that is being measured. Ethno-sectarian divisions within such units have never been adequately determined and as a result of this the extent of segregation is hidden within asocial units of reference.

As shown in Table 15.1, the majority of persons from a Catholic or Protestant community background live in places that are at least 81 per cent Catholic or Protestant. Just over two-thirds of Catholics (67.3 per cent) and 73 per cent of Protestants live in such places. A mere 10.7 per cent of Catholics and 7.0 per cent of Protestants live in places that are between 41–60 per cent Catholic or Protestant, places that could be described as mixed.

A common source used in order to determine if segregation is growing or declining is that of the Northern Ireland Housing Executive (NIHE). NIHE judges housing areas as 'segregated' if over 90 per cent of residents are from a particular community background. Its research constantly confirms that around 98 per cent of NIHE estates in Belfast are segregated compared to a rate of 71 per cent for Northern Ireland.[8] The general conclusion is that segregation within social housing estates is rising.

As shown in Table 15.1, the mosaic of segregation within the city is complex given the interlinked issues of scale and interpretation. There are evidently large areas, such as West Belfast, the Shankill and extensive parts of East Belfast, that are dominated by one of the two main communities. Such large zones are places within which the interface between communities tends towards historical lineage.

As can be seen in Map 15.1, the intricacy of territorial divisions in North Belfast is complex and acute, and this partly explains the performance of

Table 15.1: Segregation in Belfast by community background

% population bands	Community background: % of total Catholic population in band	Community background: % of total Protestant population in band
0–20	4.7	3.4
21–40	3.6	7.3
41–60	10.7	7.0
61–80	13.8	9.3
81–90	9.3	28.4
91–100	58.0	44.6

Source: Census of Population 2001.

Map 15.1: Prominent interfaces, segregation and politically motivated deaths in Belfast from 1969–(October) 2005

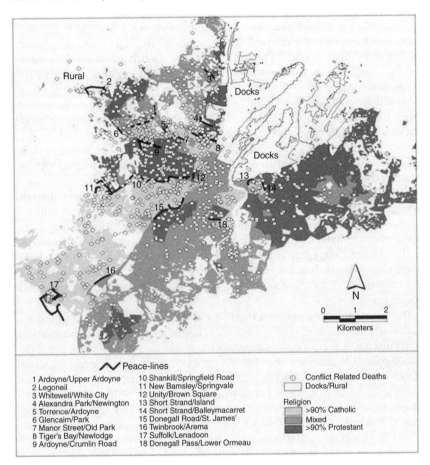

Source: author's calculations.

much recent interface violence. Within North Belfast, the borders between nationalist/republican and unionist/loyalist communities are being shaped by a series of demographic shifts which in particular are linked to the exit of Protestants. 'Exit' has been increasingly identified as a strategy for coping when the residents of a community – usually Protestant – have drifted away from interfaces and back to a hinterland that offers solace and security.[9] This is true, but it is also evident that outward migration has been linked to social mobility and poor housing stock. Associated with 'exit' is a process of residualization, whereby remaining Protestant communities tend towards marginal communities that are characterized by high rates of social deprivation and poverty. Within social housing areas dominated by Catholics there remains a higher demand for social housing and thus a claim that interface boundaries should be moved to accommodate need. Within these twin processes lie senses of territorial decline among Protestants and frustration within republican areas.[10] The ability to alter such boundaries to accommodate need remains unlikely due to the threat of violence from within Ulster loyalism.

Boundaries within North Belfast have tended to increase as mixed areas such as the Antrim Road and Cliftonville Road have become more nationalist/republican. New interfaces have also been created between private housing areas and public sector housing estates. The interface between White City and Whitewell has become a relatively new arena within which ethno-sectarian violence is being played out. This growth in violence is directly linked to the private housing community around Whitewell being redefined as a predominantly nationalist/republican community, whilst the established and predominantly loyalist/unionist White City remains unchanged due to the majority of social housing that exists there. Such increased segregation reflects the fluid nature of demographic shifts within the private housing sector, whereas the social housing stock, and the commitment to identity within such places, presents more rigidified boundaries.[11]

The most evident interfaces marked on Map 15.1 are those denoted by high walls that demarcate and disrupt the boundaries between communities. Some interfaces are not demarcated in such an obvious manner. The interface on Skegoneill Avenue in North Belfast, for example, is demarcated by a series of derelict homes and flags that mark the cessation of nationalist/republican space and the beginning of loyalist/unionist territory. Other interfaces are simply understood through a knowledge of ethno-sectarian division, and can be marked by material forms such as a lamp post or bus stop. The 25 officially recognized interfaces in Belfast cover 22 wards and of these, 17 (77 per cent) are in the top 10 per cent deprived wards as measured by the Noble Index.[12] Added to this are the daily experiences of people living in an area affected by often low-level but constant violence, pervasive fear and the threat of attack.

Geography of death

Map 15.1 illustrates conflict-related deaths in Belfast and their relationship to interface walls and segregation between 1969 and 2005. A third of the victims of politically motivated violence were murdered within 250 metres of an interface, and around 70 per cent of deaths occurred (but representing only 53 per cent of Belfast's population) within 500 metres of all segregated boundaries. In addition, over 80 per cent of deaths occurred within places that were at least 90 per cent Catholic or Protestant. Around 1400 persons died in the Belfast Urban Area as a result of the contemporary conflict. Of these 922 (65 per cent) were civilians. In relation to combatants, Royal Ulster Constabulary and Ulster Defence Regiment members made up 5.5 per cent of all deaths, compared to British soldiers constituting 9.8 per cent of all fatal casualties. Loyalist and republican paramilitaries constituted 5.9 per cent and 11.5 per cent of all fatalities, respectively.

Over three-quarters of all civilians (78.3 per cent) were killed in either North or West Belfast. Similarly, 90.6 per cent of British soldiers, 65 per cent of loyalists and 84.7 per cent of republican paramilitaries were killed within these same two geographic areas. East Belfast contained 9.1 per cent of all fatalities and most of these deaths were located around the Short Strand–Ballymacarrett interface, the only significant ethno-sectarian boundary within that part of the city. The majority of civilians killed in South Belfast were murdered within the city centre. However, pockets of death around the Ormeau Road and Donegall Pass interface are also significant. Evidently, the more prosperous parts of both East and South Belfast endured the lowest levels of politically motivated violence.

Such a high rate of violence within highly segregated places indicates the link between factors such as residential segregation, interfacing and also social class. It is not surprising that violence encouraged political and cultural retrenchment and the physical and cognitive remapping of the city. The reorganization of space due to violence increased separation and re-emphasized the fundamentals of ethno-sectarian 'difference'.[13] The share of persons who lived in Belfast and died in the city is closely correlated to their home address. Nearly one-third of all victims were murdered within their homes or only a matter of metres from their place of residence. In sum, death within one's own community was commonplace and furthered the idea that violence was based upon an assault upon community. Given the proximity of death to residence it is evident why conflict-related deaths are understood within discourses of group suffering. The proximity of so many deaths to homes forged strong and at times endurable notions of group-based losses, and in so doing diluted the capacity to see beyond violence, and see it as anything but community based assault. The parochial nature of violent enactment aided the overall process of territorial entrapment.

The imagination of difference

The initial rise in violence in the 1970s complicated – and provided depth to – what had been noticeable but relatively benign forms of separation. Violence may have become less prominent as the course of conflict altered, but the enactment of the most significant form of intercommunity violence since the formation of the Northern Ireland state polarized ideological conflict and contrasted the experience of communities. Violence sparked the imagination of difference and in so doing created new discourses concerning conflicts of non violent interest. The general failure to recognize the difference between non violent conflict and violent conflict has impeded the capacity to build meaningful political progress. The problem was never simply the enactment of violence, but that violence gave meaning and legitimacy to wider political, cultural and residential forms of separation. Violence, it should be recognized, was only one form of conflict influenced behaviour.

The negative image that brutal lines of division, physical dereliction and poverty project to a wider audience can also be a major obstacle to investment and tourism.[14] These policy costs are outlined in Table 15.2 and as shown, the extent of the problems caused by interfacing stretches from the monetary to the symbolic. It is also important to note that there are forms of masked interfacing that are based upon hidden forms of separation. In

Table 15.2: Policy costs of interfacing in Belfast

Issue	Description of need
Activity segregation	Activity segregation resulting in facilities and services 'trapped' in the territory of the 'other' out-group
Community institutions and critical mass	Locality population change undermines local institutional capacity thus accelerating 'exit' and the critical mass of the community necessary for sustainability
Deprivation	High rates of socio-economic deprivation reflecting the residents' weak bargaining power in the housing allocation and transfer system
Quality of life	Pervasive sense of fear, danger and direct violence to people and property
Death and injury	Higher rate of death and violence in areas where the ethno-sectarian map is most contested
Demographic imbalance and housing need	High demand in republican/nationalist areas fuelled by higher than average fertility rates, family sizes and younger age profiles. Protestant demographics generate comparatively less housing need, particularly given the wider choice of housing search territory
Symmetrical land and property markets	The reproduction of segregated space through symmetrical and often self-contained property markets
Direct costs	Physical construction of interfaces, buffer zones and security adaptations to property
Blight of land and property	Land and housing near interface areas blighted by fear, violence and lack of investment confidence
Image	Negative imagery produced by walls of division, sectarian graffiti and physical dereliction to investors and tourists

some instances, avoidance tactics are a benign form of removing the capacity for confrontation or respecting the dissimilar beliefs of those spoken to. However, outward friendliness towards residents from the 'other' ethnosectarian group can also be accompanied by disguised emotions based upon mistrust and even concealed loathing. These latter behaviours are founded upon masking emotions, which betray deeper senses of ethnosectarian angst.

Despite the roll out of 'conflict transformation', it is evident that violence has remained a relative and constant feature of Northern Irish society since the cease-fires of 1994. A common form of violence has been a swathe of sectarian attacks upon symbolic sites such as churches, Orange Halls and Gaelic Athletic Association clubs. There have been 594 reported attacks upon these symbolic sites. In addition, there were a staggering 6623 sectarian incidents in North Belfast between 1996 and 2004.

Living at the interface

Interfaces may vary with regard to form, style, meaning and both visibility and invisibility. However, they will most certainly be known and understood by those who live within segregated communities. This knowledge of spatial demarcation is based upon territorial marking and the twin processes of telling and spatial identification. Such processes are a common feature for many who have grown up within the city. The marking of space is thus reinforced by a sectarianized and location driven knowledge. The telling of division and the 'need' for separation are also founded upon a system of signs through which ethno-sectarian belonging is determined within both obvious and discrete spatial settings.[15]

Due to segregation and related mobility issues there are whole swathes of the city that are virtually unknown to citizens living within the city. Persons of a pensionable age seem to possess a more collective and knowledgeable geography of the city. Such knowledge predates the severe sundering of places that preceded the late 1960s. This does not mean that such persons are not aware of boundaries between communities, but these interfaces were, prior to the 1970s, easily crossed and at times traversed with enthusiasm. Similarly, for older age groups there have been more evident forms of intercommunity engagement, especially with regard to sharing space. As noted by an interview respondent, aged 68, from the predominantly republican New Lodge area:

> Do you see out there in the street? That is where we all built the bonfire for the 11th night. It was also the place where we built another bonfire to celebrate Our Lady's Day on the 15th of August.[16] There was [*sic*] never any problems living and sharing together.[17]

Fear of being attacked by the 'other' community is central in determining low levels of intercommunity contact.[18] However, a subjective reading of such information masks a series of relationships complicated by age, gender and intracommunity threat.

The following was observed from a series of surveys and interviews conducted by the author in interface areas between 2001 and 2004. Pensioners, as noted above, are those least likely to perceive the 'other' community as a menacing group. Secondly, a small group of non-pensioners are non-sectarian, and like many pensioners do not believe that the 'other' community should be represented as a homogenous cabal intent upon harming them and their community. Thirdly, around two-thirds of all respondents were found to be influenced by a highly subjective ethno-sectarian discourse. Within this group it was evident that the level of sectarianism varied and in particular, for many their sectarianism was driven by events such as Orange parades and rioting.

Interviews among pensioners disclosed that the majority are not afraid to enter 'alien' territory for four main reasons. Firstly, social relationships that existed prior to the contemporary conflict have tended to endure and there is an active desire to maintain such friendships. Secondly, pensioners were three times as likely as the other age groups to have either Catholic or Protestant relatives within each respective community. This would insinuate that intermarriages were more numerous in such places prior to the present conflict. Thirdly, older people tended to be repulsed by paramilitary activities, which they contended had destroyed a previous society within which community relations were relatively 'normalized'. Although pensioners conceded that their communities had been victimized by sectarian violence, it was also argued that sections of their community had been involved in transgressive sectarian acts. Fourthly, religious conviction and a belief that it is immoral to judge was an apparent feature of many discussions with this group. Apparently lived social histories, within which there has been an extensive form of intercommunity linkage, dilute the rationale of sectarian belief, and as a result fear of the 'other' community is somewhat tempered by more experienced forms of cultural understanding.

Stronger and more sectarian attitudes were located among those aged between 18 and 55. In general, members of this group stated that their failure to engage in cross community activities was due to fear of attack by the 'other' community. There were no observable differences in attitude that could be related to gender. For this group the experience of residential segregation was influenced by exclusive and sectarian representations and the presentation of 'tradition' as unproblematic. Sectarianism is interpreted not as a repressive relationship but as a means through which truth can be articulated. Space, for those who articulate sectarian discourses, is seen to function as an object that hosts historical 'unquestioned' and collective discourses. Community and history, for this group, serve as microterritorial constructions, which reinforce the way in which geography presents sectarian hostility as a valid politicization of space.

Among those who advance sectarian discourses, materialization of residential segregation is imperative in order to functionalize and advance topographic conflict. At every point of conversation, among those who maintain sectarian narratives, it was acknowledged that all social space is coded through a sectarian analysis. It was commonly understood, within this group, that urban space is produced by ideological and physical separation. However, one of the most pronounced factors that separates the sectarian group from the non-sectarian group was the manner in which they eulogized, through the expression of devotion, the communities within which they lived. Members of the sectarian group constantly viewed their community via utopian discourses of integrity, loyalty, kinship and symbolic purity. In comparison, non-sectarians were more likely to denote that 'their' communities contained multiple forms of impurity, transgression and deviant behaviour.

Within such a climate of ethno-sectarian cognition and telling, intercommunity contact was discussed via tales of violence and aggression. Violence from within the 'home' community which had been directed at the 'contrary' community was articulated as a strategy of defence.

Members within the non-sectarian group – who were not pensioners and who constituted around a third of all respondents – felt unthreatened by intercommunity contact. In most instances, individuals within this group contended that they were as likely to be attacked within their own community as they were if they travelled into areas dominated by the 'other' community. For these respondents it was unambiguously stated that fear of violent attack was not merely based upon a sectarianized consciousness. This non-sectarian group shared a similar profile of violent abuse from the 'other' community as those located within the larger sectarian group. However, they were twice as likely as their sectarian counterparts to be victims of physical assaults by members of their 'own' community. Many stated when interviewed that such attacks had occurred due to respondents articulating either anti-sectarian discourses or 'insolently' challenging the activities of certain groups.

This non-sectarian group was twice as likely as their sectarian counterparts to work in places dominated by the 'other' religion. This tended to be supported by a sentiment that individuals had a duty to challenge community divisions. All held meaningful friendships with either Catholics or Protestants. Reasons for being less sectarian were eclectic in range. Some stated that their anti-sectarianism was based upon religious conviction. Others stated that an interest in particular types of music had drawn them into positive relationships with members of the 'other' religious group. For some, self-education and an interest in left-wing ideology were pinpointed as catalysts in the challenge of sectarian animosities. However, non-sectarian respondents were not apolitical. Virtually all from republican areas voted for Sinn Fein but in each instance stressed that they were opposed to violence. Similarly, the Protestant respondents all supported unionist/loyalist politics, but as with their Catholic counterparts were against the use of violence. However, the factor that was most commonly mentioned among this non-sectarian group was an acknowledgement that they could no longer discuss their cross community contacts or antisectarian discourses publicly. Each stated that they had been berated when neighbours and family members had found out that they had consorted with members of the 'other' religious group. In certain cases, members of the non-sectarian group stated that they knew of instances in which people who had articulated non-sectarian views were forced to move out of their homes and who had in extreme cases been murdered.

In virtually all of the interviews with the non-sectarian group it was stressed that respondents did not want others in their 'own' community to know that they engaged in a range of cross community activities. Most stated that they would rather lie to their neighbours than tell them that they had been socializing with members of the 'other' religious group. In terms of politics, the majority of these respondents were critical of the sectarianism within the political parties that they supported but would not discuss this with people they did not trust. Several stated that they would repackage the goods they bought that were obviously purchased in shops located in the territory of the 'other' religious group.

Without doubt, the capacity of this group to undermine the power of community belonging and in so doing challenge the orthodoxy of ethno-sectarianism, through delivering new narratives of cross community camaraderie, has ensured that they remain, among sectarians, as a distrusted and disliked out-group. This non-sectarian group has the capacity to deliver an alternative process of 'telling' within which kinship and the ideological construction of space are identified as being part of a process of control and ethno-sectarian practice. However, there is a near constant refusal to state non-sectarian beliefs within public arenas. Most non-sectarians spoke of a fear of being identified as having viewpoints that contradicted the more predominant community beliefs and cultural values.

The desire, in short, of those who promote ethno-sectarianism has been to silence those who wish to promote intercommunity narratives, because of the threat non-sectarians pose to the edifice of community devotion and spatialized cultures of sectarianized affiliation.

In combining the attitude of pensioners and those who are non-sectarian it is clear that a sizeable minority of respondents hold attitudes at odds with the sectarianized nature of affiliation and habituation. In this sense, such individuals hold a belief that the 'other' group is not as menacing and threatening as is assumed by their respective neighbours. However, given the hostility that is directed by members of their own community towards those who are non-sectarian, it is evident that no arena exists within which to articulate non-sectarian beliefs. Without doubt paradigms of ethno-sectarian purity and impurity predicate social relations to such an extent, and with such power, that the capacity exists to silence the dialogue capable of challenging ethno-sectarian discourses. This implies that telling, violence and the reproduction of fear are based upon sectarianized relationships which aim not only to reproduce residential segregation but to also suppress any belief system which identifies ethno-sectarian purity as a socially constructed and imagined set of relationships. Without doubt, preserving the capacity to control the propaganda of ethno-sectarian belonging is facilitated through spreading the myth that the 'other' community is to be feared. Ensuring that sectarianized places remain will continue to be achieved through endorsing the morality of cultural and political sectarianism.

Conclusion

The evidence contained within this chapter highlights how important it is to focus upon the relative autonomy of ideology and collective consciousness as a determining factor on social action; the way, in other words, material, political and cultural change is perceived within the context of a pre-existing, if discursive, ideological framework. Evidently, among many, and despite political change, ideology still expresses a social group's need for a communal set of images whereby it can represent itself to itself and to others. However, the tradition of mythic idealizations whereby identity is aligned with a stable, predictable and repeatable order of meanings does not – within the Northern Irish context – provide inter-community senses of belonging. More crucially, community based self-representation assumes the form of a mythic reiteration of purity and self-preservation.[19]

The realities of interfacing and ethno-sectarian discord sit awkwardly with regard to the spectacle of renewed civic 'pride' and new arenas of consumption (such as Belfast's Waterfront Hall, Odyssey Project and Laganside developments). A burgeoning service sector – which offers a more sophisticated commodity mix compared to the dismal decay of the 1970s and 1980s – has been central in casting Belfast as a 'normal' and 'rehabilitated' site within which conflict transformation is delivering socio-cultural dividends. However, for many, especially those living in interfaced areas, the thriving sophistication and images of advancement that state agencies and media cast are regarded as fictitiously deep.

A further limitation is the interpretation that new environments of trust and dialogue will emerge between communities, without any consideration that identity formation in Northern Ireland is based upon a series of in-built mechanisms that aim to deny the logic of the 'other' side.[20] The success of state management of community resources has been to shift resistance to the state into new processes of lobbying and grant provision. Thus the problems that communities face can, it is assumed, be resolved via institutionalized forms at the local level.

Such a process of management founders when ethno-sectarian disputes over marching and housing issues create disorder and draw communities into confrontation with the power block that is built around the state and the police. Inhabitants now live within an environment in which financial and political resources are localized, and many of those communities and individuals who receive such support are no longer considered as being both politically deviant or socially transgressive. In practical terms the state has shifted towards a more pragmatic relationship in which the community/voluntary sector is utilized as a circuit breaker of communal angst. The goal of the state is to provide facilities which allow the community/voluntary sector to police themselves. This has been a significant development in that – especially with regard to former combatants – a relationship has been established within which communal disorder can be solved within a local context. However, as noted, the problem is that when ethno-sectarian issues arise the relationship with the state reverts to positions of open hostility. In many instances, the new relationship between the state and the community/voluntary sector is improving but ultimately it is somewhat schizophrenic.

It would be churlish to deny that there have not been positive outcomes which have emanated from reductions in political violence, cross border referenda, the creation of a Northern Ireland Assembly and the growth in a form of cross party negotiation. However, there is a need to stress that within certain areas the reproduction of ethno-sectarianism via threat, attack, fear and avoidance is still commonplace.

As such the potential to create intercommunity understandings of fear is, in terms of politics, marginalized by wider ethno-sectarian readings. Indeed, for political actors the capacity to win political support has been based upon delivering a singular narrative of victimhood and exclusion. To now accept that such political vocabularies and actions victimize the 'collective other' would be politically unwise.[21]

For those who wish to create a non-sectarian society there is a need to indicate how conceptions of identity reproduce monolithic nationalist depictions, which thrive upon ethno-sectarian readings of the 'collective self'.[22] It is only through accepting the complex relationships between place and identity – which are central to any narration or understanding of community devotion – that alternative collective action and socio-cultural modification can begin. If anything, the desire is to create a Northern Ireland within which geography, in its present representation, matters less.

Notes

1. Douglas 1997.
2. Anderson, Shuttleworth 1998.
3. Elliott 2002.
4. Feldman 1991; Murtagh 2002.
5. Shirlow 2001; Whyte 1990.
6. Boal, Murray 1977; Poole, Doherty 1996.
7. Murtagh 2002.
8. Northern Ireland Housing Executive NIHE 1999.
9. Poole, Doherty 1996.
10. Jarman 1997.
11. Coulter 1999.
12. The Noble Index (2001) is a multivariate measurement of deprivation in Northern Ireland.
13. Graham 1997.
14. Neill 2004.
15. Burton 1978.
16. 11 July is the night during which those who support the Orange Order host fires to celebrate the 12th of July. 15 August is the Feast of the Assumption, celebrated by Catholics and the Ancient Order of Hibernians.
17. Cited in Shirlow, Murtagh 2006.
18. Graham, Shirlow 1998.
19. Bairner, Shirlow 1998; Shirlow 2001.
20. Murray, Murtagh 2004.
21. Ruane, Todd 2003.
22. Shirlow, Shuttleworth 1999; Shirlow 2001.

16

Some Way to Go to a Shared Future: Groundwork in Belfast

Mary McKee and Sylvia Gordon

Northern Ireland has a recent history of civil unrest and brutal sectarian violence. Referred to locally as 'The Troubles', the period has left some 3600 people dead and upwards of 30,000 people injured. To give an idea of the scale of carnage, for a population the size of England this equates to approximately 120,000 deaths and approaching 1 million people injured. It is estimated that the number of people closely associated to those either killed or injured is about half the Northern Ireland population. Divisions exist in all societies. However, unlike many other places the divisions in Northern Ireland are still a contributing factor to violence.

Since 1994 Northern Ireland has been undergoing a 'peace process' comprising British and Irish government efforts to facilitate an internal accommodation leading to political devolution. The process has created space for a variety of attempts to counter ethnic hostility, suspicion, fear and mistrust. However, despite this:

- there is evidence of deepening community divisions in many parts of Northern Ireland;
- there have been growing levels of disillusionment in parts of the Protestant/unionist/loyalist community with the peace process in general;
- political development in Northern Ireland has been slow, and the Northern Ireland Assembly remains in suspension;
- there is a marked increase in anti-social behaviour, with associated unacceptable levels of violence and criminality;
- the Northern Ireland economy still faces major structural challenges and growing levels of economic inactivity.

It is against this background that Groundwork Northern Ireland (NI) has established, in the opinion of the authors, a distinctive approach to working within a highly segregated society. Specifically, the organization has developed a framework which draws together community safety, community relations and capacity building in neighbourhoods through environmental regeneration. At its best this is seen as a bridge across cultural difference.

This chapter describes how Groundwork NI is using environmental regeneration as a catalyst for trying to move towards a more peaceful society. Two case studies are illustrated, and as a learning organization the major self-reflexive question is posed: is the work of Groundwork NI a catalyst for moving towards a cohesive society, or is it contributing to a model of benign apartheid where there is separate development with limited contact?

Groundwork Northern Ireland

Groundwork NI is a not-for-profit organization working in partnership to effect regeneration and renewal in the most marginalized communities through a process of environmental regeneration. The work involves:

Building stronger neighbourhoods

Groundwork NI makes a long-term commitment to supporting neighbourhoods viewed as disadvantaged. Training and support are provided to help people living in these neighbourhoods get more involved in making decisions about their locality and endeavour to help them understand in direct tangible ways the benefits that peace can bring. The organization works with people to improve the appearance of their streets, parks and housing estates, and also encourages them to participate in civic networks by getting to know other people in their area and – more ambitiously – beyond, where people are also faced with problems of anti-social behaviour and fear of crime.

Reconnecting people with their surroundings

Groundwork NI helps people turn derelict land and waste ground into attractive and valuable spaces, from small community gardens or allotments to major new parks or leisure facilities.

By doing so, the aim is to create landscapes that promote better health and encourage pride in place. The organization works to ensure that people are fully involved in designing and improving new public spaces such as sports zones and community gardens. Groundwork NI also encourages people to find out more about the local history and culture of their area, and helps them understand and value the wider environment. In this regard the philosophy can be said to be loosely informed by the environmental citizenship ideals of Local Agenda 21, now Local Action 21, reaffirmed at the Earth Summit in Johannesburg in 2002.

Realizing young people's potential

Young people are being involved in a range of activities designed to bring them into contact with other people in their community and to increase their own confidence and self-esteem. Groundwork NI's aim is to make young people interested in the place where they live and to help them play a full and active part in society. This is accomplished by encouraging them to take part in practical activities such as making videos about life in their neighbourhood or planning and designing their own play areas or youth centres. Most of these activities are specifically targeted in areas where there are high levels of crime, as a way of harnessing young people's energy and reducing anti-social behaviour.

The overall approach provides synergy for addressing some of the most fundamental social and environmental problems faced by a society emerging out of conflict. These include:

- fear and mistrust of the 'other', against constant background levels of intercommunity and intracommunity violence and intimidation;
- sense of alienation, loss of sense of belonging, especially in areas of high social/economic need and where there is weak community and physical infrastructure;
- sense of powerlessness to change the environment and/or tackle key issues such as degeneration of physical space.

Conceptual framework: further considerations

Embracing the generic principle of community cohesion, it is suggested that Groundwork has developed a distinctive and innovative approach, an approach which provides a practical environmental framework for establishing mutually dependent, reciprocal and respectful relationships between the politically and physically segregated 'interface' communities of Belfast and of Northern Ireland.[1] The Groundwork model is theoretically informed by social capital theory[2] and in practice encompasses single identity work – building confidence within communities – alongside or providing a platform for cross community work. The overall objective is to build more cohesive and integrated local communities to 'promote good relations between people from different religious traditions, political outlooks and racial groups'.[3]

'Community cohesion' has developed as a key concept in response to the riots and disorder that occurred in a number of towns in the north of England during 2001. A number of government commissioned reports responded to these events: the Bradford Review team,[4] the Burnley Task Force,[5] the Oldham Independent Review,[6] the Independent Review Team,[7] and the Ministerial Group on Public Order and Community Cohesion.[8] The findings of all of these studies emphasized the need for government, and local authorities, to initiate comprehensive strategies to address increasing social fragmentation.

In a report to the UK Home Office from the Independent Review Team, social capital (which might formerly have been called a sense of neighbourliness, built up through trust which comes with common interaction) was identified as a prerequisite for community cohesion. Important are an absence of intimidation and incivility alongside the presence of tolerance, respect for diversity and inter-group co-operation.[9] A definition of a 'cohesive community' is offered here, where:

- there is common vision and a sense of belonging for all communities;
- the diversity of people's backgrounds and circumstances is appreciated and positively valued;
- those from similar backgrounds have similar life opportunities;
- strong and positive relationships are being developed between people from different backgrounds in the workplace, in schools and within neighbourhoods.[10]

Practice in Belfast: case study 1 – Tigers Bay

Situated in inner North Belfast, Tigers Bay is a Protestant housing estate located within the thirteenth most deprived ward in Northern Ireland. The community's general perception of isolation is compounded by the fact that the area is bounded by three interfaces with the Catholic/nationalist community. In Northern Ireland an 'interface' is defined as 'a common boundary line between a predominantly Protestant/unionist area and a predominantly Catholic/nationalist area. An interface community is a community which lives alongside an interface.'[11] All interface communities are typified by high social and economic deprivation. Of all deaths in Belfast due to politically motivated violence, 84 per cent have occurred within one kilometre of an interface (Chapter 15).

Interface areas have suffered disproportionately since the start of 'the Troubles' in other ways as well, as people have foregone employment – as well as access to facilities and services – that are located in places perceived as dominated by the 'other'. In some instances, people forego basic social services. Interface areas are characterized by lack of public/private investment, environmental dereliction, violence and fear.[12]

The project, developed by Groundwork NI in collaboration with the Tigers Bay community, involved regenerating a piece of derelict land directly at the interface that had become a gathering point for local youths. At this location one young man had been killed during a riot.

Community activists were keen to do something to improve the site and to develop resources for young people. The project, an all-weather multi-sports facility and games area, involved the local community in the overall design, development and implementation of the project.

Although the project did not involve any engagement with neighbouring nationalist communities, it did address displays of loyalist symbolism that are generally considered objectionable by Catholics. The site was overlooked by a provocative paramilitary mural, depicting hooded gunmen, and in its derelict state this provided ammunition for stone throwers during times of disorder. In Northern Ireland, the boundaries of interface communities are often demarcated by physical manifestations of sectarianism – visible displays designed to instil fear, not only to the 'other' community, but also within residents' own community.

Figure 16.1: Tigers Bay: before Groundwork intervention

Certain difficulties emerged during the project. These included resistance to the removal of the paramilitary mural, debate over the name of the final project and the misgivings of local politicians that persons linked to paramilitary organizations would gain credibility from the project. Each of these issues required negotiation with the local community, but eventually Groundwork NI was able to maintain its position: the mural was removed, the name was politically neutral and concerns of the politicians were acknowledged and countered. In evaluating the success of the project in fostering community cohesion, it is necessary to remember the limitations. To an extent, paramilitary structures probably did benefit from their active involvement in supporting the construction of the 'Mount Multi-Sports

Figure 16.2: Tigers Bay: after Groundwork intervention

Zone'. But such organizations play numerous roles in local communities, and it is important for them to be encouraged to engage in positive community development work and to recognize the benefits of such activities.

As mentioned above, the project did not involve dialogue with neighbouring Catholic communities, and many activists in Tigers Bay resist such engagement. They argue that if relations remain peaceful with their Catholic neighbours that is sufficient and there is no need for dialogue. Such arguments present a key challenge to organizations such as Groundwork NI. Groundwork does not accept the hard line approach of 'separate development with limited contact' that appears to be widely favoured among Protestants, according to the findings of the 'A Shared Future' consultation.[13] Practical steps which it is contended must be developed to overcome this benign apartheid model – and a key element of single identity work undertaken using the Groundwork approach – require that it is situated within a wider theoretical model which recognizes the importance of 'bridging social capital' and the need to develop cross community contact.[14]

Despite limitations, the Tigers Bay project has proved a success in transforming derelict land into a valuable resource for the community. The project has helped to consolidate relationships between Groundwork NI and the community of Tigers Bay, and between Tigers Bay and other statutory agencies. However, by creating a resource for single identity use, the question is posed whether the work of Groundwork NI is a catalyst for moving towards a cohesive society as hoped, or is it contributing to a model of benign apartheid where there is separate development with limited contact?

Practice in Belfast: case study 2 – East Belfast's Youth and Environment Programme

Based in East Belfast, the 'Youth and Environment Programme' was a Groundwork project that involved substantial cross community contact. This project was set up in 2002, following on from the Tigers Bay experience; it involved working with young people in two neighbouring interface communities (the Protestant area of Inner East Belfast and the Catholic Short Strand Estate) on issues related both to environmental improvements and mental health.

The Youth and Environment Programme employed two members of staff who were experienced community activists in the local areas and had extensive contacts with groups and individuals. The aim was to build on these contacts and develop links with young people who were not involved in organized activities and were liable to become involved in anti-social behaviour.

At the beginning the project, violent disorder and rioting broke out on the interface. The trouble was unexpected and also extremely violent, and it persisted throughout Summer and into Autumn 2002. This disrupted the planned programme, and much of the first year was spent responding to the local context, 'firefighting' activities and building relationships in single identity work within each of the communities.

Once the initial 'start up' hurdles abated, the Youth and Environment Programme developed a broad range of activities with young people, involving both single identity work in the two areas and on a cross community basis. The single identity work incorporated a range of environmental regeneration projects, including removal of paramilitary graffiti, design and painting of murals on either side of an interface barrier, a community arts project, design of community gardens, seating and signage, and organizing general clean up in the two areas.

Figure 16.3 depicts one of Belfast's newest interfaces: it divides the Catholic/nationalist Short Strand from the Protestant/unionist Inner East Belfast, which comprised the project area. At the last count, Belfast had 37 physical interfaces which is an increase of 15 since 1994, when the paramilitary ceasefires were called and the peace process began. These are powerful symbols of cultural exclusion, and hopefully not the future of the European city.

In this project Groundwork NI worked in partnership with young people on both sides of the intimidating barrier, facilitating a process where it

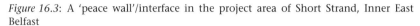

Figure 16.3: A 'peace wall'/interface in the project area of Short Strand, Inner East Belfast

is believed those involved took positive ownership of space. The project incorporated a range of cross community activities. These included building links between local football (Protestant) and Gaelic Athletic Association (Catholic) teams, and publication of two reports giving voice to the experiences of young people in the area.[15] The project provided training for young people in a range of activities such as conflict management and mediation techniques. A youth forum was created, involving ten young people, with equal numbers from both cultural backgrounds, which was involved in the design of the entire programme. Two staff members coordinated their work so that parallel activities took place on both sides of the interface simultaneously.

In evaluating the impact of the Youth and Environment Programme, it is not possible simply to gauge outcomes and outputs without taking into account the fluidity of the general political context. In many ways the positive work in East Belfast is more surprising given the fraught local circumstances. Still Groundwork asks itself the question in the spirit of taking a critical stance on the organization's interventions: is the work of Groundwork NI contributing to a more cohesive society through relationship and trust building, or is it creating better informed bigots?

Theory and practice revisited

Tigers Bay: 'benign apartheid'?

It could be argued that by providing a resource that is exclusively used by one community, the 'separate development with limited contact' approach is being supported instead of being challenged. The 'central paradox' embraced by Dumper (1996) acknowledges how planning and urban policy – even when operating with benign intent – can inadvertently reinforce as much as ameliorate divisions in contested space.[16] It could be argued that offering each community the chance to ghettoize further and to press for its factional ethnic interest over wider civic interests leads to an even more partitioned city.[17] Groundwork is aware of such critique.

In contrast, however, Lederach's (1994) work emphasizes the need for a transformative process in peace building that prioritizes relational concerns and reconciliation at various levels and over an extended period of time. He advocates three separate levels to conflict resolution, and suggests an appropriate focus with associated activities for each. No one level can deliver reconciliation on its own, rather, levels are interdependent:

- level 1, Top Leadership (political/military/religious) with the focus on negotiation and ceasefire;
- level 2, Middle Range Leaders (social partners/opinion formers) with the focus on problem solving workshops/conflict resolution;
- level 3, Grassroots Leaders (community/NGOs) with the focus on prejudice reduction/local conflict resolution.

If the work of Groundwork NI in the Tigers Bay community of North Belfast is taken and the Lederach model applied, it can be said that the majority of the work was at level 3, with contributions to level 2, while working within the overall framework of level 1 – the processes of decommissioning, demilitarization and peace building, and so on.

An evaluation of the project concluded that – while the work remained largely single identity – there was an implicit aim to progress to work involving forms of cross cultural contact with neighbouring communities incorporating engagement in wider forums.[18]

Groundwork NI would certainly argue that, as a result of the project, the following has happened:

- funding resources are coming into the area, beginning to break the cycle of decline in Interface Areas.[19] This is particularly relevant to Tigers Bay which is perceived to be an area that has not realized the potential of EU funding opportunities, amongst other funding opportunities;
- consolidation of better relationships between development agencies and statutory service providers with the community of Tigers Bay.

The multi-sports facility was supported by Urban 2 European funding, administered through the North Belfast Partnership, Department for Social Development, Northern Ireland Housing Executive and Belfast City Council;

• the community is less suspicious, residents are more willing and able to engage in other initiatives as they have seen the tangible results in building partnerships and working collaboratively. The practical support offered by Groundwork NI has been, in the assessment of the authors, very meaningful.

Short Strand/Inner East Belfast: 'better-informed bigots'?

From the outset, the programme was innovative in that intercommunity relations were an integral part of the aims and objectives. This part was particularly ambitious as the interface communities were directly adjacent to each other. Experience shows that interface communities are more able to engage with more distant 'others', where the perceived or real threat of direct attack is less acute. If Lederach's conception of a lengthy sequencing of activities across time is employed, it is known that generational vision change may take 20 years. Therefore, in reality, what can actually be expected of a three-year programme of work, especially one which commenced as relationships deteriorated and riots broke out in June 2002?

In the first twelve months, the Youth and Environment Programme was reactive and in the mode of crisis management. However, the following two years involved more proactive work and planning. Through the development of a Youth Forum, the programme has created networks for young people in the Short Strand and Inner East Belfast communities. These networks have facilitated cross community contact allowing young people to become involved in conflict transformation work. More significantly, these networks have proven robust enough to absorb and ameliorate the effect of sectarian motivated events.

An independent evaluation of the Youth and Environment programme found that:

• prejudicial sectarian attitudes remained largely unchanged, though notably none of the young people held 'very prejudiced' beliefs;
• young people reported having more friends of a different religion and less exclusively same religion friends;
• young people were marginally more optimistic about the future of Northern Ireland;
• the level and pattern of witnessing intercommunity violence remained comparatively unchanged. However, young people reported being involved in intercommunity violence markedly less frequently. 72 per cent reported not having been involved at all in intercommunity violence during the previous month;

- young people reported experiencing significantly less emotional distress;
- young people perceived themselves much more positively, and felt that significant other members in the community (parents, guardians, teachers) had a more positive view of them;
- young people reported a substantial decrease in their level of alcohol consumption: almost 50 per cent reported no intake of alcohol during the previous month.[20]

Conclusion

The success of practical environmental projects offers examples of how regeneration work can intersect with the wider agenda of building more cohesive communities, while also bringing a voice to otherwise marginalized local groups and individuals. The Groundwork NI approach advocates:

- creating *awareness*. It is important that communities have access to appropriate expertise which will allow them to engage in steering the process from identifying issues to looking at achievable solutions;
- creating *solutions*. Effective consultation to identify and raise awareness of the key issues and to develop a consensus to take these issues forward;
- creating *partnerships*. There is the potential to develop cross community partnerships which enable communities to develop, to share visions and practical solutions that mutually respect people's identities;
- creating *practical action*. Communities must have access to support which includes the technical expertise necessary to translate the vision for their area into workable proposals which will form the basis of dialogue with key stakeholders;
- creating *resources*. This approach will create opportunities to develop meaningful partnerships that influence the allocation of resources;
- creating and assessing *the change*. Monitoring and evaluation of implementation of local planning and development initiatives, and their impact on communities, should inform ongoing development. Evaluation should bring together communities, planners and social developers (public/private/voluntary/academics) in an ongoing learning process.

Problems of diversity cannot be solved simply by policy initiatives around land use, housing and the environment, but as – in the opinion of the authors – the experience of Groundwork indicates and the framework of Lederach accepts, local action, in areas where economic and social exclusion compounds cultural conflict, is necessary as part of broader conflict management and peace building. Whether this is 'motherhood and apple pie' is for other players to judge.

Notes

1. Cameron 2006.
2. Putnam 2000.
3. Northern Ireland Act 1998, Section 75.
4. Ousley 2001.
5. Clarke 2001.
6. Ritchie 2001.
7. Cantle 2001.
8. Home Office 2001.
9. Community Cohesion Unit 2002.
10. Community Cohesion Unit 2002.
11. Belfast Interface Project 1998a.
12. O'Halloran, Shirlow, Murtagh 2004.
13. Darby, Knox 2004.
14. Belfast Interface Project 2004.
15. Hall 2003.
16. Dumper 1996.
17. Gaffikin, Morrissey 2005.
18. Jarman, Keyes, Pearce, Wilson 2005.
19. O'Halloran et al. 2004.
20. Cameron 2006.

17

Bosnian Nationalism and the Rebuilding of Sarajevo[1]

Sten Engelstoft, Guy Robinson and Alma Pobric

In a peculiar way, the 'short' 20th century both started and ended in Sarajevo.[2] It started with the triggering of the First World War by the assassination of Archduke Franz Ferdinand of Austria-Hungary in 1914 in Sarajevo and was ended by the disintegration of Yugoslavia, symbolized by the siege of that haunted city.

In many ways Yugoslavia itself and its disintegration have become the symbol of that forgone century which, as it drew to its conclusion, was in many ways characterized by a significant change in the nature of its conflicts towards differences between nationalities and identities rather than between states. Originally established in 1918 as the Kingdom of Serbs, Croats and Slovenes, the country harboured one of the great lasting cultural borders of Europe separating the country in two, with Bosnia-Herzegovina as a kind of buffer between long-time enemies: on the one side, the predominantly Roman Catholic populations of Slovenes and Croats, and on the other the Orthodox Serbs.

Bosnia-Herzegovina is constituted by a relatively large territory of 51,000 sq. km situated in the geographical heart of former Yugoslavia. It is inhabited by three large ethnic groups: Serbs, Croats and Muslims (Map 17.1). However, from a linguistic point of view Bosnia-Herzegovina is the most homogeneous of the former Yugoslav republics: almost the whole population speaks variants of Serbo-Croat, and it seems to be a tragic counterpart to G.B. Shaw's characterization of the English and the Irish: three peoples separated by a mutual language.

By and large, therefore, it is religion and pre-Yugoslav history that defined national affiliations of the three populations before the civil war of 1991; together they formed an incredible mosaic of small areas, each of which was dominated by one ethnic group or the other, and with limited possibilities to create continuous territories that were connected to bordering republics of the same ethnic majority.[3] The capital, Sarajevo, had a fairly even representation of the three major ethnic groups, and furthermore a large and flourishing community of Ladino-speaking Sephardic Jews. The city was thus regarded as a free-thinking and tolerant place.[4]

The civil war of 1991–95 changed all this. The Dayton Accords of 1995 created a new Bosnian state with two 'entities', a Serb entity and a Croat–Muslim federation, both comprising a series of partitions into ethno-nationalist entities. Certainly the treaty ended the bloody fighting, which had killed over 250,000 people, the population displacement of over half the pre-war population of 4.4 million, and as a principle ensured the later return of refugees,[5] but it also de facto rewarded the wartime ethnic cleansings.

As a result and to claim and legitimize political control over space, throughout Bosnia political leaders embarked upon their own ethnically-based political agendas all containing various competing ethno-nationalist expressions, as illustrated by manifestations of what Billig (1995) terms 'banal nationalism', referring to the ideological habits that enable

Map 17.1: Important ethnic communities of former Yugoslavia

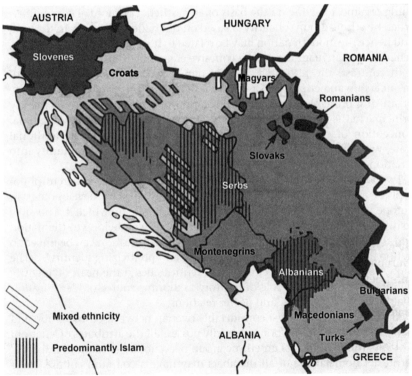

Source: after Orstrom Moller 1993; Lunden 1993; Fernandez-Armesto 1994; Pan, Pheil 2000.

nationalism to be reproduced. These expressions of nationalism can be readily observed when visiting Sarajevo.

Identity and ethno-nationalism in Sarajevo

As the establishment of the new state has unfolded, it has been possible to recognize significant aspects of the process of nation building as well as specific links between nation, state, ethnicity and territory. National identity embraces a collective political and cultural identity. The political relates to the presence of common institutions, rights and duties, whilst the cultural refers to individuals having a sense of belonging to a definite social space and a well-demarcated and bounded territory. National identity is fundamentally multi-dimensional and can subsume or combine with other types of identity such as class, ethnicity or religion.[6] However, different nationalist ideologies generally refer to variations on two broad categories of nation: the ethnic or cultural nation has ethnicity as the basis of membership, with culture as a key cohesive element. The cultural interpretation regards 'nation' as something organic, evolving on the basis of an aesthetic, primordial community, whereby ethnic group solidarity is based on ties handed down from the past, and hence the modern nation may be related to historical ethnicity.[7] History, religion and language are crucial cohesive elements of this community.

In contrast, the territorial or civic nation has territory as the basis of membership and citizenship as the cohesive force. Territoriality is the prime organizing principle in the civic conception of nation, ethnicity is the key principle in the ethnic interpretation.[8] The civic nation is based on a rational conception of community relating to a geographical area, the territorial state, with its laws and political participation welding the community into a nation.

Two ideal types of national identity have their origins in different philosophies and realities, and reflect various types of state development in Europe.[9] However, they are both organizing principles, in which it is possible to differentiate clearly between those individuals who belong to the nation and those who do not. This differentiation or identification can be linked to nationalism via 'mobilizing, territorializing and politicizing identity'.[10] The mobilization of ethnic and citizenship identities lies at the heart of 'identity politics', reinforcing the role of territory as a prime source of identification that binds peoples, states and power relations.

Although there may be a considerable overlap between ethnic group and nation, ethnic groups do not necessarily possess all the attributes of a nation. Notably, the members of an ethnic group need not be resident in a specific territorial homeland, not all members may have a common culture, there may not be a common division of labour or economic unity, and common legal codes may not apply to all.[11] However, nations tend to have an in-built ethnic component that can include certain key attributes, such as a collective proper name, a myth of common ancestry, shared historic memories, differentiating elements of common culture, an association with a specific home territory, and a sense of solidarity for significant sectors of the population.[12] Therefore, an ethnic group without a recognizable nation to which it belongs represents a potential nation, perhaps awaiting a set of circumstances to awaken nationalist ideals based upon an ethnic underpinning.

In Bosnia-Herzegovina and Sarajevo, three potential 'nation states' have been associated with long-term ethnic cleavages between Croats, Serbs and Muslims. The Bosnian Croats and Bosnian Serbs have been able to link themselves to a greater Croatia and a greater Serbia respectively, whilst the Muslims have had an identity defined by their religious affiliation and a territorial dimension related to the former Yugoslav republic of Bosnia-Herzegovina that includes large areas dominated by Croats and Serbs. Hence, in the past, there has been a less clearly stated link between the Muslims and a well-defined territorial claim embracing the whole of the new state of Bosnia-Herzegovina than there has been for their Croatian and Serbian counterparts.[13] However, in recent times, especially amongst the Croats, Serbs and Slovenes, nationalist sentiments have been inextricably linked to demands for statehood. In this context nationalism has exhibited political, ideological and cultural dimensions, but strongly linked to the ethnic characteristics embodied within the various nationalist enterprises.[14] It can be argued therefore that the several nationalist discourses based on ethnicity, group membership and solidarity have been used to develop and consolidate political independence in the former Yugoslavia.

In this context ethnicity can be viewed as something relating to ongoing social processes, in which individuals have been forced to consider how they demarcate themselves from others. A group of people may recognize a common descent and kinship, with cultural demarcations such as religion reinforcing a sense of ethnic identity. However, it is a particular set of circumstances that can create a need for an individual to identify themselves with an ethnic group. A mind-set reinforcing an ethnic identity is created by certain types of interaction with others, as in a conflict over territory or a perceived 'external' threat to the group.[15]

The changes to the ethnic map of Bosnia-Herzegovina have been substantial, establishing a closer relationship between the ethnic map and the newly created political boundaries, themselves based on attempts to maintain or create ethno-cultural homogeneity within the political units ('ethnic cleansing').[16] In effect, the Bosnian Muslims have been 'ethnicized' by the effects of the recent conflicts,[17] and to survive within the new political context, the Bosnian Muslim political leadership is laying stronger claims to the territory of the new state, establishing a clearer identity and assimilating the constituent elements of nationhood. In so doing, there is a tension between this and the desire of some intellectuals and outside agencies to develop the contested notion of *Bosnja Etvo* (Bosnian-ness/Bosnian-hood), with the category *Bosnjak* (Bosnia) established to denote independent Bosnians as opposed to Croatians or Serbians.[18] This is not an uncontested term, but 'Bosniak' is now commonly recognized in the country and is widely used instead of 'Bosnian Muslim'. In part the non-application of the label 'Muslim' reflects a strong and ongoing secular tendency amongst the Bosnian Muslims, despite recent investment from Muslim nations, notably Saudi Arabia, to rebuild damaged mosques. Even in Sarajevo, long acknowledged as a cosmopolitan city and home to both ethnically distinct and mixed communities, Bosniak is the term overwhelmingly used now by the Muslim population to distinguish themselves from other Bosnians.

The remaking of place: Sarajevo street names

Street names are laden with political meanings and are often supportive of the hegemonic socio-political order. Hence 'the political aspect of a renaming operation involves both ideological considerations and decision-making procedures which control and direct the eventual process'.[19] Street names may be embedded into structures of power and authority, and they can be used as a means of enshrining a particular vision of the past in the contemporary urban landscape. The naming process can represent 'a register of sacred history',[20] in which street names are part of an authorized, official version of history accompanying various mass-producing traditions utilized within broader 'discourses of nationalism'.[21] They are at the heart of the banal nationalism by which nation states are reproduced: part of the daily routine and a backdrop to everyday life, but containing a message about identity that is absorbed into the environment.[22]

In Sarajevo, one of the first aspects of renewal and revival post-Dayton was performed by a newly appointed administrative commission for the city, established by the new government for the canton of Sarajevo, one of ten in the Muslim–Croat controlled part of the republic. The 15-member commission included artists, writers and historians, all resident in Sarajevo and mainly Bosniaks deemed to be representative of the community that had survived the siege. They were charged with the specific task of renaming the streets. Whilst the commission was not an elected body, its activities carried a political legitimation and also had popular support for removing symbols associated with Sarajevo's wartime enemies, principally connections with Serbs and Serbian territorial aggrandisement.

The commission removed old street signs and names in Cyrillic script and replaced all the street-name signs, renaming many of them in the process. This renaming has been a conscious effort to remove certain names, especially those relating to Serbs or events associated primarily with Serbia rather than Bosnia-Herzegovina. These changes had popular support throughout the city because they helped remove the previous commemoration of Serbian (and partly also Croatian) history in the street names. It was an act that

Table 17.1: Renaming the streets of Sarajevo, 1994–2000

central area:	no.	%
individuals	124	56.1
families	13	5.9
historical events	31	14.0
geographical locations	22	10.0
local significance	31	14.0
total	*221*	*100.0*
Ilidza (a neighbouring township):		
number of streets renamed	105	69.5
total number of streets in Ilidza	*151*	
Sarajevo urban area:		
number of streets renamed	403	38.6
total number of streets	*1044*	

the public regarded as a legitimate response to the siege of the city, and symbolic of an emergent awareness of a history largely hidden within the former Yugoslav Federation. In the place of existing street names came a stress upon events and people associated directly with Sarajevo and Bosnia-Herzegovina, some (but not all) of whom were Bosniaks held in high regard within the contemporary society. In all, nearly 40 per cent of streets in the city and two-thirds in the neighbouring settlement of Ilidza, formerly with a large Bosnian Serb community, have been renamed (Table 17.1).

The commission's aim was to restore many old, traditional names for the streets that had been removed or lost under federal Yugoslav influence. In particular, there was the intention to remember key events and individuals from the period of the Ottoman Empire (dating back to 1434), but including some significant events and individuals from the period of control by the Austro-Hungarian Empire from 1878 to 1918. Many of the streets had previously been given names relating to World War Two, especially people active as fighters against the Nazis and also supporters of the Communist regime. However, streets bearing such names were now deemed by the commission to be unsuitable for the central part of the city. So it completely removed some names from the map, whilst others were moved to streets in the outlying suburbs.

In the city centre (*Baščaršija*), with its nucleus of buildings dating from the 15th century, names relating to old families and individuals have been remembered. These street names often represent reintroductions, as they had been removed at the end of the Ottoman Empire. During the 20th century new street names had tended to bear the names of writers, poets, military, political and mythological heroes. In the aftermath of the recent conflict the Bosniak-dominated commission identified many of these individuals as

'Serbs' and 'Croats', and removed their names. In their place the names of Bosniaks have appeared, primarily Bosniaks from Sarajevo or from other parts of the new state.

Names referring to places in Serbia and Croatia have gone, whilst place names from the Muslim-controlled parts of Bosnia remain. Nine streets referring to partisans of World War Two have been renamed, as have streets with references to Communist worthies, including former Yugoslav president, Marshall Tito, though one of the main thoroughfares still bears the latter's name. It seems that the sentiments of the commission were generally against commemoration of those associated with the post-war Yugoslav regime and its ideology, although popular regard for Tito appears to remain high – a hint of the multi-layered identities present in Bosnia-Herzegovina, where some people in all ethnic groups still hold in high regard ideals of unity and identity not rigidly fixed by ethno-nationality.

One of the most notable replacements is of Gavrila Princip Street, Princip being the assassin of Archduke Franz Ferdinand in Sarajevo in 1914, the incident credited as the flash point that ignited World War I. The bridge where the assassination took place has reverted to its old name, which is translated into English as the 'Latin Bridge', providing a link to the period when the area around the bridge was called Latinluk and was dominated by Bosnian Croats. Hence Princip is regarded locally as essentially a Serb nationalist rather than a Bosnian. His organization, *Mlade Bosne* (Young Bosnians), has also disappeared from street signs.

Despite the emphasis upon the primacy of an explicitly Bosniak history within the street-renaming process, there is also evidence of attempts to recognize the cosmopolitan character of Sarajevo. Hence non-Bosniaks with strong links to the city are commemorated: for example, Miss Irby Street refers to an English teacher, Adelene Paula Irby (1833–1911), who ran a school for Serbian children in Sarajevo in the 1870s. Her high standing within the community 130 years ago is now recalled in a street name in the heart of the city, even though she was primarily connected to Bosnian Serbs. This represents perhaps an alternative discourse to that based on contrasts between ethnic groups. Kaldor terms this the 'new nationalism', and portrays it as non-violent, open and inclusive. It stresses cultural diversity, not cultural homogeneity, by embracing democratic processes to create a cosmopolitan entity incorporating openness towards different peoples, places and experiences. Anyone walking around the streets of central Sarajevo can observe that elements of the cosmopolitan are still present at every turn in the streets of this city, reflecting the fact that different cultures have survived there side by side for centuries: 'the mosque, the orthodox church, the catholic church and the synagogue are all within a hundred yards of each other' (2004, 174). It is possible then that at least in this part of Bosnia there may be potential for the development of a non-ethnically based 'cosmopolitan' nationalism.

Cosmopolitanism respects diversity, different religious practices and conditions that maintain their co-existence, but it must be emphasized that attempts to retain diversity in Sarajevo exist alongside a much narrower nationalism that seeks to claim ownership of the city for Bosnian Muslims: an instance of one imagination, constructed identity or historical interpretation competing with a different version. This competition can be seen quite strikingly in another manifestation of the remaking of place, namely the reconstruction of the Bosnian National Museum.

The remaking of place: the National Museum

The establishment of a National Museum of Bosnia-Herzegovina is being accomplished as part of aid for reconstruction from both Sweden and Norway. The former State Museum was badly damaged by shellfire during the siege of Sarajevo, but most of its contents have survived. The collections are now being restored to establish a facility with a national, rather than just a local dimension. There is an opportunity to develop a more specifically Bosniak character by emphasizing a distinctive history associated with Turkish influence in the region,[23] and so there is scope for what Anderson (1991, 181–3) terms 'political museumizing', enabling those in authority to determine exactly what is represented in the collections and so to influence the 'message' conveyed. In effect, this can provide support to particular views regarding the specific characteristics of nationality. In applying this to Bosnia-Herzegovina at present, the difficulty lies in the fact that there are competing nationalisms, and that a distinctive Bosniak nationality is still emerging and being shaped by this very competition.

The initial stages of the Museum's restoration have focused on archaeology and ethnology, emphasizing a Bosnian history that embraces the long-term presence of the three main ethno-nationalist groups, but especially the Bosnian Muslims, as a recognizable and distinct group, and defined in ethno-nationalist terms alongside Croats and Serbs. This parallels the Dayton Accords' conception of three distinctive groups within the new state. The Museum's ethnographic section portrays the life of a well-to-do Muslim family in Sarajevo towards the end of Ottoman rule. There are also exhibits showing traditional craft skills of Bosnian Muslims. Other sections portray history, fauna and flora from across the newly created state. However, amidst the ongoing reconstruction, the Museum's centrepiece presents a distinctive message: that of a multi-ethnic Bosnia. The exhibit, housed in a climate-controlled room, is the Haggadah, an ancient Jewish codex which was smuggled out of Spain in the late 15th century during a purge of Sephardic Jews, when small communities of Sephardic Jews were established in Bosnia in Mostar, Sarajevo and Travnik.

The Haggadah is a 109-page lavishly illustrated manuscript with illuminated paintings. It is a traditional book of prayers, poems and stories about the Jewish exodus from Egypt, produced in 14th century Spain, then its whereabouts is unknown until it was offered to the Museum in Sarajevo in 1894. Its presence in the city has had wide significance, initially symbolizing Jewish presence in the Balkans. However, its protection, first against the Nazis in the 1940s and more recently from shellfire in the recent conflict, has also symbolized the resistance of Sarajevo to external aggressors and a desire to preserve a multicultural character. Today, the celebration of a holy Jewish tome emphasizes Sarajevo's multi-ethnic history, as does the city's retention of an old Jewish synagogue and a Jewish Museum. Although the restoration and prominence of the Haggadah owes much to funding from the United Nations and various Western organizations, it is a reminder that, within the more dominant context of ethnic division and separation within Bosnia, an important strand of Bosniak identity is not exclusively Muslim but embraces a history of ethnic diversity and tolerance, especially in the context of Sarajevo. This is a key facet of 'new nationalism', though in the example of the Haggadah it is the western powers that have provided the finance and the commitment to support this particular nationalism.

Symbols of the new state: banknotes and postage stamps

Although the renaming of streets is one of the most visible manifestations of the remaking of place in Sarajevo, there are numerous other examples of reconstruction that have incorporated an element of nationalism within them, as the new state strives to create a distinct identity to be legitimated by the support of its people. In particular, there has been further use of symbols in the issuing of banknotes and stamps bearing the portraits of writers, poets and artists from Bosnia's past. The currency and stamps are parts of the everyday life that form the state's official iconography. They 'create a link between the state's political identity project and its citizens.'[24] This is critical to the building of an 'imagined community'. In particular, money and stamps are excellent exemplars of Billig's (1995) 'banal nationalism', as they both build the state's boundaries and provide a territorial sense of 'us'.[25]

Of special significance is the use of ethno-nationalist symbols on some of the banknotes issued by the Central Bank of Bosnia-Herzegovina from 1998. The images on the back of several new notes are of 14th and 15th century fragments of tombstones and stone reliefs relating to the Bogumil church. A widely-held belief by Bosnian Muslims is that the Bogumils were independent of both the Catholic and Orthodox churches, and so their presence facilitated the widespread conversion of the Bosnian population to Islam at the beginning of Ottoman rule.[26] So Bosnian Muslims today can possibly trace their ethnic distinctiveness not only to their current religion but also to a Christian past, accepting this as part of their own tradition.[27] In contrast, the Yugoslav Nobel laureate, Ivo Andric (1990, 16), portrays those Bosnian Slavs who converted to Islam as cowardly and greedy and as 'heathen elements of a young race'. Serbian and Croatian politicians frequently repeated this view of Bosnian Muslims during the recent conflict.

In the 19th century, the Franciscan monk Franjo Jukic propagated the idea of a common heritage for Bosnians as adherents to the Bogumil church. He now appears as the front image of the one marka note, as a symbol of both a distinctive Bosnian Muslim nationalism and also of a wider pan-Slavic nationalism. This multi-layered symbolism embraces both the idea of Bosnia comprising people with a common past and Bosnia with Muslims at its core. Ironically, the possibility that the Muslims are descended from forebears who were Christians has enabled some Croats and Serbs to claim that the Muslims are really either Croats or Serbs and that all of Bosnia-Herzegovina therefore 'belongs' to either a greater Croatia or a greater Serbia.[28] There are mixed messages within this appeal to a 'greater' Bosnia. It hints at a single 'Bosnian' identity, devoid of the current ethno-nationalist categories of 'Croat', 'Serb' or 'Muslim', but it also confers a distinction upon Bosnian Muslims as having historic differences with their neighbours through their conversion to Islam, whilst possibly introducing the notion of Muslim Bosnia with wider territorial boundaries.

Postage stamps represent official visual images authorized by the state as a means of representing its history, culture, society and its place in the world. They 'have become useful ideological and cultural artefacts, and a means for governments to . . . promote certain images at home and abroad'.[29] So there is nation building power in stamps comparable with the naming of streets and the designs on banknotes.[30] Stamps, like banknotes and street names, are an everyday reminder of particular aspects of the state. Their ubiquity and 'taken for granted' nature gives them a particular role in conveying messages about the state, and their character provides insights into educational, political, ideological and financial goals of the state. However, deriving these insights is not straightforward, because of the complexity involved in interpreting visual representations in postage stamps.[31] Nevertheless, the symbolism within stamps is receiving an increasing amount of attention, with growing recognition of their semiotic status.[32]

The content of postage stamps is extremely diverse, reflecting the multiplicity of purposes underlying their production. Political considerations can certainly be one determinant of content, as seen in Russian stamps depicting technological achievements[33] and Argentinian representations of the disputed Malvinas (Falkland Islands).[34] However, there are also commercial considerations as post offices can make higher profits from the sales of stamps to collectors than to the general public.[35] This last point tends to support the proliferation of commemorative issues, mini-sheets and presentation packs that have no specific postal function but which can both convey a particular message and be attractive to collectors. The need for postage stamps to be attractive has led to worldwide development of thematic issues, in which subjects associated with the natural world are especially popular.

Stamps linked to buildings, famous people, places, the arts, science, folklore and particular events have all been significant elements incorporated in the design of stamps, though the varied usage and portrayal of the different types reflect both the underlying rationale for their adoption and the nature of the 'messages' they convey to the general public.[36]

In Bosnia-Herzegovina, the current postal service was created as part of the new state in 1995. The number of designs has been limited by the lack of readily available printing facilities within the country, but the potential for earning income from overseas sales has promoted an expansion in production, from 14 issues in 1995 to an average of 21 per annum in the period 1995–2004 (Table 17.2).[37]

The Bosnian postage stamp issues contain one overriding division: between stamps celebrating events with no specific connection to Bosnia and those depicting people, places, events and characteristics pertaining directly to the country. It was the latter that were dominant (73.9 per cent of all issues). However, the fact that around one in four issues related to events outside Bosnia seems partly to be making a statement that the new state is now a member of a world of sovereign states, with its own participants in Olympic Games, World Expos, soccer world cups, Mediterranean Games and European cultural conventions (all celebrated in Bosnian postage stamps). Indeed, a strong vein of the normal and the everyday runs through the various series: football teams, chess players, the Union of Scouts, the theatre, mail carriers' uniforms, journalism, fire-fighters and amateur radio enthusiasts. The stamps also announced the birth of the new state to the rest of the world, with issues depicting the Assembly in Sarajevo, the new flag, Sovereignty Day and a summit of world leaders in Sarajevo in 1999. The fact that Bosnia is now an independent European state is attested to in the third issue of stamps in 1995, simply entitled 'Europe 1995'. Similar reminders of 'Bosnia in Europe' appear at regular intervals, in part also as statements that normal everyday affairs have been resumed in the country after the destruction and conflict of the early 1990s. However, the conflict is not forgotten, with some powerful statements made regarding the destruction and subsequent rebuilding of the old bridge (*Stari Most*) at Mostar (a symbol both of Turkish presence in Bosnia and of the links between the Islamic and the Catholic worlds), the massacre of Bosniaks at Srebrenica, and the presence of land mines left by the conflicts (including a stamp of Diana, Princess of Wales, who campaigned against the use of land mines).

The stamps' portrayals of events, people and places contain messages that both emphasize particular Bosniak characteristics and convey a broader cosmopolitan message. The Islamic dimension of Bosniak life is present in several issues depicting Bairam, a Persian-Turkish word for the two principal festivals of Islam. There are also stamps showing the Library of Sarajevo's Islamic High School, Ferhadija Mosque, the mosque at Stanski Most, and some historical series, depicting people and events from the

Table 17.2: Postage stamps issued in Bosnia-Herzegovina, 1995–2005

Category	'95	'96	'97	'98	'99	'00	'01	'02	'03	'04	'05*	Total	%
Bosnian themes:													
religion	2	3	4	1	1	2		1	4			18	8.0
historical events	2	1	5					1	1	1		11	5.0
flora/fauna/gastronomy	1	2	2	3	3	2	2	3	2	4	3	27	12.2
places/buildings	1	3	2	3	6	2	2		2	6	3	30	13.5
people	3	2	3	2	2	3	2	5	5	3	1	31	14.0
current events	2	6	2	3	5	2	1	5	3	2	2	33	14.9
arts/science/sport	1		2	2		1	1	2	4	1		14	6.3
general/world themes:													
miscellaneous	2	5	7	7	6	7	12	5	2	5	1	58	26.1
total	*14*	*22*	*27*	*20*	*23*	*19*	*20*	*22*	*23*	*22*	*10*	*222*	

(*) to July 2005.

Ottoman period,[38] and Sarajevo's town-twinning with Doha, the capital of Qatar. However, in contrast, the stamps are inclusive of some non-Bosniak elements: for example, the jubilee of the Croatian Cultural Society is commemorated, and in one religious series both Orthodox and Roman Catholic Christianity are depicted. The Franciscan Monastery at Kaljeva Sutjestia is in one issue, and Pope John Paul II appears in two issues, one marking his visit to Bosnia in 1997. The Haggadah is portrayed in a 1997 issue. Bosniaks are to the fore amongst the writers, painters and scientists featured, whereas the Nobel Prize-winning writer, Ivo Anric, a Bosnian Serb, has not appeared on a Bosnian postage stamp.

Life in Sarajevo is a frequent theme, again with a mixture of messages. The Bosniak dimension is present via issues depicting the Bosniak Institute, the Oriental Institute and the Svrzo House (*Svrzina Kuca*), showing the architecture and lifestyle of a grand urban house from the Ottoman period. Survival and resistance are also repeated themes, via an issue depicting the Sarajevo Tunnel,[39] several issues marking the Sarajevo Film Festival, which was launched in 1995 as a statement of resistance, rebuilding the city's colleges, and the city and country 'ten years after the aggression'. The cultural and governmental roles of the city are strongly emphasized in the form of the Assembly of the new post-Dayton government, the City Hall, University, Bosnian Sovereignty Day, the centenary of the Bosniak Cultural Union, and the only politician to be featured to date, Alija Izetbegovic, leader of the Bosniaks during the conflict.

Ethno-nationalism or multi-ethnic identity?

Nationalism as the bearer of identity has both external and internal functions. The former refer to territorial, economic and political issues, whilst the internal capacities include means whereby individuals are socialized as members through the provision of shared values, symbols and traditions. So symbols provide a means whereby individuals can define and locate themselves as part of a larger collective identity. Names are symbolic elements of landscape and place, reflecting abstract or concrete national and local sentiments and goals. The evocation of a shared heritage through the use of historical figures and events depicted on stamps and banknotes and in the street names of Sarajevo is reinforcing the bonds between the Muslim (Bosniak) population and its occupation of Sarajevo and territory in the newly created state of Bosnia-Herzegovina.

Researching the reconstruction of Sarajevo discloses symbols and events being invoked as part of the new Bosniak nationalism, but it also reveals an emerging interplay of conflicting forces, including tensions between the desire by the government in Sarajevo for closer economic links with the EU, and the increased importance of Islam as a force to bind together a new nation, as Bosnian Muslims increasingly identify themselves as distinct to Bosnian Croats and Bosnian Serbs. With control of much Bosnian territory still in the hands of Serbs and Croats, it remains to be seen to what extent the new identity being created in Sarajevo can avoid further emphasizing the schism along ethnic lines that has been a central outcome of the break-up of the Yugoslav federation. That schism may be unavoidable, as one clear outcome of the conflict is establishment of an even closer relationship between the distribution of ethnic groups and the newly created political boundaries. However, there are certain countervailing forces to schism that affect both identity and political development. These include impacts from many external agencies such as international authorities,[40] the geopolitical situation in the Balkans and some traditions of multi-ethnicity within Bosnia itself.

Contrasts can be drawn between the exclusivity and homogeneity associated with ethno-nationalist agendas in the former Yugoslavia and a more inclusive, liberal and tolerant 'new nationalism' closely linked to the influence of external, Western influences. Within Bosnia, the immediate legacy of the recent conflict is the dominance of ethno-nationalism, as reflected in the estimate that 90 per cent of the population now live in ethnically homogeneous communities.[41] Bosniak, Croat and Serb versions of this ethno-nationalism have become more entrenched in particular territories because of the conflict and the nature of the Dayton Accords.

Some examples of the promotion of a multi-ethnic identity for Bosnia, such as the restoration of the Haggadah to a prime position within the National Museum, are largely dependent upon the work of external agencies. However, this is in contrast to 'local' Bosniak attempts to maintain diversity in the Sarajevo street-renaming exercise, and the evident pride of the local inhabitants at having retained mosques alongside the Catholic cathedral, the Orthodox church and the synagogue, despite the three-year long siege of the city from 1992–95.

The tensions between identity and state formation based on a mono-ethnic view and one of greater plurality can be seen in some aspects of the street-renaming exercise in Sarajevo and the restoration of the National Museum. Both of these activities celebrate a mixture of a Muslim and a multi-ethnic Bosnia. Part of the evolving Bosniak identity embraces non-Muslim elements too, and has had political manifestation in the anti-ethno-nationalist coalition that succeeded in the 2000 elections. It remains to be seen how this identity is shaped by the conflicting forces of internal division and continuing commitment by the international community to a Bosnian state of three constituent groups whose 'rights' must be protected.

Notes

1. Part of the research for this chapter was carried out with financial support from the Elisabeth Barker Fund of the British Academy.
2. Hobsbawm 1995.

3. Crnobrnja 1994.
4. See Allcock (2000, 348), who refers to the 'urban ecumenism of Sarajevo'.
5. Though over one million refugees and internally displaced persons still (mid-2005) had not returned to their former homes; Black, 2002; Job 2002, 185; UNDP, 2002.
6. Kymlicka 1995.
7. Conversi 1995; Mackay 1982; Scott 1990.
8. Grosby 1995.
9. Smith 1991a; Tilly 1990.
10. Einagle 1997, 244.
11. Connor 1994; Gellner 1983.
12. Smith 1991a, 21.
13. Denich 1994; 1996.
14. Smith 1994.
15. Barth 1969; Hobsbawm 1994.
16. Burg and Shoup 1999.
17. Banac 1994.
18. Magas 2003.
19. Azaryahu 1997, 480.
20. Schwartz 1982, 377.
21. Hobsbawm 1993b.
22. Billig 1995, 41–1.
23. Sijaric 1993.
24. Raento et al. 2004, 930.
25. Raento, Brunn 2005.
26. Kniewald 1964; Racki 1931; Solovejec 1959.
27. Fine 1975; 2002; Magas 2003, 21.
28. Bringa 1995.
29. Altman 1991, 4.
30. Unwin, Hewitt 2001.
31. Rose 2001.
32. Child 2005; Reid 1984; Scott 1995.
33. Foss 1997.
34. Beck 1983.
35. Jones 2001, 405.
36. Jones 2004.
37. The definition of an issue was determined by the Bosnian Post Office, and comprised both single stamps and collections pertaining to a single theme. For example, nearly every year there has been an issue entitled 'flora', usually consisting of two stamps showing different local plant species, whereas the seven stamps issued in 2004 depicting Bosnian cities were treated as two separate issues by the Post Office as they were released at different times of year. In producing the classification shown in Table 17.2, each issue has been placed into a single category. This involved a degree of subjectivity as, for example, in 2002 commemoration of the 100th anniversary of the synagogue in Sarajevo could be classified both as religion and place/building. In this particular case it was classified as religion, as it was part of a series of religious issues that included depiction of an historic Koran and a compilation of religious texts. Similarly, writers and artists were generally classified under people, not in the arts/science/sport category, as they were generally featured as separate individuals, rather than specifically as representatives of writers, painters or scientists.

38. E.g. King Stjepan, King Bobovec's castle, and the coat of arms from the Kotromanic dynasty.
39. This ran for 700 metres under the airport, and during the siege of the city from 1992–95 provided a lifeline for Sarajevo inhabitants.
40. Caplan 2004.
41. King 2004, 42.

18
Cultural Divisions in a Changing Lisbon

Graça Moreira

The appeal that countries and cities have to the migratory choices of potential emigrants is very much related to the image projected and knowledge possessed. In the case of Portugal, recent immigration based on such knowledge has very much been mediated by a recent history of colonialism where the basis of integration exists in various degrees of competency in a shared language. Now in a post-colonial situation Portugal still has privileged contacts with various parts of the globe, where its culture and its language still prevail. Portugal has been until recently and for many centuries a country of emigration. During the 19th century and into the 20th century, part of its population emigrated to Africa (especially Angola) and to Brazil (a former colony) in search of new lives. No less than 1.2 million people emigrated between 1899 and 1940 alone mostly leaving rural areas in the northern part of the country where life became increasingly difficult with rural properties, due to inheritance, becoming ever smaller. Many, however, maintained an identification and link to Portugal by renting their land to someone in the family. Considering endogenous demographic change, Portugal parallels since the 1960s the population tendencies of later developing European countries, such as Spain, Greece and Ireland, showing a decrease of mortality and birth rates and therefore a small natural growth.[1] However, since the late 1940s until regime change in 1974, the Portuguese emigrated to Europe, mainly to France and Germany, in large numbers. Between 1960 and 1974 it is estimated that around 1.5 million people left the country, mostly for economic reasons, but also related to the fact that during this period the country maintained a war on several fronts in Africa with the compulsory conscription of all young men. Since this time Portugal and Lisbon in particular have been locales of immigration. This chapter charts this turnaround, firstly in terms of demography, and secondly reflects on the challenges posed to cultural and economic integration and the need for common post-colonial identification in the fractured context of Lisbon.

From the revolution of 1974 to 1986

First migratory flow from Africa

The first great inflow of population to Portugal in the last century happened in the second half of the 1970s, in the wake of the watershed coup of 25 April 1974 which brought to an end nearly 50 years of right-wing domination and shortly thereafter wound up the first and most enduring European empire. Portugal received a very significant inflow of population (more or less 500,000 people in a country with barely over 8,500,000 inhabitants in 1970). This immigration came from the ex-colonies, especially the previously so-called Portuguese Africa – Angola, Mozambique, Guinea-Bissau, Cape Verde and Sao Tome – nowadays designated as PALOP[2] and accounting for 70 per cent of Portuguese born abroad. This demographic flow, however, was not always statistically represented as immigration. Some people were born in Portugal and went to the Portuguese colonies when young, and others, although born in Africa and in Asia, were of Portuguese nationality.[3] The importance of this shock to Portuguese national self-identity conception is difficult to overstate. The decoupling of overseas territories from Portugal and the return of the administrative class during these years decentred the notion previously propagated that Portugal was the focal point from which history was made.[4] It is also the first time, through the centuries, that the country received inflowing population, which, despite similar cultural roots and language, shows some different ethnic and religious characteristics as markers of difference. This returning population, mainly from Africa (notably Angola and Mozambique) and spread broadly over the country, was basically the middle class of the colonies, the civil servants of the colonial administration and employees of the Portuguese private companies who did not feel comfortable in the newly independent countries. Most of them had familial connections to Portugal and land or property, which enabled them to return to the country of their origins. This gave them a very strong notion of identity even when they did not completely feel at ease with the constricting lifestyle in Portugal, especially in the less urban and more conservative areas of a country whose ethos still remains rooted in the rural and the importance of the social support of family. Those who had no familial connections to the country or a job preferred to emigrate to other countries such as South Africa, where there still exists an important Portuguese community.

First migratory flow from Europe

While after regime change in 1974 some immigration took place from the old but long independent former colony of Brazil and from people of Portuguese background in Venezuela, this was outpaced by those returning to Portugal from other parts of Europe. In some cases these people had left for political reasons during the Salazar and Marcelo Caetano regimes, objecting in many instances to the war in Africa and settling mostly in France. A larger group comprised a retired population that had migrated for economic reasons and returning to village roots found the cost of living lower. It is very easy to recognize the new houses they built, because they reproduced what they had seen abroad and considered a sign of prosperity: the house style 'maison' or 'chalet suisse'. While aesthetic integration was a problem, cultural integration was not, only growing in importance after Portugal joined the European Union in 1986.

Joining the European Union and eurozone

Since the 1980s Portugal has experienced relatively rapid economic growth. Aided by European funds, infrastructure in the form of motorways, bridges and so forth has vastly improved, drawing in, in the process, a great many workers who are less than proficient in the Portuguese language. It must be said, however, that Portugal, although now a destination for immigrants, is only a passing-through country for some who target more developed EU countries in the longer term. In fact, in 2001 the number of foreigners in Portugal, deriving in the main from other European countries, Africa and South America, remained under 4 per cent despite roughly doubling since 1991. Nevertheless, in 2001 nearly a quarter of a million foreigners, predominantly from Africa, were overwhelmingly (66 per cent) located within the Metropolitan Area of Lisbon, the largest economic driver in the country (see Table 18.1). While the Portuguese language remains an integrating force, language markers are noticeable. Those coming from PALOP now tend to be less educated and speak Creole mixed with Portuguese. Immigrants from Brazil, a growing group, while possessing mastery of Portuguese are not surprisingly recognizable through style and syntax. The Brazilians, through superior language ability, typically find jobs in commerce making them visible in society and more easily integrated. Helping here has been the importation by Portuguese television over the last 20 years or so of Brazilian

Table 18.1: Foreign population in Greater Lisbon by continent and major representative country, 2003

Origin	Total	%		Total	%
Europe	29,248	21.8	Spain	8,429	29
Africa	79,841	59.5	Cape Verde	36,216	45
America	17,638	13.1	Brazil	11,164	63
Asia	7,036	5.2	China	2,494	35
Oceania	221	0.2	Australia	179	81
Total	134,156				

Source: SEF 2003

soap operas (*telenovelas*) bringing familiarity with the nuances of Brazilian society to Portugal.

An eastern European immigrant group arriving since the end of the 1990s is now becoming important. While not sharing a Portuguese cultural background it, nevertheless, accrues goodwill because it seems like a mirror to many Portuguese who emigrated to Europe during the 1960s. This group, taking advantage of the expression of goodwill in the form of language help and assistance in professional conversion courses (many are educated professionals in health care, engineering and so forth, temporarily taking less qualified work) energetically pursues integration into Portuguese society.

With the pressure of a surrounding rural exodus of population making itself felt on the availability of housing in Greater Lisbon (especially the northern part of the Lisbon Metropolitan Area, LMA), the housing market in a region approaching 2 million people is highly competitive and segregated. The historic inner city with traces going back to a pre-Roman period and incorporating Moorish influences is highly prized. In the centre the naming of the *Rua do Ouro* (Gold Street) in the west and *Rua da Prata* in the east of downtown tells its own story. European migrants, mainly from Spain but from the EU generally, reside in integrated middle-class residential areas in the centre of the city.[5] However, the residential periphery of the city which tolerated the development of slums since the 1970s is the more common destination for migrants especially from PALOP. The Marvila area to the east of the city and the Charneca borough close to the airport are typical here. Only recently, since the 1990s, with the help of a national programme[6] to eradicate what was shanty housing and to replace it with social housing has this former legacy been somewhat overcome. Segregation still remains. The PALOP group itself is not a homogenous one, being territorially organized on the basis of nationalities, with some municipalities of LMA still looking like excluded ghettos, places apart, with issues of public safety and a dependency culture. These residential areas incorporate former refugees from Angola and Mozambique, countries which until recently were the victims of severe civil wars. The Brazilian population, not mixing with PALOP arrivals, is distributed along the residential peripheries in low to middle socio-economic areas such as Lumiar, Benfica, S. Domingos de Benfica and Arrios. One cultural cementing factor, however, remains religion, with only 4 per cent of those expressing a religious faith following a religion other than Catholicism. With only slightly over 2,000 Muslims, a Lisbon mosque was only built relatively recently.

Identity and belonging

The feeling of belonging to a place and identifying with it is partially a matter of culture but also a matter of legal status. The people who came from PALOP after 1975–76, for example, and did not choose to be Portuguese before this

Figure 18.1: Monument to the Portuguese discoveries erected in Lisbon 1960 commemorating the 500th anniversary of the death of Prince Henry the Navigator

lost the legal claim to Portuguese nationality after the independence of their countries. As pointed out in a recent study, 'Salazarist cultural practices still shape the national imagination of what it means to be Portuguese.'[7] The regime 'constructed itself as the legitimate heir to the "civilizing mission" embodied by previous explorers such as Prince Henry the Navigator and

Vasco da Gama', where Portugal occupied 'a privileged position from which to imagine and define its sense of national identity and belonging'.[8] Lisbon thus emerges as a metropolitan centre with peripheral outposts, an imagination which fractured in 1974 creating space for fresh reorientation on matters of nation and identity, even while the afterglow of empire centred narratives of Portuguese identity persist.

While the far from complete transition to a post-colonial reconception of Portuguese identity makes cultural integration of PALOP and other former colonial identities more difficult, adding to the problem is the fact that while present discussions in the Portuguese parliament seek formally to make nationality somewhat easier to acquire, in practice this may be insufficient to counteract feelings of exclusion. Requiring proof of residency combined with the level of necessary literacy may actually increase the feeling amongst those affected of being an outsider.

Conclusion

When one compares the geographical distribution of the two most important periods of immigration it is seen that:

- the first inflow was spread around the country. Everybody was legally Portuguese and most likely had family links. Most found a job and home and integrated easily;
- in the second period immigrants try to live in Lisbon and surrounds, attracted by the greater economic development prospects. Often they are foreigners with legal problems.

The situation in Lisbon is not very different from that of other western European cities, where immigrants tend to gravitate towards the traditional capital city. The specificity lies mainly in the fact that, in Portugal, most immigrants have had some previous cultural relationship with the country. The immigrants from PALOP have a pattern of distribution peripheral to the city centre, because until now most of them have been living in slums. At the northern part of the city in Charneca, these slums have been transformed to social housing in the last few years. A permanent commercial area, however, has yet to develop and as yet the population only have an open air weekend market. Infrastructure improvements in other words are seen as a necessary first step in a process seeking cultural inclusion which is aided by the advantage of shared language, a factor which cannot be overestimated The problem of newcomers speaking a different language has only arisen in the last few years with the arrival of immigrants from eastern Europe. The Chinese community also face language difficulties but less acute due to the nature of their employment. Numbers here are small. Recognizing that language is central to integration, the Ministry of Education is developing support in schools for children to whom Portuguese is not the first language, and other organizations are promoting classes for adults. In school, children from eastern European countries and Asia generally succeed well. On the contrary, PALOP children have problems in the educational system which, if major social problems are to be avoided in the future (as recently in France, for example, although in Lisbon numbers are smaller and religion does not divide), is the key challenge facing cultural inclusion in Lisbon, and Portugal more generally, and is a vital focus for presently much neglected research and even discussion.

Notes

1. Ferrao 1997.
2. PALOP – Países Africanos de Língua Oficial Portuguesa (African countries speaking Portuguese as official language).
3. Bastos, Bastos 1999.
4. Sidaway, Power 2005, 545.
5. Such as S. Domingos de Benfica, S. Mamede, Santo Condestavel, Fatima e Arroios.
6. PER – Programa Especial de Realojamento.
7. Sidway, Power 2005, 533.
8. Sidway, Power 2005, 535.

19
Beyond the Pale in Dublin: Asylum Seekers, Welfare and Citizenship

Declan Redmond

The Republic of Ireland (hereafter Ireland) has often been characterized as a culturally homogeneous state. Historically, at least, this has been mainly true. The vast majority of the population has been overwhelmingly white, and has formally, at least, adhered to the Roman Catholic religion. Indeed, the charge has been that the Irish State was closely allied to and influenced by the institutions and moral teachings of the Catholic Church and consequently Ireland was an inhospitable place for those of other religions or cultures.[1] Again, it is broadly true that this has been the case historically. Indeed, in the context of the conflict in Northern Ireland, the picture of a monocultural state is a view still held in differing measures by the Protestant and unionist section of the population. However, while there may still be some truth to this idea, the reality is that Ireland has changed rapidly over the past two to three decades, with society becoming increasingly secularized, and adherence to the formalities and teachings of the Catholic Church weakening considerably, particularly in urban areas. This increased secularization, often taking the form of conflict over social issues such as divorce and abortion, has been termed in some quarters a culture war. In economic terms, Ireland has stylized itself as being an open economy, in tune with international trends, with a highly educated and flexible workforce. The country has marketed itself as being a young and modern European state whose inhabitants are fully committed to the European ideal and like to see themselves as secularized, tolerant, pluralistic and cosmopolitan. In particular, Dublin is portrayed as a modern European city, a popular place for others to visit, an exciting and cultured city which is deeply cosmopolitan. However, even leaving aside the Northern Ireland conflict and the complex issues of religion, nationality, identity and culture which that raises, some analysts have pointed to the treatment and conditions of the indigenous travelling population in Ireland which suggest that the self-image is somewhat occluded by reality. For example, Norris and Winston (2005), Garner (2004) and Fanning (2002) present clear evidence of persistent prejudice and racism against travellers, suggesting that so-called tolerance may merely be skin-deep. They further imply that while Ireland is increasingly secularized this does not necessarily equate with tolerant multiculturalism. This very question of whether Ireland is becoming in reality a more tolerant, hospitable and multicultural place has been posed in stark terms since the middle of the 1990s. The recent and rather sudden immigration of non-nationals from Africa, eastern Europe and beyond has been presented as a shock to the political and cultural system, and has asked some difficult and complex questions of Irish society which are only beginning to be answered. The recent rioting in French cities has led to a further spate of commentary as to the implications of immigration for Ireland generally, but in particular for the main urban areas. Questions have been posed regarding integration and assimilation and the potential for ethnic segregation to develop in places such as Dublin. In comparison to many European states, Ireland has had little history or experience of immigration in the twentieth century. The history of Irish migration has primarily been outward emigration, being a net supplier of migrants to other countries, most notably the UK and the USA. Indeed, there exists an extensive literature on the history of the Irish diaspora, with much of it emphasizing the impact of the Irish on the urban centres of the UK and the USA.[2] However, the past decade has witnessed a reversal of these historic trends. Extraordinary economic growth has led to substantial return migration of Irish nationals seeking to resettle permanently in the country.[3] More pertinently, the past decade has seen significant immigration of non-nationals. The economic boom has acted as a magnet for migrant labour in general, while specific skills shortages have been remedied, in part, with the introduction of a work permit scheme, with consequent immigration of skilled workers from former EU accession states and beyond. The transformation in the economy and society has acted, it is asserted, as a lure for asylum seekers in quest of refugee status.[4] Asylum seekers have been accused of welfare tourism and of seeking to avail themselves of a supposedly generous social welfare system in Ireland. The net effect of these different immigrations and arrivals has been quite profound, generating all manner of cultural, political and legal challenges for which the state and society have been quite unprepared. In urban areas, but particularly the capital city of Dublin, which contains over one-third of the state's four million population, the presence of different national and ethnic groups is quite noticeable. Lentin (2002) argues that immigration of ethnic minorities is not something new in Ireland and, while this is true, the recent immigrations are clearly quantitatively and qualitatively of a different order. What has been a historical reality for many European cities, the presence of ethnic and national minorities, is a very recent event in Dublin. In the context of the theme of this book, this chapter examines trends and policies towards those seeking asylum status over the past decade. The increase in the numbers of asylum seekers has raised, for example, issues regarding urban policy and settlement, social welfare provision, citizenship and racism. The reaction of Irish society to asylum seekers is instructive, and is suggestive of some tentative answers to the question of whether Ireland is moving towards a more tolerant multicultural society and whether Dublin can be regarded as becoming a cosmopolitan multicultural city.

Immigration trends

While academic interest has increased in this phenomena, it would be true to say that robust data and research on this issue is relatively, although understandably, sparse. The recent work of Hughes and Quinn (2004), Quinn and Hughes (2005a, 2005b) and Hughes (2005), however, represents a significant initial assessment of immigration trends. In addition to this work, there is a plethora of work from a variety of non-governmental organizations involved in advocacy-related and support work.[5] A number of government departments and agencies also produce relevant material. The Reception and Integration Agency, which is responsible for services to asylum seekers and refugees, and the Department of Justice, Equality and Law Reform, which is responsible for overall law and policy on immigration and citizenship, also produce useful source data. From these various sources and some selected academic material, an overall picture can be constructed of the key trends and issues in immigration.

While the emphasis in this chapter is on asylum applicants, this must be set in the context of overall immigration over the past decade. Table 19.1 shows the levels of immigration (gross) over the past decade by country of origin. Since the early 1990s, the immigration trend has been steadily upward, doubling between 1993 and 2005 from 35,000 to 70,000. One of the more notable trends has been the rapid increase in immigration from the rest of the world, with the recent arrival of 26,500 people from the former EU accessions states being particularly noteworthy. When broken down by nationality, the trend has been that of a reduction of Irish nationals returning and a substantial increase of non-nationals.[6] These figures reflect flows of population and not the stock. The most recent census, taken in 2002, shows that almost 5 per cent of the population, or 182,000 people, were foreign nationals. Of these, over 45 per cent were non-EU nationals. Not surprisingly, in the Dublin area non-nationals account for over 7 per cent of the total population. With the increase in immigration since 2002, allied with EU enlargement, these figures are likely to have increased both absolutely and relatively. In particular, in so far as can be told from existing sources, the vast majority of immigrants from former accession states arrive and stay in Dublin. With a population of over one million, up to 100,000 or 10 per cent of the city's population may be non-national.

The recent immigrations into Ireland comprise returning Irish nationals, immigrants from the enlarged EU, those entering with work permits,

Table 19.1: Immigration by country of origin (thousands)

Year ending April	UK	Rest of EU	EU 10*	USA	Rest of world	Total
1993	17.5	6.6	na	5.0	5.7	34.7
1994	15.2	5.8	na	4.3	4.8	30.1
1995	15.6	6.3	na	3.8	5.5	31.2
1996	17.6	7.2	na	6.4	8.0	39.2
1997	20.3	8.1	na	6.7	9.4	44.5
1998	22.1	9.1	na	5.1	9.7	46.0
1999	22.3	10.2	na	5.9	10.5	48.9
2000	20.8	11.7	na	5.5	14.5	52.6
2001	20.6	10.3	na	6.7	21.5	59.0
2002	19.1	11.3	na	6.6	29.9	66.9
2003	13.5	9.7	na	4.7	22.5	50.5
2004	13.0	12.6	na	4.8	19.7	50.1
2005	13.8	8.9	26.2	4.3	16.8	70.0

* EU accession states were included in rest of world prior to 2005
Source: Central Statistics Office 2005

asylum seekers and non-national students. The rapid economic growth of recent years has led at various times to labour shortages and a key response of the government has been to introduce a work permit system.[7] Work permits are generally allowed for a period of one year, and the number of new and renewed permits increased from just over 6,000 in 1999 to almost 50,000 in 2003. Approximately 40 per cent of work permit holders were allocated to employers in the Dublin area. While work permits are offered on the base of skills specifications, the data show that over 40 per cent arrived from the following five countries: Latvia, Lithuania, the Philippines, Poland and Romania, and that up to 80 per cent of work permit holders work in the services sector. With nationals from EU accession states able to enter the country without a work permit since May 2004, the most recent statistics show that 26,200 people arrived from accession states in the year to April 2005. Media reports have suggested that as many as 90,000 Polish nationals have arrived in Ireland since May 2004, and that Dublin has been termed 'Warsaw West' in response. In an interesting policy response to the enlargement of the EU, Ireland decided against putting restrictions on immigration from the former accessions states, although it retains the right to change this position where the Government believe that labour market conditions have deteriorated. In 2004, in anticipation of such immigration, the Government introduced what is termed a 'Habitual Residency Test', which severely restricts the social welfare entitlements of accession state nationals for the first two years of their stay in the country. In addition to those on work permits, there has been a significant immigration of foreign students, particularly Chinese students, although reliable estimates are difficult to come by.

The past decade has also seen the arrival of asylum seekers from a variety of countries, with significant numbers coming from African and eastern European countries. In recent years the number of refugees and asylum seekers residing in Ireland has increased significantly, although from a very low base. In the context of overall immigration, the proportion seeking asylum is in fact quite low, being 20 per cent of overall immigration at its highest. However, asylum seekers have received a disproportionate amount of policy, legal and media attention. There are in effect three different sets of refugees and asylum seekers in Ireland. First, the government has admitted, from time to time, what are termed 'Programme Refugees' as part of its international responsibilities, refugees who are granted refugee status on entry to the country. Table 19.2 shows the numbers and origins of programmes refugees to date. Those admitted under such programmes are legal refugees and have similar rights to Irish citizens. However, as can be seen, the numbers have been quite low historically. Second, there are those who arrive seeking asylum and seeking to become legal refugees who are awaiting a decision by the authorities. Third, there are those whose application for asylum has been successful and who have been granted refugee status.

Of more importance in terms of numbers has been the much more recent arrival of asylum seekers seeking refugee status. Table 19.3 shows the trends in those arriving in Ireland seeking asylum since 1992. It is only since the late 1990s that the trend rises in a sharp fashion. In the three years from 2000 to 2002, over 10,000 per annum arrived seeking asylum. In 2003 this dropped significantly to approximately 8,000 – probably due to imminent

Table 19.2: Programme refugees in Ireland

Year of arrival	Numbers admitted under government decisions	Country of origin
1956	530	Hungary
1973	120	Chile
1979–2000	803	Vietnam
1985	26	Iran
1992–2000	1341	former Yugoslavia (Bosnia)
1999–2000	1063	Kosovo
2000–2004	199	resettlement quota, from various countries

Source: Reception and Integration Agency 2005

Table 19.3: Applications for asylum in Ireland

Year	Numbers	Year	Numbers
1992	39	1999	7724
1993	91	2000	10938
1994	362	2001	10325
1995	424	2002	11634
1996	1179	2003	7900
1997	3883	2004	4766
1998	4626		

Source: Office of the Refugee Applications Commissioner 2001–2004

changes in Irish citizenship law which are examined later in the chapter. The passing of a referendum in June 2004 changing constitutional provisions on citizenship acted to further reduce the number of asylum seekers, with only 4,766 applying for asylum in 2004.

While there have been some changes over the past few years with regard to the origins of asylum seekers, over the period 2001–2004 almost 40 per cent of asylum seekers came from Nigeria and this has been fairly constant since the late 1990s. The arrival of asylum seekers from Romania has also been quite consistent over the past few years, averaging about 15 per cent of all applicants. Table 19.4 shows the decisions made on these asylum applications over the period 2001–2004. Such decisions are made in the first instance by the Office of the Refugee Applications Commissioner on the basis of whether the applicants are in fear of persecution, in line with the Geneva Convention, and Table 19.4 shows that on average only 6 per cent of applicants were granted refugee status, the remainder either being refused or withdrawn. There is an appeal process to the Refugee Appeals Tribunal where there is a higher success rate, but nonetheless the overall figures suggest that only 10 per cent of asylum seekers are successful in obtaining legal refugee status to remain in the state.

Table 19.4: Decisions on asylum

	Total cases decided on	Granted refugee status	Granted as % of total cases decided on
2001	7098	467	6.6
2002	8362	893	10.7
2003	8192	345	4.2
2004	6890	430	6.2

Source: Office of the Refugee Applications Commissioner 2001–2004

Asylum seekers, welfare and housing

One of the key issues which has arisen from the increase in asylum seekers is how best to supply them with housing and accommodation. Since 2000 asylum seekers have been accommodated directly by the government in centres outside Dublin. If granted legal status to stay and remain in Ireland, they can seek accommodation in the private market or through a variety of social housing options. The past decade has seen an extraordinary growth in the Irish economy with growth rates far higher than EU averages. One of the consequences of such growth has been rapid house price inflation in the private market both in purchase prices and in rents. New house prices have increased by over 300 per cent in some cases since the mid-1990s and at an even faster rate in the Dublin area.[8] This explosion in prices has led to all manner of problems of access to housing and affordability, with the number of households defined as being in housing need increasing substantially since the mid-1990s. There has been a severe undersupply of social housing which has led to pressure on the private rented sector. The number of households receiving rent supplement, a form of housing benefit, has more than trebled to 60,000 households in recent years. One of the key points to mention is that these problems were at their worst in the capital city of Dublin and, in the late 1990s, when the number of asylum seekers started to increase, most of them arrived in Dublin where there was in effect already an accommodation crisis.

As the number of asylum seekers arriving every month began to increase in 1999 and 2000, it became necessary to accommodate asylum seekers in hotel, bed and breakfast and hostel-type accommodation in the Dublin area. Towards the end of 1999, with asylum seekers arriving at over 1,000 per month, it became increasingly difficult to accommodate asylum seekers in the Dublin area. It has been suggested that 'within the city there were clear patterns of concentration, especially within the north inner city area. This sometimes led to conflict between asylum seekers, a socially and economically marginalized community, and other communities who were themselves disadvantaged within an increasingly polarized city'.[9] For these two reasons, shortage of accommodation in Dublin and fear of locating asylum seekers in proximity to already disadvantaged areas, a new policy direction was sought. The government introduced a system known as 'Dispersal and Direct Provision'.[10] Dispersal meant that asylum seekers would, as soon as possible, be relocated out of Dublin to accommodation centres around the country. Direct provision meant that the government would directly provide accommodation through renting premises itself. In other words, asylum seekers would not be allowed to avail themselves of any social housing option or of any private rented option but must go to the centre directly provided by government.

Asylum seekers are accommodated in three reception centres in Dublin while initial bureaucratic procedures are undertaken. Thereafter, they are relocated to a direct provision centre while their application for asylum is being processed, and to date approximately 35,000 asylum applicants have lived in such accommodation.[11] The available evidence suggests that they could be waiting up to two years in these centres while awaiting a decision or an appeal.[12] The agency has a total of 75 centres consisting of the following: three reception centres located in Dublin; 64 direct provision accommodation centres located throughout 20 local authorities; and eight self-catering accommodation centres. These centres are located throughout the country; most are in small towns and villages and not in the major urban areas. The centres consist of a mixture of state-owned and commercial premises and consist of hotels, guesthouses, hostels, former convents/nursing homes, mobile home sites, system-built facilities and apartments. Accommodation in reception and accommodation centres is provided on a full-board basis which includes provision of bed and three meals per day: residents are generally not allowed to cook their own food while living in an accommodation centre. One of the key rules is that residents are required to remain living in the centre until such time as their application is decided on, and failure to remain can be taken to mean that they have withdrawn their request for asylum. As the accommodation and meals are directly provided, a bare minimum social welfare payment of €19 is payable to each adult per week (€9.50 for children). In addition – and crucially – those applying for asylum since early 2000 are not legally entitled to work and are also precluded from receiving rent supplements towards the cost of accommodation in the private rented sector. In short, the system of accommodation for asylum applicants is heavily regulated.

In the period 1998 to 2000, prior to the direct provision and dispersal policy being formulated, there was considerable public and media debate regarding the location of asylum seekers. This debate resulted in a view, certainly among government, that there be a 'balanced' spatial distribution of asylum seekers and that various communities accept their 'fair share'. The official case for direct provision and dispersal is made clear in the quotation below.

A key determinant in providing accommodation for asylum seekers is maintaining in as much as possible a sensitive, balanced and proportional approach nationwide. The distribution of asylum seekers in direct provision across Health Board areas indicate that in no case do the numbers exceed one third of 1 per cent of the population of a Board's area.[13]

It is quite clear that official government policy is based on the premise that locating asylum seekers in major urban areas would create problems in the long term with respect to spatial concentrations of asylum seekers of different racial and ethnic origin, and this policy is seen by government as having been quite successful in countering any arguments by locals that they have received a disproportionate number of asylum applicants in their community. Thus, the key policy decision was to locate asylum seekers outside the major urban areas in general, and outside Dublin in particular. It can also be suggested that the strict rules regarding dispersal and the regulations on asylum seekers are intended to discourage applications for asylum. This system has been heavily criticized by many non-governmental organizations who see it as being a form of segregation. Interestingly, even welfare officials see serious problems with the direct provision method. Table 19.5 is taken from a study of Community Welfare Officers who are front-line staff with daily dealings with asylum seekers. Many are critical of the system as it creates boredom, depression and institutionalization. Further, the quality of the accommodation is seen by many as being substandard, with overcrowding problems common, and the weekly allowance is meagre at best. A recent qualitative study of a small sample of asylum seekers and refugees reveals strong dissatisfaction with the quality of accommodation and problems of boredom and so on which arise from not being able to legally work.[14]

If an asylum seeker is granted refugee status the person can access housing in the same way as Irish citizens, that is, by means of owner occupation, renting private accommodation or applying for social housing provided by the local authorities or from the voluntary sector. That is, they are free to leave the direct accommodation centre and move where they wish. In such circumstances it seems, although there is little hard research on this, many migrate to the major urban areas and in particular to Dublin. However, as discussed earlier, there remains a serious problem with regard to accessing

Table 19.5: Perceived weaknesses of direct provision as seen by welfare officers

Weaknesses	Frequency	%
creates boredom, depression, institutionalization	34	30.9
overcrowding, lack of facilities, poor quality food and accommodation	29	26.4
should only be a short-term measure	27	24.5
allowances paid are too low	24	21.8
ghettoizes and marginalizes asylum seekers	24	21.8
leads asylum seekers to disappear from the system	11	10.0
little attention given to ethnic composition	10	9.1
unsuitable for families	6	5.5
discriminatory system	5	4.5
very costly to the state	3	2.7
other	1	0.9

Source: Faughnan, Humphries and Whelan 2002

accommodation generally in the Dublin area. In these circumstances, it is likely to be extremely difficult for refugees to obtain appropriate accommodation at an affordable price. In all likelihood the vast majority of refugees will be unable to afford to purchase a house on the open market and will resort to social housing, the private rented sector or emergency hostel accommodation. To date there has been limited research on what happens to refugees once granted legal status. It is known, however, that approximately 6,000 non-national households (probably up to 15,000 people), which are not necessarily refugee households, avail themselves of rent allowance in the private rented sector. Moreover, it is known that, of the 48,000 households deemed as being in housing need in 2002, almost 2,700 of these households were refugee households.[15] It is likely that the majority of refugee households end up in the private rented sector. However, increasingly, many are applying for access to social rented housing.[16] To date there is little or no information available which indicates numbers of refugees who are accommodated in social housing, still less is there any information regarding their experiences with respect to integration.

Asylum, the city and citizenship

In the context of the urban realm and experience of Dublin as a city, how have these changes manifested themselves? One of the clearest and most visible ways in which the presence of immigrants has been registered has been in the rapid transformation of certain retail streets. For example, Moore Street in the centre of Dublin is well known as a street where predominantly working class women traditionally had street stalls to sell food and other goods. This remains so, but Moore Street is also now known as 'Little Africa', and the street has been transformed into a thriving and bustling area which sells all manner of African foods and goods, provides various community and entrepreneurial services and also clearly acts as a social centre for many African immigrants.[17] One would expect such changes in the city centre but in certain inner suburban neighbourhoods,[18] there has also been the development of a mix of African, Polish and Latvian shops with the attendant activity by these immigrants. With respect to religion, some older church buildings in Dublin are now being reused either as mosques or as places of worship for Protestant congregations, thus adding to the cultural diversity of the city. As would be expected with very recent immigrant communities, many of them are active in terms of forming social and community networks within their own communities and are also active in a variety of community media ventures.[19] These positive developments have, in the main, either been the product of the efforts of the communities themselves or in combination with a number of advocacy and support groups.

However, it must be made clear that the arrival of immigrants from Africa in particular, and the presence of black people on the streets of Dublin, has resulted in some atavistic responses, ranging from mild prejudice to outright racism. The initial discourse surrounding the arrival of asylum seekers brought forth responses which suggested that there was a 'flood' of asylum seekers arriving in Dublin. In the context of the overall figures on immigration this was clearly not the case. Some of the political debate revolved around defining asylum seekers as 'genuine' as opposed to 'bogus', with an inference that 'genuine' applicants were the minority. Incorrectly, some public debate suggested that asylum applicants were the recipients of more generous social welfare payments than those given to Irish citizens, to the extent that the National Consultative Committee on Racism and Interculturalism issued a corrective document on the myths surrounding these issues. As the system for assessing asylum applicants is now seen as being strict, and numbers of asylum seekers have declined substantially, this discourse has waned somewhat. It is in stark contrast to the lack of such discourse around the more recent immigration of people from the enlarged EU. In what is clearly a somewhat problematic analysis, it has sometimes been suggested that, as Ireland is a postcolonial society and has also had a history deeply scarred by emigration, there would be a certain sympathy for immigrants. In the 1980s the spectacle was to be seen of Irish politicians arguing for special treatment of the Irish in America, with pleas for illegal Irish immigrants to be granted special exemption.

However, the argument that such generosity should be shown in Ireland towards immigrants has often fallen on rather stony ground. Indeed, there has been little evidence that this historical background has made it a more tolerant society and the evidence to date would suggest that Irish people are not more virtuous than other nations in this regard. Hughes and Quinn (2004) point to a number of surveys, one of which shows that almost half the population believes that Ireland is a racist society, with a greater proportion of the Dublin population believing so. A survey of immigrants in 2001 found that almost 80 per cent of those surveyed had experienced racism of some form. More concretely, Peillon (2002) points to some protests in urban areas against asylum seekers and refugees, particularly with regard to the provision of accommodation, perhaps a form of racist NIMBYism. Even more seriously and tragically, in 2002 a Chinese student was murdered in what was most probably a racist attack. Figures from the National Consultative Committee on Racism and Interculturalism (2001–2004), which collates reported racist incidents, show that on average since 2001 almost 100 incidents are reported annually. However, approximately 60 per cent of such incidents are recorded in Dublin, indicating that the city may be a harder place to live than outside it. While this analysis is pessimistic and negative in content it is, however, difficult to place it in comparative context, and thus difficult to make a reasoned judgement as to whether it is similar to or different from the experience of other EU countries.

The reality of the arrival of asylum seekers has, in a very short timeframe, led to a significant change in the law on citizenship in Ireland. The constitutional provision for citizenship was essentially based on the concept of *jus soli* so that any child born on the island of Ireland automatically had a right to Irish citizenship. However, in the view of the Government and others, it was leading to an abuse of the system whereby non-national women (mainly African) would arrive in Ireland late in their pregnancy to give birth, thereby bestowing citizenship status on their newborn child and, it was assumed, rights to stay in Ireland for the parents. The referendum proposed to amend the Irish constitution to abolish this right and to make the question of citizenship mainly legislative. It was passed by a large majority in June 2004 and seems to have had a direct impact in reducing numbers arriving seeking asylum, and the present government has new legislation on immigration and residency in preparation subsequent to this constitutional change. In general terms it can be seen that the Irish Government has pursued a policy of attempting to discourage the arrival of asylum seekers through these changes in citizenship law and through the system of assessment and accommodation. Thus, where the government has had the power to act independently in making policy, they have tended to act in a restrictive manner. Nonetheless, the fact remains that many asylum seekers and legal refugees are already here and it is necessary to promote and implement polices which seek to include rather than exclude and segregate. What then is the position with regard to policy on integration? With respect to government policy, the Reception and Integration Agency (2005) has a set of laudable, if quite vague, aims, such as 'to create opportunities to enable newcomers to effectively participate in the economic, social and cultural aspects of Irish society and by so doing to exercise their rights and to discharge their responsibilities'. The government has also published an 'Action Plan Against Racism' and is promoting a more equal opportunity agenda, such as attempting to bring ethnic minorities into the police force.[20] However, no matter in what way the idea of integration might be defined, it is reasonably clear that at this point the level of integration and multiculturalism in Ireland and Dublin is quite low. The presence of new ethnic populations may be clear, but their long term future as equal citizens in a multicultural society is not.

Conclusions

This chapter has presented an analysis of policy development with respect to asylum seekers in Ireland. What can tentatively be concluded is that the system of welfare and accommodation for asylum seekers is de facto a segregated system which is punitive in many ways and seeks to discourage asylum seekers from coming to Ireland. Moreover, it is a system which is explicitly anti-urban in intent, which seeks to keep asylum seekers out of the capital city of Dublin. More generally, it can be argued that policy developments on asylum seekers and on citizenship are a very clear statement on behalf of the Irish State and society that immigration from non-EU states will be discouraged. Amin (2002, 2004) presents what is in essence an optimistic view of how multicultural cities and nations might operate, recognizing that there are atavistic forces at work, but hoping that a more multicultural society can be achieved. This analysis of immigration by asylum applicants into Ireland and Dublin suggests that Irish policy responses have tended to be on the 'fortress Europe' side of the debate and that broadly, as evidenced by the referendum on citizenship, society is happy with that. However, with the enlarged EU now reality, immigration by other nationalities and groups is bound to continue and the challenges facing Ireland to create a working multicultural society are only beginning.

Notes

1. Fanning 2002; Ferriter 2004.
2. Coogan 2000.
3. Central Statistics Office 2005.
4. Hughes, Quinn 2004; Quinn, Hughes 2005a.
5. Irish Refugee Council 2004; Immigration Council of Ireland 2003a, 2003b, 2004.
6. Hughes, Quinn 2004.
7. Hughes, Quinn 2004.
8. National Economic and Social Council 2004; Norris, Winston 2004.
9. Irish Centre for Migration Studies 2000.
10. Quinn, Hughes 2005a.
11. Hughes 2005; Quinn, Hughes 2005b.
12. Quinn, Hughes 2005b.
13. Reception and Integration Agency 2005.
14. Vincentian Refugee Centre 2004.
15. Department of the Environment, Heritage and Local Government 2002.
16. Clann Housing Association 2002.
17. White 2002.
18. Such as Inchicore and Rialto.
19. Quinn, Hughes 2005a; Ugba 2005.
20. Department of Justice, Equality and Law Reform 2004.

Part 4
Conclusions

20
Within the City Limits: Tolerance and the Negotiation of Difference

William J.V. Neill and Hanns-Uve Schwedler

While progressive thought often hides behind platitudes, the construction of tolerant multicultural cities in Europe at the beginning of the 21st century remains difficult work in progress. Partly driven by identity fears of where European integration is leading, negative referenda results were returned on the European Constitution in 2005 in the Netherlands and France. In the former, a famous liberal model of multiculturalism is now in retreat especially since the murder of Theo van Gogh, a critic of Islamic extremism, in 2004. A controversial official Dutch immigration video in 2006 has brought accusations of cultural exclusion through portraying images of female nakedness and gay expressions of intimacy.[1] The contrasting French model of cultural assimilation, which has also failed to deliver integration, is under question following the eruption of urban violence in ethnic estates in Autumn 2005 in the worst outbreak of civil unrest since 1968. However, nothing has epitomized more the cultural chasm between secular Europe and Islam than the global repercussions in early 2006, emanating from publication by a Danish newspaper, and subsequent reproduction by others, of 'blasphemous' cartoons depicting the prophet Mohammed. Against such a culturally charged background, this chapter, drawing on the variety of case studies presented in the book and on earlier chapters presenting theoretical perspectives and resources, can at best offer modest signposts for the resolution of a problem that will ultimately define the character of the European city in the 21st century. Given the positive link between tolerance of diversity and the creative city of innovation,[2] this also has economic ramifications. The chapter proceeds by way of considering the historical narrative of the European city and the challenge now posed in an information age of new migrant milieus and a neoliberal economic framework. The negotiation of accommodation between difference – in what can seem like a cultural minefield where some fear to tread for fear of giving offence – is re-examined. Taking a contrary view to the ideal expressed by Hillier in this volume (p. 84), which posits that in negotiation between difference 'transformation cannot only be concerned with "them", "the others"; it must also dislocate the position and rupture the prerogative of "us" ', the argument is made that decentering has boundaries and that, in the last instance, tolerance within the city has its limits. Here the dilemma presents itself that in confronting intolerance it is sometimes not possible to reply with tolerance. With this caveat, the chapter returns to the need to craft a more inclusive and participatory urban civic culture. The recent European 'common basic principles' on integration[3] are considered in this light.

The narrative of the European city

In a recent contribution Akbar and Kremer (2005, 30) usefully point out that Max Weber saw the special contribution of Europe to the history of the city as residing in its political and cultural character rather than in its physical form. Central was the concept of citizen, the city as the cohabitation of strangers but embodying a solidarity coming out of mutual recognition of equals in a common place. Dealing with the strange and foreign was part of the condition, a view shared by Georg Simmel. In this reconstruction of the city discourse of the Enlightenment:

> [T]he great narrative of the European city begins with Greek antiquity and the polis, cites the Roman republic, the virtuous citizen, and the free imperial cities of the Middle Ages, and it has continued to write these traditions without interruption until the present day – the agora, the polis and the forum are cited again and again in sketches, essays and studies by architects and urban researchers.[4]

Criticisms of the perspective articulated by Weber and Simmel include the observations that the urban citizenship of the former was bound up with property and ownership, and that the individuality given expression in the anonymity of the city and celebrated by the latter, was that of the bourgeois male citizen. More telling, however, for present preoccupations is the accusation of a limiting 'Eurocentricity', with Weber developing the identity of the European city within a symbolic field contrasting Occident and Orient (and Asian despotic forms of government in particular), in a narrative with a background dichotomy between civilization and the primitive – ignoring the fact that the European city has also been shaped by non-European, foreign cultures. Such criticisms evoke the link between the Enlightenment and colonialism exposed by Edward Said in his polemical book *Orientalism*,[5] where a discourse on the Orient, it is argued, has 'served as an instrument of rule and to shore up a European cultural identity by setting it off against the Arab world'.[6] Akbar and Kremer (2005, 32) frame the problem thus:

The problem is not only that the 'we' – the European identity – is founded on a disregard for and rejection of other cultures. Even more problematic is that such an understanding of self fails to register that the European traditions are multifarious and complex; that they do not draw the line at any geographical boundaries; that other, foreign cultures have also had an influence on European culture, becoming a part of the European identity – of that 'we'.

As the cultural geographer Günter Meyer (2004, 5) points out, dialogue between Orient and Occident since the terrorist attack of 11 September 2001 has now taken on a whole new meaning. However, this he says presumes well-founded knowledge of the 'other' culture – on respective sides – and an understanding of each other's life world. Without such knowledge in depth, dialogue surely cannot be productive and the risk is present that it remains at the level of prejudice and unexamined attributions.

In this remaking of a European 'we', work in progress will of necessity be multiscalar, recognizing the multiple publics within which citizenship these days is constructed and experienced. In the age of the translocal there are identities and civic networks, as Staeheli points out, not necessarily mediated by the neatness of a territorially defined nation state with migrants, often striving for a balance between 'hereness' and 'thereness', identifying with new homes but keeping connections to place of origin:

> The new language of citizenship must recognise the varied experiences of people living in cities, who build complex connections with people and places and who negotiate identities structured in more than one place and at more than one scale . . . No one is the disembodied, rational, universal citizen removed from the contexts of place that is postulated in liberal theories of citizenship.[7]

Here the city, with identity and citizenship constructed across scales, may be a more appropriate anchor point in the future for civic engagement than the nation state or EU citizenship. The economic milieu for such interaction and the challenge ahead will increasingly be a neoliberal one with claims on citizenship, social capital, connections and commitments made in the name of Third Way inspired new localism, putting responsibility, in particular for social welfare, on to localities.[8] The contribution by Morphet in this volume takes an optimistic view of possibilities in this regard. Not all are so sanguine.[9]

Towards a new urbanity?

If there is one loose connection that binds the contributions to this volume, writing as authors do from a variety of locales and viewpoints, it is the notion that to achieve cultural inclusion in the European city of the future it will be necessary to devise governance structures that enable the active negotiation between difference of a shared civic culture and sense of belonging to the city. In a sense President Kennedy's declaration of identification with the city of Berlin in 1963 as a symbol of tolerance and bulwark against forces which seek to exclude and crush (*'Ich bin ein Berliner'*) needs to ring in a new way and to be writ large in European cities. Yet the recent cold water poured by Baudrillard on what can appear as utopian aspirations, writing in the wake of the torching of the French *banlieues*, gives room for pause:

> If French – if European – society were to succeed in 'integrating' them, it would in its own eyes cease to exist. Yet French or European discrimination is only the micro-model of a world wide divide which, under the ironical sign of globalisation is bringing two irreconcilable universes face to face . . . Of course, nothing will prevent our enlightened politicians and intellectuals from considering the autumn riots as minor incidents on the road to a democratic reconciliation of all cultures.[10]

Taking a more optimistic view it would, nevertheless, be dishonest not to confront the elephant in the living room circumvented by various contributors to this book and embodied in the question: within the city, what are the limits of tolerance? Here the chanting of cosmopolitan mantras and the evocation of urban dreams are of little help. The question is approached through an examination of recent developments in urban planning theorizing, recognizing the intractably agonistic nature of city governance, and secondly, through an examination of some concrete views on an issue where liberal opinion is divided. The conclusion is reached that, based on negotiation over what constitutes 'the good city', in the last instance, despite laying oneself open to the charge of being 'only willing to accommodate a "filtered Other" ',[11] order must, nevertheless, be imposed on difference.[12]

Dealing with agonism

The chapter by Murtagh et al. in this volume draws attention to the cracks that have appeared in recent years in the dominant normative academic procedural planning paradigm, communicative planning, inspired by the German philosopher Jürgen Habermas. While the premium placed on reaching democratic consensus within an open dialogic context remains a laudable aspiration of Habermas, the criticism that such a model insufficiently engages with power relations in society, especially when measured against the Foucaultian insight that components of power are present in all communicative relations (discourse as transmitting, producing and reinforcing power) has proved telling.[13] More recent theory derived from the psychoanalytical work of Jacques Lacan and applied to planning practice[14] turns the search for consensus in urban planning into the 'quest for the snark'. The human subject is simply always divided against itself, is traumatized, with contradictory desires and identifications, the Habermasian ideal thus being in fact an impossibility. Rather, the call is made for an approach to planning and urban governance that does not seek one dominant consensus, but is based on an acceptance of 'affable but agonistic dis-sensus', an agonistic pluralism involving an approach to planning that is capable of accommodating conflict and emotion.[15] It is an approach going beyond a liberal model of civil society with a stress on individualism within a framework of rights, to nest within a more civic republican view as articulated by Honohan in this volume. Here the stress is on active citizenship rooted in the reality of interdependence. There is perhaps a danger of exaggerating the novelty of this. As Bernard Crick wrote in his famous book *In Defence of Politics* which argues that politics is about dialogue:

> Politics arises from accepting the fact of the simultaneous existence of different groups, hence different interests and different traditions, within a territorial unit under a common rule... politics represents at least some tolerance of different truths, some recognition that government is possible, indeed is best conducted amid the open canvassing of rival interests. (1982, 18)

With the need more than ever to negotiate coherence in a context of cultural diversity, Gunder usefully warns against any multicultural planning fantasy that a utopian state of security and inclusiveness for both 'us' and the 'Other' can be achieved. The desire for tolerance to the 'Other' 'may run counter to society's most fundamental desire for security, inclusiveness, and completeness'.[16] Still there must be negotiation between difference. Here the chapter by Wilson in this book suggests various bridges worth cultivating. In more general terms, despite current critique of its utopian aspirations, the concept of the processual aspect of public life in Habermas' work continues to inspire:

> ... the European traditions of the city must be separated from their past definitions and made flexible. An understanding of urban development as an everyday, continual process of negotiation between various milieus and different interest groups on the political level is now constituent of the European city. Such a concept of urbanity extends beyond simple participation, for it recognises and demands the active participation and contribution of urban protagonists.[17]

In this city, as Amin (2005a, 73) puts it, practical ways are needed of affirming an ideal of inclusion based on 'fellow feeling' developed through 'dense

everyday networks of institutional relations that bind difference', a view
shared by Benhabib (2000, 13) who makes the point that when groups articulate 'good reasons' in public to convince others in a multicultural society, the
likelihood of the emergence of a civic point of view of 'enlarged community'
is enhanced. Arguing that difference may 'more easily coexist in relation to
the civic identity of a city than in the concept of a nation', urban planning
in the broadest sense, Neill and Schwedler (2001, 207–09) have argued, must
take place with an 'ethic of cultural inclusion'. The chapter by Murtagh
et al. in this book provides some practical guidance on how this can be
taken forward. Yet the big question can no longer be avoided. What are the
barriers that cannot be crossed in a democratic multicultural city? Leonie
Sandercock (1998, 198–9) even while dreaming of post modernist 'togetherness in difference' in a utopian 'Cosmopolis' which has had some success
in capturing urban planning imagination, required that this be 'grounded
in a basic humanistic respect for others'. The updated dream addressing the
issue of living together in the 'mongrel city' of the 21st century now grounds
such a multicultural city firmly within 'an agonistic democratic politics that

Figure 20.1: Agonism in the city: public art in Berlin

demands active citizenship and daily negotiations of difference in all the banal sites of intercultural interaction'.[18]

This reverberates with what seems to be an emerging progressive discourse on conducting civic life in the multicultural city, incorporating aspects of a communitarian concept of citizenship, where the latter is concerned about respect for and preservation of cultural identity, the essential problem being not the agreement of a moral universalism, but the integration of self and other.[19] The attempt to apply such thinking to a conception of Britain as 'a community of communities' as advocated by the influential Parekh Report[20] has, however, not been without its critics. Too much tolerance of difference brings the accusation that it can impede the development of a binding civic culture of belonging, a point strongly made by the current chair of Britain's Commission for Racial Equality in 2005 and bringing what has been labelled an intemperate response from the Muslim Council of Britain.[21] In turn, majority imposition of values on a minority can be seen as an application of the doctrine that 'might' makes 'right'.[22] This is a 'fuzzy dilemma' unlikely to disappear in the near future. Here the issue is not one of reaching pragmatic accommodation over issues such as acceptable burial practices or the design features of mosques in the city, for example – where experience indicates that intercultural dialogue does allow cultures to successfully rub along together in a spirit of give and take,[23] although in a context where cultural minorities still face considerable intolerance and difficulties living in a dominant culture.[24] While it has been said that 'lofty declarations of old universals will not do',[25] difficulty is more evidently manifest when the chasm over basic values is wide and where moral relativism can create space for more extreme positions. Here issues concerning freedom of expression, human rights (the rights of women in particular) and the principle of the secular nature of Europe's democracies are central. In essence, the limits to the decentering of 'the dominant culture' in practice must be drawn at the extension of group rights to oppressive cultural practices. Here it is useful to recall Kant's categorical imperative and the principle that freedom may have to be limited when it infringes on the freedom of others. It is certain that honour rapes and killings fall into this category. Forced marriages, discrimination against homosexuals and polygamy would add to the list. It is also not so certain that the uproar caused by the Danish cartoons can be put down to an act of provocation, even with the recognition that freedom of speech is a social construct and far from being an absolute. While maximum room must be left for cultural self-definition, and while no attempt should be made to equate the violent actions of a radicalized minority with the opinions of majority ethnic society, one prominent commentator of recent immigrant stock in Britain caught the mood of popular discourse and feeling in stating, in the wake of the London Tube bombing in July 2005:

... the time for sophistry has passed. Our citizens and our society are under threat from those who believe that difference is a justification for terror and murder. Our country has the right to assert its values and require from everyone living here compliance with our laws and respect for our standards... Tolerance was clearly never meant to mean that Britain should allow those with roots outside the country to flout human rights and the laws of the land on the pretext that things were done differently where they came from... [26]

It might be added, of course, that tolerance was never meant to accept the violation of human rights, whatever the root or the sources.

Walking a tightrope between not decentering 'host' society values, alongside accepting the obligation of tolerance to respect difference, can be seen as expressed in the common basic principles on integration recently adopted by the European Council (Figure 20.2). This precedes, however, a much needed broad, open and rational public discussion on the future complexion of European values and principles.

These principles, adopted at the informal ministerial conference in the Netherlands in November 2004, now endorsed by the European Commission as laying the basis of a coherent European framework for integration, bear the stamp of the good governance guidance policies on cultural integration approved by the annual general meeting of EuroCities (Chapter 4 in this volume) in 2003. The latter, 'keeping the separation of church and state intact', is 'in agreement with the Convention on the Protection of Human Rights and Fundamental Freedoms of the Council of Europe' (2003, 8). In conformity with the tenor of EuroCities, integration, as conceived through the common basic principles, is a two way process of mutual engagement, where immigrants are expected to respect the fundamental norms and values of the host society and to participate actively in the integration process – all of which must be made possible and actively permitted by the host society. This process, however, presumes equally valid opportunities to participate for everyone in the resources of a society.[27] If this is not the case, integration and dialogue must remain euphemisms (Chapter 9 of this volume).

A European Year of Inter-Cultural Dialogue is envisaged for 2008 as an awareness raising initiative. Of particular interest for cities is acknowledgement, in the most recent Commission thinking on the matter, of 'the value of a concept of "civic citizenship" as a means of promoting the integration of immigrants who do not have national citizenship'.[28] However, the 'fuzzy dilemma' of the Parekh report in Britain, referred to above, as ultimately failing to justify why, in the last instance in intercultural dialogue, the public values of the wider society should trump the values of minority communities, may be seen as writ large on the European stage in the Common Basic Principles. In the last instance, it might be said, order must be imposed on difference due to the fact that there is a much commented upon difficulty with liberal politics. It embodies a deep contradiction:

Figure 20.2: Towards common principles?

Principles on Integration adopted by European Council, Groningen, November 2004

- Integration is a dynamic, two-way process of mutual accommodation by all immigrants and residents of Member States.
- Integration implies respect for the basic values of the European Union.
- Employment is a key part of the integration process and is central to the participation of immigrants, to the contributions immigrants make to the host society and to making such contributions visible.
- Basic knowledge of the host society's language, history, and institutions is indispensable to integration; enabling immigrants to acquire this basic knowledge is essential to successful integration.
- Efforts in education are critical to preparing immigrants, and particularly their descendants, to be more successful and more active participants in society.
- Access for immigrants to institutions, as well as to public and private goods and services, on a basis equal to national citizens and in a non-discriminatory way is a critical foundation for better integration.
- Frequent interaction between immigrants and Member State citizens is a fundamental mechanism for integration. Shared forums, intercultural dialogue, education about immigrants and immigrant cultures, and stimulating living conditions in urban environments enhance the interactions between immigrants and Member State citizens.
- The practice of diverse cultures and religions is guaranteed under the Charter of Fundamental Rights and must be safeguarded, unless practices conflict with other inviolable European rights or with national law.
- The participation of immigrants in the democratic process and in the formulation of integration policies and measures especially supports their integration at the local level.
- Mainstreaming integration policies and measures in all relevant policy portfolios and levels of government and public services is an important consideration in public policy formation and implementation.
- Developing clear goals, indicators and evaluation mechanisms are necessary to adjust policy, evaluate progress on integration and to make the exchange of information more effective,

---

Source: EC Commission of the European Communities (Com(2005)389/1-9-2005).

On the one hand cultural differences must be respected and preserved; on the other culture is subordinate to a political theory of universalism in which difference is transcended in the doctrines of equality and human rights.[29]

Conclusion

This book can make but a modest contribution to a fundamental challenge opening up to increasingly diverse European cities. The problem to be addressed is the reconciliation of diversity with the need for societal coherence – and at its worst how to prevent difference and diversity becoming division and warfare – by constructing a politics which channels and negotiates conflict. As MacGregor (1993, 10) rightly said surveying this emerging landscape over a decade ago 'there must be some shared notions or things will fall apart – the centre will not hold ... The old certainties about values may have gone but the awareness of the abyss beyond if we do not step cautiously has led to a searching for some agreed pathways and directions.' Recent evidence of the abyss in Europe has been all too apparent. Accepting the admonition that there should be no analysis of power without an accompanying analysis of hope,[30] there are, even in the present cold climate, reasons for optimism that initiatives such as the EuroCities charter and EU Common Basic Principles on Integration have made a start in helping to chart pathways and directions for the tolerant negotiation of difference within the city limits.

Notes

1. C4 News UK, 16 March 2006.
2. Florida 2005.
3. CEC 2005.
4. Akbar, Kremer 2005, 31.
5. Said 1978.
6. Ali 2003, 61.
7. Staeheli 2005, 146.
8. Staeheli 2005, 145; Amin 2005a, 64.
9. Phillips 2005.
10. Baudrillard 2006. 6–7.
11. Gunder 2005a, 97.
12. Neill 2004, 7.
13. Gunder 2003, 289.
14. Gunder, Hillier 2004.
15. Gunder 2005b, 177.
16. Gunder 2005a, 85.
17. Akbar, Kremer 2005, 34.

18. Sandercock 2003a, 103.
19. Neill 2004, 224.
20. FMEB 2000.
21. *Times* leader column, 23 September 2005.
22. Barry 2001, 67.
23. Manço 2006, 5–11.
24. Dittrich 2006, 16–19.
25. Amin 2005b.
26. Portillo 2005.
27. Schwedler 1985, 197ff.
28. COM 2005, 22.
29. Inglis 2001, 17.
30. Sandercock 2004, 142.

Appendix 1: EUROCITIES' Contribution to Good Governance Concerning the Integration of Immigrants and the Reception of Asylum Seekers

The charter on good governance concerning the integration of migrants has been adopted in 2003 and published in August 2004. In twelve points it outlines both common general, and more specific principles relating to the delivery of key services:

Concerning common principles

City governments commit themselves to:

- Fully inform their population about the fact that immigration is a common phenomenon in all European cities and that immigrants have a permanent place in the life of their cities.
- Fully inform their population about the rights of asylum and their obligations concerning the protection of asylum seekers and refugees.
- Promote the fact that immigration is an enriching and positive phenomenon as well as a sometimes challenging process to adapt to – on the part of the established population as well as the newcomers.
- Promote the perspective that integration demands a two-sided response, from the established population as well as the newcomer; in fact that integration requires a joint venture in adaptation to a common future involving all parties concerned.
- Act in fairness and equity on behalf of all parties.
- Prevent racist behaviour and combat it in all its forms. They will – if not yet existing – develop initiatives to sensitize public officials and the police to racist and xenophobic behaviour.
- Always preserve and promote the common and basic values of democracy, gender equality, equal rights, social cohesion, respect for cultural diversity, and participation as the basis to construct and strengthen our societies.
- Take appropriate measures against the dissemination of misleading information relating to immigration.

Concerning participation

In agreement with the Convention for the Protection of Human Rights and Fundamental Freedoms of the Council of Europe, and considering the participation of all residents in public life at the local level to be the life-blood of local democracy, city governments will:

- Develop and/or invest in direct and open communication with all communities of immigrant background, to involve them in the design and implementation of all policies directly affecting their life-chances and living environment.
- Promote serious dialogue between the groups of residents of different origin in the neighbourhoods of their cities on all issues relevant to those communities and especially on issues which may lead to inter-group tension, gender gap and conflict. They will provide communities with the conditions and resources to prevent conflict and to join forces to solve common problems.
- Promote effective participation, they will aim to provide resources to communities to organize themselves – managerial expertise, accommodation and finances.
- Promote, if not yet existent, the right to vote and to be elected to neighbourhood and municipal councils, for all legal residents, whatever their nationality.
- Promote the dissemination of both the full rights and the obligations of immigrants as citizens in their society.

Concerning the reception of newcomers

In agreement with the commitment of the Tampere European Council for a common European immigration and asylum system, including the establishment of minimum quality standards in the reception of asylum seekers, city governments will:

- Promote investment in the provision of decent reception centres and housing, the provision of adequate health care and legal counsel, and the provision of sufficient income to enable newcomers to survive decently in accordance with the minimum necessary standards of their communities.
- Promote the provision of educational, language and vocational courses, to start as soon as possible after the beginning of asylum procedures, irrespective of whether a procedure leads to a residence permit or the refusal thereof. In case a claimant is refused residence, he or she would then leave the receiving society better equipped than when he or she arrived.
- Promote the enlargement of possibilities to obtain gainful employment during procedures. A prolonged period of unemployment is damaging to prospects for successful integration in the formal labour market. Waiting a long time in forced idleness and insecurity is damaging to human dignity and mental health.
- Pay special attention to the situation of unaccompanied minors seeking asylum and those granted refugee status, in taking over parental care eventually by proxy of private guardian institutions to adequately protect this particularly vulnerable group.
- Invite all relevant public bodies and non-governmental organizations to join forces in an organized, integrated way in order to carry out these tasks. City governments will promote the commitment of the private and voluntary sectors to these activities.

Concerning integration

Cities fully recognize the responsibility of local authorities as the entity at local level ultimately responsible for integration issues, based on their responsibility for local social cohesion. Taking into account that integration is a mutual process between a receiving society and the newcomer, and conscious of the fact that integration is intrinsically linked to the promotion of social cohesion and progress, city governments commit themselves to:

- Make a maximum effort to develop, if not yet in place, an organized and integrated set of policies to support newcomers to find their place in society rapidly and efficiently as fully functioning citizens in all areas of urban life, economically, socially, politically and culturally.
- Maintain and improve appropriate public services to deal with issues concerning immigrants and their integration.
- Invest in developing joint ventures of all parties concerned: NGOs, the private sector and the urban residents in general, in order to commit all forces to a common strategy.
- Invest in ethnic minority and refugee community organizations, because they are positioned to play a pivotal role in the integration process.
- Inform all newcomers about the commitments on both sides of the integration process and the consequences of not fulfilling their role in this process. As integration is a mutual obligation of the receiving society and the newcomer, they expect the newcomer to take advantage of any opportunity offered to progress on the road to full independent citizenship.
- Invest in full and transparent information for all residents on the realities of immigration and the necessary conditions for effective integration. They consider it of utmost importance that integration is a matter for the whole urban community. They will develop strategies to promote not only tolerance but also receptive attitudes among the 'general population', and to inform all urban residents about what is expected from them in terms of support to newcomers.

Concerning education

As education is the key to independent and informed citizenship, cities consider full access to and participation in the formal education system essential to successful integration. This applies to obligatory education as well as second chance or adult education. It applies equally to newcomers and established minorities. City governments will:

- Invest in promoting access to all educational provisions.
- Develop, with the involvement of all parties concerned, education systems which take into account the diversity of backgrounds and needs of students. They will promote the evaluation and updating of the curricula of their education programmes in order to adapt them to the reality of new students.
- Promote the development of special programmes for teaching the language of the receiving society, as a fundamental tool to enable integration in local society.
- Adequately address the educational needs of the children of newcomers and established ethnic minorities, by investing in special programmes if needed. City governments will develop strategies, if not yet existent, to prevent pupils from dropping out of the school system.
- Promote positive recognition of the language skills of immigrants in education and training programmes.

- Promote the simplification of international recognition procedures for qualifications.
- Invest in sensitizing educational institutions, their management and teachers towards the increasing diversity of their students, in providing the necessary expertise in this respect.
- Facilitate for children from ethnic minorities the teaching of their mother tongue and culture and, in this respect, they will search for collaboration with the countries of origin, where appropriate.

Concerning the labour market

Considering employment to be a fundamental right and basic need in terms of social and economic integration, city governments will:

- Defend the principle of equal rights and equal obligations for all with regard to the labour market.
- Develop, if they are not already in existence, special programmes to enhance the labour market opportunities for all newcomers and established minorities.
- Address the particular needs and difficulties of young people regarding their inclusion in the labour market and develop special programmes and services for them.
- In accordance with the European directives on anti-discrimination, strongly fight against any kind of discrimination based on cultural, racial, religious, ethnic or gender differences.
- Fight against exploitation, employment segregation and abuse of any kind, in terms of salary, working hours, conditions of work, contracts, etc.
- Actively work towards the prevention and elimination of illegal and clandestine work, as well as the protection of both legal immigrants and undocumented workers from exploitation.
- Promote the role and active participation of all relevant parties, from entrepreneurs to workers' associations.

Concerning health

In agreement with the Convention on the Protection of Human rights and Fundamental Freedoms of the Council of Europe, city governments will:

- Actively promote the access of immigrants and asylum seekers to health services, regardless of their legal and administrative situation.
- Guarantee the necessary information and orientation in order to access health services.
- Develop mediation programmes within the health services as much as possible, so as to facilitate communication and understanding between professionals and different ethnic groups.
- Develop specific health prevention and action programmes addressing the special needs of new populations, including asylum seekers of both genders.
- Promote counselling and medical treatment in the mother tongue, if necessary.
- Promote educational programmes on cultural diversity for health workers.

Concerning housing

City governments will:

- Promote the equal rights of newcomers and established ethnic minorities to access decent housing in order to establish a home as fully-fledged citizens. Equal rights will include access to decent housing in the formal market, as well as to protected accommodation.
- Promote and enhance support services for newcomers and established ethnic minorities for access to decent housing.
- Design specific policies for the upgrading of housing in deprived areas, with the objective of promoting better housing conditions for immigrants and other residents in those areas, while also taking action to prevent the social and spatial segregation of immigrants and established ethnic minorities in the more deprived urban areas and in poor quality housing.
- Prevent competition for cheap and irregular accommodation between homeless people, asylum seekers and undocumented immigrants by investing in adequate housing.

Concerning social services

City governments will:

- Promote the adaptation of social services to meet the needs of a diverse population. They will aim to enhance the human and financial resources of the local social services to adequately address the specific needs of immigrants and asylum seekers. This includes the provision of individual counselling in the mother tongue, if necessary.
- Facilitate cultural mediation in the social services, as appropriate to their users
- Enhance the expertise of social services' staff to adequately respond to the needs of new populations.
- Monitor and evaluate social services, with the participation of users, in order to adapt the design and delivery of services as deemed necessary.

Concerning cultural identity and diversity

In agreement with the Convention on the Protection of Human Rights and Fundamental Freedoms of the Council of Europe, city governments will:

- Develop cultural programmes that promote and enhance the visibility of the cultural diversity of their cities.
- Promote access to the cultural facilities of the city and participation in cultural life for all immigrants.
- Provide the necessary services and resources to minority ethnic groups to promote their own culture.
- Develop special cultural programmes and events to facilitate the dissemination and exchange of the different cultures represented in their cities, including the receiving society's culture, with the aim of promoting common understanding and fruitful exchange.

- Develop strategies to prevent tensions and conflicts arising in the cities' shared public spaces. They will promote the respect of common rules in the use of public spaces as a first step to enhancing social cohesion.
- Defend the right to freedom of expression and religion. This right should include the freedom to manifest one's religion or belief in worship, observance, practice and teaching, within the limits of the law and keeping the separation of church and state intact.

Concerning the eviction of refused asylum claimants, refugees and immigrants

In agreement with the Convention on the Protection of Human Rights and Fundamental Freedoms of the Council of Europe, if there is no convention, humanitarian or political grounds on which to grant an asylum claimant permission to stay, city governments will:

- Act within the limits of their legal competencies and practical constraints, and in accordance with the distribution of competencies between the international, national and local level, to promote and develop policies to support the return of those persons who have been denied access to their countries, to a safe and secure future in the framework of national cooperation.

Concerning monitoring and evaluating progress

City governments will:

- Develop monitoring and evaluation systems to enable the adequate collection of data relating to the position of immigrants in the city, and to successfully monitor and evaluate the effectiveness of actions taken to promote integration.
- Develop follow-up mechanisms to adequately assess the development of their policies with regard to this Contribution to Good Governance.

Bibliography

Abizadeh, A. (2002): Does liberal democracy presuppose a cultural nation? Four arguments; *American Political Science Review*, 96, 495–509

Abu-Lughod (1991): Writing against culture; in: R. Fox, *Recapturing Anthropology*, (Santa Fe: School of American Research Press) pp. 137–62

Akbar, O; Kremer, E. (2005): Shrinking – a challenge for the European city; in: International Building Exhibition (IBA), Stiftung Bauhaus Dessau (ed.): *The Other Cities, Volume 1: Experiment* (Berlin: Jovis Verlag)

Alesina, A.; Spolaore, E. (2003): *The Size of Nations* (Cambridge, MA: MIT Press)

Ali, T. (2003): Remembering Edward Said; *New Left Review*, 24, 59–65

Allasino, E.; Bobbio, L.; Neri, S. (2000): Crisi urbane: che cosa succede dopo? Le politiche per la gestione della conflittualità legata ai problemi dell'immigrazione, Working paper 135 (Turin: IRES)

Allcock, J.B. (2000): *Explaining Yugoslavia* (London: Hurst)

Allen, J.; Göran, C.; Madanipour, A. (eds) (1998): *Social Exclusion in European Cities: Processes, Experiences and Responses* (London: Jessica Kingsley)

Allmendinger, P.; Gunder, M. (2005): Applying Lacanian insights and a dash of Derridean deconstruction to planning's 'dark side'; *Planning Theory*, 4 (1), 87–112

Altman, D. (1991): *Paper Ambassadors: the Politics of Stamps* (North Ryde: NSW)

Ambrosini, M.; Molina, S. (eds) (2004): *Seconde generazioni. Un'introduzione al futuro dell'immigrazione in Italia* (Turin: Edizioni Fondazione Giovanni Agnelli)

Amin, A. (2001): Immigrants, cosmopolitans and the idea of Europe; in: H. Wallace (ed.): *Interlocking Dimensions of European Integration* (Basingstoke: Palgrave – now Palgrave Macmillan) pp. 280–301

Amin, A. (2002): Ethnicity and the multicultural city: living with diversity; *Environment and Planning*, 34 (6), 959–80

Amin, A. (2004): Multi-ethnicity and the idea of Europe; *Theory, Culture & Society*, 21(2), 1–24

Amin, A. (2005a): Local community on trail; in: International Building Exhibition (IBA), Stiftung Bauhaus Dessau (ed.): *The Other Cities, Volume 1: Experiment* (Berlin: Jovis Verlag)

Amin, A. (2005b): In the west, we love to hate; *Guardian*, 21 January

Amin, A.; Thrift, N. (2002): *Cities: Reimagining the Urban* (Cambridge: Polity Press)

Amselle, J.-L. (1999): *Logiques Métisses. Anthropologie de l'identité en Afrique et ailleurs* (Paris: Editions Payot)

Amselle, J.-L. (2001): *Branchements. Anthropologie de l'universalité des cultures* (Paris: Flammarion)

Anderson, B. (1991): *Imagined Communities: Reflections on the Origin and Spread of Nationalism* (London: Verso)

Anderson, J.; Shuttleworth, I. (1998): Sectarian demography, territoriality and political development in Northern Ireland; *Political Geography*, 187–208

Andric, I. (1990): *The Development of Spiritual Life in Bosnia under the Influence of Turkish Rule* (Durham, NC: Duke University Press)

Ardener, E. (1989): Remote places; in: E. Ardener (ed.): *The Voice of Prophecy and Other Essays* (Oxford: Basil Blackwell)

Ardener, S. (1993): *Women and Space: Ground Rules and Social Maps*, 2nd edn (London: Croom Helm)

Arendt H. (1958): *The Human Condition* (Chicago: University of Chicago Press)

Arendt, H. (1977): What is freedom?; in: H. Arendt (ed.): *Between Past and Future* (Harmondsworth: Penguin) pp. 143–72

ARGEBAU: (2000): Leitfaden zur Ausgestaltung der Gemeinschaftsinitiative 'Soziale Stadt', (http://www.sozialestadt.de/veroeffentlichungen/arbeitspapiere/band 3 /3_argebau.shtml)

Atkinson, J.; Flint, J. (2004): Fortress UK? Gated communities, the spatial revolt of the elites and time – space trajectories of segregation; *Housing Studies*, 19 (6), 875–92

Audit Commission (2004): *People Places and Prosperity London* (www.audit-commission.gov.uk)

Audit Commission (2005): *Area Profiles* (www.audit-commission.gov.uk)

Azaryahu, M. (1997): German reunification and the politics of street names: the case of East Berlin; *Political Geography*, 16, 479–93

Bader, V. (2001): Institutions, culture and identity of transnational citizenship: how much integration and communal spirit is needed?; in: C. Crouch, K. Eder, D. Tambini (eds): *Citizenship, Markets and the State* (Oxford: Oxford University Press)

Bairner, A.; Shirlow, P. (1998): Loyalism, Linfield and the territorial politics of soccer fandom in Northern Ireland; *Space and Polity*, 2, 163–78

Banac, I. (1994): The recent history of the Bosnian Muslims; in: M. Pinson (ed.): *The Muslims of Bosnia-Herzegovina: their Historic Development from the Middle Ages to the Dissolution of Yugoslavia* (Cambridge, MA: Harvard University Press) pp. 129–53

Barnett, A. (1997): *This Time: Our Constitutional Revolution* (London: Vintage)

Barrucci, T.; Liberti, S. (2004): *Lo stivale meticcio. L'immigrazione in Italia oggi* (Rome: Carocci)

Barry, B. (2001): The muddles of multiculturalism; *New Left Review*, 8

Barth, F. (ed.) (1969): *Ethnic Groups and Boundaries: Social Organization of Culture Differences* (London: Athlone Press)

Bartlett, R. (1993): *The Mabo Decision*: commentary by R.H. Bartlett and the full text of the decision (Sydney: Butterworths)

Bastos, J.G.; Bastos, S. (1999): *Portugal Multicultural* (Lisbon: Fim de Século)

Baubock, R. (2003): Reinventing urban citizenship; *Citizenship Studies*, 7(2), 139–60

Baudrillard, J. (2006): Pyres of Autumn; *New Left Review*, 37, 5–7

Bauman, Z. (2001): *Community: Seeking Safety in an Insecure World* (Cambridge: Polity Press)

Baumann, G. (1994): *Contesting Culture, Ethnicity and Community in West London* (Cambridge: Cambridge University Press)

Baumann,G. (1996): *Contesting Culture: Discourses of Identity in Multi-ethnic London* (Cambridge: Cambridge University Press)

Baxter, H. (2002a): Habermas' discourse theory of law and democracy; *Buffalo Law Review*, 30(1), 205–340

Baxter, H. (2002b): System and lifeworld in Habermas' theory of law; *Cardozo Law Review*, 23(2), 473–615

BBC (2005): Born abroad web site (www.bbc.co.uk/bornabroad)

Beck, P.J. (1983): Argentina's 'philatelic annexation' of the Falklands; *History Today*, February, 39–44

Beck, U. (1998): *Democracy Without Enemies* (Cambridge: Polity Press)

Begg, I. (1998): Structural Fund Reform in the Light of Enlargement; Sussex University: Centre on European Political Economy Working Paper No. 1

Belfast Interface Project (1998): Interface Communities and the Peace Process, Belfast

Bell, D. (1998): *Ngarrindjeri Warruwarrin: a World that is, was and will be* (Melbourne: Spinifex)

Bellamy, R. (2001): The 'right to have rights': citizenship practice and the political constitution of the EU; in: R. Bellamy, A. Warleigh (eds): *Citizenship and Governance in the European Union* (London: Continuum) pp. 42–71

Bellamy, R.; Castiglione, D.; Shaw, J. (eds) (2006): *Making European Citizens* (Basingstoke: Palgrave Macmillan)

Belpiede, A. (ed.) (2002): *Mediazione culturale. Esperienze e percorsi formativi* (Turin: Utet)

Benhabib, S. (1988): Judgement and the moral foundations of politics in Arendt's thought; *Political Theory*, 16(1), 29–51

Benhabib, S. (2000): Democracy and identity; in: Swiss Federal Office of Culture, *Humanity, Urban Planning, Dignity*, pp. 12–22

Benhabib, S. (2002): *The Claims of Culture* (Princeton: Princeton University Press)

Bickford, S. (2000): Constructing inequality – city spaces and the architecture of citizenship; *Political Theory*, 28(3), 355–76

Billig, M. (1995): *Banal Nationalism* (London: Sage)

Black, R. (2002): Conceptions of 'home' and the political geography of refugee repatriation: between assumption and contested reality in Bosnia-Herzegovina; *Applied Geography*, 22, 123–38

Blomley, N. (2003): Law, property, and the geography of violence: the frontier, the survey, and the grid; *AAAG*, 93(1), 121–41

Bloomfield, J.; Bianchini, F. (2004): *Planning for the Intercultural City* (Stroud: Comedia)

Boal, F. (ed.) (2000): *Ethnicity and Housing. Accommodating Differences* (Aldershot: Ashgate)

Boal, F.; Murray, R. (1977): A city in conflict; *Geographical Magazine*, 44, 364–71

Booher, D.; Innes, J. (2002): Network power in collaborative planning; *Journal of Planning Education and Research*, 21(3), 221–36

Borneman, J.; Fowler, N. (1997): Europeanization; *Annual Review of Anthropology*, 26, 487–514

Borzel, T. (1999): Towards convergence in Europe? Institutional adaptation to Europeanization in Germany and Spain; *Journal of Common Market Studies*, 37(4), 573–96

Bourquin, J.-F. et al. (2004): *(Re)Thinking Stereotypes: Constructing Intercultural and Inter-religious Dialogue* (Strasbourg: Council of Europe)

Braccesi, C.; Sacchini, G.; Selmini, R. (2004): Le politiche per la sicurezza urbana: l'esperienza italiana nel contesto europeo; *Inchiesta*, XXXIV(143)

Braidotti, R. (2002): *Metamorphoses* (Cambridge: Polity)

Bringa, T.R. (1995): *Being Muslim the Bosnian way: Identity and Community in a Central Bosnian Village* (Princeton NJ: Princeton University Press)

Brubaker, R. (2002): Ethnicity without groups; *Archives Européenes de Sociologie*, 13(2), 163–89

Buck, N.; Gordon, I.; Hall, P.; Harloe, M.; Kleinman, M. (2002): *Working Capital: Life and Labour in Contemporary London* (London: Routledge)

Burg, S.L.; Shoup, P.S. (1999): *The War in Bosnia-Herzegovina: Ethnic Conflict and International Intervention* (Armonk: M.E. Sharpe)

Burton, F. (1978): *The Politics of Legitimacy: Struggles in a Belfast Community* (London: Routledge and Kegan Paul)

Buttimer, A. (1994): Edgar Kant and Balto-Skandia: Heimatkunde and regional identity; in: D. Hooson (ed.): *Geography and National Identity* (Oxford: Blackwell) pp.161–83

Cameron, David (2006): Independent Evaluation of the Youth and Environment Programme; Groundwork N. Ireland

Campbell, D. (1998): *National Deconstruction: Violence, Identity and Justice in Bosnia* (Minneapolis: University of Minnesota Press)

Cantle, T. (2001): *Community Cohesion: a Report of the Independent Review Team on the Disturbances in Oldham and Burnley in 2001* (London: Home Office)

Capello, C. (2003): Torino, Maghreb. La costruzione di identità trasversali tra i migranti marocchini; in: P. Sacchi, P. Viazzo (eds.): *Più di un Sud. Studi antropologici sull'immigrazione a Torino* (Turin: Rosenberg e Sellier)

Caplan, R. (2004): International authority and state building: the case of Bosnia and Herzegovina; *Global Governance*, 10, 53–65

Castree, N. (2004): Differential geographies: place, indigenous rights and 'local' resources; *Political Geography*, 23, 133–67

CEC – Commission of the European Communities (2005): *A Common Agenda for Integration. Framework for the Integration of Third-Country Nationals in the European Union*, COM(2005) 389 final (Brussels: CEC)

Central Statistics Office (2005): *Population and Migration Estimates* (Dublin: Central Statistics Office)

Certeau, M. de (1980): *L'invention du quotidien*. Arts de faire (Paris: UGE)

Chambers, S. (2004): Democracy, popular sovereignty, and constitutional legitimacy; *Constellations*, 11(2), 153–73

Cheshire, P.; Carbonaro, G.; Hay, D. (1986): Problems of urban decline and growth in EEC countries: or measuring degrees of elephantness; *Urban Studies*, 2, 131–49

Chiang-Liang Low, C. (1996): *White Skins/Black Masks: Representations and Colonialism* (London: Routledge)

Child, J. (2005): The politics and semiotics of the smallest icons of popular culture: Latin American postage stamps; *Latin American History Review*, 40(1), 108–37

Cicero, M.T. (1991): *On Duties* (reprint) (Cambridge: Cambridge University Press)

Clann Housing Association (2002): *Housing and Refugees: A New Challenge – Conference Proceedings* (Dublin: Clann Housing Association)

Clarke, Lord (2001): *Burnley Task Force Report* (Burnley: Burnley Task Force)

Closa, C. (1995): Citizenship of the Union and nationality of Member States; *Common Market Law Review*, 32, 487–518

Closa, C. (1998a): Some foundations for the normative discussion on supranational citizenship and democracy, in European citizenship, multiculturalism, and the state; in: K.U. Preuss, F. Requejo (eds.): *European Citizenship, Multiculturalism, and the State* (Baden-Baden: Nomos Verlagsgessellschaft) pp. 105–24

Closa, C. (1998b): Supranational citizenship and democracy: normative and empirical dimensions; in: M. Torre (ed.): *European Citizenship: an International Challenge* (Dordecht: Kluver Law International) pp. 416–43

Cohen, A. (1974): Introduction: the lesson of ethnicity; in: A. Cohen: *Urban Ethnicity* (London: Tavistock)

Cohen, A. (1974a): *Urban Ethnicity* (London: Tavistock)

Cohen, S.B.; Kliot, N. (1992): Place-names in Israel's ideological struggle over the Administered Territories; *Annals of the Association of American Geographers*, 82, 653–80

Colombo, A.; Sciortino G. (2004): *Gli immigrati in Italia. Assimilati o esclusi: gli immigrati, gli italiani, le politiche* (Bologna: Il Mulino)

Commissie-Blok (Parlementaire Commissie Integratiebeleid) (2002): *Bruggen bouwen* (The Hague: Sdu Uitgevers)

Commission of Enquiry (Enquete-Kommission) (2001): *Local Agenda 21/Fit for the Future* (Berlin: House of Representatives – 14th term of office)
Commissione per le politiche di integrazione degli immigrati (2002): Vol II, Cap.IV, La sicurezza (http://www.cestim.it/integr2/integr2_hl.htm)
Community Cohesion Unit, United Kingdom Home Office (2002): Community Cohesion: A Report of the Independent Review Team
Community Relations Council (1998): *Into the Mainstream: Strategic Plan 1998–2001* (Belfast: Community Relations Council)
Connolly, A.; Day, S.; Shaw, J. (eds) (2006): The contested case of EU voting rights; in: R. Bellamy, D. Castiglione, J. Shaw (eds.): *Making European Citizens* (Basingstoke: Palgrave Macmillan)
Connor, W.: (1994): *Ethnonationalism: the Quest for Understanding* (Princeton NJ: Princeton University Press)
Conversi, D. (1995): Reassessing current theories of nationalism: Nationalism as boundary maintenance and creation; *Nationalism and Ethnic Politics*, 1(1), 42–57
Coogan, T.P. (2000): *Wherever Green is Worn: the Story of the Irish Diaspora* (London: Hutchinson)
Corry, D.; Stoker, G. (2003): *New Localism: Refashioning the Centre–Local Relationship* (London: NLGN)
COS – Centrum voor Onderzoek en Statistiek (2003): *Prognose Bevolkingsgroepen 2017* (Rotterdam: COS)
Coulter, C. (1999): The absence of class politics in Northern Ireland; *Capital and Class*, Special Issue, 69, 77–100
Crick, B. (1982): *In Defence of Politics* (London: Penguin)
Crnobrnja, M. (1994): *The Yugoslav Drama* (Montreal: McGill-Queen's University Press)
Dahl, R.A. (1986): *Democracy, Liberty and Equality* (Oslo: Norwegian University Press)
Dahrendorf, R. (1988): *The Modern Social Contract: an Essay on the Politics of Liberty* (London: Weidenfeld and Nicolson)
Dallmayr, F. (1997): An 'inoperative' global community? Reflections on Nancy; in: D. Sheppard, S. Sparks, C. Thomas (eds.): *On Jean-Luc Nancy: the Sense of Philosophy* (London: Routledge) pp. 174–96
Darby, John; Knox, Colin (2004): A Shared Future: A Consultative Paper on Improving Relations in N. Ireland; Office of the First and Deputy First Minister, Belfast
De Boeck, F. (2004): *Kinshasa. Tales of the Invisibile City* (Brussels: Ludion)
De Decker, P.; Vranken, J.; Beaumont, J.; Van Nieuwerhuyze, I. (eds) (2003): *On the Origin of Urban Development Programmes in nine European Countries* (Antwerp: Garant)
Denich, B. (1994): Dismembering Yugoslavia: Nationalist ideologies and the symbolic revival of genocide; *American Ethnologist*, 21(2), 367–90
Denich, B. (1996): *Ethnic Nationalism: The Tragic Death of Yugoslavia* (Minneapolis: University of Minnesota Press)
Department of Justice, Equality and Law Reform (2004): *Planning for Diversity: the National Action Plan Against Racism* (Dublin: Stationery Office)
Department of the Environment, Heritage and Local Government (2002): *Quarterly Bulletin of Housing Statistics – Assessment of Housing Need* (Dublin: Stationery Office)
Dittrich, M. (2006): Muslims in Europe: addressing the challenges of radicalization; European Policy Centre, Brussels. Working Paper 23
Donin, R.J. (1994): *Bosnia and Hercegovina: a Tradition Betrayed* (London: Hurst)
Douglas, N. (1997): Political structures, social interaction and identity change in Northern Ireland; in: B. Graham (ed.): *In Search of Ireland* (London: Routledge) pp. 151–73

Downs, T. (2001): Market citizenship: functionalism and fig-leaves; in: R. Bellamy, A. Warleigh (eds): *Citizenship and Governance in the European Union* (London: Continuum) pp. 93–106

Dumper, M. (1996): *The Politics of Jerusalem since 1967* (New York: University of Columbia Press)

Duncan, O.D.; Duncan B. (1955): A methodological analysis of segregation indexes; *American Sociological Review*, 20, 210–17

Dunford, M.; Hudson, R. (1996): *Successful European Regions: Northern Ireland Learning From Others* (Belfast: Northern Ireland Economic Council)

Durkheim, E. (1991): *De la division du travail social* (Paris: Puf, coll. Quadrige)

EC – Commission of the European Communities, DG IV (ed.) (2004): Core Values for Intercultural Dialogue: Towards a Europe of all Citizens (Brussels: EC)

EC – Commission of the European Communities (2005): Green Paper 'Confronting demographic change: a new solidarity between the generations' (COM(2005) 94 final)

EC – Commission of the European Communities (2005a): *Treaty Establishing a Constitution for Europe* (Luxembourg: Office for Official Publications of the European Communities)

EC – Commission of the European Communities (2005b): Green Paper on an EU Approach to Managing Economic Migration (COM(2004): 811 final)

Eckardt, F. (2003): *Pim Fortuyn und die Niederlande: Populismus als Reaktion auf die Globalisierung* (Marburg: Tectum-Verlag)

Einagle, V.I. (1997): Lasting peace in Bosnia? Politics of territory and identity; in: O. Tunander, P. Baev, V.I. Einagel (eds): *Geopolitics in Post-wall Europe: Security, Territory and Identity* (Oslo: International Peace Research Institute) pp. 235–52

Elliott, M. (2002): Religion and identity in Northern Ireland; in: M. Elliott (ed.): *The Long Road to Peace in Northern Ireland* (Liverpool: Liverpool University Press) pp. 169–88

Etienne, B.(2002): Expert Colloquy: Dialogue serving intercultural and inter-religious communication, paper presented at Council of Europe, Strasbourg, 7–9 October 2002 (www.coe.int/T/E/Cultural_Co-operation/Culture/Action/Dialogue/pub_DGIV_CULT_PREV-ICIR%282002%293_Etienne_E.PDF?L=E)

EuroCities (2003): *Contribution to Good Governance Concerning the Integration of Immigrants and the Reception of Asylum Seekers* (Brussels: EuroCities)

Eyben, K.; Morrow, D.; Wilson, D. (1997): *A Worthwhile Venture? Practically Investing in Equity Diversity and Interdependence in Northern Ireland* (Coleraine: University of Ulster)

Fanning, B. (2002): *Racism and Social Change in the Republic of Ireland* (Manchester: Manchester University Press)

Faughnan, P.; Humphries, N.; Whelan, S. (2002): *Patching up the System: the Community Welfare Service and Asylum Seekers* (Dublin: Social Science Research Centre, University College Dublin)

Feld, S.; Basso, K.H. (eds) (1996): *Senses of Place* (Santa Fé: School of American Research Press)

Feldman, A. (1991): *Formations of Violence: the Narrative of the Body and Political Terror in Northern Ireland* (Chicago: University of Chicago Press)

Fenger, M.; Klok, P.J. (2001): Interdependency, beliefs and coalition behaviour: a contribution to the advocacy coalition framework; *Policy Sciences*, 34, 157–70

Fenster, T. (1996): Ethnicity and citizen identity in planning and development for minority groups; *Political Geography*, 15(5), 405–18

Fernández-Armesto, F. (1994): *The Times Guide to Peoples of Europe* (London: The Times)

Ferrao, J. (1997): Três décadas de consolidação do Portugal demográfico 'Moderno'; in: A. Barreto (ed.): *A Situação Social em Portugal, 1960–1995* (Lisbon:ICS)

Ferriter, D. (2004): *The Transformation of Ireland 1900–2000* (London: Profile Books)

Fine, J.V.A. (1975): *The Bosnian Church: a New Interpretation* (Boulder, CO: East European Quarterly)

Fine, J.V.A. (2002): The various faiths in the history of Bosnia: Middle Ages to the present; in: M. Shatzmiller (ed.): *Islam and Bosnia: Conflict Resolution and Foreign Policy in Multi-ethnic States* (Montreal and Kingston: McGill-Queen's University Press)

Firth, R. (1973): *Symbols Public and Private* (Ithaca, New York: Cornell University Press)

Florida, R. (2005) An introduction to the creative class, Ch 1; in: S. Franke, E. Verhagen (eds): *Creativity and the City* (Rotterdam: NAi Publishers)

Flynn, P. (1986): Urban deprivation: What it is and how to measure it; *Public Money*, September, 37–41

Flyvbjerg, B. (1998): *Rationality and Power: Democracy in Practice* (Chicago IL: University of Chicago Press)

Flyvbjerg, B. (2001): Beyond the limits of planning theory: response to my critics; *International Planning Studies*, 6 (3), 285–92

Flyvbjerg, B. (2002): Bringing power to planning research. One researchers praxis story; *Journal of Planning Education and Research*, 21(2), 353–66

Flyvbjerg, B. (2004): Phronetic planning research: theoretical and methodological reflections; *Planning Theory and Practice*, 5(3), 83–306

Forgacs, D.; Lumley, R. (eds) (1996): *Italian Cultural Studies: an Introduction* (Oxford: Oxford University Press)

Foss, C. (1997): Russia's romance with the airship; *History Today*, 10–16 December

Foucault, M. (1967): Of Other Spaces: Heterotopias (http://www.foucault.info)

Foucault, M. (1991): Politics and the study of discourse; in: G. Burchell, C. Gordon, P. Miller P. (eds): *The Foucault Effect: Studies in Governmentality* (Chicago IL: University of Chicago Press) pp. 53–72

Fox, R. (1991): *Recapturing Anthropology* (Santa Fe: School of American Research Press)

Friedrichs, J. (1995): *Stadtsoziologie* (Opladen: Leske + Budrich)

Friedrichs, J. (1998): Do poor neighbourhoods make their residents poorer? Context effects of poverty neighbourhoods on residents; in: H.-J. Andress, (ed.): *Empirical Poverty Research in a Comparative Perspective* (Aldershot: Ashgate) pp. 77–99

Future of Multi-ethnic Britain, The Parekh Report (2000): London: Profile Books

Gaffikin, Frank; Morrissey, Mike (2005): Planning for Peace in Contested Space; Queen's University Belfast. Available from the authors

Galligan, Y.; Clavero, S.; Sloat, A.: (ongoing research project) Enlargement, Gender and Governance (Belfast: Centre for the Advancement of Women in Politics, School of Politics, International Studies and Philosophy, Queen's University Belfast) (www.qub.ac.uk/cawp/)

Gardner, J.P. (ed.) (1997): *Citizenship: The White Paper* (London: The Institute for Citizenship Studies and The British Institute of International and Comparative Law)

Garland, R. (2001): *Gusty Spence* (Belfast: Blackstaff Press)

Garner, S. (2004): *Racism in the Irish Experience* (London: Pluto Press)

Gaspar, J. (1994): O desenvolvimento do sitio de Lisboa; in: I. Moita (ed.): *O livro de Lisboa* (Lisbon: Livros Horizonte)

Gellner, E. (1983): *Nations and Nationalism* (Oxford: Blackwell)

Gemeentebestuur Rotterdam (2003): *Rotterdam zet door. Op weg naar een stad in balans* (Rotterdam: Gemeente Rotterdam)

Gerard, A. (1970): *La Revolution Française: Mythes et interpretations, 1789–1970* (Paris: Editions)

Gesemann, F. (ed.): *Migration und Integration in Berlin* (Opladen: Leske + Budrich)

Gibson, J.J. (1979): The Ecological Approach to Visual Perception (Boston: Houghton Mifflin)

Giddens, A. (1994): *Beyond Left and Right: the Future of Radical Politics* (Cambridge: Polity Press)

GLA (2005): *Sustaining Success* (London: GLA)

GLA (2005a): London's changing population: Diversity of a world city in the 21st century DMAG briefing 2005/39 November (London: GLA)

Glenny, M. (1999): *The Balkans: Nationalism, War and the Great Powers* (London: Granta Books)

Glick Schiller, N.; Basch, L.; Szanton-Blanc, C. (eds) (1992): *Towards Transnational Perspectives on Migration: Race, Class Ethnicity and Nationalism* (New York: New York Academy of Sciences)

Graham, B. (1997): The imagining of place: representation and identity in contemporary Ireland; in: B. Graham (ed.): *In Search of Ireland* (London: Routledge) pp. 192–212

Graham, B.; Shirlow, P. (1998): An elusive agenda: the development of the middle ground in Northern Ireland; *Area*, 30(3), 245–54

Graham, S.; Marvin, S. (2001): *Splintering Urbanism* (London: Routledge)

Grigorievs, A. (1996): The Baltic predicament; in: R. Caplan, J. Feffer (eds): *Europe's New Nationalism: States and Minorities in Conflict* (New York: Oxford University Press), pp. 120–37

Grillo, R.; Pratt, J. (eds) (2002): *The Politics of Recognizing Difference* (Aldershot: Ashgate)

Grosby, S. (1995): Territoriality: the transcendental, primordial feature of modern societies; *Nations and Nationalism*, 1, 143–62

Gunder, M. (2003): Passionate planning for the others' desire: an agonistic response to the dark side of planning; Progress in Planning, 60, 235–319

Gunder, M. (2004): Obscuring difference through shaping debate: a Lacanian view of planning for diversity; paper presented at Planning Research and Development conference, Aberdeen, 31 March–2 April

Gunder, M. (2004a): Shaping the planner's ego-ideal: a Lacanian interpretation of planning education; *Journal of Planning Education and Research*, 23(3), 299–311

Gunder, M. (2005a): Obscuring difference through shaping debate: a Lacanian view of planning for diversity; *International Planning Studies*, 10(2), 83–103

Gunder, M. (2005b) The production of desirous space: mere fantasies of the utopian city?; *Planning Theory*, 4(2), 173–99

Gunder, M.; Hillier, J. (2004): Conforming to the expectations of the profession: a Lacanian perspective on planning practice, norms and values; *Planning Theory and Practice*, 5(2), 217–35

Habermas, J. (1987): *The Philosophical Discourse of Modernity* (Cambridge: Polity Press)

Habermas, J. (1987a): *Theory of Communicative Action, Lifeworld and System* (Boston: Beacon Press)

Habermas, J. (1995): Citizenship and national identity; in: R. Beiner (ed.): *Theorizing Citizenship* (Albany NY: State University of New York Press)

Habermas, J. (1996): *Between Facts and Norms* (Cambridge: Polity Press)

Habermas, J. (1998): *The Inclusion of the Other* (Cambridge: Polity Press)

Habermas, J. (1999): *On the Pragmatics of Communication* (Cambridge: Polity Press)

Habermas, J. (2000): Richard Rorty's pragmatic turn; in: R. Brandom (ed.): *Rorty and his Critics* (Oxford: Blackwell)

Habermas, J. (2001): *The Postnational Constellation* (Cambridge, MA: MIT Press)

282 *Bibliography*

Habermas, J. (2004): Religious tolerance – the pacemaker for cultural rights; *Philosophy*, 79, 5–18

Hage, G. (1998): *White Nation: Fantasies of White Supremacy in a Multicultural Nation* (Sydney: Pluto Press)

Hall, P. (2003): *Cities in Civilization* (London: Phoenix Giant)

Hammer, M. (1989): Putting Ireland on the map; *Textual Practice*, 3, 184–201

Hannerz, U. (1980): *Exploring the City. Enquiries towards an Urban Anthropology* (New York: Columbia University Press)

Hannerz, U. (1996): *Transnational Connections. Culture, People, Places* (London: Routledge)

Harley, J.B. (1988a): Maps, knowledge and power; in: D. Cosgrove, S. Daniels (eds): *The Iconography of Landscape* (Cambridge: Cambridge University Press) pp. 283–98

Harley, J.B. (1988b): Silences and secrecy: the hidden agenda of cartography in early modern Europe; *Imago Mundi*, 40, 57–76

Harley, J.B. (1989): Deconstructing the map; *Cartographica*, 26, 1–20

Haseler, S. (1996): *The English Tribe* (Basingstoke: Macmillan 1–1 now Palgrave Macmillan)

Häussermann, H. (2001): Marginalisierung als Folge sozialräumlichen Wandels in der Großstadt; in: F. Gesemann (ed.): *Migration und Integration in Berlin. Wissenschaftliche Analysen und politische Perspektiven* (Opladen: Leske + Budrich) pp. 63–85

Häussermann, H.; Kapphan, A. (2002): *Berlin – von der geteilten zur gespaltenen Stadt? Sozialräumlicher Wandel seit 1990* (Opladen: Leske + Budrich)

Häussermann, H.; Kronauer, M.; Siebel, W. (eds) (2004): *An den Rändern der Städte. Armut und Ausgrenzung* (Frankfurt/Main: Suhrkamp)

Häussermann, H; Kapphan; A. Gerometta, J. (2005): Berlin – Integration through multicultural empowerment and representation; in: M. Balbo (ed.): *International Migrants and the City* (Venice: UB-HABITAT, 2005) pp. 53–89

Häussermann, H.; Läzer, K.-L.; Wurtzbacher, J. (2006): *Das dichte Netz der dünnen Fäden – Politische Integration und Repräsentation in der fragmentierten Stadt* (Wiesbaden: VS Verlag)

Hayden, R.M. (1998): Bosnia: the contradictions of 'democracy' without consent; *East European Constitutional Review*, 7, 47–51

Haymes, T. (1997): What is nationalism really? Understanding the limitations of rigid theories in dealing with the problems of nationalism and ethnonationalism; *Nations and Nationalism*, 3(4), 541–57

Healey, P. (1997): *Collaborative Planning: Shaping Places in Fragmented Societies* (Basingstoke: Macmillan 1–1 now Palgrave Macmillan)

Healing Through Remembering (2002): The Report of the Healing Through Remembering Project (www.healingthroughremembering.org)

Heater, D. (1990): *Citizenship: the Civic Ideal in World History, Politics and Education* (London, New York: Longman)

Heikkila, E. (2001): Identity and inequality: race and space in planning; *Planning Theory and Practice*, 2 (3), 261–75

Held, D. (1995): *Democracy and the Global Order: From the Modern State to Cosmopolitan Governance* (Cambridge: Polity Press)

Held, D. (2003): From executive to cosmopolitan multilateralism; in: D. Held, M. Koenig-Archibugi (eds): *Taming Globalization: Frontiers of Governance* (Cambridge: Polity Press)

Hillier, J. (2002): *Shadows of Power* (London: Routledge)

Hillier, J. (2003): 'Agonizing over consensus: why Habermasian ideals cannot be 'Real'; *Planning Theory*, 2(1), 37–59

Hilson, C. (2006): EU citizenship and the principle of affectedness; in: R. Bellamy, D. Castiglione, J. Shaw (eds): *Making European Citizens* (Basingstoke: Palgrave Macmillan)

HMG – Her Majesty's Government (2005): Together We Can (http://www.together wecan.info)

HMT – Her Majesty's Treasury (2004): Devolved Decision Making: 2 Meeting the regional economic challenge: Increasing regional and local flexibility (www.hmt.gov.uk)

Hobbes T. (1982): *De Cive – Le citoyen ou les fondements de la politique* (Paris: Garnier-Flammarion)

Hobsbawm, E.J. (1993a) Introduction: inventing traditions; in: E.J. Hobsbawm, T. Ranger (eds): *The Invention of Tradition* (Cambridge: Canto) pp. 1–14

Hobsbawm, E.J. (1993b) Mass-producing traditions: Europe, 1870–1914; in: E.J. Hobsbawm, T. Ranger (eds): *The Invention of Tradition* (Cambridge: Canto) pp. 263–308

Hobsbawm, E.J. (1994): What is ethnic conflict and how does it differ from other conflicts?; in: A. McDermott (ed.): *Ethnic Conflict and International Security* (Oslo: Norwegian Institute of International Affairs) pp. 37–46

Hobsbawm, E.J. (1995): *Age of Extremes: the Short Twentieth Century* (London: Michael Joseph)

Hobsbawm, E.J. (1996): Ethnicity and nationalism in Europe today; in: G. Balakrishnan (ed.): *Mapping the Nation* (London: Verso Hutchinson) pp. 255–66

Home Office (2001): *Building Cohesive Communities: a Report of the Ministerial Group on Public Order and Community Cohesion* (London: Home Office)

Honohan, I. (2002): *Civic Republicanism* (London: Routledge)

Honohan, I. (2004): Active Citizenship in Contemporary Democracy. Paper for the Democracy Commission (Dublin: TASC-Think-tank for Action on Social Change) (www.tascnet.ie)

Honohan, I. (2005): Educating citizens: nation-building and its republican limits; in: I. Honohan; J. Jennings (eds): *Republicanism in Theory and Practice* (London: Routledge)

Horowitz, D.L. (2001): *The Deadly Ethnic Riot* (Berkeley: University of California Press)

Howitt, R. (2001): A nation in dialogue: recognition, reconciliation and indigenous rights in Australia; *Hagar*, 2(2) 261–75

Howitt, R.; Suchet-Pearson, S. (2003): Ontological pluralism in contested cultural landscapes; in: K. Anderson et al. (eds): *Handbook of Cultural Geography* (London: Sage) pp. 557–69

Hughes, G. (2005): *Annual Report on Statistics on Migration, Asylum and Return: Ireland 2002* (Dublin: Economic and Social Research Institute and European Migration Network)

Hughes, G.; Quinn, E. (2004): *The Impact of Immigration on Europe's Societies: Ireland* (Dublin: Economic and Social Research Institute and European Migration Network)

Hughes, J.; Knox, C.; Murray, M.; Greer, J. (1998): *Partnership Governance in Northern Ireland* (Dublin: Oak Tree Press)

Huntington, S.P. (1993): The clash of civilizations?; *Foreign Affairs*, 72(3), 22–49

Huntington, S.P. (1996): *The Clash of Civilizations and the Remaking of World Order* (New York: Simon & Schuster)

Hutton, W. (2004): Transcript of speech at Senior Civil Service Seminar on A Wider Role for the Voluntary and Community Sector in Public Service Delivery (Belfast: Department of Social Development and the Chief Executives' forum, 29 April)

IfS – Institut für Stadtforschung und Strukturpolitik (2004): Die Soziale Stadt. Ergebnisse der Zwischenevaluierung. Bewertung des Bund-Länder-Programms 'Stadtteile mit besonderem Entwicklungsbedarf – die soziale Stadt' nach vier Jahren Programmlaufzeit (Berlin: Bundesministeriums für Verkehr, Bau- und Wohnungswesen)

Immigrant Council of Ireland (2003a): *Labour Migration into Ireland* (Dublin: Immigrant Council of Ireland)

Immigrant Council of Ireland (2003b): *Handbook on Immigrants Rights and Entitlements in Ireland* (Dublin: Immigrant Council of Ireland)

Immigrant Council of Ireland (2004): *Voices of Immigrants: the Challenges of Inclusion* (Dublin: Immigrant Council of Ireland)

Indovina, F. (ed.) (1987): *La città diffusa* (Venice: Daest)

INE – Instituto Nacional de Estatística (1991): *Recenseamento da População e Habitação de 1991 – resultados definitivos* (Lisbon: INE)

INE – Instituto Nacional de Estatística (2001): *Recenseamento Geral da População e Habitação de 2001 – resultados definitivos* (Lisbon: INE)

Inglis, F. (2001): Universalism and Difference: the separation of culture and politics. Paper presented to Canadian Studies Conference (Belfast: Queen's University, Centre for Canadian Studies, 19–21 October)

Ingram, A. (1996): Constitutional patriotism; *Philosophy and Social Criticism*, 22, 1–18

Innes, J. (1998): Information in communicative planning; *Journal of the American Planning Association*, 64 (1), 52–75

IPPR – Institute for Public Policy Research (ed.) (2005): Labour Migration to the UK – an ippr factfile (London: IPPR) (www.ippr.org.uk)

Irigaray, L. (1985a) *The Sex Which is Not One* (Ithaca NY: Cornell University Press)

Irigaray, L. (1985b) *Speculum of the Other* (Ithaca NY: Cornell University Press)

Irish Centre for Migration Studies (2000): Asylum Seekers and Housing Rights in Ireland (http://migration.ucc.ie/asylumhousing.htm)

Irish Refugee Council (2004): *Information Note on Asylum Seekers and Accommodation Centres* (Dublin: Irish Refugee Council)

Ivison, D. (2002): *Postcolonial Liberalism* (Cambridge: Cambridge University Press)

Jacquier, C. (2004): La politique de la ville: towards a more integrated urban governance in France; in: P. de Decker, J. Vranken, J. Beaumont, I. Van Nieuwenhuyze (eds): *On the Origin of Urban Development Programmes* (Antwerp/Apeldoorn: Garant) pp. 59–72

Jarman, N. (1997): *Material Conflicts: Parades and Visual Displays in Northern Ireland* (London: Berg)

Jarman, N. (2005): *Demography, Development and Disorder* (Belfast: Community Relations Council)

Jarman, Neal; Keyes, Libby; Wilson, Derick (2005): Community Cohesion: Applying Learning from Groundwork; Groundwork, Belfast

Jenkins, R. (1996): *Social Identity* (London: Routledge)

Job, C. (2002): *Yugoslavia's Ruin: the Bloody Lessons of Nationalism, a Patriot's Warning* (Lanham, MD: Rowman and Littlefield)

Jones, R.A. (2001): Science in national cultures: the message of postage stamps; *Public Understanding of Science*, 13, 75–81

Jones, R.A. (2004): Heroes of the nation? The celebration of scientists on the postage stamps of Great Britain, France and West Germany; *Journal of Contemporary History*, 36, 403–22

Joppke, C. (2004): The retreat of multiculturalism in the liberal state: theory and policy; *British Journal of Sociology*, 55(2), 137–57

Jung; A. (2005): Taming the monster; *Spiegel International Edition*, 7, 136–41

Kaldor, M. (2004): Nationalism and globalisation; *Nations and Nationalism*, 10, 161–77

Katunaric, V. (2003): *Peace enclaves/cradles: Final Report – main findings and policy proposals* (Strasbourg: Council of Europe) (www.coe.int/T/E/Cultural_Cooperation/Culture/Action/Dialogue/pub_DGIV_CULT_PREV_PE%282003%294_Katunaric_E.PDF?L=E)

Keane, J. (1998): *Civil Society: Old Images, New Visions* (Cambridge: Polity Press)

King, A. (ed.) (1996): *Re-presenting the city: Ethnicity, Capital and Culture: the 21st C Metropolis*, (London: Macmillan)

King, H. (2004): Has Dayton facilitated the building of a multi-ethnic Bosnia? An examination of refugee return and reintegration after the Dayton accords (London: Kingston University, unpublished MSc thesis)

King, L. (2004): Democracy and city life; *Philosophy, Politics and Economics*, 3(1), 97–124

King, R. (ed.) (1993): *Mass Migrations in Europe. The Legacy and the Future* (London: Belhaven)

Kirkling, G.A. (1999): *A Search for Understanding: Untangling Bosnia-Hercegovina* (Madison WI: RealWorld Press)

Kitchen, T.; Rydin, Y.; Thornley, A. (2004): *Skills for Planning Practice* (London: Palgrave Macmillan)

Kniewald, D. (1964): Hierarchie und Kultus bosnischer Christen; *Accademia nazionale deilincei L'Oriente christiano nella storia della civilita*, 62

Komesar, N. (2001): *Law's Limits* (Cambridge: Cambridge University Press)

Korpi, W. (2000): Faces of inequality: gender, class and patterns of inequalities in different types of welfare states; *Social Politics*, 7(2), 127–91

Kostakopoulou, D. (1998): Is there an alternative to 'Schengenland'?; *Political Studies*, 46(4), 886–902

Kostakopoulou, T. (2001a): *Citizenship, Identity and Immigration in the European Union: Between Past and Future* (Manchester: Manchester University Press)

Kostakopolou, T. (2001b): Invisible citizens? Long-term resident third-country nationals in the EU and the struggle for recognition; in: R. Bellamy, A. Warleigh (eds): *Citizenship and Governance in the European Union* (London: Continuum) pp. 189–205

Kumar, R. (1997): *Divide and Fall: Bosnia and the Annals of Partition* (London: Verso)

Kyambi, S. (2005): *Beyond Black and White: Mapping New Immigrant Communities* (London: IPPR)

Kymlicka, W. (1995): *Multicultural Citizenship: a Liberal Theory of Minority Rights* (Oxford: Clarendon Press)

Laclau, E. (ed.) (1994): *The Making of Political Identities* (London: Verso)

Laclau, E.; Mouffe, C. (2001): *Hegemony and Socialist Strategy: Towards a Radical Democratic Politics* (London: Verso)

Ladrech, R. (1994): Europeanization of domestic politics and institutions: the case of France; *Journal of Common Market Studies*, 32(1), 69–88

Landry, C. (2003): *Imagination and Regeneration: Culural Policy and the Future of Cities* (Strasbourg: Council of Europe)

Landry, C.; Bianchini, F. (1995): *The Creative City* (London: Demos)

Lawless, P. (1986): *The Evolution of Spatial Policy* (London: Pion)

Le Gales, P.; Mawson, J. (1994): *Management Innovations in Urban Policy Lessons from France* (Luton: LGMB)

Lebon, F. (2002): Cultural Diversity – Interculturality – Cultural policy, paper presented at 'Expert Colloquy: Dialogue serving intercultural and inter-religious communication', Strasbourg, 7–9 October (Strasbourg: Council of Europe) (www.coe.int/T/E/Cultural_Cooperation/Culture/Action/Dialogue/pub_DGIV_CULT_PREV-ICIR%282002%295_Lebon_ E.PDF?L=E)

Lederach, J.P. (1994): *Preparing for Peace: Conflict Transformation across Cultures* (Syracuse: University Press)

Lentin, R. (2002): At the heart of the Hibernian post-metropolis: spatial narratives of ethnic minorities and diasporic communities in a changing city; *City* 6(2), 229–49

Leonard, M. (1998): *Rediscovering Europe* (London: Demos/Interbrand Newell and Sorrell)

Low, S.M.; Lawrence-Zuniga, D. (2003): *The Language of Space and Place. Locating Culture* (Oxford: Blackwell)

Lunden, T. (1993): *Sprakens landskab I Europa* (Lund: Studentlitteratur)

Lynch, K. (1981): *A Theory of Good City Form* (Cambridge MA.: MIT Press)

Maalouf, A. (2000): *On Identity* (London: Harvill Press)

MacDonald, M. (1993): The construction of difference: an anthropological approach to stereotypes; in: S. MacDonald (ed.): *Inside European Identities* (Oxford: Berg) pp. 219–36

MacGregor, S. (1993): Reconstructing the divided city: problems of pluralism and governance. Paper presented at Fulbright Colloquium, Managing Divided Cities, Centre for the Study of Conflict, University of Ulster at Magee College, 6–8 September

Mackay, J. (1982): An exploratory synthesis of primordial and mobilizationist approaches to ethnic phenomena; *Ethnic and Racial Studies*, 5(4), 66–78

Macpherson, W. (1999): *Inquiry into the Death of Stephen Lawrence* (London: The Stationery Office)

Magas, B. (2003): On Bosnianness; *Nations and Nationalism*, 9, 19–24

Maher, V. (1996): Immigration and social identities; in: D. Forgacs, R. Lumley (eds): *Italian Cultural Studies: an Introduction* (Oxford: Oxford University Press) pp. 160–77

Manço, A.A. (2006): *Dialogue with Muslim Communities: Suggested Practices for Resolving and Preventing Problems Related to the Multicultural Society* (Brussels: Institute for Research, Teaching and Action on Migration – IRFAM)

March, A. (2004): Planning as a Democratic Practice: antinomy and mediatisation (Melbourne: University of Melbourne, unpublished PhD thesis)

March, A.; Low, N. (2004): Knowing and steering: mediatisation, planning and democracy in Victoria, Australia; *Planning Theory*, 3(1), 41–69

Maritano, L. (2002): An obsession with cultural difference: representations of immigrants in Turin; in: R. Grillo, J. Pratt (eds): *The Politics of Recognizing Difference* (Aldershot: Ashgate) pp. 59–77

Markell, P. (2003): *Bound by Recognition* (Princeton: Princeton University Press)

Märker, A. (2001): Zuwanderungspolitik in der Europäischen Union; *Aus Politik und Zeitgeschichte*, B8, 3–10

Marshall, A. (1920): *Principles of Economics* (London: Macmillan)

Marshall, T.H. (1963): *Citizenship and Social Class* (London: Heinemann)

Marshall, T.H. (ed.) (1973): *Class, Citizenship and Social Development* (Westport, CT: Greenwood Press)

Mason, A. (2000): *Community, Solidarity and Belonging* (Cambridge: Cambridge University Press)

Mayer, I.; Mayer, P. (1980): Migrancy and the study of Africans in towns; in: I. Press, E. Smith (eds): *Urban Place and Process. Readings in the Anthropology of Cities* (New York: Macmillan, 1980) pp. 223–40

McCarthy, T. (1978): *The Critical Theory of Jürgen Habermas* (London: Hutchinson)

McDonough, G. (1993): The geography of emptiness; in: R. Rotenberg, G. McDonough: *The Cultural Meaning of Urban Space* (Westport, CT: Bergin and Garvin) pp. 3–17

Meehan, E. (1993): *Citizenship and the European Community* (London: Sage)

Melegari, C. (2002): Gli immigrati a Verona. Osservazioni su alcuni indicatori di integrazione (http://www.cestim.it/integr2/integr2_hl.htm)

Melossi, D.; Silverman, E.B. (2004): Migrazioni, conflitti culturali, Zero Tolerance; *Inchiesta*, XXXIV(143), 5–22

Meyer, G. (2004): Foreword; in: G. Meyer (ed.): *Die Arabische Welt im Spiegel der Kulturgeographie* (Mainz: Zentrum für Forschung zur Arabischen Welt – ZEFAW) p. 5

Miliband, D. (2005): The Politics of Community, speech given 24th October (http://www.odpm.gov.uk/index.asp?id=1122746)

Miller, D. (1993): In defence of nationality; *Journal of Applied Philosophy*, 10, 3–16

Montgomery, A.; Fraser, G.; McGlynn, C.; Smith, A.; Gallagher, T. (2003): *Integrated Education in Northern Ireland: Integration in Practice* (Coleraine: University of Ulster UNESCO Centre)

Morphet, J. (2006): New Localism; in: M. Tewdwr-Jones, P. Allmendinger (eds): *Territory, Identity and Space: Spatial Governance in a Fragmented Nation* (London: Routledge)

Morris, R; Carstairs, V. (1991): Which deprivation? A comparison of selected deprivation indexes; *Journal of Public Health*, 13(4), 318–26

Morrow, D.; Eyben, K; Wilson, D. (2003): From the margin to the middle: taking equity, diversity and interdependence seriously; in: O. Hargie, D. Dickson (eds): *Researching the Troubles: Social Science Perspectives on the Northern Ireland Conflict* (Edinburgh: Mainstream Publishing) pp. 163–81

Mouffe, C. (1992): Democratic citizenship and the political community; in: C. Mouffe (ed.): *Dimensions of Radical Democracy, Pluralism, Citizenship, Community* (London: Verso)

Mouffe, C. (1999): Deliberative democracy or agonistic pluralism; *Social Research*, 66(3), 745–58

Mouffe, C. (2000): *The Democratic Paradox* (London: Verso)

Müller, H. (1998): Der Mythos vom Kampf der Kulturen. Eine Kritik an Huntingtons kulturalistischer Globaltheorie; *E + Z – Entwicklung und Zusammenarbeit*, 10, 262–64

Müller, R. (2001): Turkish commercial and business activities in Berlin: a case of organic urban development and contact; in: W.J.V. Neill, H.-U. Schwedler (eds): *Urban Planning and Cultural Identity: Lessons from Belfast and Berlin* (New York: Palgrave – now Palgrave Macmillan) pp. 121–33

Murray, M.; Murtagh, B. (2004): *Equity, Diversity and Interdependence: Reconnecting People through Authentic Dialogue* (Aldershot: Ashgate)

Murtagh, B. (2002): *The Politics of Territory* (London: Palgrave – now Palgrave Macmillan)

Murtagh, B. (2004): Collaboration, equality and land use planning; *Planning Theory and Practice*, 5(4), 453–69

Nancy, J.-L. (1990): *The Inoperative Community* (Paris: Christian Bourgois)

Nash, C. (1998): Narratives and names: Irish landscape meanings; in: T. Unwin (ed.): *A European Geography* (Harlow: Longman) pp. 73–6

National Consultative Committee on Racism and Interculturalism (2001–2004): *Reported Incidents Relating to Racism* (Dublin: National Consultative Committee on Racism and Interculturalism)

National Economic and Social Council (2004): *Housing in Ireland: Policy and Performance* (Dublin: National Economic and Social Council)

Negri, A. (1999): *Insurgencies: Constituent Power and the Modern State* (Minneapolis: University of Minnesota Press)

Neill, W.J.V. (2004): *Urban Planning and Cultural Identity* (London: Routledge)

Neill, W.J.V. (ed.) (2000): *Planning and Cultural Pluralism, A Report to the Royal Town Planning Institute – RTPI, Irish Branch, Northern Section* (Belfast: RTPI)

Neill, W.J.V.; Schwedler, H.-U. (eds) (2001): *Urban Planning and Cultural Identity: Lessons from Belfast and Berlin* (New York: Palgrave – now Palgrave Macmillan)

Newham Borough (2005a): Local Development Scheme (www.newham.gov.uk)

Newham Borough (2005b): Olympic web site (www.newham.gov.uk)

Norris, M.; Winston, N. (2004): *Housing Policy Review 1990–2002* (Dublin: Stationery Office)

Norris, M; Winston, N. (2005): Housing and accommodation of Irish travellers: from assimilationism to multiculturalism and back again; *Social Policy and Administration*, 39(7), 802–21

ODPM – Office of the Deputy Prime Minister (2004): Local Area Agreements: a prospectus

ODPM – Office of the Deputy Prime Minister (2004a): Local Vision: the future of local government – developing the ten year vision

ODPM – Office of the Deputy Prime Minister (2004b): Competitive European Cities: Where do the core cities stand?

ODPM – Office of the Deputy Prime Minister (2004c): *The Egan Review: Skills for Sustainable Communities* (London: ODPM)

ODPM – Office of the Deputy Prime Minister (2005): The Government's proposals for additional powers and responsibilities for the Mayor and Assembly

ODPM – Office of the Deputy Prime Minister (2005b): Devolving to Deliver – more freedom to secure better outcomes

ODPM – Office of the Deputy Prime Minister (2005c): Extended terms of reference of the Lyons Inquiry Press notice 20 September

OECD – Organization for Economic Cooperation and Development (ed.) (2003): *Urban Renaissance Study: Towards an Integrated Strategy for Social Cohesion and Economic Development* (Berlin: OECD)

OECD – Organization for Economic Cooperation and Development (ed.) (2004): *Education Policy Analysis* (Paris: OECD)

OECD – Organization for Economic Cooperation and Development (ed.) (2006): *Where Immigrant Students Succeed – a Comparative Review of Performance and Engagement in PISA 2003* (Paris: OECD)

Office of the Refugee Applications Commissioner (2001–2004): *Statistics on Asylum Applicants* (Dublin: Office of the Refugee Applications Commissioner)

O'Halloran, Chris; Shirlow, Peter; Murtagh, Brendan (2004): A Policy Agenda for the Interface; Belfast Interface Project, Belfast

Ohliger, R.; Raiser, U. (2005): *Integration und Migration in Berlin, Zahlen – Daten – Fakten* (Berlin: Commissioner of the Berlin *Senat* for Integration and Migration)

Orstrom Moller, J. (1993): *Folkeslag I Central- og Osteuropa* (Copenhagen: Thorup)

Osborne, T. (2003): What is neo-Enlightenment? Human rights culture and juridical reason; *Journal of Human Rights*, 2(4), 523–30

Ousley, H. (2001): *Community Pride not Prejudice: Making Diversity Work in Bradford* (Bradford: Bradford Vision)

Pan, C.; Pfeil, S.B. (2000): *Die Volksgruppen in Europa. Ein Handbuch* (Vienna: Braumüller)

Parekh Report (2000): *Future of Multi-ethnic Britain* (London: Profile Books)

Parekh, B. (2000): Rethinking Multiculturalism (Cambridge, MA.: Harvard University Press)

Pateman, C. (1988): *The Sexual Contract* (Oxford: Basil Blackwell/Polity Press)

Payrow Shabani, O. (2004): Language policy and diverse societies: constitutional patri-otism and minority language rights; *Constellations*, 11(2), 193–216

Peillon, M. (2002): Exclusionary protests in urban Ireland; *City*, 6(2), 193–204

Peritz, D. (2004): Toward a deliberative and democratic response to multicultural politics: post-Rawlsian reflections on Benhabib's 'The Claims of Culture'; *Constellations*, 11(2), 266–90

Permezel, M.; Duffy, M. (2003): What about we hold another cultural festival? Negoti-ating cultural difference in local communities; paper presented at State of Australian cities Conference, Sydney, 3–5 December

Perroux F. (1991): *L'économie du 20ᵉ siècle* (Grenoble: PUG)

Petaux, J. et al. (2002): Analysis of the Debate, Reflection of the Rapporteur General, Working Session Conclusions – Expert Colloquy: Dialogue serving intercultural and inter-religious communication, Strasbourg, 7–9 October (Strasbourg: Council of Europe) (www.coe.int /T/E/Cultural_Cooperation/Culture/Action/Dialogue/pub_DGIV_CULT_PREV-ICIR%282002%299_Conclusions_E.PDF?L=E)

Pettit, P. (1997): *Republicanism* (Oxford: Oxford University Press)

Phillips M. (2005): *Londonistan* (London: Encounter Books)

Pimlott, B.; Rao, N. (2002): *Governing London* (Oxford: Oxford University Press)

Pinelli, D.; Ottaviano, G.; Maignan C. (2004): Development and growth; in: P. Wood (ed.): *Intercultural City Reader* (Stroud: Comedia)

Pitkin, H. (1981): Justice: on relating private and public; *Political Theory*, 9(3), 327–52

Platt, L. (2005): *Migration and Social Mobility: the Life Chances of Britain's Ethnic Communities* (Bristol: JRF/Polity Press)

Pløger, J. (2001): Public participation and the art of governance, environment and planning; *Planning and Design*, 28(2), 219–41

Pløger, J. (2004): Strife – urban planning and agonism; *Planning Theory*, 3(1), 71–92

Poole, M. (1997): In search of ethnicity in Ireland; in: B. Graham (ed.): *In Search of Ireland* (London: Routledge) pp. 128–47

Poole, M.; Doherty, P. (1996): *Ethnic Residential Segregation in Northern Ireland* (Coleraine: University of Ulster, Centre for the Study of Conflict)

Porter, L. (2004): Unlearning one's privilege: reflections on cross-cultural research with indigenous peoples in South-eastern Australia; *Planning Theory and Practice, Interface*, 5(1) 104–09

Porter, R.; Porter, K.-A. (2003): Habermas and the pragmatics of communication: a Deleuze – Guattarian critique; *Social Semiotics*, 13(2), 129–45

Portillo, M. (2005): Multiculturalism has failed but tolerance can save us (London: *Sunday Times*, 17 July)

Prager, J.U.; Wieland, C. (2005): *Repräsentativumfrage zur Selbstwahrnehmung der Jugend in Deutschland* (Gütersloh: Bertelsmann Stiftung)

Pred, A. (2004): *The Past is not Dead* (Minneapolis: University of Minnesota Press)

Press, I., Smith E. (eds.) (1980): *Urban Place and Process. Readings in the Anthropology of Cities* (New York: Macmillan)

Priemus, H. (1993): In Nederland gebeurt alles vijftig jaar later. Langetermijn perspectieven voor de sociale huursector in de grote stad [In The Netherlands everything happens fifty years later. Long term perspectives for the social rented sector in the big city]; in: Jaarverslag 1992 Gemeentelijk Woningbedrijf Rotterdam [Annual report 1992 Municipal Housing Company Rotterdam] (Rotterdam: GWR) pp. 1–7

Priemus, H. (1995): Kleurrijke wijken: het multi-cultureel samenwonen als volkshuis-vestingsopgave [Colourful districts: multi-cultural co-habitation as a housing chal-lenge]; *Bouw*, 50 (3), 14–15

Priemus, H.; Smid I.S. (eds) (1995): *Kleurrijke wijken: multi-etniciteit als opgave en uitdaging* [Colourful districts: multi-ethnicity as a challenge] (Delft: Delftse Universitaire Pers)

Priemus, H. (2000): Colourful districts: West European cities moving towards multi-ethnicity; in: F.W. Boal (ed.): *Ethnicity and Housing. Accommodating Differences* (Aldershot: Ashgate) pp. 225–32

Priemus, H. (2004): Stedelijk beleid uit balans; *Tijdschrift voor de Volkshuisvesting*, 10(3), 6–11

Putnam, R.D. (2000): *Bowling Alone: the Collapse and Revival of American Community* (New York: Simon and Schuster)

Putnam, R.D. (ed.) (1993): *Making Democracy Work: Civic Traditions in Modern Italy* (Princeton NJ: Princeton University Press)

Quinn, E.; Hughes, G. (2005a) *Policy Analysis Report on Asylum and Migration: Ireland 2003 to mid-2004* (Dublin: Economic and Social Research Institute and European Migration Network)

Quinn, E.; Hughes, G. (2005b): *Reception Systems, their Capacities and the Social Situation of Asylum Applicants within the Reception System in Ireland* (Dublin: Economic and Social Research Institute and European Migration Network)

Racki, F. (1931): Bogumil i patareni; *Srpska kraljeva akademija, posebna izdanja*, 87

Raento, P.A.; Brunn, S.D. (2005): Visualizing Finland: postage stamps as political messengers; *Geografiska Annaler*, 87B, 145–63

Raento, P.A.; Hamalainen, H.; Ikonen, H.; Mikkonen, N. (2004): Striking stories: a political geography of European coinage; *Political Geography*, 23, 929–56

Rahola, F. (2003): *Zone definitivamente temporanee. I luoghi dell'umanità in eccesso* (Verona: Ombre corte)

RCN – Rural Community Network (2003): *Workbook on Equity, Diversity and Interdependence in Rural Society* (Cookstown: RCN) (www.ruralcommunitynetwork.org)

RCN – Rural Community Network (2005): *Rural Community Network: Good Relations Duty* (Cookstown: RCN)

Reception and Integration Agency (2005): The Asylum Process: Reception and Dispersal (http://www.ria.gov.ie/the_asylum_process/reception_and_dispersal/)

Reeves, D. (2005): *Planning for Diversity: Policy and Planning in a World of Difference* (London: Routledge)

Reid, D.M. (1984): The symbolism of postage stamps: a source for the historians; *Journal of Contemporary History*, 19(2), 223–49

Reissert, B.; Brake, K.; Einem E. von; Heine, M. et al. (2001): *The Berlin Study – Strategies for the City* (Berlin: The Governing Mayor of Berlin, Regioverlag)

Ritchie, D. (2001): *One Oldham, One Future, Panel Report 11 December* (Oldham: Oldham Independent Review)

Ritchie, D. (2002): Report on the Oldham Riots (http://www.oldhamir.org.uk/OIR%20Report.pdf)

Robinson, G.M.; Engelstoft, S.; Pobric, A. (2001): Remaking Sarajevo: Bosnian nationalism after the Dayton Accords; *Political Geography*, 20, 957–80

Rogers, R. (1997): *Cities for a Small Planet* (London: Faber and Faber)

Roller, N. (2006): Von brennenden Autos und anderen urbanen Unannehmlichkeiten; *Telepolis* (09.03.)

Rorty, R. (2000): Universality and truth; in: R. Brandom (ed.): *Rorty and his Critics* (Oxford: Blackwell)

Rosa, M.J.; Seabra, H.E.; Santos, T. (2003): *Contributos dos 'imigrantes' na demografia portuguesa* (Porto: ACIME)

Rose, D.B. (1996): *Nourishing Terrains: Australian Aboriginal Views of Landscape and Wilderness* (Canberra: Australian Heritage Commission)

Rose, G. (2001): *Visual Methodologies. An Introduction to the Interpretation of Visual Materials* (London: Sage)

Rotenberg, R.; McDonough, G. (1993): *The Cultural Meaning of Urban Space* (Westport: Bergin and Garvin)

Roxburgh, A. (2002): *Preachers of Hate: the Rise of the Far Right* (London: Gibson Square Books)

Ruane, J.; Todd, J. (2003): Northern Ireland: religion, ethnic conflict and territoriality; in: J. Coakley (ed.): *The Territorial Management of Ethnic Conflict* (London: Frank Cass) pp. 45–72

Rubin, J. (1991): Some wise and mistaken assumptions about conflict and negotiation; in: W. Breslin, J. Rubin (eds): *Negotiation Theory and Practice* (Cambridge MA: Harvard Law School)

Sacchi, P.; Viazzo, P. (eds) (2003): *Più di un Sud. Studi antropologici sull'immigrazione a Torino* (Turin: Rosenberg e Sellier)

Sachverständigenrat für Zuwanderung und Integration (2004): Migration und Integration – Erfahrungen nutzen, Neues wagen; Jahresgutachten 2004 (http://www.dstgb.de/index_inhalt/homepage/top_themen/inhalt/archiv_2004/newsitem 00997/997_3_1092.pdf)

Safier, M. (1996): The cosmopolitan challenge in cities on the edge of the millennium: moving from conflict to co-existence; *City*, 3–4 June

Said, E.W. (1978): *Orientalism* (New York: Pantheon Books)

Salecl, R. (1994): The crisis of identity and the struggle for new hegemony in the Former Yugoslavia; in: E. Laclau (ed.): *The Making of Political Identities* (London: Verso) pp. 205–32

Salgueiro, T. (1992): *A cidade em Portugal. Uma Geografia Urbana* (Lisbon: Ed.Afrontamento)

Saloojee, A.; van Heelsum, A. (2002): Introduction; in: A. Saloojee, A. van Heelsum (eds): Civic Participation by Newcomer Communities; *Journal of International Migration and Integration*, 3(2), 151–5

Sandercock, L. (1998): *Towards Cosmopolis* (Chichester: John Wiley)

Sandercock, L. (2003a): *Cosmopolis II, Mongrel Cities* (London: Continuum)

Sandercock, L. (2003b): Planning in the ethno-cultural diverse city: a comment; *Planning Theory & Practice*, 4(3): 319–23

Sandercock, L. (2004): Editorial; *Planning Theory and Practice, Interface*, 5(2), 141–4

Sandercock, L. (2004a): Planning and Indigenous Communities; *Planning Theory and Practice, Interface*, 5(1), 95–7

Sandercock, L. (2004b): Commentary: indigenous planning and the burden of colonialism; *Planning Theory and Practice, Interface*, 5(1), 118–24

Sandercock, L. (2005): Difference, fear and habitus: a political economy of urban fears; in: J. Hillier, E. Rooksby (eds): *Habitus: a Sense of Place* (Aldershot: Ashgate) pp. 219–34.

Scarman, L.G. (1981): Report on the Brixton Riots, 25 November (www.bbc.co.uk/on)

Schopflin, G. (1995): Nationhood, communism and state legitimation; *Nations and Nationalism*, 1, 81–91

Schopflin, G. (1996): Nationalism and ethnic minorities in post-communist Europe; in: R. Caplan, J. Feffer (eds): *Europe's New Nationalism: States and Minorities in Conflict* (New York: Oxford University Press) pp. 151–68

Schwartz, B. (1982): The social context of commemoration: a study in collective memory; *Social Forces*, 82, 374–402

292   *Bibliography*

Schwedler, H.-U. (1985): *Arbeitsmigration und urbaner Wandel. Eine Studie über Arbeitskräftewanderung und räumliche Segregation in orientalischen Städten am Beispiel Kuwaits* (Berlin: Reimer)

Schwedler, H.-U. (2001): Berlin – eine zweimalige Stadt. Stadtplanung im Spannungsfeld vieler Interessen; in: *Aus Politik und Zeitgeschichte*, 34/35, 25–30

Schwedler, H.-U. (2001b): The urban planning context in Berlin: a city twice unique; in: W.J.V. Neill, H.-U. Schwedler (eds): *Urban Planning and Cultural Inclusion: Lessons from Belfast and Berlin* (New York: Palgrave – now Palgrave Macmillan)

Schwedler, H.-U. (ed.) (2005): *New Citizens for Europe – Demographic Changes and Impacts on Urban Policy Fields* (Berlin: EA.UE)

Scott, G.M. Jr (1995): A resynthesis of the primordial and circumstantial approaches to ethnic group solidarity: toward an explanatory model; *Ethnic and Racial Studies*, 13(2), 147–71

SCP – Sociaal en Cultureel Planbureau (2003): *Minderheden 2003* (The Hague: SCP)

SEF – Serviço de Estrangeiros e Fronteiras (2003): População estrangeira residente em Portugal (http://www.sef.pt/estatisticas/por_sexo_04_new.pdf)

Seglow, J. (2005): The ethics of immigration; *Political Studies Review*, 3(3), 317–34

Senat von Berlin (2005): Integrationskonzept für Berlin, Abgeordnetenhaus Berlin, Drucksache (Berlin Parliament printing) 15/4208, 23 August

Senghaas, D. (1998): Die fixe Idee vom Kampf der Kulturen; in: K.P. Fritzsche, F. Frank (eds): *Frieden und Demokratie* (Baden-Baden: Nomos) pp. 31–8

Sennett, R. (1994): *Flesh and Stone: the Body and the City in Western Civilization* (Harmondsworth: Penguin)

Shachar, A. (2001): *Multicultural Jurisdictions: Cultural Differences and Women's Rights* (Cambridge: Cambridge University Press)

Shamir, R. (2001): Suspended in space: Bedouins under the Law of Israel; in: N. Blomley, D. Delaney, R. Ford (eds): *The Legal Geographies Reader: Law, Power and Space* (Oxford: Blackwell) pp. 135–42

Shields, R. (1996): A guide to urban representation and what to do about it: alternative traditions of urban theory; in: A. King: *Re-presenting the city: Ethnicity, Capital and Culture: the 21st C Metropolis* (London: Macmillan) pp. 227–52

Shirlow, P. (1997): Class, materialism and the fracturing of traditional alignments; in: Graham, B. (ed.): *In Search of Ireland* (London: Routledge) pp. 87–107

Shirlow, P. (2001): Devolution in Northern Ireland; *Regional Studies*, 35(8), 743–52

Shirlow, P. (2003): Who fears to speak? Fear, mobility and ethno-sectarianism in the two Ardoynes; *Global Review of Ethnopolitics*, 3(1), 76–91

Shirlow, P.; Murtagh, B. (2004): Capacity-building, representation and intracommunity conflict; *Urban Studies*, 41(1), 57–70

Shirlow, P.; Murtagh, B. (2006): *Belfast: Segregation, Violence and the City* (London: Pluto Press)

Shirlow, P.; Shuttleworth, I. (1999): Who is going to toss the burgers; *Capital and Class*, 67, 27–46

Sidaway, J.D.; Power, M. (2005): The tears of Portugal: empire, identity, 'race', and destiny in Portuguese geopolitical narratives; *Environment and Planning D: Society and Space*, 23, 527–54

Siebel, S. (2004): *Stadtsoziologie. Eine Einführung* (Frankfurt/M: Campus-Verlag)

Sijaric, R. (1993): World of museums: update on the Zemaljski Muzej, Sarajevo; *Museum Management and Curatorship*, 12, 195–206

Simmel, G. (1999): *Sociologie: études sur les formes de la socialisation* (Paris: puf)

Simons, M. (2003): *The Meeting of the Waters* (Sydney: Hodder)

Smith, A.D. (1991a): *National Identity* (London: Penguin)

Bibliography 293

Smith, A.D. (1991b): The nation: invented, imagined, reconstructed; *Millennium Journal of International Studies*, 20, 353–68

Smith, A.D. (1994): Nationalism and peace: theoretical notes for research and political agendas; *Innovation*, 7, 219–36

Smith, G. (ed.), (1994): *The Baltic States: the National Self-determination of Estonia, Latvia and Lithuania* (London: Macmillan)

Smith, T. (1998): Re-casting Citizenship: From Apathy and Alienation to Active Participation. Thirteenth T.H. Marshall Memorial Lecture University of Southampton, 23 February 1998

Soja, E. (2000): *Postmetropolis: Critical Studies of Cities and Regions* (London: Blackwell)

Solovejec, A. (1959): Bogumilentum und Bogumilengräber in den südslawischen Ländern; in: W. Gülich (ed.): *Völker und Kulturen Südosteuropas* (Munich: Südosteuropa Gesellschaft) pp. 182–6

Staeheli, L.A. (2005): Reconfiguring citizenship in a transnational perspective; in: International Building Exhibition (IBA) Saxony-Anhalt: *The Other Cities, Volume 2: Civic Culture* (Berlin: Jovis Verlag)

Stanley, C. (1996): *Urban Excess and the Law: Capital, Culture and Desire* (London: Cavendish)

Stavrakakis, Y. (1999): *Lacan and the Political* (London: Routledge)

Steiger, C. (1989): Serbian, Croatian – Serbo-Croatian?; *Swiss Review of World Affairs*, 6–7 April

Stewart, G.B. (1975): *Names on the Globe* (New York: Oxford University Press)

Takei, M. (1998): Collective memory as the key to national and ethnic identity: the case of Cambodia; *Nationalism and Ethnic Politics*, 4(3), 59–78

Tewdwr-Jones, M.; Allmendinger, P. (1998): Deconstructing communicative rationality: a critique of Habermasian collaborative planning; *Environment and Planning A*, 30(4), 1975–1989

Thompson, G. (2005): Toleration and the art of international governance: how is it possible to 'live together' in a fragmenting international system?; in: J. Hillier, E. Rooksby (eds): *Habitus: a Sense of Place* (Aldershot: Ashgate) pp. 83–108

Threadgold, T. (1999): Law as/of property, judgement as dissension: feminist and postcolonial interventions in the networks; *International Journal for the Semiotics of Law*, 12, 369–96

Thrift, N. (2004): A non-representational geography; paper presented at IGU – UK Conference, Glasgow, 16–20 August

Tibi, B. (1995): *Krieg der Zivilisationen. Politik und Religion zwischen Vernunft und Fundamentalismus* (Hamburg: Hoffmann und Campe)

Tibi, B. (1998): *Europa ohne Identität? Leitkultur oder Wertebeliebigkeit* (Munich: Bertelsmann)

Tilly, C. (1990): *Coercion, Capital and European States, AD 900–1990* (Oxford: Basil Blackwell)

Tonnies, F. (1946): *Communauté et société* (Paris: puf)

Travers, T. (2004): *The Politics of London: Governing an Ungovernable City* (Basingstoke: Palgrave Macmillan)

Tully, J. (1999): The agonic freedom of citizens; *Economy & Society*, 28(2), 151–82

Tully, J. (2000): Struggles over recognition and distribution; *Constellations*, 7(4), 469–82

Turner, B. (1990): Outline of a theory of citizenship; *Sociology*, 22(2), 189–217

Tzfadia, E.; Yiftachel, O. (2004): Between urban and national: political mobilization among Mizrahim in Israel's 'development towns'; *Cities*, 21 (1), 41–55

Ugba, A. (2005): Active Civic Participation of Immigrants in Ireland (http://www.uni-oldenburg.de/politis-europe)

Ulrich, B. (1998): *Democracy Without Enemies* (Cambridge: Polity Press)
UNDP – United Nations Development Programme (2002): *Early Warning System. Bosnia and Hercegovina 2002 Election Special* (Sarajevo: UNDP)
United Nations Population Division (2004): *World Population in 2300*, ESA/P/WP.187 (New York: UN)
Unwin, T.; Hewitt, V. (2001): Banknotes and national identity in central and eastern Europe; *Political Geography*, 20, 1005–28
Urban Task Force (1999): *Towards an Urban Renaissance: Final Report of the Urban Task Force Chaired by Lord Rogers of Riverside* (London: Department of the Environment, Transport and the Regions)
Varshney, A. (2002): *Ethnic Conflict and Civic Life: Hindus and Muslims in India* (New Haven: Yale University Press)
Veltz, P. (1996): *Mondialisation villes et territoires. L'économie d'archipel* (Paris: puf)
Vile, M.J.C. (1999): *Politics in the USA* (London: Routledge)
Vincentian Refugee Centre (2004): *Housing and Refugees – the Real Picture* (Dublin: Vincentian Refugee Centre)
Viveret, P. (1993): Du savoir faire au savoir vivre, Projet no. 235; *Espace local, espace mondial*, Automne
Walker, D. (2002): *In Praise of Centralism: a Critique of New Localism* (London: Catalyst)
Wallerstein, D. (1991): *Geopolitics and Geoculture* (Cambridge: Cambridge University Press)
Walther, U.-J. (ed.) (2002): *Soziale Stadt – Zwischenbilanzen: ein Programm auf dem Weg zur sozialen Stadt?* (Opladen: Leske+Budrich)
Warleigh, A. (2001): Purposeful opportunists? EU institutions and the struggle over European citizenship; in: R. Bellamy, A. Warleigh (eds): *Citizenship and Governance in the European Union* (London: Continuum) pp. 19–40
Weber, M. (1959): *Le Savant et le politique* (Paris: Plon)
Weiler, J.H.H. (1997a): To be a European citizen – eros and civilization; *Journal of European Public Policy*, 4, 495–519
Weiler, J.H.H. (1997b): The European Union belongs to its citizens: three immodest proposals; *European Law Review*, 22 April, 150–6
White, E.J. (2002): Forging African diaspora places in Dublin's retro-global spaces; *City* 6(2), 251–70
Whyte, J. (1990): *Interpreting Northern Ireland* (Oxford: Clarendon)
Wilkinson, R.G. (2005): *The Impact of Inequality: How to Make Sick Societies Healthier* (London: Routledge)
Wittgenstein, L. (1951): *Tractatus Logico-Philosophicus* (Paris: Gallimard)
Yiftachel, O. (1995): Planning as control: policy and resistance in a deeply divided society; *Progress in Planning*, 44(2), 116–84
Yiftachel, O. (2001): Can theory be liberated from professional constraints? On rationality and explanatory power in Flyvbjerg's Rationality and Power; *International Planning Studies*, 6(3), 251–55
Young, I.M. (1990): *Justice and the Politics of Difference* (Princeton: Princeton University Press)
Zincone, G. (ed.) (2001): *Primo rapporto sull'integrazione degli immigrati in Italia, Commissione per le politiche di integrazione degli immigrati* (Bologna: Il Mulino)
Zizek, S. (1999): *The Ticklish Subject* (London: Verso)
Zizek, S. (2000): Holding the place; in: J. Butler, E. Laclau, S. Zizek (eds): *Contingency, Hegemony, Universality* (London: Verso) pp. 308–29
Zizek, S. (2004): *Organs without Bodies* (London: Routledge)

Index

Abu-Lughod, Lila, 181–2
acquis, 30 n9
  and European citizenship, 19
Advisory Council for Integration and
  Migration (Berlin), 166
agonism
  and dealing with, 260–6
  and dimensions of, 92–3
  and planning, 90, 91, 98
Akbar, O, 258–9
Algeria, and France, 121
alienation, and European citizenship, 21
Allmendinger, P, 89, 94
Amin, A, 24–5, 253, 261–2
  and citizenship, 36–7
  and cultural hybridization, 36
  and urban life, 35
Amsterdam, and ethnic population of,
  104, 106
Amsterdam, Treaty of (1997), 9
  and protection against discrimination,
  21
Anderson, Benedict, 41, 225
Andric, Ivo, 226, 230
Antwerp, and xenophobic reaction in,
  33–4
Arendt, Hannah, 64, 68
Aristotle, 34, 69
arts
  and integration, 42
  and role of, 38
assimilation
  and France, 22, 37, 257
  and migration, 64
asylum seekers, *see* Ireland
Athens, in classical period, 34
Atkinson, J, 88
Audit Commission (UK), 171–2
Australia
  and Aboriginal peoples:
    marginalization, 75; restriction of
    rights, 75; transmission of
    knowledge, 77

  and Kumarangk case, 75, 76–7:
    Ngarrindjeri women, 76–7
  and land use, 74, 75
  and multiculturalism, 75
  and place-making: Gunder's approach,
    81–2; Habermasian concepts,
    77–81; informal negotiations,
    84–5; Ivison's approach, 81;
    Sandercock's approach, 81, 84;
    state law, 75; tensions in law,
    74–5, 76

Baltic states, and porous borders, 44–5
bank notes, and Bosnia-Herzegovina,
  226–7
Barth, Frederik, 2–4, 182
Baudrillard, J, 260
Bauman, Z, 36
Baumann, Gerd, 182
Beck, Ulrich, 36
Belfast, 33
  and conflict-related deaths 196–7
  and Equity, Diversity and
    Interdependence (EDI), 95–7
  and Groundwork Northern Ireland:
    Tigers Bay, 209–12, 214–15; Youth
    and Environment Programme,
    212–13, 215–16
  and identity construction, 192:
    ideological framework, 203
  and interfacing, policy costs of, 198–9
  and living at the interface, 199–203:
    18–55 age group, 200–1; attitudes
    towards community, 201;
    hostility to non-sectarians, 202–3;
    ignorance of city, 199; knowledge
    of interfaces, 199; non-sectarians,
    200, 201–2; pensioners, 199, 200;
    variation in sectarianism, 200
  and media stereotypes, 41–2
  and mixed marriages, 44
  and museums, 41
  and non-sectarians, 193, 200, 201–2

Belfast – *continued*
and physical divisions, 39
and segregation: boundaries, 196; by
community background, 194;
desire for, 191; 'exit', 195; growth
of, 194; impact of, 192; as
instrument of animosity, 192;
mobile Catholic community, 193;
relative nature of, 193; residential,
192–3; residualization, 195–6;
shortcomings of census data, 194;
territorial divisions, 194–5
and strife, dimensions of, 92–3
and 'the lack', 91
and violence, 191: constancy of, 199;
geography of, 197; imagination of
difference, 197–8; reproduction
of, 192
see also Northern Ireland
Bellamy, R, 26
Benhabib, S, 68–9, 262
Berlin
and economic decline, 136, 139
and immigration/immigrants:
education, 140, 161; ethnic
Germans, 137, 139; guest workers,
137; history of, 137–8; income
levels, 139; numbers of, 137, 160;
residential segregation, 138–9,
160; socio-economic position of,
139–42; Turks, 137–8, 160–1;
unemployment, 136, 139, 161
and integration of immigrants:
Advisory Council for Integration
and Migration, 166;
Commissioner for Integration and
Migration, 162, 163, 164;
immigrant involvement, 163–4;
immigrant organizations, 162–3,
165–6; integration plan (2005),
142; Migration Council, 166; new
policy on, 164–5; policy, 162–3;
policy reorientation, 163;
problems with, 161; *Senat's*
integration concept, 164
and neighbourhood management,
142, 143–4: economy and
employment, 144–5;
Neighbourhood Council, 145–6;
obstacles facing residents, 144;
promoting tolerant coexistence,
145; schools and education, 144
and Socially Integrative City
programme, 136, 142
and urban policy: challenges faced by,
136, 146; differentiated
approaches to, 143; identifying
areas in need, 143;
neighbourhood management,
142, 143–6
see also Germany
Bianchini, F, 34–5
Biffi, Cardinal, 181
Billig, M, 219–20, 226
Birmingham, 170
Bloomfield, J, 34–5
Booher, D, 89
borders
and cities, 130
and porous borders, 44–5
and spatial migration patterns, 126–8
Borneman, J, 22
Bos, Wouter, 104
Bosnia-Herzegovina, 218
and Central Bank of, 226
and characteristics of, 218
and creation of, 219
and Croats, 221
and ethno-nationalism, 219–22, 231
and linguistic homogeneity, 218
and multi-ethnic identity, 231
and Muslims, 221: Bosniak
nationalism, 230–1; as Bosniaks,
221–2; secular tendency of, 222
and potential nation states, 221
and remaking of place: bank notes,
226–7; national identity, 230;
National Museum, 225–6; postage
stamps, 227–30
and Serbs, 221
see also Sarajevo
Bradford, 168
and integrated education, 43
and separate communities, 40
Brazil, 236–7
British National Party, 42–3
Brixton riots, 168, 170
Brubaker, Rogers, 41
Burnley, and separate communities, 40

Caetano, Marcelo, 235
Calicut, and civic networks, 40
Cantle report (2001), 39, 40, 42–3
Capello, C, 189
case studies, and use of, 4–5
Castiglione, D, 26
Castree, N, 74
Centre for Research and Statistics
  (Netherlands), 105
Chicago School, and urban
  development, 6
cities
  and agonistic democratic politics,
    262–3
  and borders, 126–8, 130
  and challenge facing, 35
  and citizenship, 17, 258, 259
  and civic republicanism, 69–71
  and conflictual relationships, 118–19
  and confusion surrounding, 118
  and cultural diversity, 130, 272–3
  and immigration, 49–50, 58
  as laboratory, 133–4
  and narrative of European, 258–9
  and nature of, 34–7: community, 36;
    creative city, 34; economic strains
    on, 36; ethnic diversity, 35;
    interculturalism, 34–5;
    organization of urban space, 35–6;
    outsider, 34
  and political/cultural character, 258
  and racial, economic and gender
    contests, 88
  and segregation, 5–6
  and social fragmentation, France,
    124–8
  and social/political role of, 134
  see also Council of Europe, and 'shared
    cities'; entries for individual
    countries and cities; EuroCities
    Cities Overcoming Division in
    Europe (CODE), 45
citizenship
  and cities, 17, 258, 259
  and civic citizenship, 19, 22, 264
  and communitarianism, 18, 25, 64
  and cultural difference, 63–4
  and encouragement of, 36–7
  and France, 119–20
  and integrated education, 43–4

  and Ireland, 252
  and Italy, 180–1
  and liberalism, 18
  and migrants, 53
  and nationality, 18, 23–6
  and political disillusionment, 21, 66
  and supranational polity, 23–6
  see also civic republicanism; European
    citizenship
city-states, and civic republicanism, 65,
  69–70
civic associations, 26
civic citizenship, 19, 264
  and third-country migrants, 22
civic leadership
  and integration, 42–3
  and role of, 38
civic networks, 36, 37–8
  and integration, 39–40
civic pride, and role of, 38
civic republicanism
  and citizenship, 18, 64–6
  and the city, 69–71
  and cultural difference, 66–9, 73:
    compensatory support, 66–7;
    interdependence, 68–9, 73;
    Ireland, 71–3; nature of public
    realm, 68; recognition of groups,
    67–8; sharing of common fate,
    68–9, 73; and planning, 261
civilizations, and 'clash of', 1–2
civil rights, and European citizenship, 20
Closa, C, 18, 25, 26, 27, 28
Cohen, Abner, 182
collaborative planning, 88, 89
  and criticisms of, 90–1, 93
Commission for Racial Equality (UK),
  43, 263
Common Agricultural Policy, 17
communitarianism
  and citizenship, 18, 25, 64
  and immigration policy, 31 n29
community
  and civic republicanism, 65, 73
  as divisive concept, 41
  and nature of, 36
  and separate communities, 40
  and sharing of common fate,
    68–9
  and uses of notion of, 182

community cohesion
  and Groundwork Northern Ireland,
    208–9
  and United Kingdom, 169–73
Community Relations Council (CRC)
    (Belfast), 95
conflict resolution, and levels of, 214
Convention on the Future of Europe, 25,
    28
corruption, and civic republicanism, 65
cosmopolitanism, and Sarajevo, 224–5
Council of Europe, and 'shared cities',
    33, 45
  and arts, 42
  and challenge facing cities, 35
  and Cities Overcoming Division in
    Europe (CODE), 45
  and civic leadership, 42–3
  and integration: civic networks, 39–40;
    education, 43–4; media/museums,
    41–2; public space, 38–9
  and lessons for policy makers, 37–8
  and mixed marriages, 44
  and nature of cities, 34–7:
    community, 36; creative city, 34;
    economic strains on, 36; ethnic
    diversity, 35; interculturalism,
    34–5; organization of urban space,
    35–6; outsider, 34
  and origins of project, 33
  and porous borders, 44–5
creative city, 34
  and the arts, 42
  and interculturalism, 34–5
Crick, Bernard, 261
Croatia, 23
cultural diversity
  and cities, 130
  and civic republicanism, 66–9, 73:
    compensatory support, 66–7;
    interdependence, 68–9, 73;
    Ireland, 71–3; nature of public
    realm, 68; recognition of groups,
    67–8; sharing of common fate,
    68–9, 73
  and common citizenship, 63–4
  and construction of, 4
  and EuroCities 'Contribution to Good
    Governance . . . ', 272–3
  and European city, 258–9

  and imposition of order, 264–6
  and increase in, 9
  and intercultural dialogue, 37
  and Italy, 181–2
  and liberalism, 63
  and limits of tolerance, 258, 260, 261,
    263–4
  and negotiation of accommodation,
    257–8, 261
  and responses to, 63
  and use of concept, 181–2
  see also multiculturalism
cultural hybridization, 36
cultural identity, and political solidarity,
    64
cultural inclusion
  and affirming ideal of, 261–2
  and controversy surrounding, 1
  and European approach to, 9–12
  and governance structures, 259–60
  and imposition of order, 264–6
  and limits of tolerance, 258, 260, 261,
    263–4
  and methodological approach to, 4–5
  and planning, 262
  and theoretical dilemma: academic
    uncertainty, 4; 'clash of
    civilizations', 1–2; domestic
    cultural conflict, 2; failure of
    metatheories, 5; identity
    construction, 2–4
cultural mediation, and Italy, 188

Dayton Accords (1995), 219, 231
de Boeck, Filip, 183
deliberative democracy, 79
democracy
  and bridging social capital, 35
  and deliberative democracy, 79
  and law, 78
  and participation, 66
democratic citizenship, and
    supranational polity, 23–6
demographic change
  and Europe, 7–9
  and European Commission, 10
Denmark, and Mohammed cartoon
    controversy, 257, 263
De Valera, Eamon, 71
discrimination

and immigrants, 57–8
and protection against, 21
Draft Constitutional Treaty, 25
and Dutch/French rejection of, 29
   n1, 257
and engagement of citizens, 28
and European citizenship, 17, 18,
   19–20, 26
Dublin
and asylum seekers: accommodation
   of, 247–8, 249–50; dispersal of,
   248–9; responses to, 251
and immigration/immigrants, 72, 243:
   formation of networks, 250;
   impact on retailing, 250; novelty
   of, 242; Poles, 244; racism, 251;
   responses to, 250–1; work permit
   holders, 244
and portrayal of, 241
Duffy, M, 84
Dumper, M, 214
Dunford, M, 17

education
and EuroCities 'Contribution to Good
   Governance . . . ', 270–1
and Germany: Berlin's immigrants,
   140, 161; Socially Integrative City
   programme, 155–6
and integration, 38, 43–4
and planners, 97–8, 99–100
environmental regeneration, *see*
   Groundwork Northern Ireland
equality, and different understandings
   of, 23
Equity, Diversity and Interdependence (EDI)
and applications of, 96
and implications for critical discursive
   practice, 96–8
as model of agonistic practice, 88
and planning, 94–9
ethnic diversity
and increase in, 9
and scapegoating, 36
and social capital, 35
ethnic identity, and construction of, 4
ethnicity
and ethnic identity, 221
and instrumental theory of, 182
and nationality, 220–1

ethnic minorities, and human rights, 22
ethno-nationalism, and
   Bosnia-Herzegovina, 219–22, 231
EuroCities
and 'Contribution to Good
   Governance . . . ', 50–1, 264, 268–73
and establishment of, 47
and future priorities of, 58
and government of, 48
and membership of, 47
and migration and integration, 48–9,
   58: reasons for interest in, 49–50
and organization of, 48
and political lobbying, 48–9
and response to 'Common Agenda for
   Integration', 53–4: facilitating
   exchange and learning, 55–6;
   improving governance, 55;
   monitoring, evaluation and
   research, 56–7; sustainable
   integration, 54
and response to EU Green Paper on
   Economic Migration, 51: flawed
   document, 51–2; undocumented
   migrants, 52–3
European Charter of Fundamental
   Rights (2000), 19
European citizenship
and challenges facing, 20–3
and characteristics of, 18–20
and cities, 17
and civic citizenship, 19
and civic republicanism, 18
and civil rights, 20
and communitarianism, 18
and complementary nature of, 19
and consensus on, 26
and Draft Constitutional Treaty, 17,
   18, 19–20, 26
and European Commission working
   parties, 19–20
and freedom of movement, 17, 18
and human rights, 19, 20, 22, 30 n16
and liberalism, 18
and migrants, 53
and nationality, 18, 23–6
and new member states, 22–3
and political rights, 20
and public space, 25, 26–7
and social citizenship, 20

European citizenship – *continued*
  and state's control of naturalization,
    27–8
  and supranational polity, 23–6
  and third-country migrants, 19, 22
  and unresolved tension in, 27–8
European Commission
  and civic citizenship, 264
  and 'Common Agenda for
    Integration', response to, 53–7
  and demographic change, 10
  and European citizenship, 19–20
  and migration, 9–10
  and nationality, 28
European Court of Justice, 28
European Parliament, and EuroCities, 49
European Policy Centre Programme on
    Multicultural Europe, 49
European Social Fund, 188
European Spatial Development
    Perspective (1999), 5
European Union
  and Common Basic Principles on
    Integration, 51, 54, 264–5
  and demographic change, 7–9
  and EuroCities, 49
  and Green Paper on Economic
    Migration, 51: EuroCities response
    to, 51–3
  and migration, 9–12, 49: lack of joint
    policy, 111
  see also European citizenship;
    European Commission
European Year of Inter-Cultural
    Dialogue, 264
Eyben, K, 95

family, and support for mixed marriages,
    38, 44
Fanning, B, 241
Fenster, T, 93–4
Ferdinand, Archduke Franz, 218, 224
Fiat Industries, 187
Fiennes, Ralph, 42
Flint, J, 88
Flyvbjerg, B, 90, 91
Fortuyn, Pim, 1, 13 n2, 103
Foucault, M, 90
Fowler, N, 22
France

and Algeria, 121
and assimilation, 22, 37, 257
and citizenship, 119–20: political
  rights, 120; Republican
  conception of, 119, 120
and conflictual urban relationships,
  118–19
and euphemisms for conflict, 118–19
and historic legacy: colonial period,
  121; French Revolution, 120;
  separation of Church and State,
  121
and immigration/immigrants, 123:
  attitudes towards, 124; children
  of, 129; economic cycles, 123–4
and minorities/communities: in cities,
  128–9; need for new governance,
  129–33; non-recognition of,
  119–21; uncertainty over
  designation of, 129
and nationality, 119–20
and rejection of Draft Constitutional
  Treaty, 29 n1, 257
and urban periphery, 125–7: borders,
  126–8, 130; diversity of *banlieues*,
  126; insufficiency of physical
  solutions, 133; joined-up
  governance, 132; nature of
  top-down policies, 129–30; need
  for new governance, 129–33;
  potential ignored, 130; social
  fragmentation, 124–8;
  subsidiarity, 131–2; territorial
  coordination, 131; urban
  reconquest, 131
and urban riots, 1, 6, 13 n3, 191, 257:
  lack of name, 119; search for
  identity, 122
freedom, and civic republicanism, 65
freedom of movement, and European
  citizenship, 17, 18
Friedrichshafen, 45
fuzzy places, 182–3

Garner, S, 241
Germany
  and hostel burnings, 1, 13 n4
  and immigration/immigrants:
    adoption of new policy paradigm,
    159; education, 140; ethnic

Germans, 160; guest workers, 160; history of, 137–8, 159–60; integration, 156–7; integration policy, 159

and Socially Integrative City programme: aims of, 148, 150; area selection, 153–4; Berlin, 136, 142; construction-oriented urban renewal, 150; education, 155–6; establishment of, 148; identifying problems/setting goals, 150–1; impact of, 154–5; integration of immigrants, 156–7; inter-departmental cooperation, 152; involvement of external actors, 154; local economy and employment, 157–8; pooling resources, 153; recommendations for, 158; residential segregation, 151–2; variable implementation of, 149

see also Berlin

governance
and cultural inclusion, 259–60
and French cities, 129–33
and integration, 55
and new localism, 170–1, 172–3

Graham, S, 6

Greater Dandenong Council, 84–5

Grenoble, and immigration, 123: economic cycles, 123–4

Groundwork Northern Ireland
and approach of, 206–7, 208, 216
in Belfast: achievements of, 214–15, 215–16; Tigers Bay, 209–12, 214–15; Youth and Environment Programme, 212–13, 215–16
and benign apartheid model, 214–15: overcoming, 211; problems posed by, 212
and building stronger neighbourhoods, 207
and improving environment, 207
and making 'better informed bigots', 215
and problems addressed by, 208
and realizing potential of young, 207–8

and theoretical grounding of: community cohesion, 208; social capital theory, 208–9

guest workers, and Germany, 137, 160

Gunder, M, 81–2, 90, 94, 98, 261

Habermas, Jürgen, 37, 75, 260
and context independence, 79
and criticisms of, 80–1
and deliberative democracy, 79
and juridical systems, 77–8
and legitimate law, 78
and mediatization, 78
and planning-related processes, 79
and truth, 79–80

Hague, The, and ethnic population of, 104

Hague Programme, 48

Hall, Peter, 34

Häussermann, H, and segregation, 6

health, and EuroCities 'Contribution to Good Governance . . . ', 271

Heaney, Seamus, 36

Heater, D, 23

Heikkila, E, 96–7

Held, D, 24

Hillier, J, 90

Hindmarsh Island Bridge, *see* Kumarangk

Hirsi Ali, Ayaan, 13 n2

history, and integration, 41

Hobbes, Thomas, 128

Honohan, I, 24

housing
and EuroCities 'Contribution to Good Governance . . . ', 272
see also Rotterdam

Howitt, R, 75, 83

Hudson, R, 17

Hughes, G, 242, 251

human rights
and ethnic minorities, 22
and European citizenship, 19, 20, 30 n16
and migrants, 53

Huntington, Samuel, and 'clash of civilizations', 1–2

Hutton, W, 27

identity
and construction of, 2–4
and ethnic identity, 221

identity – *continued*
   and nationality, 220–1, 230
   and political solidarity, 64
illegal immigration, *see* undocumented
   migrants
immigration
   and cities, 49–50, 58
   and Europe's future reliance on, 8–9,
      10, 57
   and securitization of, 22
   see also entries for individual countries
      and cities
Independent Review Team (UK), 208–9
Innes, J, 89
integration, 37
   and the arts, 42
   and Baudrillard on, 260
   and civic leadership, 42–3
   and civic networks, 39–40
   and education, 43–4
   and EU Common Basic Principles on
      Integration, 51, 54, 264–5
   and EuroCities, 48–9, 58:
      'Contribution to Good
      Governance . . . ', 50–1, 264,
      268–73; facilitating exchange and
      learning, 55–6; improving
      governance, 55; monitoring,
      evaluation and research, 56–7;
      need for measures for, 52; reasons
      for interest in, 49–50; response to
      European Commission, 53–7;
      sustainable integration, 54;
      undocumented migrants, 52–3
   and Germany, 156–7: Advisory
      Council for Integration and
      Migration, 166; Berlin *Senat*'s
      integration concept, 164; Berlin's
      new policy, 164–5; Commissioner
      for Integration and Migration
      (Berlin), 162, 163, 164; immigrant
      involvement, 163–4; immigrant
      organizations, 162–3, 165–6;
      Migration Council, 166; policy in
      Berlin, 162–3; policy
      reorientation, 163; problems
      with, 161
   and governance, 55
   and history, 41
   and integrated education, 43–4

   and Ireland, 252
   and lack of consensus over meaning, 57
   and lessons for policy makers, 37–8
   and media/museums, 41–2
   and mixed marriages, 44
   and need for new measures, 6
   and porous borders, 44–5
   and Portugal, 235–7, 239–40
   and public space, 38–9
   and sustainable integration, 54
   as two-way process, 264
Integration of Third Country Nationals
   programme (INTI), 56
Intercultural Centres, and Italy, 188
Intercultural Dialogue and Conflict
   Prevention programme, 33
interculturalism
   and creative city, 34
   and definition of, 34–5
   and European citizenship, 21
   and organization of urban space, 35–6
   and positive freedom, 21
interdependence
   and civic republicanism, 64–5, 68–9,
      73
   and collaborative planning, 89
International Migration Integration
   Social Cohesion (IMISCOE), 49, 57
Irby, Adelene Paula, 224
Ireland
   and asylum seekers, 242, 252–3:
      accommodation of, 247–8,
      249–50; criticism of system, 249;
      decline in, 251, 252;
      discouragement of, 252; Dispersal
      and Direct Provision, 247–9;
      dispersal of, 248–9; increase in,
      245–6; issues raised by, 242–3;
      origins of, 246; 'Programme
      Refugees', 245; responses to, 251;
      welfare payments, 248
   and citizenship law, 252
   and cultural diversity, 71–3
   and cultural homogeneity, 241
   and economic development, 242, 247
   and emigration from, 242
   and immigration/immigrants, 252–3:
      EU accession states, 244; Habitual
      Residency Test, 244; impact of,
      242; racism, 251; sparse research

on, 243; trends in, 243–4; work
permit system, 244
and integration policy, 252
and Roman Catholicism, 241
and secularization, 241
and travellers, 241–2
Islam, and Mohammed cartoon
controversy, 257, 263
Italy
and cultural difference, 181–2
and demographic change, 8
and immigration/immigrants, 179–80:
citizenship, 180–1; cultural
mediation, 188; demand for
labour, 180; factors affecting, 180
see also Turin; Verona
Ivangorod, and porous borders, 44–5
Ivison, D, 81

Jarman, Neil, 41
Jukic, Franjo, 227
juridical systems
and Habermas, 77–8
and legitimate law, 78

Kaldor, M, 224
Kant, Immanuel, 263
Katunaric, Vjeran, 41
Kaufmann, Margarita, 45
Kennedy, John F, 260
King, Russell, 110
Kok, Wim, 113
Kostakopoulou, T, 22, 26, 27, 28
Kremer, E, 258–9
Kumarangk, 75
and Hindmarsh Island Bridge
controversy, 76–7

labour market
and EuroCities 'Contribution to Good
Governance . . . ', 271
and predicted shortages in, 9
Lacan, Jacques, 90–1, 261
lack, and Lacanian theory, 90–1
Laclau, E, 27
Landry, Charles, 34
land use
and Australia, 74, 75
and incommensurable values, 80–1
see also place, and negotiation of

law
and juridical systems, 77–8
and legitimate law, 78
and mediatization, 78
and negotiation of place, 74
and place-making, 74–5
Lawrence, Steven, 170
Lebon, F, 36
Lederach, J P, 214, 215
Leinen, Jo, 32 n41
Leitkultur, 2
Lentin, R, 242
liberalism
and citizenship, 18
and cultural diversity, 63
liberty, and different understandings of,
23
Lisbon
and immigration/immigrants, 236
and national identity, 239
and residential segregation, 237, 239
see also Portugal
Local Agenda 21, 207
Local Area Agreements (LAAs) (UK), 170,
172
local authorities, *see* EuroCities; new
localism
London
and government of, 173–4
and immigrants, origin of, 167, 169
and London bombings (2005), 176–7,
263–4
and multiculturalism, 176–7:
acceptance of, 168; adjustment
difficulties, 168; ethnic diversity,
167; impact on schools, 168;
promoting localism, 174–6; spatial
policy, 173–4; as strength, 177
and Olympic Games (2012) bid, 168,
175–6
see also United Kingdom
London Docklands, 175
Los Angeles, 35
Low, N, 78

Maalouf, Amin, 42
Maastricht Treaty (1992), 9
MacGregor, S, 266
Machiavelli, Niccolo, 69
Madison, James, 66

March, A, 78
Maritano, Laura, 181
Markell, P, 66
Märker, A, 10
Marseilles, and civic networks, 40
Marshall, T H, 180
Marvin, S, 6
master signifiers, 94
Mayer, Iona, 182
Mayer, Philip, 182
McAleese, Mary, 72
media
   and integration, 41–2
   and role of, 38
   and stereotypes, 41–2
mediatization, 78
Melossi, D, 187
Metropolis Project, 49
Meyer, Günter, 259
migration
   and demographic change in Europe,
      7–9
   and EU Green Paper on Economic
      Migration, 51: EuroCities response
      to, 51–3
   and EuroCities, 48–9: reasons for
      interest in, 49–50
   and European approach to, 9–12
   and human rights, 53
   and undocumented migrants, 52–3
Migration Council (Berlin), 166
Milan, and cultural mediation, 188
Mitrovica, 33
   and physical divisions, 39
   and separate communities, 40
mixed marriages
   and integration, 44
   and support for, 38
Morrow, D, 95–6
Mouffe, C, 26–7, 91
multiculturalism, 37
   and agonistic democratic politics,
      262–3
   and Australia, 75
   and challenge of, 167
   and civic republicanism, 73
   and cultural diversity, 63
   and European citizenship, 21
   and imposition of order, 264–6

   and limits of tolerance, 258, 260, 261,
      263–4
   and positive freedom, 21
   and United Kingdom, 21–2:
      multicultural community
      cohesion, 169–73
   as western construct, 82
   as work in progress, 257
   see also London; Netherlands
multiethnicity, and spatial planning, 74,
      82–6, 93–4
   and Gunder, 81–2
   and Habermasian concepts, 77–81
   informal negotiations, 84–6
   and Ivison, 81
   and Kumarangk case, 76–7
   and Sandercock, 81, 84
Murray, M, 96
Murtagh, B, 93, 96, 97
museums
   and integration, 41–2
   and National Museum of
      Bosnia-Herzegovina, 225
   and role of, 38
Muslim Council of Britain, 263

naming
   and Sarajevo street names, 222–5
   and urbanism, 118, 119
Nancy, Jean-Luc, 83–4
Narva, 33
   and porous borders, 44–5
National Contact Points for Integration
      (NCPs), 55
nationality
   and citizenship, 18, 23–6
   and ethnicity, 220–1
   and France, 119–20
   and identity, 220–1, 230
   and state's control of naturalization,
      27–8
National Museum of
      Bosnia-Herzegovina, 225–6
naturalization, and different practices of,
      27–8
N'Dour, Youssou, 72
Negri, A, 85
Neill, W J V, 262
neo-liberalism, and impact of, 5

Netherlands, 1
and ethnic population of, 104–5
and immigrants, urban concentrations
of, 103
and multiculturalism, planning for,
103: approaches to, 106–7; denial
of problems of, 106–7; evaluation
of Rotterdam's approach, 108–13;
Fortuyn approach to, 107–8;
future of, 112–15; Major Cities
Policy/urban renewal, 113;
pre-Fortuyn period, 104–7;
recommendations for, 115–16;
retreat from, 257; Zuidvleugel
Administrative Platform, 113–15
and Pim Fortuyn List (LPF – Lijst Pim
Fortuyn), 103–4
and rejection of Draft Constitutional
Treaty, 29 n1, 257
and Rotterdam housing policy: dealing
with multiculturalism, 107–8;
enforcement/implementation
problems, 111–12; focus on
ethnicity, 110–11; housing
associations, 112; as management
by speech, 109; overvaluation of
databases, 111; regulatory
complexity, 110; social
engineering, 109–10; structural
problems ignored, 112
and unemployment by ethnicity, 105–6
network power, and collaborative
planning, 89
new localism, 259
and United Kingdom, 170–1, 172–3:
London, 174–6
New York, 177
Ngarrindjeri women, and Kumarangk
case, 76–7
Nicosia, 33
and education, 43
and museums, 41
and physical divisions, 38–9
Norris, M, 241
Northern Ireland
and continuing problems in, 206
and control of place, 192
and cultural identity, 64
and Equity, Diversity and
Interdependence (EDI), 88, 95–7
and identity construction, 192:
ideological framework, 203
and integrated education, 43, 44
and interface communities, 209
and non-sectarians, 193
and paramilitary groups, 192
and 'peace process', 206
and progress in, 204
and reconciliation, 84
and segregation 191–3
and state's role, 203–4
and strife, dimensions of, 92–3
and violence, 191: constancy of, 199;
reproduction of, 192; scale of, 206
see also Belfast; Groundwork Northern
Ireland
Northern Ireland Housing Executive, 194

Oldham, 168
and separate communities, 40
order, and imposition of, 264–6
Orwell, George, 39
Osijek, 41–2

Parekh Report, 263, 264
participation
and civic republicanism, 66
and EuroCities 'Contribution to Good
Governance . . . ', 268–9
Pastors, Marco, 104
Patterson, Glenn, 41
Peillon, M, 251
periphery, and cities, 125–7
see also France, and urban periphery
Permezel, M, 84
Petaux, Jean, 41
Pettit, P, 70
Phillips, Trevor, 40, 263
Pim Fortuyn List (LPF – Lijst Pim
Fortuyn), 103–4
Pitkin, H, 66
place, and negotiation of
and Gunder, 81–2
and Habermasian concepts, 77–80:
criticisms of, 80–1
and informal approach to, 84–6
and Ivison, 81
and Kumarangk case, 76–7
and law, 74–5
and multiethnicity, 82–6

place, and negotiation of – *continued*
 and past and present, 76
 and Sandercock, 81, 84
 and Sarajevo: bank notes, 226–7;
  National Museum, 225–6; postage
  stamps, 227–30; renaming streets,
  222–5
 and spatial planning, 74
planning
 and agonism, 90, 91, 98: agonistic
  pluralism, 261; dimensions of,
  92–3
 and alternative vision of, 98
 and Assimilation/Pluralist/
  Discriminatory models, 94
 and civic republicanism, 261
 and collaborative planning, 88, 89
 criticisms of, 90–1, 93
 and cultural inclusion, 262
 and discursive planning, 94
 and education for, 97–8, 99–100
 and empowerment, 91
 and Equity, Diversity and
  Interdependence (EDI), 88, 94–9
 and master signifiers, 94
 and multiethnicity, 74, 82–6, 93–4:
  Gunder's approach, 81–2;
  Habermasian concepts, 77–81;
  informal negotiations, 84–6;
  Ivison's approach, 81; Kumarangk
  case, 76–7; Sandercock's
  approach, 81, 84
 and reinforcement of division, 214
 and strife, 91: in community settings,
  92–3
 and 'the lack', 90–1
 and theory, 260–1
 and winners and losers, 91
Ploeger, J, 90, 91, 92
political rights
 and European citizenship, 20
 and France, 120
politics, and Crick on, 261
Porter, L, 81
Portillo, Michael, 264
Portugal
 and demographic trends, 234
 and economic development, 236
 and emigration from, 234

and immigration/immigrants, 234:
  Brazil, 236–7; eastern Europeans,
  237; geographical distribution,
  239; as passing-through country,
  236; Portuguese Africa, 235;
  returners from Europe, 235–6
 and integration of immigrants:
  Brazilian immigrants, 236–7;
  eastern Europeans, 237; language,
  236–7, 239–40; national identity,
  239; from Portuguese Africa, 235;
  religion, 237; returners from
  Europe, 235–6
 and national identity, 237–9
postage stamps, and
  Bosnia-Herzegovina, 227–30
Powell, Enoch, 169
Pred, Allan, 76
Princip, Gavrilo, 224
public space
 and civic republicanism, 68
 and European citizenship, 25, 26–7
 and integration, 38–9
 and single or open-minded
  organization of, 35–6
 and state's restructuring of, 26–7
public sphere, and reconstruction of, 27
Putnam, R D, 35

Quinn, E, 242, 251

Reeves, D, 98
religion
 and differences between civilizations,
  1–2
 and integrated education, 43
 and Ireland, 241
 and Portugal, 237
republicanism, *see* civic republicanism
Republic of Ireland, *see* Ireland
respect, 80
reterritorialization, 189
Rogers, Richard, 35
 and organization of urban space, 35–6
Rotterdam
 and ethnic population of, 104, 106
 and housing policy: dealing with
  multiculturalism, 107–8;
  enforcement/implementation
  problems, 111–12; focus on

ethnicity, 110–11; housing associations, 112; as management by speech, 109; overvaluation of databases, 111; regulatory complexity, 110; social engineering, 109–10; structural problems ignored, 112
and population movements in, 106
and unemployment by ethnicity, 105–6
Royal Ulster Constabulary, 197
Rural Community Network, 96

Said, Edward, 258
Saleci, R, 22–3
Saloojee, A, 17
Sandercock, Leonie, 75, 81, 84, 262
Sarajevo, 218
and Bosniak nationalism, 230–1
and cosmopolitanism, 224–5
and ethnic composition of, 218–19
and ethno-nationalism, 220–2, 231
and multi-ethnic identity, 231
and remaking of place: bank notes, 226–7; national identity, 230; National Museum, 225–6; postage stamps, 227–30; renaming streets, 222–5
see also Bosnia-Herzegovina
Saudi Arabia, 222
scapegoating, and ethnic diversity, 36
Scarman report (1986), 170
Schengen Agreement, 9
Schwedler, H -U, 262
security, and immigration, 22
Seglow, J, 19
segregation
and cities, 5–6
and Germany, 151–2: Berlin, 138–9, 160
and Lisbon, 237, 239
and marginalization, 191
and Northern Ireland, 191–6
and space, 183
shared cities, *see* Council of Europe, and 'shared cities'
Shaw, George Bernard, 218
Shaw, J, 26
Shields, R, 183
Shirlow, P, 93, 193

Simnel, Georg, 258
Slovenia, 23
social capital
and bridging social capital, 35, 211
and ethnic diversity, 35
and Groundwork Northern Ireland, 208–9
and types of, 35
social citizenship, and European citizenship, 20
Socially Integrative City programme
and aims of, 148, 150
and area selection, 153–4
and Berlin, 136, 142
and construction-oriented urban renewal, 150
and establishment of, 148
and future activity of, 155: education, 155–6; integration of immigrants, 156–7; local economy and employment, 157–8
and identifying problems/setting goals, 150–1
and impact of, 154–5
and inter-departmental cooperation, 152
and involvement of external actors, 154
and pooling resources, 153
and recommendations for, 158
and residential segregation, 151–2
and variable implementation of, 149
social security, and failures of, 6
social services, and EuroCities 'Contribution to Good Governance . . . ', 272
Spain, and foreign population of, 7
spatial perception, 182–3, 189–90
and fuzzy spaces, 183
and habitus, 183
and representations of, 183
and reterritorialization, 189
and social segregation, 183
and Turin, 185–7
and Verona, 184
spatial planning, *see* planning
Spence, Gusty, 84
Staeheli, L A, 259
stereotypes, and media, 41–2

strife, and planning, 91: in community
    settings, 92–3
subsidiarity, 131–2
    and European Union, 174
    and United Kingdom, 170–1
Suchet-Pearson, S, 83
supranational polity, and democratic
    citizenship, 23–6
sustainable integration, 54
Szabo, Istvan, 42

Tampere Process, 48, 54
    and EuroCities 'Contribution to Good
    Governance . . . ', 269
Tebbit, Norman, 21
Tewdr-Jones, M, 89
Thames Gateway, 175
Thatcher, Margaret, 24, 64, 173
third country nationals
    and European citizenship, 19, 22
    and naturalization procedures, 27–8
Thrift, Nigel
    and citizenship, 36–7
    and cultural hybridization, 36
    and urban life, 35
Tibi, Bassam, 2
Tito, Marshall, 224
tolerance, 37
    and limits of, 258, 260, 261, 263–4
transnational networks, 189
Turin, 179
    and attitudes toward immigrants, 181
    and citizens' committees, 179, 185
    and cultural mediation, 188
    and economic decline, 186–7
    and immigrants, 185
    and perceptions of space, 185–7
    and physical refurbishment, 185–6
Tuzla
    and civic leadership, 43
    and civic networks, 40

Ulster Defence Regiment, 197
undocumented migrants, 52–3
unemployment
    and Berlin, 136, 139, 161
    and Netherlands, 105–6
United Kingdom
    and Modernizing Government
    Programme, 27

and multicultural community
    cohesion, 169–73: Inner Area
    Studies, 169; Local Area
    Agreements, 170, 172; local
    governance, 170; Local
    Government Act (2000), 171;
    Neighbourhood Development
    Companies, 170–1; New Local
    Government Network, 171; new
    localism, 170–1, 172–3;
    partnership arrangements, 171–2;
    Urban Programme, 169–70
    and multiculturalism, 21–2
    and riots, 170
    and Urban Task Force, 45
    see also London
United Nations, and European
    demographic change, 8
United States, and 'clash of civilizations', 1
urban planning, *see* planning
urban space, and organization of, 35–6
Urban Task Force (UK), 45
Utrecht, and ethnic population of, 104
Uzhgorod, 33
    and mixed marriages, 44

van Gogh, Theo, 1, 13 n2, 57, 257
van Heelsum, A, 17
Varshney, A, 35
    and civic networks, 39–40
Verona, 179
    and citizens' committees, 184
    and Intercultural Centres, 188
    and perceptions of space, 184
    and use of space, 183

Warleigh, A, 18–19
Weber, Max, 258
Weiler, J H H, 25, 26
welfare systems, and failures of, 6
Wilkinson, Richard, 36
Wilson, D, 95
Winston, N, 241
women
    and migration to Italy, 179–80
    see also Ngarrindjeri women

Yiftachel, O, 88, 93
Yugoslavia, and disintegration of, 218–19

Zizek, S, 82